Mastering
Financial Calculations

TO MY PARENTS
without whom none of this would have been possible

AND TO MY FAMILY
who have suffered while I've been writing it

Mastering
Financial Calculations

A step-by-step guide to the
mathematics of financial
market instruments

Second edition

BOB STEINER

An imprint of **Pearson Education**
Harlow, England • London • New York • Boston • San Francisco • Toronto
Sydney • Tokyo • Singapore • Hong Kong • Seoul • Taipei • New Delhi
Cape Town • Madrid • Mexico City • Amsterdam • Munich • Paris • Milan

PEARSON EDUCATION LIMITED

Edinburgh Gate
Harlow CM20 2JE
Tel: +44 (0)1279 623623
Fax: +44 (0)1279 431059
Website: www.pearsoned.co.uk

First published in Great Britain 1998
Reprinted and updated 1999
This second edition published 2007

ISBN 978-0-273-70444-7

British Library Cataloguing in Publication Data
A CIP catalogue record for this book can be obtained from the British Library

10 9 8 7 6 5 4 3 2 1
11 10 09 08 07

Typeset by 30
Printed and bound by Ashford Colour Press Ltd., Gosport.

The Publishers' policy is to use paper manufactured from sustainable forests.

Author's note

Throughout this book, I have aimed to put the calculations used in the financial markets in context, by explaining the ideas behind them, and the background and situations in which they arise. However, the reader must be aware that different situations might give rise to significant differences in the detail of the calculation method that is most appropriate, and also that different markets – and also different people within the same market – might use different conventions. The formulas and methods here cannot be used as an off-the-peg prescription for pricing any specific instrument, without checking carefully the assumptions made, and the details of the underlying situation.

The author

Bob Steiner is Managing Director of Markets International Ltd, an independent company specialising in training in a range of areas related to the international financial markets, treasury and banking. The company also provides advice to finance directors and treasurers of international companies on foreign exchange, money markets and other treasury matters. This advice ranges from written studies reviewing existing management policies and procedures, through the development of appropriate hedging strategies, to short-term market advice.

Bob was previously senior consultant with HongKong and Shanghai Banking Corporation, where he worked in London and New York in the dealing area as consultant to major US and European companies on treasury management. He has also been treasurer and fund manager of H P Bulmer Holdings PLC and English and American Insurance Group PLC, active in currency and interest rate management. He has thus been closely involved in treasury management as consultant and practitioner. He has also worked in the Overseas Department of the Bank of England, and with the European Commission in Brussels.

Bob spends a considerable amount of time training bankers, systems staff, corporate staff and others involved in the financial markets. In particular, he personally runs courses for several of the ACI exams – the ACI Diploma, the Dealing Certificate, Repo Markets and the Settlements Certificate. He is the author of *Mastering Repo Markets* and *Key Market Concepts*, also published by Financial Times Prentice Hall and of *Foreign Exchange and Money Markets* published by Butterworth Heineman.

His academic background is an honours degree in mathematics from Cambridge University followed by further studies in economics with London University. He is an associate member of ACI UK, and a member of the Association of Corporate Treasurers.

Contents

Part 3: FOREIGN EXCHANGE

Part 4: SWAPS AND OPTIONS

Part 5: GOLD AND OTHER COMMODITIES

Part 6: HINTS AND ANSWERS TO EXERCISES

Foreword

ACI's Board of Education (BoE) is the educational division of ACI – the Financial Markets Association. For half a century, ACI has represented its members and is considered to have the largest membership of any international association in the wholesale financial markets with 14,000 members from 80 countries, of which 64 currently have affiliated National Associations.

ACI BoE, the main pillar of ACI, is responsible for the ongoing strategy, implementation and marketing for ACI's education programmes. It administers the delivery of examinations, working closely with regulators and trainers on the development and delivery of high quality examinations designed to enable the certification of skill levels in the international financial markets. The BoE achieves this through the development of cutting-edge products and close understanding of market trends and needs, spearheaded by the innovation and widespread marketing of education and accreditation.

ACI Education has established three internationally recognised benchmark certificate courses that test skills, knowledge and understanding of wholesale financial market products and awareness of the market environment and the professional behaviour expected within it. Specialised examinations cover foreign exchange, money markets, related derivatives, risk management, and settlement for front, middle and back office staff.

In its continuous striving to adapt to the needs of the markets and to build understanding between the trading community and back office operations staff, ACI Education is launching the new "ACI Operations Certificate" that will ultimately replace the ACI Settlements Certificate in order to reflect the changing market landscape.

ACI BoE perceives professional trainers, publishers and authors as being close partners who provide huge support both for ACI and for the candidates considering sitting ACI exams. We at ACI are extremely enthusiastic about Bob Steiner and Financial Times Prentince Hall publishing the second edition of *Mastering Financial Calculations*. Bob, over and above being a great friend and supporter of ACI, has a long and professional track record as an author and trainer and we believe his new publication will be an asset and a great guide for market practitioners in general and for candidates preparing to sit both the ACI Dealing Certificate and the ACI Diploma in particular.

Saad Jamaluddin
Chairman Board of Education
ACI – the Financial Markets Association

Introduction

THE AIM OF THE BOOK

This book is aimed at the very many people in financial institutions, universities and elsewhere who will benefit from a solid grounding in the calculations behind the various financial instruments – dealers, treasurers, investors, programmers, students, auditors and risk managers – but who do not necessarily do complex mathematical puzzles for fun. There is also a strong emphasis on the mechanics, background and applications of all the various instruments.

Many dealers would claim to be able to perform their job – essentially buying and selling – very profitably, without using much maths. On the other hand, the different dealing areas in a bank overlap increasingly and it is essential to understand the basis for pricing each instrument, in order to understand how the bank's position in one relates to a position in another.

Almost all the concepts in this book regarding pricing the different instruments can be reduced to only two basic ideas. The first concerns the "time value of money": a hundred dollars is worth more if I have it in my hand today than if I do not receive it until next year; or alternatively, for a given amount of cash which I will receive in the future, I can calculate an equivalent "present value" now. The second is the "no free lunch" principle: in theory, it should not generally be possible to put together a series of simultaneous financial transactions which lock in a guaranteed no-risk profit. For example, if a dealer buys an interest rate futures contract and simultaneously reverses it with an FRA, he will in general make no profit or loss if we ignore minor mechanical discrepancies and transaction costs. This concept links the pricing calculations for the two instruments. If the reader has a clear grasp by the end of the book of how to apply these two crucial concepts, he or she will be well equipped to cope. Much of the difficulty lies in seeing through the confusion of market terminology and conventions.

There is a significant jump between the arithmetic needed for most instruments and the complex mathematics needed to construct option pricing formulas from first principles. I have deliberately excluded much of the latter from this book, because many readers are more likely to be discouraged than helped, and because that subject alone warrants an entire book. On the other hand, I have discussed the ideas behind option pricing, particularly volatility, which introduce the concepts without being mathematically frightening. I have also included the Black–Scholes formula for reference and mentioned standard books on the subject for those interested.

The book has been conceived as a workbook, as well as a reference book, with an emphasis on examples and exercises. It has grown out of workshops on financial mathematics which I have run for many years, including some for the ACI's former Financial Calculations exam. The book is therefore also suitable for the student who chooses to take exams without any formal tuition course. There is however considerably more background material than is required for any exam aimed specifically at calculations. The intention is to benefit the reader technically as well as making the book more readable.

THE STRUCTURE OF THE BOOK

The book is set out in six parts:

Part 1: The basics

This covers the fundamental concepts of time value of money, discounting, present values and calculations with interest rates.

Part 2: Interest rate instruments

This looks at the range of instruments based on interest rates or yields in both the money markets and capital markets – simple deposits, CDs, bills and CP, FRAs and futures, bonds, repos, buy/sell-backs and securities lending. The market background and use for each instrument are given as a structure within which to see the calculations. This section also covers zero-coupon rates, yield curves, duration and convexity.

Part 3: Foreign exchange

This looks at all the foreign exchange instruments from basic spot, through swaps, outrights, short dates and forward-forwards to time options. Again, the context of each instrument in the market is explained, together with the link with the money markets.

Part 4: Swaps and options

This part explains both interest rate and currency swaps, and options. Examples are given of the basic uses as well as some of the combination option strategies. It also introduces option pricing concepts and the "Greeks".

Part 5: Gold and other commodities

This looks at gold in particular as a traded instrument, and considers briefly the complexity involved in commodities generally.

Part 6: Hints and answers to exercises

This section gives hints and answers to the exercises which are found throughout the book.

KEY FEATURES OF THE BOOK

Key points

Throughout the book, key points have been highlighted for emphasis.

Calculation summaries

The procedures for all the necessary calculations have been summarised in the text to ensure the reader's understanding. These have also been collected together into a reference section in Appendix 3.

Glossary

The market terminology is explained throughout the text, with a glossary for reference in Appendix 4.

Market interest conventions

A constant source of confusion is the range of different conventions used for interest and coupon calculations in different markets. These are also summarised in Appendix 2 for various countries' markets.

Examples

Many examples to help the reader's understanding have been included throughout the text.

Exercises

Fully worked answers for each chapter's exercises are provided at the end of the book in Chapter 12. The exercises form an important part of the book as they provide further examples of the calculations covered in the text. Readers who do not wish to attempt them as exercises should therefore read them as worked examples. For the reader who is struggling with a particular question but who wishes to persevere, there is a section of hints, which will lead him or her through the procedure to be followed for each question.

Calculator keystrokes

Many of the examples and answers include the full keystroke procedures necessary using a Hewlett-Packard calculator. The use of an HP calculator is described in detail in Appendix 1.

A FINAL WORD

However hard one tries, there are always mistakes. I apologise for these and welcome comments or suggestions from readers – particularly on other areas which might usefully be included in the book without making it too boffin orientated. As always, I am hugely indebted to my wife for her support throughout.

Part 1

The Basics

"The fundamental principle behind market calculations is the time value of money: as long as interest rates are not negative, any given amount of money is worth more sooner than it is later because you can place it on deposit to earn interest."

■ ■ ■

Financial Arithmetic Basics

SOME OPENING REMARKS ON FORMULAS

There are three important points concerning many of the formulas in this book. These have nothing to do with the business of finance, but rather with how mathematical formulas are written in all areas of life.

First, consider the expression "$1 + 0.08 \times \frac{92}{365}$". In this, you must do the multiplication *before* the addition. It is a convention of the way mathematical formulas are written that any exponents (5^4, x^2, $4.2^{\frac{1}{4}}$ etc.) must be done first, followed by multiplication and division (0.08×92, $x \div y$, $\frac{17}{38}$ etc.) and addition and subtraction last. This rule is applied first to anything inside brackets "(...)" and then to everything else. This means that "$1 + 0.08 \times \frac{92}{365}$" is the same as "$1 + (0.08 \times \frac{92}{365})$" and is equal to 1.0202. This is *not* the same as "$(1 + 0.08) \times \frac{92}{365}$", which is equal to 0.2722. If I mean to write this latter expression, I must write the brackets. If I mean to write the first expression, I do not need to write the brackets and it is in fact usual to leave them out.

Second, the expression "percent" means "divided by 100". Therefore "4.7%", "$\frac{4.7}{100}$" and "0.047" are all the same. When writing a formula which involves an interest rate of 4.7 percent for example, this usually appears as "0.047" rather than "$\frac{4.7}{100}$", simply because "0.047" is neater. Similarly, when we speak of an "interest rate i", we mean a decimal such as 0.047, not a number such as 4.7.

Third, the symbol $\sum$ is shorthand for "the sum of all". Thus for example, "$\sum (\text{cashflow})_i$" is shorthand for "$\text{cashflow}_1 + \text{cashflow}_2 + \text{cashflow}_3 + ...$". Where there are many cashflows, this is a very useful abbreviation.

USE OF AN HP CALCULATOR

Some of the calculations used in financial arithmetic are most easily performed using a specialist calculator. The ones most widely used in the markets are probably Hewlett-Packard calculators. In many of the worked examples and exercises in this book, as well as showing the method of calculation, we have therefore also given the steps used on an HP. It is important to understand that you do not *need* an HP in order to work through these examples. An ordinary non-financial calculator is fine for many calculations, and you can use an alternative specialist calculator – or a computer spreadsheet – for the rest. We have chosen to show the steps for an HP simply because many readers will already have access to one, as they are widely used in the financial markets.

In order to make these steps intelligible to anyone new to an HP, we have explained the basics of operating the calculator in Appendix 1. We have certainly not tried to give full instructions for using an HP – the calculator's own instruction manual is clearly the best place for that – but have set out only those operations which are necessary for our examples.

SIMPLE AND COMPOUND INTEREST

Simple interest

On short-term financial instruments, interest is usually "simple" rather than "compound". Suppose, for example, that I place £1 on deposit at 8 percent for 92 days. As the 8 percent is generally quoted as if for a whole year rather than for only 92 days, the interest I expect to receive is the appropriate proportion of 8 percent:

$$£0.08 \times \tfrac{92}{365}$$

The total proceeds after 92 days are therefore the return of my principal, plus the interest:

$$£(1 + 0.08 \times \tfrac{92}{365})$$

If I place instead £73 on deposit at 8 percent for 92 days, I will receive a total of:

$$£73 \times (1 + 0.08 \times \tfrac{92}{365})$$

Total proceeds of short-term investment = principal $\times \left(1 + \text{interest rate} \times \dfrac{\text{days}}{\text{year}}\right)$

Calculation summary

By $\dfrac{\text{" days "}}{\text{year}}$ we mean $\dfrac{\text{" number of days in the period "}}{\text{number of days in the year}}$.

In this chapter "number of days in the year" generally means 365. In some markets, however (as explained in Chapter 2), this number is 360 by convention. Where this might be the case, we have therefore used "year" to cover either situation.

Compound interest

Now consider an investment of 1 made for two years at 10 percent per annum. At the end of the first year, the investor receives interest of 0.10. At the end of the second year he receives interest of 0.10, plus the principal of 1. The total received is 0.10 + 0.10 + 1 = 1.20. However, the investor would in practice reinvest the 0.10 received at the end of the first year, for a further year. If he could do this at 10 percent, he would receive an extra 0.01 (= 10 percent × 0.10) at the end of the second year, for a total of 1.21.

In effect, this is the same as investing 1 for one year at 10 percent to receive 1 + 0.10 at the end of the first year and then reinvesting this whole (1 + 0.10) for a further year, also at 10 percent, to give (1 + 0.10) × (1 + 0.10) = 1.21.

The same idea can be extended for any number of years, so that the total return after N years, including principal, is:

$$\text{Principal} \times (1 + \text{interest rate})^N$$

This is "compounding" the interest, and assumes that all interim cashflows can be reinvested at the same original interest rate. "Simple" interest is when the interest is not reinvested.

> Total proceeds of long-term investment for N years
> $= \text{principal} \times (1 + \text{interest rate})^N$

Nominal rates and effective rates

Now consider a deposit of 1 made for only one year at 10 percent per annum, but with quarterly interest payments. This would mean interest of 0.025 received each quarter. As above, this could be reinvested for a further quarter to achieve interest-on-interest of $0.025 \times 0.025 = 0.000625$. Again, this is the same as investing 1 for only three months at 10 percent per annum (that is, 2.5 percent per quarter) to receive $(1 + 0.025)$ at the end of the first quarter and then reinvesting this whole $(1 + 0.025)$ for a further quarter, also at the same interest rate, and so on for a total of four quarters. At the end of this, the total return, including principal, is:

$$(1 + 0.025) \times (1 + 0.025) \times (1 + 0.025) \times (1 + 0.025) = (1 + 0.025)^4 = 1.1038$$

The same idea can be extended for monthly interest payments or semi-annual (6-monthly) interest payments, so that in general the proceeds at the end of a year including principal, with n interest payments per year, are:

$$\text{Principal} \times \left(1 + \frac{\text{interest rate}}{n}\right)^n$$

It is often useful to compare two interest rates which are for the same investment period, but with different interest payment frequency – for example, a 5-year interest rate with interest paid quarterly compared with a 5-year rate with interest paid semi-annually. To do this, it is common to calculate an equivalent annualised rate. This is the rate with interest paid annually which would give the same compound return at the end of the year as the rate we are comparing. From this it follows that:

$$\text{Principal} \times \left(1 + \frac{\text{interest rate}}{n}\right)^n = \text{principal} \times (1 + \text{equivalent annual rate})$$

Thus if the interest rate with n payments per year is i, the equivalent annual interest rate i* is:

$$i* = \left[\left(1 + \frac{i}{n}\right)^n - 1\right]$$

Calculation summary

This equivalent annual interest rate i* is known as the "effective" rate. The rate i from which it is calculated is known as the "nominal" rate. It follows that:

$$i = \left[(1 + i*)^{\frac{1}{n}} - 1\right] \times n$$

Calculation summary

Example 1.1

8% is the nominal interest rate quoted for a 1-year deposit with the interest paid in quarterly instalments. What is the effective rate (that is, the equivalent rate quoted when all the interest is paid together at the end of the year)?

$$\left[\left(1 + \frac{0.08}{4}\right)^4 - 1\right] = 8.24\%$$

Answer: 8.24%

> **Using an HP19BII**
> .08 ENTER
> 4 ÷ 1 +
> 4 ☐ ∧
> 1 −

Example 1.2

5% is the nominal interest rate quoted for a 1-year deposit when the interest is paid all at maturity. What is the quarterly equivalent?

$$\left[(1.05)^{\frac{1}{4}} - 1\right] \times 4 = 4.91\%$$

Answer: 4.91%

> 1.05 ENTER
> 4 ☐ $^1/x$ ☐ ∧
> 1 − 4 ×

In the same way, we might for example wish to compare the rate available on a 40-day investment with the rate available on a 91-day investment. One approach, as before, is to calculate the effective rate for each. In this case, the effective rate formula above can be extended by using the proportion $\frac{365}{days}$ instead of the interest rate frequency n.

Example 1.3 The interest rate for a 5-month (153-day) investment is 10.2%. What is the effective rate?

$$\text{Effective rate} = \left(1 + i \times \frac{\text{days}}{\text{year}}\right)^{\frac{365}{\text{days}}} - 1$$

$$= \left(1 + 0.102 \times \frac{153}{365}\right)^{\frac{365}{153}} - 1 = 10.50\%$$

.102 ENTER 153 x 365 ÷ 1 +
365 ENTER 153 ÷ □ ∧ 1 −

Calculation summary

$$\text{Effective rate} = \left(1 + i \times \frac{\text{days}}{\text{year}}\right)^{\frac{365}{\text{days}}} - 1$$

Continuous compounding

The effect of compounding increases with the frequency of interest payments, because there is an increasing opportunity to earn interest on interest. As a result, an annual rate will always be greater than the semi-annual equivalent, which in turn will always be greater than the monthly equivalent, etc. In practice, the limit is reached in considering the daily equivalent rate. Thus the equivalent rate with daily compounding for an annual rate of 9.3% is:

$$\left[(1 + 0.093)^{\frac{1}{365}} - 1\right] \times 365 = 8.894\%$$

1.093 ENTER 365 □ ¹/x □ ∧ 1 − 365 ×

In theory, however, the frequency could be increased indefinitely, with interest being compounded each hour, or each minute. The limit of this concept is where the frequency is infinite – that is, "continuous compounding". The equivalent interest rate in this case can be shown to be LN(1.093), where LN is the natural logarithm $\log_e$. The number e – approximately 2.7183 – occurs often in mathematical formulas; e^x and $\log_e x$ can both usually be found on mathematical calculators, sometimes as EXP and LN. Thus:

Continuously compounded rate = LN(1.093) = 8.893%

1.093 □ MATHS LOG LN

In general:

Calculation summary

> The continuously compounded interest rate r is:
>
> $$r = \frac{365}{\text{days}} \times LN\left(1 + i \times \frac{\text{days}}{\text{year}}\right) \text{ where i is the nominal rate for that number of days}$$
>
> In particular:
>
> $$r = LN(1 + i) \text{ where i is the annual effective rate}$$

These relationships can be reversed to give:

Calculation summary

> $$i = \frac{\text{year}}{\text{days}} \times \left(e^{r \times \frac{\text{days}}{365}} - 1\right)$$

The 91-day interest rate is 6.4%. What is the continuously compounded equivalent?   **Example 1.4**

$$r = \frac{365}{\text{days}} \times LN\left(1 + i \times \frac{\text{days}}{\text{year}}\right)$$

$$= \frac{365}{91} \times LN\left(1 + 0.064 \times \frac{91}{365}\right) = 6.35\%$$

> .064 ENTER 91 × 365 ÷ 1 + □ MATH LOGS LN 365 × 91 ÷

The continuously compounded rate is 7.2%. What is the effective rate?   **Example 1.5**

$$i = e^r - 1 = e^{0.072} - 1 = 7.47\%$$

> .072 □ MATH LOGS EXP 1 −

Reinvestment rates

The assumption we have used so far for compounding interest rates, calculating effective rates, etc. is that interest cashflows arising during an investment can be reinvested at the same original rate of interest. Although these calculations are very important and useful, reinvestment of such cashflows is in practice likely to be at different rates.

To calculate the accumulated value by the end of the investment in this case, account must be taken of the different rate paid on the interim cashflows.

Example 1.6 £100 is invested for 3 years at 3.5% (paid annually). By the end of the first year, interest rates for all periods have risen to 4.0% (paid annually). By the end of the second year, rates have risen to 5.0% (paid annually). Whenever an interest payment is received, it is reinvested to the end of the 3-year period. What is the total cash returned by the end of the third year?

The cashflows received from the original investment are:

> 1 year: + £3.50
> 2 years: + £3.50
> 3 years: + £103.50

At the end of year 1, the £3.50 is reinvested at 4.0% to produce the following cashflows:

> 2 years: + £3.50 × 4% = £0.14
> 3 years: + £3.50 × (1 + 4%) = £3.64

At the end of year 2, the £3.50 from the original investment plus the £0.14 arising from reinvestment of the first year's interest is reinvested at 5.0% to produce the following cashflow:

> 3 years: + £3.64 × (1 + 5%) = £3.82

The total return is therefore £103.50 + £3.64 + £3.82 = £110.96.

Note that the result would be slightly different if the interim interest payments were each reinvested only for one year at a time (and then rolled over), rather than reinvested to the maturity of the original investment.

```
3.5 ENTER .04 ×
3.5 +
.05 ENTER 1 + ×
.04 ENTER 1 + 3.5 × +
103.5 +
```

NOMINAL AND EFFECTIVE RATES

We have seen that there are three different elements to any interest rate. Confusion arises because the words used to describe each element can be the same.

1. The period for which the investment/loan will last

In this sense, a "6-month" interest rate is one for an investment which lasts six months and a "1-year" interest rate is one for an investment which lasts one year.

2. The absolute period to which the quoted interest rate applies

Normally, this period is always assumed to be one year, regardless of the actual period of investment. Thus, if the interest rate on a 6-month investment is quoted as 10 percent, this does not mean that the investor in fact receives 10 percent after six months; rather, the investor receives only 5 percent, because the quoted rate is expressed as the 1-year *simple* equivalent rate, even though there is no intention to hold the investment for a year. Similarly, a 5-year zero-coupon rate of 10 percent means that the investor will in fact receive 61.05 percent after five years. Again, the quoted rate is the *decompounded* one-year equivalent, even though the investment is fixed for five years and pays no actual interest at the end of one year.

The reason for this "annualising" of interest rates is to make them approximately comparable. If this were not done, one would not be able immediately to compare rates quoted for different periods. Instead, we would be trying to compare rates such as 0.0274 percent for 1 day, 5 percent for 6 months and 61.05 percent for 5 years (all in fact quoted as 10 percent). A yield curve drawn like this would be difficult to interpret at a glance.

One exception is the interest paid on personal credit cards, which is sometimes quoted for a monthly period rather than annualised (for cosmetic reasons). In the UK, for example, credit card companies are obliged also to quote the effective rate (known as APR, annualised percentage rate).

3. The frequency with which interest is paid

If interest on a 1-year deposit is paid each 6 months, the total interest accumulated at the end of the year, assuming reinvestment of the interim interest payment, will be greater than the interest accumulated if the deposit pays the same quoted rate, but all in one amount at the end of the year. When the interest rate on a money market investment is quoted, it is generally quoted on the basis of the frequency which the investment does actually have. For example, if a 1-year deposit pays 2.5 percent each 3 months, the interest is quoted as 10 percent; the rate is quoted on the basis that all parties know the payment frequency is 3 months. Similarly, if a 1-year deposit pays 5 percent each 6 months, or 10 percent at the end, the rate is quoted as 10 percent on the basis that all parties know the payment frequency is 6 months, or 1 year. The economic effect is different in each case, but no adjustment is made to make the quotations comparable; they are simply stated as "10 percent quarterly" or "10 percent semi-annual" or "10 percent annual".

Yields for financial instruments are generally quoted in the market in this *simple* way, regardless of whether they are short-term money market instruments such as treasury bills and deposits, or long-term capital markets instruments such as bonds and swaps. One exception is zero-coupon rates, where the interest rate is *compounded* downwards when expressed as an annualised rate. Other exceptions may arise in specific markets – for example treasury bills in Norway are quoted on the basis of an *effective* annual equivalent yield. Furthermore, because an investor does need to be able to compare rates, they are often all converted by the investor to a common effective basis. In this way, "10 percent quarterly" is converted to an effective

"10.38 annual equivalent", or "10 percent annual" to an effective "9.65 per-cent quarterly equivalent" or "9.532 percent daily equivalent".

FUTURE VALUE / PRESENT VALUE; TIME VALUE OF MONEY

This section is probably the most important in this book, as present value calculations are the key to pricing financial instruments.

Short-term investments

If I deposit 100 for 1 year at 10 percent per annum, I receive:

$$100 \times (1 + 0.10) = 110$$

at the end of the year. In this case, 110 is said to be the "future value" (or "accumulated value") after 1 year of 100 now. In reverse, 100 is said to be the "present value" of 110 in a year's time. Future and present values clearly depend on both the interest rate used and the length of time involved.

Similarly, the future value after 98 days of £100 now at 10 percent per annum would be $100 \times (1 + 0.10 \times \frac{98}{365})$.

The expression above can be turned upside down, so that the present value now of 102.68 in 98 days' time, using 10 percent per annum, is:

$$\frac{102.68}{(1 + 0.10 \times \frac{98}{365})} = 100$$

In general, the present value of a cashflow C, using an interest rate i, is:

$$\frac{C}{(1 + i \times \frac{days}{year})}$$

We can therefore now generate a future value from a present value, and vice versa, given the number of days and the interest rate. The third calculation needed is the answer to the question: if we know how much money we invest at the beginning (= the present value) and we know the total amount at the end (= the future value), what is our rate of return, or yield (= the interest rate) on the investment? This is found by turning round the formula above again, to give:

$$\text{Yield} = \left(\frac{\text{future value}}{\text{present value}} - 1\right) \times \frac{\text{year}}{\text{days}}$$

This gives the yield as normally expressed – that is, the yield for the period of the investment. This can of course then be converted to an effective rate by using:

$$\text{Effective yield} = \left(1 + i \times \frac{\text{days}}{\text{years}}\right)^{\frac{365}{\text{days}}} - 1$$

Combining these two relationships gives:

$$\text{Effective yield} = \left(\frac{\text{future value}}{\text{present value}}\right)^{\frac{365}{\text{days}}} - 1$$

The calculation of present value is sometimes known as "discounting" a future value to a present value and the interest rate used is sometimes known as the "rate of discount".

In general, these calculations demonstrate the fundamental principles behind market calculations, the "time value of money". As long as interest rates are not negative, any given amount of money is worth more sooner than it is later because if you have it sooner, you can place it on deposit to earn interest. The extent to which it is worthwhile having the money sooner depends on the interest rate and the time period involved.

For short-term investments

$$FV = PV \times \left(1 + i \times \frac{\text{days}}{\text{year}}\right)$$

$$PV = \frac{FV}{\left(1 + i \times \frac{\text{days}}{\text{year}}\right)}$$

$$i = \left(\frac{FV}{PV} - 1\right) \times \frac{\text{year}}{\text{days}}$$

$$\text{Effective yield (annual equivalent)} = \left(\frac{FV}{PV}\right)^{\frac{365}{\text{days}}} - 1$$

Calculation summary

Long-term investments

The formulas above are for investments where no compound interest is involved. For periods more than a year where compounding is involved, this compounding must be taken into account.

The future value in three years' time of 100 now, using 10 percent per annum, is:

$$100 \times (1 + 0.10)^3 = 133.10$$

This expression can again be turned upside down, so that the present value now of 133.10 in three years' time, using 10 percent per annum, is:

$$\frac{133.10}{(1 + 0.10)^3} = 100$$

In general, the present value of a cashflow C in N years' time, using an interest rate i, is:

$$\frac{C}{(1 + i)^N}$$

Calculation summary	**For long-term investments over N years**

$$FV = PV \times (1 + i)^N$$

$$PV = \frac{FV}{(1 + i)^N}$$

$$i = \left(\frac{FV}{PV}\right)^{\frac{1}{N}} - 1$$

Example 1.7

What is the future value in 5 years' time of £120 now, using 8% per annum?

$$120 \times (1.08)^5 = 176.32$$

(The interest rate is compounded because interest is paid each year and can be reinvested.)

Answer: £176.32

```
1.08 ENTER
5 □ ∧
120 ×
```

Example 1.8

What is the future value in 92 days' time of £120 now, using 8% per annum?

$$120 \times \left(1 + 0.08 \times \frac{92}{365}\right) = 122.42$$

(Simple interest rate, because there is only one interest payment, at maturity.)

Answer: £122.42

```
.08 ENTER
92 × 365 ÷
1 + 120 ×
```

Example 1.9

What is the present value of £270 in 4 years' time, using 7% per annum?

$$\frac{270}{(1.07)^4} = 205.98$$

(The interest rate is compounded because interest is paid each year and can be reinvested.)

Answer: £205.98

```
1.07 ENTER
4 □ ∧
270 □ x≷y ÷
```

What is the present value of £270 in 180 days' time, using 7% per annum? **Example 1.10**

$$\frac{270}{\left(1 + 0.07 \times \frac{180}{365}\right)} = 260.99$$

(Simple interest rate, because there is only one interest payment, at maturity.)

Answer: £260.99

```
.07 ENTER
180 × 365 ÷
1 +
270 □ x⪌y ÷
```

I invest £138 now. After 64 days I receive back a total (principal plus interest) of £139.58. What is my yield on this investment? **Example 1.11**

$$\text{Yield} = \left(\frac{139.58}{138.00} - 1\right) \times \frac{365}{64} = 0.0653$$

Answer: 6.53%

```
139.58 ENTER
138 ÷
1 −
365 ×
64 ÷
```

DISCOUNT FACTORS

So far, we have discounted from a future value to a present value by dividing by $(1 + i \times \frac{\text{days}}{\text{year}})$ for simple interest and $(1+i)^N$ for compound interest. An alternative way of expressing this, also commonly used, is to multiply by the reciprocal of these numbers, which are then usually called "discount factors".

What is the 92-day discount factor if the interest rate for the period is 7.8%? What is the present value of £100 in 92 days' time? **Example 1.12**

$$\text{Discount factor} = \frac{1}{1 + 0.078 \times \frac{92}{365}} = 0.9807$$

£100 × 0.9807 = £98.07

```
.078 ENTER 92 × 365 ÷ 1 + □ 1/x        (Discount factor)
100 ×                                   (Present value)
```

Example 1.13

What is the 3-year discount factor based on a 3-year interest rate of 8.5% compounded annually? What is the present value of £100 in 3 years' time?

$$\text{Discount factor} = \frac{1}{(1 + 0.085)^3} = 0.7829$$

£100 × 0.7829 = £78.29

1.085 ENTER 3 ☐ ∧ ☐ ¹/ₓ	(Discount factor)
100 ×	(Present value)

Calculation summary

For simple interest

$$\text{Discount factor} = \frac{1}{1 + i \times \frac{\text{days}}{\text{year}}}$$

For compound interest

$$\text{Discount factor} = \left(\frac{1}{1 + i}\right)^N$$

Note that we know from an earlier section that using a continuously compounded interest rate r, $i = \frac{\text{year}}{\text{days}} \times \left(e^{r \times \frac{\text{days}}{365}} - 1\right)$.

Using a continuously compounded interest rate therefore, the discount factor becomes:

$$\frac{1}{1 + i \times \frac{\text{days}}{\text{year}}} = \frac{1}{1 + \left(e^{r \times \frac{\text{days}}{365}} - 1\right)} = e^{-r \times \frac{\text{days}}{365}}$$

This way of expressing the discount factor is used commonly in option pricing formulas.

Calculation summary

Using a continuously compounded interest rate

$$\text{Discount factor} = e^{-r \times \frac{\text{days}}{365}}$$

CASHFLOW ANALYSIS

NPV

Suppose that we have a series of future cashflows, some of which are positive and some negative. Each will have a present value (PV), dependent on the time to the cashflow and the interest rate used. The sum of all the positive and negative present values added together is the net present value or NPV.

What is the NPV of the following future cashflows, discounting at a rate of 7.5%?　**Example 1.14**

After 1 year:	+ $83
After 2 years:	− $10
After 3 years:	+$150

$$\frac{83}{(1.075)} - \frac{10}{(1.075)^2} + \frac{150}{(1.075)^3} = 189.30$$

Answer: +$189.30

```
83 ENTER 1.075 ÷
10 ENTER 1.075 ENTER 2 ☐ ∧ ÷ −
150 ENTER 1.075 ENTER 3 ☐ ∧ ÷ +
```

An NPV is the sum of a series of PVs, of which some might be positive and some negative.　**Key Point**

IRR

An internal rate of return (IRR) is the one single interest rate which it is necessary to use when discounting a series of future values to achieve a given net present value. This is equivalent to the interest rate which it is necessary to use when discounting a series of future values *and* a cashflow *now*, to achieve a *zero* present value. Consider the following cashflows, for example, which might arise from some project:

Now:	−87
After 1 year:	+25
After 2 years:	−40
After 3 years:	+60
After 4 years:	+60

What interest rate is needed to discount +25, −40, +60 and +60 back to a net present value of +87? The answer is 5.6 percent. It can therefore be said that an initial investment of 87 produces a 5.6 percent internal rate of return if it generates these subsequent cashflows. This is equivalent to saying that, using 5.6 percent, the net present value of −87, +25, −40, +60 and +60 is zero.

Calculating an NPV is relatively simple: calculate each present value separately and add them together. Calculating an IRR however requires a repeated "trial and error" method and is therefore generally done using a specially designed calculator.

Example 1.15 What is the IRR of the following cashflows?

Now:	−$164
After 1 year:	+$45
After 2 years:	+$83
After 3 years:	+$75

Answer: 10.59% (If you do not have a calculator able to calculate this, try checking the answer by working backwards: the NPV of all the future values, using the rate of 10.59%, should come to +$164.)

> *See below for an explanation of how to use the HP19 to solve this.*

Key Point

> The internal rate of return is the interest rate which discounts all the known future cashflows to a given NPV.
>
> This is equivalent to the interest rate which discounts all the cashflows *including* any cashflow *now* to zero.

Money-weighted, and time-weighted, rates of return

An internal rate of return is sometimes known as a money-weighted rate of return, because the rate so calculated varies according to the cashflows arising over the period. Consider for example a fund which has 100 at the beginning of the year. This increases in value to 105 after six months. At that point, a further 50 is added to the fund. By the end of the year, the value of the fund has risen to 170. What is the rate of return on the fund?

Over the first six months, the absolute rate of return (i.e. *not* per annum) is 5.00%:

$$\frac{105}{100} - 1 = 0.0500$$

Over the second six months, the absolute rate of return is 9.68%:

$$\frac{170}{155} - 1 = 0.0968$$

The money-weighted rate of return over the year is the internal rate of return of the cashflows: −100 at time zero, −50 at time six months and +170 at time one year. This comes to 16.12%. This gives a greater weighting to the second half of the year than to the first, because there is more money in the fund for the second half, due to the extra 50 added.

The time-weighted rate of return over the year, however, excludes the effect of the addition of extra money, by compounding the rates of return for the two halves of the year to give 15.16%:

$$\frac{105}{100} \times \frac{170}{155} - 1 = 0.1516$$

In general, the time-weighted rate of return is a geometric average. It can be calculated by compounding the growth for periods between flows of new money. It might be preferred for comparing the management of two funds for example, because the addition of new money is outside the control of the fund manager.

ANNUITIES

An annuity is a regular stream of future cash receipts which can be purchased by an initial cash investment. An annuity is also known as an annuity certain. When the payments are made at the end of each period, it is known as a deferred annuity and when they are at the beginning of each period, an annuity due.

An annuity is an investment designed to provide a regular stream of income rather than a lump sum at maturity. This would suit for example an investor's need to provide for a particular expense (such as school fees) over a number of years. A house mortgage structured with regular monthly payments over a number of years but no lump sum payment at maturity is similarly an annuity structure.

The regular payments are not necessarily equal. They can for example increase at a regular predetermined rate. This would be useful for an income stream designed to increase with forecast inflation.

The payment stream can also last indefinitely, in which case the annuity is known as a perpetual.

The size of the future cash amounts is determined by the yield appropriate to the investment. This is the same as the internal rate of return on all the cashflows (initial outflow and subsequent inflows).

A bond paying a fixed coupon rate can also be seen as a combination of an annuity (representing the coupon payments) plus a zero-coupon bond (representing the face value of the bond redeemed at maturity). This is one approach to interpreting the conventional formula for the price of a bond.

Annuity paying a constant amount at the end of each year — *Calculation summary*

$$\text{Initial cost} = \frac{\text{annual amount}}{\text{yield}} \times \left(1 - \left(\frac{1}{(1 + \text{yield})^{\text{number of years}}}\right)\right)$$

$$\text{Annual amount} = \frac{\text{initial cost} \times \text{yield}}{\left(1 - \left(\frac{1}{(1 + \text{yield})^{\text{number of years}}}\right)\right)}$$

▶

Annuity paying a constant amount at the beginning of each year

$$\text{Initial cost} = \frac{\text{annual amount}}{\text{yield}} \times \left(1 + \text{yield} - \left(\frac{1}{(1 + \text{yield})^{(\text{number of years} - 1)}}\right)\right)$$

$$\text{Annual amount} = \frac{\text{initial cost} \times \text{yield}}{\left(1 + \text{yield} - \left(\frac{1}{(1 + \text{yield})^{(\text{number of years} - 1)}}\right)\right)}$$

Perpetual annuity paying a constant amount at the end of each year

$$\text{Initial cost} = \frac{\text{annual amount}}{\text{yield}}$$

$$\text{Annual amount} = \text{initial cost} \times \text{yield}$$

All the following examples assume that yields are quoted on a bond basis (effectively a 365-day year basis), rather than a money market basis (effectively a 360-day year basis).

Example 1.16 What is the cost of a 10-year annuity paying $5,000 at the end of each year and yielding 6%?

$$\text{Initial cost} = \frac{\$5,000}{0.06} \times \left(1 - \left(\frac{1}{(1.06)^{10}}\right)\right) = \$36,800.44$$

1.06 ENTER 10 □ ∧ □ $^1/x$ 1 □ $x \gtrless y$ − 5,000 × .06 ÷

Example 1.17 How much is payable at the end of each year on a 7-year annuity yielding 6%, if the initial investment is $60,000?

$$\text{Annual amount} = \frac{\$60,000 \times 0.06}{\left(1 - \left(\frac{1}{(1.06)^{7}}\right)\right)} = \$10,748.10$$

1.06 ENTER 7 □ ∧ □ $^1/x$ 1 □ $x \gtrless y$ − 60,000 □ $x \gtrless y$ ÷ .06 ×

Example 1.18 What is the cost of a 10-year annuity paying £5,000 at the beginning of each year and yielding 6%?

$$\text{Initial cost} = \frac{£5,000}{0.06} \times \left(1.06 - \left(\frac{1}{(1.06)^{9}}\right)\right) = £39,008.46$$

1.06 ENTER 9 □ ∧ □ $^1/x$ 1.06 □ $x \gtrless y$ − 5,000 × .06 ÷

A 25-year mortgage of £100,000 is structured with equal payments at the beginning of each month and no lump sum paid at maturity. The interest rate is 7.5% per annum (monthly basis).

Example 1.19

$$\text{Monthly payment} = \frac{\dfrac{£100,000 \times 0.075}{12}}{\left(12.075 - \left(\left(1 + \left(\dfrac{0.075}{12}\right)\right)^{((12 \times 25)-1)}\right)\right)} = £734.40$$

.075 ENTER 12 ÷ 1 + 12 ENTER 25 × 1 − ☐ ∧ 12 ☐ $x \gtreqless y$ ÷ 12.075 ☐ $x \gtreqless y$
−100,000 ☐ $x \gtreqless y$ ÷ .075 ×

What is the cost of a perpetual annuity paying $5,000 at the end of each year?

Example 1.20

$$\text{Initial cost} = \frac{\$5,000}{0.06} = \$83,333.33$$

5,000 ENTER .06 ÷

USING AN HP CALCULATOR FOR CASHFLOW ANALYSIS

There are various functions built into the HP calculator relating to the time value of money. These involve using five keys: N for the number of time periods involved, I%YR for the yield, PV for the initial cashflow or present value, PMT for a regular cashflow recurring at the end of each period and FV for an additional final cashflow or the future value. Any of the cashflows (PV, PMT or FV) may be zero. Before any cashflow operation, we suggest setting the calculator by entering g END (for the HP12C) or selecting the FIN menu, selecting the TVM menu, selecting OTHER and then selecting END (for the other calculators). Note that you must always pay strict attention to the sign of each cashflow: a cash outflow is negative and a cash inflow is positive.

HP calculator example

Example

What is the net present value of the following cashflows using an interest rate of 10%?

$11 at the end of each year for 7 years.
$80 at the end of the seventh year in addition to the $11.

Answer: $94.61

HP12C	HP19BII (RPN mode)	HP19BII (algebraic)
7 n	Select FIN menu	Select FIN menu
10 i	Select TVM menu	Select TVM menu
11 PMT	7 N	7 N
80 FV	10 I%YR	10 I%YR
PV	11 PMT	11 PMT
	80 FV	80 FV
	PV	PV

Example   **HP calculator example**

What is the internal rate of return of the following cashflows?

Outflow of $94.6053 now.
Inflow of $11 at the end of each year for 7 years.
Inflow of $80 at the end of the seventh year in addition to the $11.

Answer: 10%

HP12C	HP19BII (RPN mode)	HP19BII (algebraic)
7 n	Select FIN menu	Select FIN menu
94.6053 CHS PV	Select TVM menu	Select TVM menu
11 PMT	7 N	7 N
80 FV	94.6053 +/– PV	94.6053 +/– PV
i	11 PMT	11 PMT
	80 FV	80 FV
	I%YR	I%YR

Example   **HP calculator example**

What regular cash inflow is needed at the end of each year for the next seven years to achieve an internal rate of return of 10%, assuming an additional final cash inflow of $80 at the end of the seventh year and a net present value of $94.6053?

Answer: $11

HP12C	HP19BII (RPN mode)	HP19BII (algebraic)
7 n	Select FIN menu	Select FIN menu
10 i	Select TVM menu	Select TVM menu
94.6053 CHS PV	7 N	7 N
80 FV	10 I%YR	10 I%YR
PMT	94.6053 +/– PV	94.6053 +/– PV
	80 FV	80 FV
	PMT	PMT

You can see that the last three examples all involve the same five data: the number of time periods (N = 7), the interest rate or internal rate of return per period (I%YR = 10), the net present value (PV = –94.6053), the regular cashflow each period (PMT = 11) and the additional final cashflow or future value (FV = 80). Once four of these five data have been entered, the fifth can be calculated by pressing the relevant key.

HP calculator example

Example

What is the internal rate of return of the following cashflows?

> Outflow of $60 now.
> Inflow of $10 at the end of each year for 10 years.

Answer: 10.5580%

HP12C	HP19BII (RPN mode)	HP19BII (algebraic)
10 n	Select FIN menu	Select FIN menu
60 CHS PV	Select TVM menu	Select TVM menu
10 PMT	10 N	10 N
0 FV	60 +/– PV	60 +/– PV
i	10 PMT	10 PMT
	0 FV	0 FV
	I%YR	I%YR

For the TVM function to be appropriate, the time periods between each cashflow must be regular. They do not need to be 1 year. If the periods are shorter than a year however, the absolute interest rate for that period and the total number of periods (rather than years) must be entered.

HP calculator example

Example

What is the net present value of the following cashflows using an interest rate of 10% per annum paid quarterly?

> $100 at the end of each quarter for 5 years.
> $1,000 at the end of the fifth year in addition to the $100.

Answer: $2,169.19

HP12C	HP19BII (RPN mode)	HP19BII (algebraic)
20 n	Select FIN menu	Select FIN menu
2.5 i	Select TVM menu	Select TVM menu
100 PMT	20 N	20 N
1000 FV	2.5 I%YR	2.5 I%YR
PV	100 PMT	100 PMT
	1000 FV	1000 FV
	PV	PV

In the example above, instead of entering the interest rate per period as 2.5 percent, it is possible with the HP19BII to enter the interest rate per year as 10% and the number of payments per year as 4 as follows. This merely avoids dividing by 4.

	HP19BII (RPN mode)	HP19BII (algebraic)
	Select FIN menu	Select FIN menu
	Select TVM menu	Select TVM menu
	OTHER 4 P/YR EXIT	OTHER 4 P/YR EXIT
	20 N	20 N
	10 I%YR	10 I%YR
	100 PMT	100 PMT
	1000 FV	1000 FV
	PV	PV

The built-in TVM functions can be used when all the cashflows are the same except for the initial cashflow now or present value, and the additional final cashflow or future value. For bonds and swaps, this is often the case. In cases where the cashflows are irregular however, an alternative function must be used.

Example   **HP calculator example**

What is the IRR of the following cashflows?

Now:	−$120
After 1 year:	+$20
After 2 years:	+$90
After 3 years:	−$10
After 4 years:	+$30
After 5 years:	+$30
After 6 years:	+$30
After 7 years:	+$40

Answer: 20.35%

HP12C	HP19BII (RPN mode)	HP19BII (algebraic)
f CLEAR REG	Select FIN menu	Select FIN menu
120 CHS g CFo	Select CFLO menu	Select CFLO menu
20 g Cfj	☐ CLEAR DATA	☐ CLEAR DATA
90 g Cfj	Select yes	Select yes
10 CHS g Cfj	120 +/− INPUT	120 +/− INPUT
30 g Cf	20 INPUT INPUT	20 INPUT INPUT
3 g Nj	90 INPUT INPUT	90 INPUT INPUT
40 g Cfj	10 +/− INPUT INPUT	10 +/− INPUT INPUT
f IRR	30 INPUT 3 INPUT	30 INPUT 3 INPUT
	40 INPUT INPUT	40 INPUT INPUT
	CALC	CALC
	IRR%	IRR%

(If several successive cashflows are the same, the amount need be entered only once, followed by the number of times it occurs.)

HP calculator example

Using the same cashflows as above, what is the NPV of all the cashflows using an interest rate of 10%?

Answer: 41.63%

HP12C	HP19BII (RPN mode)	HP19BII (algebraic)
f CLEAR REG	Select FIN menu	Select FIN menu
120 CHS g Cfo	Select CFLO menu	Select CFLO menu
20 g Cfj	☐ CLEAR DATA	☐ CLEAR DATA
90 g Cfj	Select yes	Select yes
10 CHS g Cfj	120 +/– INPUT	120 +/– INPUT
30 g Cfj	20 INPUT INPUT	20 INPUT INPUT
3 g Nj	90 INPUT INPUT	90 INPUT INPUT
40 g Cfj	10 +/– INPUT INPUT	10 +/– INPUT INPUT
10 i	30 INPUT 3 INPUT	30 INPUT 3 INPUT
f NPV	40 INPUT INPUT	40 INPUT INPUT
	CALC	CALC
	10 I%	10 I%
	NPV	NPV

Solution to Example 1.15 using HP19BII
FIN CFLO GET ☐ CLEAR DATA YES
164 +/– INPUT
45 INPUT INPUT
83 INPUT INPUT
75 INPUT INPUT
CALC
IRR%

Solution to Example 1.16 using HP19BII
FIN TVM
10 N
6 I%YR
5,000 PMT
0 FV
PV

INTERPOLATION AND EXTRAPOLATION

In the money market, prices are generally quoted for standard periods such as 1 month, 2 months, etc. If a dealer needs to quote a price for an "odd date" between these periods, he needs to "interpolate".

Suppose for example that the 1-month rate (30 days) is 8.0 percent and that the 2-month rate (61 days) is 8.5 percent. The rate for 1 month and 9 days (39 days) assumes that interest rates increase steadily from the 1-month rate to the 2-month rate – a *straight line* interpolation. The increase from 30 days to 39 days will therefore be a $\frac{9}{31}$ proportion of the increase from 30 days to 61 days. The 39-day rate is therefore:

$$8.0\% + (8.5\% - 8.0\%) \times \tfrac{9}{31} = 8.15\%$$

The same process can be used for interpolating exchange rates.

Example 1.21   The 2-month (61 days) rate is 7.5% and the 3-month (92 days) rate is 7.6%.

What is the 73-day rate?

$$7.5 + (7.6 - 7.5) \times \tfrac{12}{31} = 7.5387$$

Answer: 7.5387%

```
7.6 ENTER 7.5 –
12 × 31 ÷
7.5 +
```

If the odd date required is just before or just after the known periods, rather than between them, the same principle can be applied (in this case "extrapolation" rather than interpolation).

Example 1.22   The 2-month (61 days) rate is 7.5% and the 3-month (92 days) rate is 7.6%.

What is the 93-day rate?

$$7.5 + (7.6 - 7.5) \times \tfrac{32}{31} = 7.6032$$

Answer: 7.6032%

```
7.6 ENTER 7.5 –
32 × 31 ÷
7.5 +
```

An alternative is "exponential" (or "logarithmic") interpolation, in which a straight line interpolation is performed on the logarithms of the data rather than on the data themselves. This can provide a smoother interpolation and, although the difference between the two methods can be rather small, it can be significant for capital market calculations.

Example 1.23

The 2-month (61 days) rate is 7.5% and the 3-month (92 days) rate is 7.6%.

What is the 73-day rate using logarithmic interpolation?

$$\text{Log}_e 7.5 + (\text{Log}_e 7.6 - \text{Log}_e 7.5) \times \tfrac{12}{31} = 2.02003$$

$$e^{2.02003} = 7.5386$$

Answer: 7.5386%

What is the 93-day rate using logarithmic interpolation?

$$\text{Log}_e 7.5 + (\text{Log}_e 7.6 - \text{Log}_e 7.5) \times \tfrac{32}{31} = 2.02858$$

$$e^{2.02858} = 7.6032$$

Answer: 7.6032%

☐ MATH LOGS 7.6 LN
7.5 LN STO 1 –
12 × 31 ÷
RCL 1 +
EXP

☐ MATH LOGS 7.6 LN
7.5 LN STO 1 –
32 × 31 ÷
RCL 1 +
EXP

Straight line interpolation

$$i = i_1 + (i_2 - i_1) \times \frac{(d - d_1)}{(d_2 - d_1)}$$

Exponential interpolation

$$\log(i) = \log(i_1) + (\log(i_2) - \log(i_1)) \times \frac{(d - d_1)}{(d_2 - d_1)}$$

or equivalently:

$$i = i_1 \times \left(\frac{i_2}{i_1}\right)^{\left(\frac{d - d_1}{d_2 - d_1}\right)}$$

where: i is the rate required for d days
i_1 is the known rate for d_1 days
i_2 is the known rate for d_2 days

MEAN, VARIANCE, STANDARD DEVIATION AND VOLATILITY

The arithmetic mean (or simply mean) of a series of numbers is the average of the numbers as we normally understand it. If we have the following five numbers:

52, 53, 57, 58, 60

then their mean is:

$$\frac{(52 + 53 + 57 + 58 + 60)}{5} = 56$$

The mean is useful, because it gives us an idea of how big the numbers are – "about 56". However, if we knew only this mean, 56, it would not give us any idea of how "spread out" all the numbers are around 56; perhaps they are all very close to 56, or perhaps they are very spread out.

The standard deviation of the same numbers is a measure of how spread out the numbers are around this mean. If all the numbers were exactly the same, the standard deviation would be zero. If the numbers were very spread out, the standard deviation would be very high. Effectively, the standard deviation gives an idea of the answer to the question: "On average, how far are the numbers away from their mean?" The standard deviation is defined as the square root of the "variance". The variance in turn is defined as the average of the squared difference between each number and their average.

Consider the two following sets of numbers (see Figures 1.1 and 1.2). They also each have a mean of 56, but the first set is closely packed together and the second set is very spread out. In fact, the first set has a

Figure 1.1

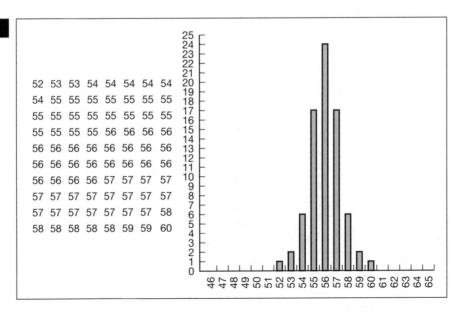

```
52  53  53  54  54  54  54  54
54  55  55  55  55  55  55  55
55  55  55  55  55  55  55  55
55  55  55  55  56  56  56  56
56  56  56  56  56  56  56  56
56  56  56  56  56  56  56  56
56  56  56  56  57  57  57  57
57  57  57  57  57  57  57  57
57  57  57  57  57  57  57  58
58  58  58  58  58  59  59  60
```

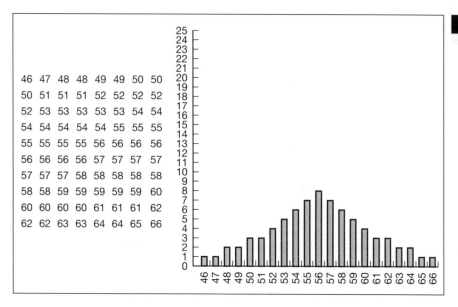

Figure 1.2

standard deviation of 1.4 and the second set has a standard deviation of 4.3. If the standard distribution or variance is lower, the histogram is compressed horizontally – it looks taller and thinner – and there is a lower probability that any particular number is a long way from the mean. If the standard distribution or variance is greater, the histogram is more stretched out horizontally – it looks lower and fatter – and more numbers are further from the mean.

This gives the variance of a set of numbers, given that all the numbers are known. Very often however, a sample only of the numbers is used. For example, a representative sample of prices for a particular instrument might be the daily closing prices over a period of only 1 year, rather than over the entire history of that instrument since it began trading. In this case, a better estimate of the variance of all the numbers is:

$$\text{Estimated variance} = \frac{\text{sum of all the (difference from the mean)}^2}{\text{(the number of values} - 1)}$$

Whichever formula is used,

$$\text{Standard deviation} = \sqrt{\text{variance}}$$

The symbol μ is sometimes used for the mean, the symbol σ for the standard deviation and the symbol σ^2 for the variance.

Calculation summary

Mean (μ) = sum of all the values divided by the number of values

Variance (σ^2) = mean of (difference from mean)^2

$$= \frac{\text{sum of all the (difference from the mean)}^2}{\text{the number of values}}$$

When estimating the variance from only a sample of the data rather than all the data, divide by 1 less than the number of values used.

Standard deviation (σ) = $\sqrt{\text{variance}}$

Example 1.24 What are the mean, variance and standard deviation of the following numbers?

83, 87, 82, 89, 88

Their mean is:

$$\frac{(83 + 87 + 82 + 89 + 88)}{5} = 85.8$$

Numbers	Difference between the numbers and 85.8	(Difference)^2
83	−2.8	7.84
87	+1.2	1.44
82	−3.8	14.44
89	+3.2	10.24
88	+2.2	4.84
Mean = 85.8		Total = 38.80

The variance is therefore $\dfrac{38.80}{5} = 7.76$ and the standard deviation is $\sqrt{7.76} = 2.79$.

83 ENTER 87 + 82 + 89 + 88 + 5 ÷	(Mean)
STO 1	
83 RCL 1 − 2 ☐ ∧	
87 RCL 1 − 2 ☐ ∧ +	
82 RCL 1 − 2 ☐ ∧ +	
89 RCL 1 − 2 ☐ ∧ +	
88 RCL 1 − 2 ☐ ∧ +	
5 ÷	(Variance)
☐ $\sqrt{x}$	(Standard deviation)

Example 1.25

If the numbers above were only a sample of all the possible numbers, a better estimate of the variance of all the numbers would be found by dividing by 4, rather than by 5. The estimated variance would therefore be $\frac{38.80}{4} = 9.70$ and the estimated standard deviation would be $\sqrt{9.7} = 3.11$.

Calculating historic volatility

The volatility of an option is defined formally as the annualised standard deviation of the logarithm of relative price movements. This is the standard deviation of the continuously compounded return over a year.

Example 1.26

Given five daily price data for an exchange rate, the volatility is calculated as follows:

Day	Exchange rate	LN($\frac{1.8345}{1.8220}$) etc.	Difference from mean	(Difference)^2
1	1.8220			
2	1.8345	0.00684	0.00622	0.000039
3	1.8315	−0.00164	−0.00226	0.000006
4	1.8350	0.00191	0.00129	0.000002
5	1.8265	−0.00464	−0.00526	0.000028
		Mean = 0.00062		Total = 0.000074

$$\text{Variance} = \frac{\text{sum of (differences)}^2}{(\text{number of data} - 1)} = \frac{0.000074}{3} = 0.000025$$

$$\text{Standard deviation} = \sqrt{\text{variance}} = 0.00497$$

$$\text{Volatility} = \text{standard deviation} \times \sqrt{\text{frequency of data per year}}$$

$$= 0.00497 \times \sqrt{252} = 7.9\%$$

The frequency per year of the data in Example 1.27 assumes that weekends and bank holidays are ignored for daily data. If "dummy" data are included for these days, then the frequency per year is 365. If the data are weekly, the annualised volatility is:

$$0.00497 \times \sqrt{52} = 3.6\%$$

Note that we began with 4 data. Although there are 5 exchange rates, there are only 4 relative price changes. In calculating the variance, we then divided by 3, rather than 4 because, as mentioned earlier, when only a part of the historical data is used rather than all possible data, a better estimate of the true variance is achieved by dividing by (number of data − 1).

What we have calculated is the historic volatility – that is, the volatility of actual recorded prices. When a dealer calculates an option price, he will not in practice use an historic volatility exactly. Instead, he will use a blend of his own forecast for volatility, the current general market estimate of volatility, his own position and recent actual experience of volatility.

The volatility which is used to calculate an option premium – either the price quoted by a particular dealer or the current general market price – is known as the "implied volatility", or simply the "implied". This is because, given the pricing model, the price and all the other factors, it is possible to work backwards to calculate what volatility is implied in that calculation. Implied volatility therefore means current volatility as used by the market in its pricing.

Calculation summary

$$\text{Historic volatility} =$$
$$\text{standard deviation of LN(relative price movement)} \times$$
$$\sqrt{\text{frequency of data per year}}$$

CORRELATION AND COVARIANCE

Correlation and covariance are measures of the extent to which two things do, or do not, move together. The precise mathematical definitions are given below.

Consider for example the price of a 10-year government bond and the price of an 11-year government bond (issued by the same government). Generally, the price of one will rise and fall in line with the price of the other. The two prices are therefore closely correlated. When house prices rise, however, a government bond price might fall (because rising inflation pushes up interest rates) and vice versa. There might therefore be a negative correlation between government bond prices and the value of shares in a building materials producer. There might well be very little relationship at all between government bond prices and the price of rubber, so that the price of one moving up or down suggests no information about whether the other has risen or fallen (no correlation).

A correlation coefficient lies between +1 and −1. If two series of numbers are perfectly correlated – they move exactly in line – their correlation co-efficient is +1. If they move exactly in line but in opposite directions, their correlation coefficient is −1. If there is no link at all between the two series, their correlation coefficient is 0.

First series	Second series	Correlation coefficient	First series	Second series	Correlation coefficient	First series	Second series	Correlation coefficient
1	2		1	-2		1	10	
2	4		2	-4		2	2	
3	6	+1	3	-6	-1	3	4	0
4	8		4	-8		4	6	
5	10		5	-10		5	9	

Covariance is a concept linking correlation and variance. Whereas variance quantifies how much the value of one particular thing varies, covariance measures how much two things vary, relative to each other.

Calculation summary

Correlation coefficient

$$= \frac{\text{sum of } (x \times y) - (n \times (\text{mean of } x) \times (\text{mean of } y))}{\sqrt{[((\text{sum of } x^2) - (n \times (\text{mean of } x)^2)) \times (\text{sum of } (y^2) - (n \times (\text{mean of } y)^2))]}}$$

Covariance

$$= \text{correlation coefficient} \times (\text{standard deviation of } x) \times (\text{standard deviation of } y)$$

$$= \frac{\text{correlation coefficient}}{n} \times \sqrt{(\text{sum of } (x - \text{mean of } x)^2 \times \text{sum of } (y - \text{mean of } y)^2}$$

where n is the number of pairs of data

What are the correlation coefficient and covariance of the following prices?

Example 1.27

	First price x	Second price y	$x \times y$	x^2	y^2	$(x - \text{ave of } x)^2$	$(y - \text{ave of } y)^2$
Day 1:	94	75	7,050	8,836	5,625	1	4
Day 2:	95	74	7,030	9,025	5,476	4	1
Day 3:	93	73	6,789	8,649	5,329	0	0
Day 4:	91	72	6,552	8,281	5,184	4	1
Day 5:	92	71	6,532	8,464	5,041	1	4
Totals:	465	365	33,953	43,255	26,655	10	10

Average of $x = \dfrac{465}{5} = 93$ Average of $y = \dfrac{365}{5} = 73$

Correlation coefficient $= \dfrac{33,953 - (5 \times 93 \times 73)}{\sqrt{((43,255 - (5 \times (93)^2)) \times (26,655 - (5 \times (73)^2)))}} = 0.80$

This is a reasonably high level of correlation, indicating that the price of x and the price of y move to some extent in parallel:

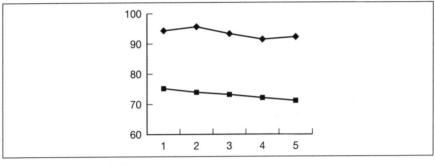

$$\text{Covariance} = \frac{0.80}{4} \times \sqrt{(10 \times 10)} = 2.0$$

THE 'NORMAL' PROBABILITY FUNCTION

Probability density

The "probability density" of a series of numbers is a description of how likely any one of them is to occur. Thus the probability density of the results of throwing a die is $\frac{1}{6}$ for each possible result. The probability density of the heights of 100 adult men chosen at random will be relatively high for around 170 cm to 180 cm, and extremely low for less than 150 cm or more than 200 cm. The "shape" of the probability density therefore varies with the type of results being considered.

A particular probability density which is used as an approximate description of many circumstances in life is known as the "normal" probability function (see Figure 1.3).

Figure 1.3

Normal probability density function

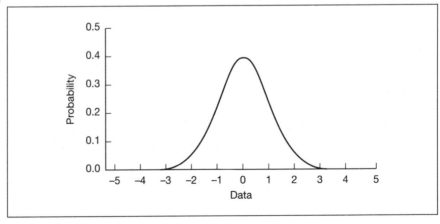

If the probabilities are as shown in Figure 1.3, for example, a number less than −3 or more than +3 is extremely unlikely, while a number between say −1 and +1 is rather likely.

The normal probability function is not straightforward – the equation for Figure 1.3 is:

$$\text{Probability density} = \frac{1}{\sqrt{2\pi}\ e^{\frac{x^2}{2}}}$$

This function is important here because it is used in option pricing. A standard assumption used for pricing options is that movements in the logarithm of relative prices can be described by this function. By this we mean $\text{LN}\left(\frac{\text{current price}}{\text{previous price}}\right)$. If we are looking at daily price changes for example, this means that a series of data such as $\text{LN}\left(\frac{\text{today's price}}{\text{yesterday's price}}\right)$ is expected to have a normal probability density.

This relative price change $\frac{\text{current price}}{\text{previous price}}$ is the same as $\left(1 + i \times \frac{\text{days}}{\text{year}}\right)$, where i is the rate of return being earned on an investment in the asset. We have seen that $\text{LN}\left(1 + i \times \frac{\text{days}}{\text{year}}\right)$ is equal to $r \times \frac{\text{days}}{\text{year}}$ where r is the continuously compounded rate of return. Therefore the quantity $\text{LN}\left(\frac{\text{current price}}{\text{previous price}}\right)$ which we are considering is in fact the continuously compounded return on the asset over the period.

Probability distribution

The "cumulative probability distribution" of a series of numbers is the probability that the result will be no greater than a particular number. Thus the probability distribution for throwing the die is:

probability ⅙ that the number thrown will be 1
probability ²⁄₆ that the number thrown will be 1 or 2
probability ³⁄₆ that the number thrown will be 1, 2 or 3
probability ⁴⁄₆ that the number thrown will be 1, 2, 3 or 4
probability ⁵⁄₆ that the number thrown will be 1, 2, 3, 4 or 5
probability ⁶⁄₆ that the number thrown will be 1, 2, 3, 4, 5 or 6

The normal probability function shown above has the probability distribution shown below (Figure 1.4). With this particular normal probability distribution, there is a probability of around 84.1% that the outcome will be less than or equal to 1 standard deviation higher than the mean; a probability of around 97.7% that the outcome will be less than or equal to 2 standard deviations higher than the mean; a probability of around 99.9% that the outcome will be less than or equal to 3 standard deviations higher than the mean, and so on.

In each of these examples, we are considering a range which goes down to minus infinity but goes up only to a certain defined level (1, 2, 3 and so on), leaving a "tail" excluded at the top. Often however, we are interested in a range

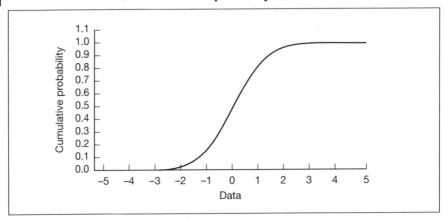

Figure 1.4

Normal cumulative probability distribution

of a certain width around the mean which excludes a tail at each end – one of relatively very high values and one of relatively very low values. This is a "two-tailed" measurement rather than "one-tailed". For example, with the same normal probability distribution, 68.3% of values will lie within a range of 1 standard deviation either side of the mean, 95.4% of values will lie within a range of ± 2 standard deviations either side of the mean, 99.7% of values will lie within a range of ± 3 standard deviations either side of the mean, etc.

EXERCISES

1. What is the future value after 120 days of £43 invested at 7.5%?

2. You will receive a total of £89 after 93 days. What is the present value of this amount discounted at 10.1%?

3. You invest £83 now and receive back a total of £83.64 after 28 days. What is the yield on your investment?

4. What is the future value in 10 years' time of £36 now, using 9% per annum?

5. You have a choice between receiving DEM 1,000 now or DEM 990 in 3 months' time. Assuming interest rates of 8.0%, which do you choose?

6. If you invest £342 for 5 years at 6% per annum (interest paid annually), how much interest do you receive at the end of 5 years assuming that all interim cashflows can be reinvested also at 6%?

7. What is the present value, using a rate of discount of 11%, of a cashflow of DEM 98.00 in 5 years' time?

8. You place £1,000 in a 4-year investment which makes no interest payments but yields 5.4% per annum compound. How much do you expect to receive at the end of 4 years?

9. You invest £1,000 and receive back a total of £1,360.86 at the end of 7 years. There are no interest payments during the 7 years. What annual yield does this represent?

10. You deposit £1 million for 10 years. It accumulates interest at 6% quarterly for the first 5 years and 6.5% semi-annually for the next 5 years. The interest is automatically added to the capital at each payment date. What is the total accumulated value at the end of 10 years?

11. You place £1 million on deposit for 1 year at 8.5%. What total value will you have accumulated by the end of the year, assuming that the interest is paid quarterly and can be reinvested at the same rate? What would the total value be if the interest payments could be reinvested at only 8.0% paid quarterly?

12. You buy a 10-year annuity, with a yield of 9% per annum. How much must you invest in the annuity now to receive £5,000 at the end of each year?

13. You borrow £90,000 for 25 years at 7.25% per annum (interest paid monthly). You repay the loan by making equal payments which cover principal plus interest at the end of each month for the 25 years. How much are the monthly payments?

14. You receive 11.4% paid semi-annually. What is the effective rate (annual equivalent)?

15. You receive 12% paid annually. What are the equivalent quarterly rate and monthly rate?

16. If 7.0% is a continuously compounded interest rate, what is the total value accumulated at the end of a year at this rate, on a principal amount of £1 million, and what is the effective rate (annual equivalent)? If 9.0% is an effective (annual equivalent) rate, what is the equivalent continuously compounded rate?

17. You receive 6.5% per annum on a 138-day deposit. What is the effective rate? What is the daily equivalent rate? What is the 138-day discount factor?

18. The 30-day interest rate is 5.2% and the 60-day rate is 5.4%. Interpolate (straight line) to find the 41-day rate.

19. What is the NPV of the following cashflows using an effective annual interest rate of 10% per annum?

Now:	−$105
6 months:	−$47
12 months:	−$47
18 months:	−$47
24 months:	−$93
36 months:	+$450

20. What is the IRR of the cashflows in the previous question?

21. What is the estimated standard deviation of the price of a cup of coffee in Manchester? You have the following sample data from six cafes:

95 pence
250 pence
160 pence
124 pence
180 pence
175 pence

22. Assume that the price of coffee in Manchester is in fact normally distributed. Based on the mean price and estimated standard deviation from the previous question, what is the maximum that you will need to pay for a coffee 84.1% of the time?

Part 2

Interest Rate Instruments

"For any instrument, the price an investor is prepared to pay is the present value of the future cashflows which he or she will receive because of owning it."

■ ■ ■

2

The Money Market

OVERVIEW

The "money market" is the term used to include all *short-term* financial instruments which are based on an interest rate (whether the interest rate is actually paid or just implied in the way the instrument is priced). Traditionally, the money market covered instruments up to 1 year in maturity. Now however, it also includes instruments which are based on such short-term instruments, but are themselves longer term – for example, a 2-year interest rate swap, which could be priced from a series of 3-month interest rate futures (see later).

The underlying instruments are essentially those used by one party (the borrower, seller or issuer) to borrow and by the other party to lend (the lender, buyer or investor). The main such instruments are:

- Treasury bill — borrowing by government
- Time deposit
- Certificate of deposit (CD) } — borrowing by banks
- Commercial paper (CP) — borrowing by companies (or in some cases, banks)
- Bill of exchange — borrowing by companies
- Repurchase agreement — used to borrow short term but using another instrument (such as a bond) as collateral

Each of these instruments represents an obligation on the borrower to repay the amount borrowed at maturity, plus interest if appropriate. As well as these underlying borrowing instruments, there are other money market instruments which are linked to these, or at least to the same interest rate structure, but which are not direct obligations on the issuer in the same way:

- Futures contract
- Forward rate agreement (FRA) } — used to trade or hedge short-term interest rates for future periods
- Interest rate swap — used to trade or hedge interest rates for different periods

Negotiable security

There are two slightly different procedures for borrowing money. The first is simply that an organisation borrows money from a lender and agrees to repay the money to that lender in the future.

The second procedure involves giving the lender a "security" in return for the money. The lender can, if he wishes, then sell this security on to someone else. By doing so, he is effectively passing on the borrowing. At maturity of the borrowing, the original borrower still owes the money, and repays it. However, rather than repaying it to the original lender, he repays it instead to whoever currently holds the security. The borrower is said to have "issued" the security at the beginning. The security is thus a financial asset sold initially for cash by the issuer. A security which can be sold and bought again subsequently in this way – i.e. transferred from one party to another – is referred to as "negotiable".

A security can be represented by something physical – a paper certificate showing the issuer, the amount of money, the interest rate and the maturity date. Alternatively, it can be represented merely by an entry on a physical or a computerised register.

"Securitisation" is the process of creating a security out of a loan. For example, bank B lends cash to company C. In order to fund the loan, bank B issues a CD (i.e. a security). The bank has thereby securitised the loan.

| Negotiable security = sellable instrument representing a loan | **Key Point** |

A "secured" transaction is one where a party taking the credit risk has some claim on the assets of the other party. For example, when a bank lends cash to an individual to buy a house, the loan is usually secured by the bank having some claim on the value of the house if the individual fails to repay the money (a mortgage in this case). The house in this instance is, confusingly, also referred to as the "security" for the loan. Note that it is possible for a negotiable security to be secured or unsecured, and also for a simple borrowing to be either secured or unsecured.

The money market is linked to other markets through arbitrage mechanisms. Arbitrage occurs when it is possible to achieve the same result in terms of position and risk through two alternative mechanisms which have a slightly different price; the arbitrage involves achieving the result via the cheaper method and simultaneously reversing the position via the more expensive method – thereby locking in a profit which is free from market risk (although still probably subject to credit risk). For example, if I can buy one instrument cheaply and simultaneously sell at a higher price another instrument or combination of instruments with identical characteristics, I am arbitraging. In a completely free market with no other price considerations involved, the supply and demand effect of arbitrage tends to drive the two prices together.

For example, the money market is linked in this way to the forward foreign exchange market, through the theoretical ability to create synthetic deposits in one currency, by using foreign exchange deals combined with money market instruments. Similarly, it is linked to the capital markets (long-term financial instruments) through the ability to create longer-term instruments from a series of short-term instruments (such as a 5-year swap from a series of 3-month futures contracts).

| **Terminology** | **Eurocurrency** | Historically, the term "Euro" has been used to describe any instrument which is held outside the country whose currency is involved. The term does not imply "European" specifically. For example, a sterling deposit made by a UK resident in London is domestic sterling, but a sterling deposit made in New York is Eurosterling. Similarly, US dollar commercial paper issued outside the USA is Euro-commercial paper while US dollar commercial paper issued inside the USA is domestic commercial paper. Confusingly, this term has nothing whatever to do with the European Monetary Union currency also called "euro". |
| | **Face value** | For securities, the principal amount is generally known as the "face value" (which can be thought of as the principal amount written on the face of the instrument). It is also sometimes called the "nominal amount". |

Key Point	Face value = nominal amount = principal

| **Terminology** | **Notional principal** | With some instruments such as an FRA (see Chapter 3), the principal amount is never actually transferred to either party, but is used as a reference amount for calculation purposes. In this case, it is referred to as a "notional" principal. |
| | **Coupon/yield** | A certificate of deposit pays interest – usually only at maturity but sometimes also during the CD's life – as well as repaying the principal. For example, a CD might be issued with a face value of £1 million, which is repaid on maturity together with interest of say 10% calculated on the number of days between issue and maturity. The 10% interest rate is called the "coupon". The coupon is fixed once the CD is issued. This should not be confused with the "yield", which is the current rate of return available in the market when investing, or buying and selling an instrument, and varies continually. |

Key Point	A coupon, or the method for calculating it, is determined for an instrument at the outset. The yield is the market-determined rate of return, which changes continually.

Fixed rate or floating rate

Many instruments pay a "fixed" rate – that is, an interest rate or coupon which is determined when the instrument is issued and remains fixed throughout its life, regardless of whether the interest is paid only at maturity or on several occasions. Others pay a "floating" coupon rate. This means that the coupon rate is changed in line with market conditions at certain predetermined times (for example, refixed each 6 months to the current LIBOR (see below)).

Bid, offer and spread

As in other markets, money market dealers quote a "two-way" rate. This means that the dealer quotes two rates simultaneously – one at which he buys something or borrows money, and the other at which he sells something or lends money.

The "bid" price or rate is the rate at which the dealer quoting the price is prepared to buy or borrow. The "offer" (or "ask") rate is the rate at which he is prepared to sell or lend. The difference between them, representing a profit to the dealer, is called the "spread".

It is important to note that with cash, the dealer's bid means that he is willing to receive the cash (i.e. *borrow* cash) at that interest rate. However, with a negotiable security, his bid means that he is willing to receive the security and pay cash (i.e. *invest* cash) at that rate. Also, the bid and offer are not always quoted in that order (bid first, then offer) – they might be quoted the other way round. None of this creates ambiguity however. The higher interest rate is always the rate at which the dealer quoting the rate will lend or invest cash, regardless of whether he calls this his bid or his offer, and regardless of whether it is the first number quoted or the second. The lower interest rate is always the rate at which the dealer quoting the rate will borrow or receive cash.

LIBOR, EURIBOR

"LIBOR" means "London interbank offered rate" – the interest rate at which one London bank offers a cash deposit to another London bank of top creditworthiness. "LIBID" means "London interbank bid rate" – the rate at which a London bank of top creditworthiness bids for a cash deposit from another bank. LIBOR is always the higher side of a two-sided interest rate quotation (quoted high–low in some markets and low–high in others). "LIMEAN" is the average of the two sides. In practice, the offered rate for a particular currency at any moment is generally no different in London than in any other major centre, although reserve costs, credit

▶

considerations, etc. might make a slight difference. LIBOR is therefore often just shorthand for "offered interest rate".

Specifically however, LIBOR for a particular currency also means the average offered rate for that currency quoted by a group of banks in London at around 11:00 a.m. This is a reference rate (known as a "fixing") calculated on behalf of the BBA (British Bankers' Association) each day and used as a benchmark for agreeing rates between two parties for loans, FRAs and other instruments. LIBOR for GBP refers to GBP loans/deposits starting today. LIBOR for other currencies, and also EURIBOR, which is specifically for EUR, refer to loans/deposits starting in 2 days' time ("spot").

STIBOR is the reference in Stockholm for Swedish kronor, BUBOR for forints in Budapest, etc.

EONIA

Whereas EURIBOR is published at a particular time of day for a range of maturities for the EUR interest rate, EONIA ("Euro overnight index average") is a benchmark rate published by the European Central Bank (ECB) specifically for the EUR overnight interest rate. It is an average of the EUR overnight rate as traded throughout the day, weighted by the volume of business dealt at each rate. EURONIA is a similar rate published in the London market. The equivalent indexes published for GBP and USD are SONIA ("Sterling overnight index average") and "Fed funds effective" respectively.

Transactions are often based on such an overnight index even when the period of the transaction is longer than 1 day. In this case, the interest is settled not each day but after the end of the transaction, or periodically at agreed intervals, and is compounded to take account of the settlement delay. In some markets, the overnight index is published the morning after the day to which it relates. In Swiss francs, similar transactions are based on the tom/next rate rather than the overnight rate. The tom/next rate used in this case is not an average, but a fixing at 11:00 am.

Basis point

When discussing interest rates, a "basis point" is always 0.01% (which is the same as 0.0001). Note that this is not necessarily the same as a "point" in foreign exchange, which can vary according to the size of the exchange rate.

Key Point	1 basis point = 0.01%

Discount	1. An instrument which does not carry a coupon is a "discount" instrument. Because there is no interest paid on the principal, a buyer will only ever buy it for less than its face value – that is "at a discount" (unless yields are negative!). For example, almost all treasury bills are discount instruments.
	2. The word "discount" is also used in the very specialised context of a "discount rate" quoted in the US and UK markets on certain instruments. This is explained in detail below.
	3. To "discount" a cashflow means to calculate its present value, as discussed earlier.

Terminology

"Discount instrument" = instrument with a zero coupon
"Discount rate" = a special method of quoting a market rate
"To discount" = to calculate a present value

Key Point

Tenor	The "tenor" of an instrument is the length of time until it matures.
Primary market and secondary market	When a security is issued, the original purchaser is said to be buying it in the primary market. All subsequent transactions – whether they are on the same day or much later during the life of the security – are said to be secondary market transactions.

Terminology

"Primary market" is at issue.
"Secondary market" is everything thereafter.

Key Point

Bearer / registered	A "registered" security is one where the owner is considered to be whoever is registered centrally as the owner; this registration is changed each time the security changes hands. A "bearer" security by contrast is one where there is no registration of ownership; the issuer pays the principal at maturity (and coupon if there is one) to whoever is holding the security at maturity. This enables the security to be held anonymously.
Asset / liability	An "asset" is an investment or lending. A "liability" is a borrowing.

Terminology

DAY/YEAR CONVENTIONS

As a general rule in the money markets, the calculation of interest takes account of the exact number of days in the period in question, as a proportion of a year. Thus:

Key Point | Interest paid = interest rate quoted × days in period/days in year

A variation between different money markets arise, however, in the conventions used for the number of days assumed to be in the base "year". Domestic UK instruments, for example, assume that there are 365 days in a year, even when it is a leap year. Thus a sterling time deposit at 10 percent which lasts exactly one year but includes 29 February in its period (a total of 366 days) will actually pay slightly more than 10 percent – in fact:

$$10\% \times \frac{366}{365} = 10.027\%$$

This convention is usually referred to as ACT/365 – that is, the actual number of days in the period concerned, divided by 365. Some money markets, however, assume that each year has a conventional 360 days. For example, a dollar time deposit at 10 percent which lasts exactly 365 days pays:

$$10\% \times \frac{365}{360} = 10.139\%$$

This convention is usually referred to as ACT/360. The ACT/360 convention is also often known as the "money market basis" (because USD money markets, for example, use this basis). The ACT/365 convention is often known as the "bond basis" (because USD bond markets, for example, use a basis which is approximately equivalent to this).

Most money markets assume a conventional year of 360 days. There are however some exceptions, which assume a year of 365 days. These include the international and domestic markets in the following currencies:

- sterling
- Hong Kong dollar
- Singapore dollar
- Malaysian ringgit
- Taiwan dollar
- Thai baht
- South African rand

and the domestic (but not international) markets in the following currencies:

- Japanese yen
- Canadian dollar
- Australian dollar
- New Zealand dollar

In order to convert an interest rate i quoted on a 360-day basis to an interest rate i* quoted on a 365-day basis:

$$i* = i \times \frac{365}{360}$$

Similarly,

$$i* = i \times \frac{360}{365}$$

Calculation summary

Interest rate on 360-day basis = interest rate on 365-day basis $\times \frac{360}{365}$

Interest rate on 365-day basis = interest rate on 360-day basis $\times \frac{365}{360}$

Example 2.1

The yield on a security on an ACT/360 basis is 10.5%. What is the equivalent yield expressed on an ACT/365 day basis?

$$10.5 \times \frac{365}{360} = 10.6458$$

Answer: 10.6458%

```
10.5 ENTER
365 × 360 ÷
```

There are some exceptions to the general approach above. Yields on Icelandic T-bills and some short-term German securities, for example, are calculated on a "bond basis" (discussed in Chapter 5).

We have given a list of the conventions used in some important markets in Appendix 2.

Effective rates

The concept of "effective rate" discussed in Chapter 1 normally implies an annual equivalent interest rate on the basis of a calendar year – that is, 365 days. It is possible however to convert the result then to a 360-day basis.

Example 2.2 An amount of 83 is invested for 214 days. The total proceeds at the end are 92. What are the simple and effective rates of return on an ACT/360 basis?

$$\text{Simple rate of return (ACT/360)} = \left(\frac{\text{total proceeds}}{\text{initial investment}} - 1\right) \times \frac{\text{year}}{\text{days}}$$

$$= \left(\frac{92}{83} - 1\right) \times \frac{360}{214} = 18.24\%$$

$$\text{Effective rate of return (ACT/365)} = \left(\frac{\text{total proceeds}}{\text{initial investment}}\right)^{\frac{365}{\text{days}}} - 1$$

$$= \left(\frac{92}{83}\right)^{\frac{365}{214}} - 1 = 19.19\%$$

$$\text{Effective rate of return (ACT/360)} = 19.19\% \times \frac{360}{365} = 18.93\%$$

---

92 ENTER 83 ÷ 1 − 360 × 214 ÷	(Simple rate ACT/360)
92 ENTER 83 ÷ 365 ENTER 214 ÷ ☐ ∧ 1 −	
360 × 365 ÷	(Effective rate ACT/360)

Note that in Example 2.2 the effective rate on an ACT/360 basis is not $\left(\frac{92}{83}\right)^{\frac{360}{214}} - 1$ = 18.91%. This would instead be the equivalent 360-day rate (ACT/360 basis) – that is, the rate on a 360-day investment which is equivalent on a compound basis to 18.24 percent on a 214-day investment. The effective rate we want instead is the equivalent 365-day rate (ACT/360 basis) – that is, the rate on a 365-day investment which is equivalent on a compound basis to 18.24 percent (ACT/360) on a 214-day investment. The difference between these two is however usually not very significant.

MONEY MARKET INSTRUMENTS

Time deposit / loan

A time deposit or "clean" deposit is a deposit placed with a bank. This is not a security which can be bought or sold (that is, it is not "negotiable") and it must normally be held to maturity.

Time deposit/loan	
Term:	From 1 day to several years, but typically not longer than 1 year
Interest:	Usually all paid on maturity, but deposits of over a year (and sometimes those of less than a year) pay interest more frequently – commonly each year. A sterling 19-month deposit, for example, generally pays interest at the end of one year and then at maturity
Quotation:	As an interest rate
Registration:	There is no registration
Negotiable security?	No

Certificate of deposit (CD)

A certificate of deposit is a security issued to a depositor by a bank or building society, to raise money in the same way as a time deposit. A CD is however negotiable. This gives the investor flexibility in two ways. First, he can liquidate the CD if he needs the cash back sooner than anticipated. Second, it allows him to take a view on how interest rates will move, which is linked to the price at which the CD can be bought and sold. For example, if he buys a 6-month CD at 5% and one week later interest rates have fallen to 4.5%, he can then sell the CD and make a capital profit. Because of this flexibility, the yield on a CD (which is generally the same as the coupon when it is first issued) should be slightly lower than the yield on a deposit for the same term with the same bank.

For the bank, this gives the advantage of slightly cheaper funding, and also the possibility of managing its liabilities, in that the bank can buy its own CDs back in the market. It also enables the bank to raise longer-term funds, given the availability of CDs longer than a year.

In most countries, a CD is issued only by a bank or similar institution. CDs are purchased largely by professional depositor (rather than individuals) – companies, fund managers, banks, government bodies, etc. The CD is issued specifically for that depositor and the terms of that particular CD are negotiated between the issuing bank and the depositor, or via a broker.

CD	
Term:	Generally from 1 day up to 1 year, although CDs can be issued for up to 5 years in the London market
Interest:	Usually pays a coupon, although occasionally not. Interest is usually all paid on maturity, but CDs of over a year (and sometimes those of less than a year) pay interest more frequently – commonly each year or each 6 months. Some CDs pay a floating rate (FRCD), which is paid and refixed at regular intervals
Quotation:	As a yield
Negotiable security?	Yes

Treasury bill (T-bill)

Treasury bills are issued to raise short-term government finance. The exact name of the instrument varies from country to country.

A T-bill is issued by a government, or on behalf of a government by a central bank or government debt-issuing organisation. Investors are usually professional investors – companies, fund managers, banks, etc. – although some T-bills are issued in denominations small enough to allow for individuals to invest in them. T-bills are generally issued on a regular cycle (typically each quarter or each month) and generally for regular maturities (3 months, 6 months, etc.), in amounts reflecting the government's need for funds. Issue is generally by auction. This means that investors, particularly large banks, submit bids for the price or rate at which they would be willing to buy a given face value of bills, and the bills are issued to these bidders according to a predetermined procedure.

T-bill	
Term:	Typically 4, 13, 26 or 52 weeks but it does vary from country to country
Interest:	Generally non-interest-bearing, issued at a discount
Quotation:	T-bills in the UK and the US are quoted as a discount rate. T-bills in other countries are quoted as a yield
Negotiable security?	Yes

Commercial paper (CP)

Commercial paper is issued usually by a company (although some banks and governments also issue CP) in the same way that a CD is issued by a bank. CP is however usually not interest-bearing. The maturity can be anything from 1 to 365 days, depending on where it is issued, and in some countries can even be issued for several years. Unlike banker's acceptances (see below), no underlying trade transactions are necessary for issuing CP.

CP is generally unsecured (an "unsecured promissory note"), so that a company usually needs to have a good rating from a credit agency for its CP to be widely acceptable. A good quality corporate can borrow more cheaply than by using bank borrowing. This is because the borrowing is disintermediated – the end-investor is lending directly to the company, rather than there being a bank effectively intermediating between the investor and the borrower (as there is when a company borrows from a bank).

Governments generally issue T-bills on a regular schedule and for regular periods. Banks generally issue CDs when an investor requests them. CP issuance, by contrast, is initiated by the borrower and is very flexible in timing and maturity.

A company intending to issue CP generally arranges a CP programme with a bank (although it is possible for the corporate to run its own CP sales programme). The bank is acting as salesman in this role, not as lender. Whenever the corporate wishes to borrow, it calls the bank to arrange the sale of new paper to investors. CP borrowing can be arranged at very short notice – it is possible to arrange within the same day – and is completely flexible in terms of maturity. By repeatedly rolling over its short-term issues, the company can sell the paper to a range of investors, thereby widening its available funding sources (while still keeping its bank credit lines in reserve) and spreading the name of the company.

Investors in CP come from the professional market. For the investor, CP allows for investment in short-term assets unrelated to the banking industry. The bank selling the CP on behalf of the issuer is generally obliged to make a market in the CP, so that an investor is able to sell the paper again if he wishes.

Details vary between markets. For example:

Domestic US CP	
Term:	From 1 day to 270 days; usually very short term
Interest:	Non-interest-bearing
Quotation:	As a discount rate
Negotiable security?	Yes

Euro-commercial paper (ECP)	
Term:	From 1 to 365 days; usually between 30 and 180 days
Interest:	Usually non-interest-bearing
Quotation:	As a yield, calculated on the same year basis as other money market instruments in that Eurocurrency
Negotiable security?	Yes

Bill of exchange

A bill of exchange is used by a company essentially for trading purposes. It is an unconditional order in writing from one party to another, requiring the second party to pay an amount on a future date. The party originating the bill (this is the party to whom the money is owed) is called the "drawer" of the bill. The party to whom the bill requires the money to be paid (usually the same as the drawer) is the "payee". The party owing the money is the "drawee" of the bill. When the drawee accepts liability to pay the amount by signing the bill, it becomes the "acceptor". If a bank stands as guarantor to the drawer, it is also said to accept the bill by endorsing it appropriately. A bill accepted in this way is a "banker's acceptance" (BA) or a "bank bill". Because the holder of a BA has recourse to both the drawer of the bill and the accepting bank, it is known as a "two-name" instrument.

A commercial or finance company can also address a bill directly to a bank, rather than to a trading partner, and discount it immediately at the bank, in order to raise funds for general purposes rather than to finance a specific sale of goods.

Investors in bank bills again come from the professional market and in practice are generally the accepting banks.

Bill of exchange	
Term:	From 1 week to 1 year but usually less than 6 months
Interest:	Non-interest-bearing
Quotation:	In the US and UK quoted as a discount rate, but elsewhere as a yield
Negotiable security?	Yes, although in practice banks often tend to hold until maturity the bills they have discounted

Repurchase agreement (repo)

A repo (covered in more detail in Chapter 6) is an arrangement whereby one party sells a security to another party and simultaneously agrees to repurchase the same security at a subsequent date at an agreed price. This is equivalent to the first party borrowing from the second party against collateral, and the interest rate reflects this – that is, it is slightly lower than an unsecured loan. The security involved will often be of high credit quality, such as a government bond. A reverse repurchase agreement (reverse repo) is the same arrangement viewed from the other party's perspective. The deal is generally a "repo" if it is initiated by the party borrowing money and lending the security and a "reverse repo" if it is initiated by the party borrowing the security and lending the money.

Repo	
Term:	Usually very short term, although in principle can be for any term
Interest:	Usually implied in the difference between the purchase and repurchase prices
Quotation:	As a yield
Negotiable security?	No

MONEY MARKET CALCULATIONS

When a CD is issued in the primary market, it is issued at par. In other words, the first investor pays exactly the CD's face value to buy it. At that point, the yield at which the CD is purchased is the same as the coupon rate.

For any instrument, the price an investor is prepared to pay is essentially the present value, or NPV, of the future cashflow(s) which he will receive because of owning it. This present value depends on the interest rate (the "yield"), the time to the cashflow(s) and the size of the cashflow(s).

Price = present value	Key Point

For an instrument such as a CD which has a coupon rate, the price in the secondary market will therefore depend not only on the current yield but also on the coupon rate, because the coupon rate affects the size of the cash-flow received at maturity.

Consider first a CD paying only one coupon (or in its last coupon period). The maturity proceeds of the CD are given by:

$$F \times \left(1 + \text{coupon rate} \times \frac{\text{days}}{\text{year}}\right)$$

where: F = face value of the CD
days = number of days in the coupon period
year = either 360 (e.g. in the USA) or 365 (e.g. in the UK)

The price P of this CD now is the investment needed at the current yield i to achieve this amount on maturity – in other words, the present value now of the maturity proceeds:

$$P = \frac{F \times \left(1 + \text{coupon rate} \times \frac{\text{days}}{\text{year}}\right)}{\left(1 + i \times \frac{d_{pm}}{\text{year}}\right)}$$

where: d_{pm} = number of days from purchase to maturity

The price would normally be quoted based on a face value amount of 100.

We saw earlier that the simple return on *any* investment can be calculated as:

$$\left(\frac{\text{total proceeds at maturity}}{\text{initial investment}} - 1\right) \times \frac{\text{year}}{\text{days held}}$$

Following this, the yield E earned on a CD purchased after issue and sold before maturity will be given by:

$$E = \left(\frac{\text{price achieved on sale}}{\text{price achieved on purchase}} - 1 \right) \times \left(\frac{\text{year}}{\text{days held}} \right)$$

From the previous formula, this is:

$$E = \left[\frac{\left(1 + i_p \times \dfrac{d_{pm}}{\text{year}} \right)}{\left(1 + i_s \times \dfrac{d_{sm}}{\text{year}} \right)} - 1 \right] \times \left(\frac{\text{year}}{\text{days held}} \right)$$

where: i_p = yield on purchase
i_s = yield on sale
d_{pm} = number of days from purchase to maturity
d_{sm} = number of days from sale to maturity

Example 2.3 A CD is issued for $1 million on 17 March for 90 days (maturity 15 June) with a 6.0% coupon. On 10 April the yield is 5.5%. What are the total maturity proceeds? What is the secondary market price on 10 April?

$$\text{Maturity proceeds} = \$1 \text{ million} \times \left(1 + 0.06 \times \tfrac{90}{360} \right) = \$1,015,000.00$$

$$\text{Price} = \frac{\$1,015,000.00}{\left(1 + 0.055 \times \tfrac{66}{360} \right)} = \$1,004,867.59$$

On 10 May, the yield has fallen to 5.0%. What is the rate of return earned on holding the CD for the 30 days from 10 April to 10 May?

$$\text{Return} = \left[\frac{1 + 0.055 \times \tfrac{66}{360}}{1 + 0.050 \times \tfrac{36}{360}} - 1 \right] \times \frac{360}{30} = 6.07\%$$

.06 ENTER 90 × 360 ÷ 1 +	
1,000,000 ×	(Maturity proceeds)
.055 ENTER 66 × 360 ÷ 1 + ÷	(Secondary market cost)
.055 ENTER 66 × 360 ÷ 1 +	
.05 ENTER 36 × 360 ÷ 1 +	
÷	
1 −	
360 × 30 ÷	(Return over 30 days)

Calculation summary

For a CD

$$\text{Maturity proceeds} = \text{face value} \times \left(1 + \text{coupon rate} \times \frac{\text{days from issue}}{\text{year}}\right)$$

$$\text{Secondary market price} = \frac{\text{maturity proceeds}}{\left(1 + \text{market yield} \times \frac{\text{days left to maturity}}{\text{year}}\right)}$$

$$\text{Return on holding a CD} = \left[\frac{\left(1 + \text{purchase yield} \times \frac{\text{days from purchase to maturity}}{\text{year}}\right)}{\left(1 + \text{sale yield} \times \frac{\text{days from sales to maturity}}{\text{year}}\right)} - 1\right] \times \frac{\text{year}}{\text{days held}}$$

Note that, in the formula above, if the yield increases, the secondary market proceeds are less – assuming the number of days does not change. Similarly, if the yield falls, the secondary market proceeds are more. In general, the following is true for all securities:

Yield goes up implies that price goes down.
Yield goes down implies that price goes up.

Key Point

DISCOUNT INSTRUMENTS

Some instruments are known as "discount" instruments. This means that only the face value of the instrument is paid on maturity, without a coupon, in return for a smaller amount paid originally (instead of the face value paid originally in return for a larger amount on maturity). Treasury bills, for example, are generally discount instruments.

Consider, for example, sterling commercial paper with face value £10 million issued for 91 days. On maturity, the investor receives only the face value of £10 million. If the yield on the CP is 10%, the price the investor will be willing to pay now for the CP is its present value calculated at 10%:

$$\text{Price} = \frac{\text{£10 million}}{\left(1 + 0.10 \times \frac{91}{365}\right)} = \text{£9,756,749.53}$$

| Example 2.4 | A French T-bill with face value €10 million matures in 74 days. It is quoted at 8.4%. What is the price of the bill? |

$$\frac{\text{€10 million}}{\left(1 + 0.084 \times \frac{74}{360}\right)} = \text{€9,830,264.11}$$

.084 ENTER 74 × 360 ÷ 1+
10,000,000 ☐ x⇄y ÷

| Key Point | **Secondary market price = present value**
(again!) |

| Calculation summary | **For a discount instrument**

Maturity proceeds = face value

$$\text{Secondary market price} = \frac{\text{face value}}{\left(1 + \text{market yield} \times \frac{\text{days left to maturity}}{\text{year}}\right)}$$ |

Note that, unlike with a CD, the original investor who buys a discount instrument at issue (the primary market) does not pay the face value of the instrument, but instead pays less.

Discount / true yield

In the USA and UK, a further complication arises in the way the interest rate is quoted on discount instruments – as a "discount rate" instead of a yield. If you invest 98.436 in a sterling time deposit or CD at 10 percent for 58 days, you expect to receive the 98.436 back at the end of 58 days, together with interest calculated as:

$$98.436 \times 0.10 \times \frac{58}{365} = 1.564$$

In this case, the total proceeds at maturity – principal plus interest – are 98.436 + 1.564 = 100.00.

This means that you invested 98.436 to receive (98.436 + 1.564) = 100 at the end of 58 days. If the same investment were made in a discount instrument, the face value of the instrument would be 100 and the amount of discount would be 1.564. In this case, the *discount rate* is the amount of discount expressed as an annualised percentage of the face value, rather than as a percentage of the original amount paid. The discount rate is therefore:

$$(1.564 \div 100) \times \frac{365}{58} = 9.84\%$$

> Terminology can be confusing. What we are calling "discount rate" can also be known in the USA as "discount yield" or even just "yield". When we use the term "yield" in this documentation, we always mean yield as we have already described – also known as "true yield", "CD yield", "money market yield" or "investment yield"; we never mean discount rate.

Beware!

The discount rate is always less than the corresponding yield. If the discount rate on an instrument is D, then the amount of discount is:

$$F \times D \times \frac{\text{days}}{\text{year}}$$

where F is the face value of the instrument.

The price P to be paid is the face value less the discount:

$$P = F \times \left(1 - D \times \frac{\text{days}}{\text{year}}\right)$$

If we expressed the price in terms of the equivalent yield rather than the discount rate, we would still have the same formula as earlier:

$$P = \frac{F}{\left(1 + i \times \frac{\text{days}}{\text{year}}\right)}$$

Combining these two relationships, we get:

$$D = \frac{i}{1 + i \times \frac{\text{days}}{\text{year}}}$$

where i is the equivalent yield (often referred to as the "true yield"). This can perhaps be understood intuitively, by considering that because the discount is received at the beginning of the period whereas the equivalent yield is received at the end, the discount rate should be the "present value of the yield". Reversing this relationship:

$$i = \frac{D}{1 - D \times \frac{\text{days}}{\text{year}}}$$

Instruments quoted on a discount rate in the USA and UK include treasury bills and trade bills, while a yield basis is used for loans, deposits and certificates of deposit. USA CP is also quoted on a discount rate basis, while ECP and sterling CP are quoted on a yield basis.

Example 2.5 A USA treasury bill of $1 million is issued for 91 days at a discount rate of 6.5%. What is the amount of the discount and the amount paid?

$$\text{Amount of discount} = \$1 \text{ million} \times 0.065 \times \tfrac{91}{360} = \$16,430.56$$

Price paid = face value – discount = $983,569.44

1,000,000 ENTER .065 × 91 × 360 ÷	(Amount of discount)
1,000,000 ☐ $x \gtrless y$ –	(Amount paid)

Example 2.6 A UK treasury bill with remaining maturity of 70 days is quoted at a discount rate of 7.1%. What is the equivalent yield?

$$\frac{7.1\%}{1 - 0.071 \times \tfrac{70}{365}} = 7.198\%$$

Answer: 7.198%

.071 ENTER 70 × 365 ÷ 1 ☐ $x \gtrless y$ –
7.1 ☐ $x \gtrless y$ ÷

Calculation summary

$$\text{Rate of true yield} = \frac{\text{discount rate}}{\left(1 - \text{discount rate} \times \tfrac{\text{days}}{\text{year}}\right)}$$

$$\text{Discount rate} = \frac{\text{rate of true yield}}{\left(1 + \text{yield} \times \tfrac{\text{days}}{\text{year}}\right)}$$

$$\text{Amount of discount} = \text{face value} \times \text{discount rate} \times \frac{\text{days}}{\text{year}}$$

$$\text{Amount paid} = \text{face value} \times \left(1 - \text{discount rate} \times \frac{\text{days}}{\text{year}}\right)$$

Key Point

Instruments quoted on a discount rate

USA: T-bills   UK: T-bills
      BA   BA
      CP

Bond-equivalent yields

For trading or investment purposes, a government treasury bond which has less than a year left to maturity may be just as acceptable as a treasury bill with the same maturity left. As the method used for quoting yields generally differs between the two instruments, the rate quoted for treasury bills in the USA is often converted to a "bond-equivalent yield" for comparison. This is considered in Chapter 5.

CDs PAYING MORE THAN ONE COUPON

Most CDs are short-term instruments paying interest on maturity only. Some CDs however are issued with a maturity of several years. In this case, interest is paid periodically – generally every 6 months or every year. The price for a CD paying more than one coupon will therefore depend on all the intervening coupons before maturity, valued at the current yield. Suppose that a CD has three more coupons yet to be paid, one of which will be paid on maturity together with the face value F of the CD. The amount of this last coupon will be:

$$F \times R \times \frac{d_{23}}{\text{year}}$$

where: R = the coupon rate on the CD
d_{23} = the number of days between the second and third (last) coupon
year = the number of days in the conventional year

The total amount paid on maturity will therefore be:

$$F \times \left(1 + R \times \frac{d_{23}}{\text{year}}\right)$$

The value of this amount discounted to the date of the *second* coupon payment, at the current yield i, is:

$$\frac{F \times \left(1 + R \times \frac{d_{23}}{\text{year}}\right)}{\left(1 + i \times \frac{d_{23}}{\text{year}}\right)}$$

To this can be added the actual cashflow received on the same date – that is, the second coupon, which is:

$$F \times R \times \frac{d_{12}}{\text{year}}$$

where d_{12} = the number of days between the first and second coupons.

The total of these two amounts is:

$$F \times \left[\frac{\left(1 + R \times \frac{d_{23}}{year}\right)}{\left(1 + i \times \frac{d_{23}}{year}\right)} + R \times \frac{d_{12}}{year} \right]$$

Again, this amount can be discounted to the date of the first coupon payment at the current yield i and added to the actual cashflow received then, to give:

$$F \times \left[\frac{\left(1 + R \times \frac{d_{23}}{year}\right)}{\left(1 + i \times \frac{d_{23}}{year}\right)\left(1 + i \times \frac{d_{12}}{year}\right)} + \frac{R \times \frac{d_{12}}{year}}{\left(1 + i \times \frac{d_{12}}{year}\right)} + \left(R \times \frac{d_{01}}{year}\right) \right]$$

where d_{01} = the number of days up to the first coupon since the previous coupon was paid (or since issue if there has been no previous coupon).

Finally, this entire amount can be discounted to the purchase date, again at the current yield of i, by dividing by:

$$\left(1 + i \times \frac{d_{p1}}{year}\right)$$

where d_{p1} = the number of days between purchase and the first coupon date.

The result will be the present value of all the cashflows, which should be the price P to be paid. This can be written as:

$$P = \frac{F}{\left(1 + i \times \frac{d_{p1}}{year}\right)\left(1 + i \times \frac{d_{12}}{year}\right)\left(1 + i \times \frac{d_{23}}{year}\right)}$$

$$+ \frac{F \times R \times \frac{d_{23}}{year}}{\left(1 + i \times \frac{d_{p1}}{year}\right)\left(1 + i \times \frac{d_{12}}{year}\right)\left(1 + i \times \frac{d_{23}}{year}\right)}$$

$$+ \frac{F \times R \times \frac{d_{12}}{year}}{\left(1 + i \times \frac{d_{p1}}{year}\right)\left(1 + i \times \frac{d_{12}}{year}\right)}$$

$$+ \frac{F \times R \times \frac{d_{01}}{year}}{\left(1 + i \times \frac{d_{p1}}{year}\right)}$$

In general, for a CD with N coupon payments yet to be made:

$$P = F \times \left[\frac{1}{A_N} + \left(\frac{R}{year} \times \sum_1^N \left[\frac{d_{k-1;k}}{A_k} \right] \right) \right]$$

where: A_k $= \left(1 + i \times \frac{d_{p1}}{year}\right)\left(1 + i \times \frac{d_{12}}{year}\right)\left(1 + i \times \frac{d_{23}}{year}\right)...\left(1 + i \times \frac{d_{k-1;k}}{year}\right)$

F = face value of the CD

R = coupon rate of the CD

year = number of days in the conventional year

$d_{k-1;k}$ = number of days between $(k-1)^{th}$ coupon and k^{th} coupon

d_{p1} = number of days between purchase and first coupon

What is the amount paid for the following CD?

Example 2.7

Face value:	$1 million
Coupon:	8.0% semi-annual
Maturity date:	12 September 2011
Settlement date:	14 January 2010
Yield:	7%

The last coupon date was 14 September 2009 (12 September was a Saturday). Future coupons will be paid on 12 March 2010, 13 September 2010 (12 September is a Sunday), 14 March 2011 (12 March is a Saturday) and 12 September 2011.

With the previous notation:

$d_{01} = 179$, $d_{p1} = 57$, $d_{12} = 185$, $d_{23} = 182$, $d_{34} = 182$

$$Price = \frac{\$1 \text{ million} \times \left(1 + 0.08 \times \frac{182}{360}\right)}{\left(1 + 0.07 \times \frac{57}{360}\right)\left(1 + 0.07 \times \frac{185}{360}\right)\left(1 + 0.07 \times \frac{182}{360}\right)\left(1 + 0.07 \times \frac{182}{360}\right)}$$

$$+ \frac{\$1 \text{ million} \times 0.08 \times \frac{182}{360}}{\left(1 + 0.07 \times \frac{57}{360}\right)\left(1 + 0.07 \times \frac{185}{360}\right)\left(1 + 0.07 \times \frac{182}{360}\right)}$$

$$+ \frac{\$1 \text{ million} \times 0.08 \times \frac{185}{360}}{\left(1 + 0.07 \times \frac{57}{360}\right)\left(1 + 0.07 \times \frac{185}{360}\right)}$$

$$+ \frac{\$1 \text{ million} \times 0.08 \times \frac{179}{360}}{\left(1 + 0.07 \times \frac{57}{360}\right)}$$

$$= \$1,042,449.75$$

```
TIME CALC
12.092011 DATE2 14.032011 DATE1 DAYS                        (d₃₄)
360 ÷ .08 × 1 +
RCL DAYS 360 ÷ .07 × 1 + ÷
13.092010 DATE2 DAYS +/−                                    (d₂₃)
☐ x≥y↓360 ÷ .08 × +
RCL DAYS +/− 360 ÷ .07 × 1 + ÷
12.032010 DATE1 DAYS                                        (d₁₂)
☐ x≥y↓360 ÷ .08 × +
RCL DAYS 360 ÷ .07 × 1 + ÷
14.092009 DATE2 DAYS +/−                                    (d₀₁)
☐ x≥y↓360 ÷ .08 × +
14.012010 DATE2 DAYS +/−                                    (dₚ₁)
☐ x≥y↓360 ÷ .07 × 1 + ÷
1,000,000 ×
```

EXERCISES

23. You invest in a 181-day sterling CD with a face value of £1 million and a coupon of 11%. What are the total maturity proceeds?

24. You buy the CD in the previous question 47 days after issue, for a yield of 10%. What amount do you pay for the CD?

  You then sell the CD again after holding it for only 63 days (between purchase and sale), at a yield to the new purchaser of 9.5%. What yield have you earned on your whole investment on a simple basis? What is your effective yield?

25. At what different yield to the purchaser would you need to have sold in the previous question in order to achieve an overall yield on the investment to you of 10% (on a simple basis)?

26. You place a deposit for 91 days at 11.5% on an ACT/360 basis. What would the rate have been if it had been quoted on an ACT/365 basis? What is the effective yield on an ACT/365 basis and on an ACT/360 basis?

27. You purchase some sterling Euro-commercial paper as follows:

Purchase value date:	8 July 2008
Maturity value date:	8 September 2008
Yield:	8.2%
Amount:	£2,000,000.00

What do you pay for the paper?

28. An investor seeks a yield of 9.5% on a sterling 1 million 60-day banker's acceptance. What is the discount rate and the amount of this discount?

29. If the discount rate were in fact 9.5%, what would the yield and the amount paid for the banker's acceptance be?

30. If the amount paid in the previous question is in fact £975,000.00, what is the discount rate?

31. The rate quoted for a 91-day US treasury bill is 6.5%.

a. What is the amount paid for US$1,000,000.00 of this T-bill?

b. What is the equivalent true yield on a 365-day basis?

32. You buy a US treasury bill 176 days before it matures at a discount rate of 7% and sell it again at a discount rate of 6.7% after holding it for 64 days. What yield have you achieved on a 365-day year basis?

33. What would be the yield in the previous question if you sold it after only 4 days at a discount rate of 7.5%?

34. The market rate quoted for a 91-day T-bill (or the local equivalent) is 5% in the USA, UK, Australia and France. Each T-bill has a face value of 1 million of the local currency. What is the amount paid for the bill in each country?

35. Place the following instruments in descending order of yield, working from the rates quoted:

30-day UK T-bill	$8\frac{1}{4}\%$
30-day UK CP (£)	$8\frac{3}{16}\%$
30-day ECP (£)	$8\frac{1}{8}\%$
30-day US T-bill	$8\frac{5}{16}\%$
30-day interbank deposit (£)	$8\frac{1}{4}\%$
30-day US CP	$8\frac{1}{2}\%$
30-day US$ CD	$8\frac{5}{8}\%$
30-day French T-bill	$8\frac{1}{2}\%$

36. A US $1 million CD with semi-annual coupons of 7.5% per annum is issued on 25 March 2008 with a maturity of 5 years. You purchase the CD on 19 May 2011 at a yield of 8.0%. What is the amount paid?

"An important point is to consider which comes first. Are forward-forward rates (and hence futures prices and FRA rates) the mathematical result of the yield curve? Or are the market's expectations of future rates the starting point?"

■ ■ ■

Forward-Forwards and Forward Rate Agreements (FRAs)

FORWARD-FORWARDS, FRAs AND FUTURES

Overview

Forward-forwards, forward rate agreements (FRAs) and futures are very similar and closely linked instruments, all relating to an interest rate applied to some period which starts in the future. We shall first define them here and then examine each more closely. Futures in particular will be considered in the next chapter.

Terminology

A **forward-forward** is a cash borrowing or deposit which starts on one forward date and ends on another forward date. The term, amount and interest rate are all fixed in advance. Someone who expects to borrow or deposit cash in the future can use this to remove any uncertainty relating to what interest rates will be when the time arrives.

An **FRA** is an off-balance-sheet instrument which can achieve the same economic effect as a forward-forward. Someone who expects to borrow cash in the future can buy an FRA to fix in advance the interest rate on the borrowing. When the time to borrow arrives, he borrows the cash in the usual way. Under the FRA, which remains quite separate, he receives or pays the difference between the cash borrowing rate and the FRA rate, so that he achieves the same net effect as with a forward-forward borrowing.

A **futures** contract is similar to an FRA – an off-balance-sheet contract for the difference between the cash interest rate and the agreed futures rate. Futures are however traded only on an exchange and differ from FRAs in a variety of technical ways.

Pricing a forward-forward

Suppose that the 3-month sterling interest rate is 13.0 percent and the 6-month rate is 13.1 percent. If I borrow £100 for 6 months and simultaneously deposit it for 3 months, I have created a net borrowing which begins in 3 months and ends in 6 months. The position over the first 3 months is a net zero one. If I undertake these two transactions at the same time, I have created a forward-forward borrowing – that is, a borrowing which starts on one forward date and ends on another.

Example 3.1

If I deposit £1 for 91 days at 13%, then at the end of the 91 days, I receive:

$$£1 + 0.13 \times \frac{91}{365} = £1.03241$$

If I borrow £1 for 183 days at 13.1%, then at the end of the 183 days, I must repay:

$$£1 + 0.131 \times \frac{183}{365} = £1.06568$$

My cashflows are: an inflow of £1.03241 after 91 days and an outflow of £1.06568 after 183 days. What is the cost of this forward-forward borrowing? The calculation is similar to working out a yield earlier in the book:

$$\text{Cost} = \left(\frac{\text{cash outflow at the end}}{\text{cash inflow at the start}} - 1 \right) \times \frac{\text{year}}{\text{days}} = \left(\frac{1.06568}{1.03241} - 1 \right) \times \frac{365}{92}$$

$$= 12.785\%$$

.131 ENTER 183 × 365 ÷ 1 +   (Value after 183 days)
.13 ENTER 91 × 365 ÷ 1 +   (Value after 91 days)
÷
1 –
365 × 92 ÷   (Forward-forward interest rate)

In general:

$$\text{Forward-forward rate} = \left[\frac{\left(1 + i_L \times \dfrac{d_L}{\text{year}}\right)}{\left(1 + i_S \times \dfrac{d_S}{\text{year}}\right)} - 1 \right] \times \left(\frac{\text{year}}{d_L - d_S} \right)$$

where: i_L = interest rate for longer period
i_S = interest rate for shorter period
d_L = number of days in longer period
d_S = number of days in shorter period
year = number of days in conventional year

Note that this construction of a theoretical forward-forward rate applies only for periods up to one year. A money market deposit for longer than one year typically pays interim interest after one year (or each six months). This extra cashflow must be taken into account in the forward-forward structure. This is explained in Chapter 7.

If I am a bank customer, I could more simply ask the bank to provide the forward-forward loan from 3 months to 6 months at an agreed rate, rather than construct it myself as in the example above. However, the bank would be able to construct it in exactly the same way and then present it to me as a forward-forward loan: the bank borrows for 5 months, lends the cash in the interbank market for 2 months and then has the cash available to lend to me for the forward period from 2 months to 5 months.

If the bank did not hedge the forward-forward loan to me in this way, it would be at risk to a rise in interest rates, because it has agreed to lend to me at a certain rate. In practice however, if the bank does not wish to take this risk, it is more likely to hedge itself by using an FRA or futures (see below) than by using a borrowing and a deposit as described above. This is because of the heavy transaction costs involved in the borrowing and deposit.

Forward rate agreements (FRAs)

An FRA is an off-balance-sheet agreement to make a settlement in the future with the same economic effect as a forward-forward. It is an agreement to pay or receive, on an agreed future date, the difference between an agreed interest rate and the interest rate actually prevailing on that future date, calculated on an agreed notional principal amount. It is settled against the actual interest rate prevailing at the beginning of the period to which it relates, rather than paid as a gross amount.

| Example 3.2 | A borrower intends to borrow cash at LIBOR from 91 days forward to 183 days forward, and he fixes the cost with an FRA. His costs will be as follows: |

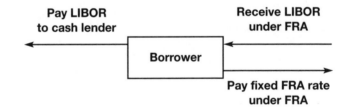

His flows will therefore be: – LIBOR
+LIBOR
– FRA rate

net cost: – FRA rate

If the cash is actually borrowed at a different rate – say LIBOR + $\frac{1}{4}$% – then the net cost will be (FRA rate + $\frac{1}{4}$%), but the all-in cost is still fixed.

Pricing

In calculating a theoretical FRA price, we can apply exactly the same ideas as in the forward-forward calculation above. As we are not actually borrowing cash with the FRA however, we might calculate using middle rates for both the 6-month and the 3-month period – rather than separate bid and offered rates. Conventionally however, FRAs are always settled against LIBOR rather than LIMEAN. As a calculation using middle rates produces a rate which is comparable to LIMEAN, we would therefore need to add the difference between LIMEAN and LIBOR – generally around $\frac{1}{16}$ percent – to this theoretical "middle price" forward-forward. An alternative approach is to base the initial theoretical price calculation on LIBOR, rather than LIMEAN, for both periods. The result is different, but generally only very slightly.

Quotation

Having established a theoretical FRA price, a dealer would then build a spread round this price.

In Example 3.1, the theoretical FRA rate could be calculated as: 12.785% + 0.0625% = 12.85%. Putting a spread of, say, six basis points around this would give a price of 12.82% / 12.88%. A customer wishing to hedge a future borrowing ("buying" the FRA) would therefore deal at 12.88 percent. A customer wishing to hedge a future deposit ("selling" the FRA) would deal at 12.82 percent.

An FRA is referred to by the beginning and end dates of the period covered. Thus a "5 v 8" FRA is one to cover a 3-month period, beginning in 5 months and ending in 8 months. Our example above would be a "3 v 6" FRA.

Settlement

Suppose that the actual 3-month LIBOR, in 3 months' time, is 11.5 percent. Settlement then takes place between these two rates. On a principal of £100, the effective interest settlement in our example would be:

$$£100 \times (0.1288 - 0.1150) \times \frac{92}{365} = £0.3478$$

As the settlement rate of 11.50 percent is lower than the agreed FRA rate, this amount is due from the FRA buyer to the other party. Conventionally however, this settlement takes place at the *beginning* of the 3-month borrowing period. It is therefore discounted to a present value at the current 3-month rate to calculate the actual settlement amount paid:

$$\frac{£100 \times (0.1288 - 0.1150) \times \frac{92}{365}}{1 + 0.1150 \times \frac{92}{365}} = £0.3380$$

In general:

> **Calculation summary**
>
> The FRA settlement amount = principal $\times \dfrac{(f - L) \times \dfrac{days}{year}}{\left(1 + L \times \dfrac{days}{year}\right)}$

where: f   = FRA rate

L   = interest rate (LIBOR) prevailing at the beginning of the period to which the FRA relates

days = number of days in the FRA period

year = number of days in the conventional year

If the period of the FRA is longer than one year, the corresponding LIBOR rate used for settlement relates to a period where interest is conventionally paid at the end of each year as well as at maturity. A 6 v 24 FRA, for example, covers a period from 6 months to 24 months and will be settled against an 18-month LIBOR rate at the beginning of the FRA period.

An 18-month deposit would, however, typically pay interest at the end of one year and after 18 months. The agreed FRA rate and the settlement LIBOR would therefore be based on this. As FRA settlements are paid at the beginning of the period on a discounted basis, each of these payments therefore needs to be discounted separately. Strictly, the net settlement payment calculated for the end of 18 months should be discounted at an appropriate compounded 18-month rate and the net settlement amount calculated for the end of the first year should be discounted at 1-year LIBOR. In practice, the FRA settlement LIBOR is generally used for both. In this case, the final discounted settlement amount would be:

Calculation summary

$$\text{Principal} \times \frac{(f - L) \times \frac{d_1}{\text{year}}}{\left(1 + L \times \frac{d_1}{\text{year}}\right)} + \frac{(f - L) \times \frac{d_2}{\text{year}}}{\left(1 + L \times \frac{d_1}{\text{year}}\right) \times \left(1 + L \times \frac{d_2}{\text{year}}\right)}$$

where: d_1 = number of days in the first year of the FRA period

d_2 = number of days from d_1 until the end of the FRA period

This same principle can be applied to the settlement of FRAs covering any period.

Dates

The reference fixing rate used to calculate the settlement amount depends on the currency. With a sterling FRA, it is generally the sterling LIBOR for the forward period that prevails on the "effective" date of the FRA – that is, the first day of the forward period. LIBOR is therefore fixed on the settlement date itself.

When an FRA in other major currencies is traded internationally, it is generally the LIBOR that prevails two business days earlier. This is because the LIBOR for a currency other than sterling is for value spot. In domestic markets in other currencies, as opposed to the international market, FRAs can be traded for settlement against a same-day value reference, as with sterling.

Suppose that an FRA is traded for a regular period – for example 7 months against 10 months. In the case of a sterling FRA, both the effective date (7 months) and the end date (10 months) are generally taken from the dealing date. In the case of foreign currency FRAs, both the effective date (7 months) and the end date (10 months) are generally taken from the spot date. In either case however, because of non-business days, it might be that, when LIBOR is fixed, the period between the two dates turns out not to be a regular period. The following example demonstrates this.

Example 3.3

It is now Thursday 13 March 2003. I will need to borrow $1 million for a 3-month period, starting in 2 months' time. I purchase a 2 v 5 FRA at 5.22% on a notional amount of $1 million.

Spot value date is Monday 17 March. The 2-month value date is Monday 19 May (because 17 and 18 May are non-business days). The 5-month value date is Monday 18 August (because 17 August is a non-business day). I have therefore purchased an FRA from 19 May to 18 August (a 91-day period).

LIBOR on 15 May for the period from 19 May to 18 August is not exactly the 3-month LIBOR fixing on that day, because 3-month LIBOR would be from 19 May to 19 August. It is therefore necessary on 15 May to interpolate between the 2-month LIBOR and 3-month LIBOR fixings, although the difference from 3-month LIBOR would be rather slight. Assume that the LIBOR so calculated for the period 19 May to 18 August is 5.05%. The FRA settlement amount is then $424.31:

$$\$1,000,000 \times \frac{(0.0522 - 0.0505) \times \dfrac{91}{360}}{\left(1 + \left(0.0505 \times \dfrac{91}{360}\right)\right)} = \$424.31$$

Because I purchased the FRA and rates went down, I will pay the FRA settlement rather than receive it.

Key Point

Dates for FRAs in GBP are based on today.

Dates for FRAs traded internationally in other currencies are generally based on spot.

The short-term yield curve

If I wish to borrow money for 3 months, the interest rate is likely to be different – possibly higher and possibly lower – from what the rate would be if I wished instead to borrow for 6 months. The "yield curve" is a graph showing how interest rates vary with term to maturity. For example, a Reuters screen might show the following rates:

1 month	9.50%
2 months	9.70%
3 months	10.00%
6 months	10.00%
12 months	10.20%

In a free market, these rates show where the market on average believes rates "should" be, as supply and demand would otherwise tend to move the rates up or down. A yield curve where longer-term rates are higher than shorter-term rates is known as a "normal" or "positive" yield curve. A curve where longer-term rates are lower than shorter-term rates is known as "negative" or "inverted". A curve where rates are approximately the same across the range of maturities is known as "flat". A curve where both short-term and long-term rates are lower than medium-term rates is known as "humped".

Clearly the rates at some maturity level or levels are influenced by central bank policy. If the market believes that the central bank is about to change official 3-month rates, for example, this expectation will already have been factored into the market 3-month rate.

If the 3-month maturity is indeed the rate manipulated by the central bank for this particular currency, a more logical curve to look at might be one that shows what the market expects 3-month rates to be at certain times in the future. For example, what is the 3-month rate now, what will it be after 1 month, after 2 months, after 3 months, etc? Given enough such rates, it is possible to work "backwards" to construct the yield curve shown above.

Suppose, for example, that the 3-month rate now is 10.0 percent and the market expects that there will be a 0.25 percent cut in rates during the next 3 months – so that at the end of 3 months, the 3-month rate will be 9.75 percent. Given these data, what should the 6-month rate be now?

The answer must be the rate achieved by taking the 3-month rate now, compounded with the expected 3-month rate in 3 months' time; otherwise there would be an expected profit in going long for 3 months and short for 6 months or vice versa, and the market would tend to move the rates. In this way, the 6-month rate now can be calculated as:

$$\left[\left(1 + 0.10 \times \frac{91}{360}\right) \times \left(1 + 0.0975 \times \frac{92}{360}\right) - 1\right] \times \frac{360}{183} = 10.00\%$$

This rate is in fact the 6-month rate shown above. If we now work in the other direction, we would find that the forward-forward rate from 3 months to 6 months ("3 v 6") would be 9.75 percent as expected:

$$\left[\frac{\left(1 + 0.10 \times \frac{183}{360}\right)}{\left(1 + 0.10 \times \frac{91}{360}\right)} - 1\right] \times \frac{360}{92} = 9.75\%$$

This shows that a "flat" short-term yield curve – in our example, the 3-month and 6-month rates are the same at 10.0 percent – does not imply that the market expects interest rates to remain stable. Rather, it expects them to fall.

An important point here is to consider the question of which comes first. Are forward-forward rates (and hence futures prices and FRA rates) the mathematical result of the yield curve? Or are the market's expectations of future rates (i.e. forward-forwards, futures and FRAs) the starting point, and from these it is possible to create the yield curve? The question is a circular one to some extent, but market traders increasingly look at constructing a yield curve from expected future rates for various periods and maturities.

The "forward yield curve" is a graph of forward interest rates of a certain forward period. This could for example be the forward 3-month rates, so it would show the 3-month cash rate and then the 1 v 4, 2 v 5, 3 v 6, 4 v 7, 5 v 8, 6 v 9, 7 v 10 rates, etc. Or it could be a graph of the forward 6-month rates, so it would show the 6-month cash rate and then the 1 v 7, 2 v 8, 3 v 9, 4 v 10, 5 v 11, 6 v 12, 7 v 13 rates, etc.

The relationship between the cash yield curve and the forward yield curve for short-term interest rates is as follows. If the cash curve is negative, the forward curve is more negative. If the cash curve is flat, the forward curve is negative (as demonstrated above). If the cash curve is positive, the forward curve could be negative, flat or (if the cash curve is sufficiently positive) positive.

Constructing a strip

In the previous section, when we compounded the 3-month rate now with the expected 3-month rate in 3 months' time, we were effectively creating a "strip" – that is, a series of consecutive legs which, compounded together, build up to a longer overall period.

Example 3.4

Suppose that it is now January and we have the following rates available. At what cost can we construct a fixed-rate borrowing for 9 months? All rates are ACT/360.

3-month LIBOR:	8.5% (92 days)
3 v 6 FRA:	8.6% (91 days)
6 v 9 FRA:	8.7% (91 days)

We construct the strip as follows:

- borrow cash now for 3 months;
- buy a 3 v 6 FRA now based on the total repayment amount in April (principal plus interest);
- refinance this total amount in April at the 3-month LIBOR in April;

- buy a 6 v 9 FRA now based on the total repayment amount in July (principal plus interest calculated at the 3 v 6 FRA rate now);
- refinance this amount in July at the 3-month LIBOR in July.

Suppose that in April when the first FRA settles, 3-month LIBOR is 9.0% and that in July when the second FRA settles, 3-month LIBOR is 9.5%. Although market practice is for the FRA settlements to be made at the beginning of the relevant period discounted at LIBOR, the economic effect is the same as if the settlement were at the end of the period but not discounted – assuming that the discounted settlement amount could simply be invested or borrowed at LIBOR for the period. For clarity, we will therefore assume that the FRA settlements are at the ends of the periods and not discounted.

This gives us the following cashflows based on a borrowing of 1:

January: $+ 1$

April: $\quad -\left(1 + 0.085 \times \frac{92}{360}\right)$ $\hfill$ (Repayment)

$\quad\quad + \left(1 + 0.085 \times \frac{92}{360}\right)$ $\hfill$ (Refinancing)

July: $\quad -\left(1 + 0.085 \times \frac{92}{360}\right) \times \left(1 + 0.09 \times \frac{91}{360}\right)$ $\hfill$ (Repayment)

$\quad\quad + \left(1 + 0.085 \times \frac{92}{360}\right) \times \left(0.09 - 0.086\right) \times \frac{91}{360}$ $\hfill$ (FRA settlement)

$\quad\quad + \left(1 + 0.085 \times \frac{92}{360}\right) \times \left(1 + 0.086 \times \frac{91}{360}\right)$ $\hfill$ (Refinancing)

October: $-\left(1 + 0.085 \times \frac{92}{360}\right) \times \left(1 + 0.086 \times \frac{91}{360}\right) \times \left(1 + 0.095 \times \frac{91}{360}\right)$ $\hfill$ (Repayment)

$\quad\quad + \left(1 + 0.085 \times \frac{92}{360}\right) \times \left(1 + 0.086 \times \frac{91}{360}\right) \times \left(0.095 - 0.087\right) \times \frac{91}{360}$ (FRA settlement)

Most of these flows offset each other, leaving the following net flows:

January: $+ 1$

October: $-\left(1 + 0.085 \times \frac{92}{360}\right) \times \left(1 + 0.086 \times \frac{91}{360}\right) \times \left(1 + 0.087 \times \frac{91}{360}\right) = -1.066891$

The cost of funding for 9 months thus depends only on the original cash interest rate for 3 months and the FRA rates, compounded together. The cost per annum is:

$$(1.066891 - 1) \times \frac{360}{274} = 8.79\%$$

In general:

Calculation summary

The interest rate for a longer period up to one year =

$$\left[\left(1 + i_1 \times \frac{d_1}{year}\right) \times \left(1 + i_2 \times \frac{d_2}{year}\right) \times \left(1 + i_3 \times \frac{d_3}{year}\right) \times \dots - 1\right] \times \frac{year}{total\ days}$$

where: i_1, i_2, i_3, ... are the cash interest rate and forward-forward rates for a series of consecutive periods lasting d_1, d_2, d_3, ... days.

APPLICATIONS OF FRAs

As with any instrument, FRAs may be used for hedging, speculating or arbitrage, depending on whether they are taken to offset an existing underlying position or taken as new positions themselves.

Hedging

Example 3.5

A company has a 5-year borrowing with 3-monthly rollovers – that is, every three months, the interest rate is refixed at the prevailing 3-month LIBOR. The company expects interest rates to rise before the next rollover date. It therefore buys an FRA to start on the next rollover date and finish 3 months later. If the next rollover date is 2 months away, this would be a "2 v 5" FRA. If the company is correct and interest rates do rise, the next rollover will cost more, but the company will make a profit on the FRA settlement to offset this. If rates fall however, the next rollover will be cheaper but the company will make an offsetting loss on the FRA settlement. The FRA settlement profit or loss will of course depend on how the 3-month rate stands after two months compared with the FRA rate now, not compared with the cash rate now. Either way, the net effect will be that the company's borrowing cost will be locked in at the FRA rate (plus the normal margin which it pays on its credit facility):

Company pays	LIBOR + margin	to lending bank
Company pays	FRA rate	to FRA counterparty
Company receives	LIBOR	from FRA counterparty
Net cost	FRA rate + margin	

The FRA payments are in practice netted and also settled at the beginning of the borrowing period after discounting. The economic effect is still as shown.

Example 3.6

A company expects to make a 6-month deposit in two weeks' time and fears that interest rates may fall. The company therefore sells a 2-week v $6\frac{1}{2}$-month FRA. Exactly as above, but in reverse, the company will thereby lock in the deposit rate. Although the company may expect to receive LIBID on its actual deposit, the FRA will always be settled against LIBOR:

Company receives	LIBID	from deposit
Company receives	FRA rate	from FRA counterparty
Company pays	LIBOR	to FRA counterparty
Net return	FRA rate – (LIBOR – LIBID)	

As the FRA rate is theoretically calculated to be comparable to LIBOR, it is reasonable to expect the net return to be correspondingly lower than the FRA rate by the (LIBID – LIBOR) spread.

Speculation

The most basic trading strategy is to use an FRA to speculate on whether the cash interest rate when the FRA period begins is higher or lower than the FRA rate. If the trader expects interest rates to rise, he buys an FRA; if he expects rates to fall, he sells an FRA.

Example 3.7

On 15 May, a dealer expects interest rates to fall and takes a speculative position. He therefore sells a 2 v 3 FRA (from 17 July to 17 August) for €60 million at 4.73%. On 15 July, 1-month EURIBOR is fixed at 4.80%. What is his profit or loss?

The interest rate has risen, so he makes a loss of €3,601.78:

$$€60,000,000 \times \frac{(0.0473 - 0.048) \times \dfrac{31}{360}}{\left(1 + \left(0.048 \times \dfrac{31}{360}\right)\right)} = €3,601.78$$

Calendar spread

In general, a "spread" of any kind is a strategy where a trader simultaneously buys something and sells another similar thing. For example, a bond spread is a strategy where a trader buys one bond and simultaneously sells another bond, because he expects the first bond to perform better than the second bond. A call option spread (discussed fully in a later chapter) is where a trader buys one put option and similarly sells another put option.

Therefore an FRA spread – in this case called a "calendar spread" – is a strategy where a trader buys one FRA and sells another FRA. For example, a trader might buy a shorter-dated FRA (say a 1 v 7) and sell a longer-dated FRA (say a 4 v 10). If all forward interest rates move up to the same extent, he will make a profit on the first deal and lose the same amount on the second deal, thereby making neither profit nor loss. If all forward rates move down to the same extent, he will lose on the first and gain on the second but still make no overall profit or loss. However if the yield curve twists clockwise – for example, the shorter rates rise and the longer rates fall – he will make an overall profit. This will happen regardless of whether the forward interest rates overall move up or down. Therefore a trader uses a spread if he expects a twist in the shape of the yield curve, but does not necessarily have any expectation about the whole forward yield curve moving up or down.

Key Point

Calendar spread

A dealer expecting the yield curve to twist anti-clockwise sells a shorter-dated FRA and buys a longer-dated FRA.

A dealer expecting the yield curve to twist clockwise buys a shorter-dated FRA and sells a longer-dated FRA.

Interest rates for euros are now as follows. For simplicity, we have ignored bid / offer spreads in this example. We have used FRA rates which are exactly in line with the cash rates.

Example 3.8

2 months (61 days):	5.00%
5 months (153 days):	5.00%
8 months (245 days):	5.00%
11 months (337 days):	5.00%
2 v 5 FRA:	4.96%
8 v 11:	4.84%

A trader expects the yield curve to become positive (i.e. to twist anti-clockwise). He therefore sells a 2 v 5 FRA and buys a 8 v 11 FRA.

Later that day, rates are as follows:

2 months (61 days):	5.01%
5 months (153 days):	5.04%
8 months (245 days):	5.07%
11 months (337 days):	5.10%
2 v 5 FRA:	5.02%
8 v 11 FRA:	5.01%

The dealer has lost 6 basis points on the 2 v 5 FRA but gained 17 basis points on the 8 v 11 FRA – a net gain of around 11 basis points because the yield curve has twisted as he expected.

Arbitrage

Arbitrage between FRAs and futures is considered later.

EXERCISES

37. Current market rates are as follows for SEK:

3 months (91 days):	9.87 / 10.00%
6 months (182 days):	10.12 / 10.25%
9 months (273 days):	10.00 / 10.12%

What is the theoretical FRA 3 v 9 for SEK now?

38. You borrow €5 million at 7.00% for 6 months (183 days) and deposit €5 million for 3 months (91 days) at 6.75%. You wish to hedge the mismatched position, based on the following FRA prices quoted to you:

3 v 6:	7.10% / 7.15%
6 v 9:	7.20% / 7.25%

    a. Do you buy or sell the FRA?

    b. At what price?

    c. For a complete hedge, what amount do you deal?

When it comes to fixing the FRA, the 3-month rate is 6.85% / 6.90%:

    d. What is the settlement amount? Who pays whom?

    e. What is the overall profit or loss of the book at the end of six months, assuming that your borrowings are always at LIBOR and your deposits at LIBID?

"In general, a futures contract in any market is a contract in which the commodity being bought and sold is considered as being delivered (even though this may not physically occur) at some future date rather than immediately."

■ ■ ■

Interest Rate Futures

OVERVIEW

In general, a futures contract in any market is a contract in which the commodity being bought and sold is considered as being delivered (even though this may not physically occur) at some future date rather than immediately – hence the name. The significant differences between a "futures contract" and a "forward" arise in two ways. First, a futures contract is traded on a particular exchange (although two or more exchanges might trade identically specified contracts). A forward however, which is also a deal for delivery on a future date, is dealt "over the counter" (OTC) – a deal made between any two parties, not on an exchange. Second, futures contracts are generally standardised, while forwards are not. The specifications of each futures contract are laid down precisely by the relevant exchange and vary from commodity to commodity and from exchange to exchange. Some contracts, for example, specifically do not allow for the commodity to be delivered; although their prices are calculated as if future delivery takes place, the contracts must be reversed before the notional delivery date, thereby capturing a profit or a loss. Interest rate futures, for example, cannot be delivered, whereas most bond futures can.

The theory underlying the pricing of a futures contract depends on the underlying "commodity" on which the contract is based. For a futures contract based on 3-month interest rates, for example, the pricing is based on forward-forward pricing theory, explained earlier. Similarly, currency futures pricing theory is the same as currency forward outright pricing theory and bond futures pricing theory is based on bond pricing.

The "underlying"

There are relatively minor differences between futures exchanges, and also between different STIR (short-term interest rate) contracts on the same exchange.

The typical contract specification for short-term interest rate futures is for a 3-month interest rate. This is very similar to an FRA for a forward period of 3 months – for example, a 1 v 4 or a 2 v 5 or a 3 v 6, etc. The contract is settled against a reference fixing rate such as LIBOR, in the same way as an FRA. A trader buying or selling a futures contract is therefore taking a view on what 3-month LIBOR will be fixed at on a certain date in the future – again, the same as if he were trading an FRA with a 3-month forward period.

In some currencies on some exchanges 1-month contracts also exist (for example, the Euro-USD 1-month interest rate contract on the CME in

Chicago). The precise specification varies from exchange to exchange but is in practice for exactly one quarter of a year (or exactly one twelfth of a year for 1-month contracts).

The price at which a STIR contract trades is quoted as 100 minus (the implied forward interest rate × 100). For example, if the forward interest rate is 5.71%, the futures price is quoted as 94.29 (= 100 − 5.71).

Futures price = 100 − (implied forward interest rate × 100)	**Key Point**

Importantly, because an FRA is traded on an interest rate and a futures contract is traded on a price, FRAs and futures are in opposite directions – as the interest rate rises, so the price falls. Therefore a buyer of an FRA will profit if the interest rate rises but a buyer of a futures contract will profit if the interest rate falls. If a trader sells an FRA to a counterparty, he must therefore also sell a futures contract to cover his position.

Futures and FRAs are in opposite directions.	**Key Point**

The size of the contract varies. For example the USD and EUR 3-month contracts are $1 million and €1 million, the USD 1-month contract is $3 million, the GBP 3-month contract is £500,000 and the JPY 3-month contract is ¥100 million.

Value dates

Most 3-month STIR contracts worldwide are based on the delivery month cycle of March, June, September and December each year. There is only one value date in the delivery month, which is the third Wednesday (or the next following business day) of that month. There are thus generally only four delivery dates in the year. It is therefore generally only possible to trade a forward period beginning on one of these four dates. This is different from an FRA, where you can trade a forward period beginning on any working date.

A futures contract is named according to the beginning of the period, when the reference rate such as LIBOR is fixed. For example, a "June" 3-month futures contract is a contract which refers to the 3-month period starting in June. The contract expires in June and is settled against the 3-month rate fixed in June.

A few contracts also include "serial months". Serial months are additional delivery months other than these four, added so that a series of consecutive months, starting with the nearest, is always available in addition to the normal quarterly cycle. The 3-month EURIBOR contract on LIFFE, for example (but not the similar contract on EUREX and also not the GBP contract on LIFFE), includes serial months, although the volume of trading in the serial month contracts is generally not great. For this LIFFE EURIBOR contract, on 5 May, the delivery months available would be May, June, July, August, September, October, December, March... . On 25 July, the delivery months available would be August, September, October, November, December, January, March, June... .

1-month STIR contracts are based on a monthly delivery cycle (also the third Wednesday of each month), rather than a quarterly cycle.

Trading in a STIR contract generally finishes at the time when the reference rate against which it is settled at expiry – such as LIBOR – is fixed. For contracts settled against a reference rate with spot value (such as EURIBOR or CHF LIBOR), this is two working days before the third Wednesday. Final settlement of any remaining profit or loss (see "margin" later) takes place on the following working day, i.e. one working day before the third Wednesday. In the case of the Euroyen contract on Euronext LIFFE, trading finishes two days before trading finishes for the equivalent contract on TIFFE in Tokyo, i.e. effectively four days before the third Wednesday.

In the case of sterling futures, both the last trading day and the LIBOR fixing used for settlement are the third Wednesday of the delivery month, rather than two business days earlier, and settlement is the following working day.

Settlement price

The "exchange delivery settlement price" ("EDSP") is the closing price for the futures contract, when it expires at the point when the reference rate such as LIBOR is fixed.

The EDSP is therefore 100 minus the reference rate fixing. The exact calculation of this settlement price varies according to both currency and exchange. For the EURIBOR contract on EUREX, the fixing is rounded to the nearest half basis point. For contracts on Euronext LIFFE, the fixing is rounded to the nearest tenth of a basis point. For the Eurodollar contract on the IMM, the fixing is rounded to the nearest one hundredth of a basis point.

Profit and loss and "basis point value"

A 3-month STIR futures contract is based on exactly one quarter of a year, as mentioned above. Therefore the profit or loss is based on the notional principal size of the contract, and the movement in the interest rate calculated for one quarter of a year. In general therefore:

Calculation summary	$$\text{Profit/loss} =$$ $$\text{number of contracts} \times \text{contract amount} \times \frac{\text{price movement}}{100} \times \frac{1}{4}$$

As mentioned above, the size of a EUR STIR futures contract is €1 million. Therefore the profit or loss on one contract arising from a movement of only one basis point in interest rates (which is equivalent to a 0.01 change in the futures price) would be:

$$€1,000,000 \times 0.0001 \times \frac{3}{12} = €25$$

The value of a one basis point change in the EUR futures is therefore €25 per contract.

A dealer buys 20 EUR 3-month futures contracts at 95.27. He closes them out subsequently at 95.20. What is his profit or loss? **Example 4.1**

The price has fallen, so he makes a loss of €3,500:

Number of contracts × contract amount × price movement × $\frac{1}{4}$

$= 20 \times €1,000,000 \times 0.0007 \times \frac{1}{4} = €3,500$

Or, using the basis point value:

20 contracts × 7bp × €25 = €3,500

Note that the calculation of profit or loss on a STIR futures on the basis of exactly one quarter of a year does not depend on the currency. The calculation is the same even for a GBP contract (despite the fact that other GBP money market instruments are calculated on a 365-day year).

"Tick" and "tick value"

The exchange determines the minimum price change allowed in trading. This is known as a "tick". For example, GBP STIR futures prices can change in increments of one basis point, while EUR STIR futures prices can change in increments of ½ basis point. The minimum price movement for the USD contract in Chicago is ¼ basis point for the nearest-dated futures contract, but ½ basis point for subsequent ones.

The "tick value" of a contract is the profit or loss made due to a one tick change in price. Tick values therefore vary in line with the tick size for a particular contract, as well as with the notional amount of the contract itself.

In calculating the profit or loss made on a position, it might be easier to think in terms of the value of a one basis point change in price (which might or might not be the same as a 1 tick change, depending on the contract) – as in the example above.

Some financial futures exchanges and contracts

There is a large number of futures exchanges, some trading financial futures and/or options, some other commodities. The following are some of the important financial exchanges and contracts:

- **Euronext LIFFE:** London International Financial Futures and Options Exchange
- **Eurex:** Combined derivatives market of Germany and Switzerland
- **IMM:** International Monetary Market, a division of the CME (Chicago Mercantile Exchange)

Contract (exchange)	Based on	Tick size	Tick value	Basis point value
Eurodollar (CME)	3-month **USD LIBOR** $1,000,000	0.0025 / 0.005	$6.25 / $12.50	$25
(Euronext LIFFE)	3-month **USD LIBOR** $1,000,000	0.005	$12.50	$25
EURIBOR (Eurex)	3-month **EURIBOR** €1,000,000	0.005	€12.50	€25
(Euronext LIFFE)	3-month **EURIBOR** €1,000,000	0.005	€12.50	€25
Short sterling (Euronext LIFFE)	3-month **GBP LIBOR** £500,000	0.01	£12.50	£12.50
Euroyen (Euronext LIFFE)	3-month **JPY TIBOR** ¥100,000,000	0.005	¥1,250	¥2,500
EuroSwiss (Euronext LIFFE)	3-month **CHF LIBOR** CHF 1,000,000	0.01	CHF 25	CHF 25

Example 4.2   3-month EURIBOR futures contract traded on Euronext LIFFE:

Exchange Euronext LIFFE (London International Financial Futures and Options Exchange). All trading is screen-based.

Underlying The basis of the contract is a deposit of €1 million lasting for 90 days based on an ACT/360 year.

Delivery It is not permitted for this contract to be delivered; if a trader buys such a contract, he cannot insist that, on the future delivery date, his counterparty makes arrangements for him to have a deposit for 90 days from then onwards at the interest rate agreed. Rather, the trader must reverse his futures contract by delivery, thereby taking a profit or loss.

Delivery months March, June, September, December, and four "serial" months, so that 24 delivery months are traded, with the nearest six delivery months being consecutive calendar months.

Settlement price On the last day of trading – usually the third Monday of the month – Euronext LIFFE declares an exchange delivery settlement price which is the closing price at which any contracts still outstanding will be automatically reversed. The EDSP is 100 minus the ACI/European Bankers Federation 3-month offered rate (EURIBOR) at 11:00 a.m. Brussels time.

Last trading day 10:00 a.m. (London time) two business days prior to the third Wednesday of the delivery month.

Settlement day First business day after the last trading day.

Price The price is determined by the free market and is expressed as 100 minus (implied interest × 100). Thus a price of 94.52 implies an interest rate of 5.48% (100 – 94.52 = 5.48).

Price movement Prices are quoted in units of 0.005. This minimum movement is called a tick.

Profit and loss The P&L is calculated on $\frac{3}{12}$ exactly of a year, regardless of the number of days in a calendar quarter. The profit or loss on a single contract is therefore:

$$\text{Contract amount} \times \text{price movement} \times \frac{3}{12}$$

Therefore the value of a 1 basis point movement is €25.00 and the value of a 1 tick movement (the tick value) is €12.50:

$$€1 \text{ million} \times 0.01\% \times \frac{3}{12} = €25.00$$

$$€1 \text{ million} \times 0.005\% \times \frac{3}{12} = €12.50$$

Yen/dollar futures contract traded on the IMM:

Example 4.3

Exchange IMM (International Monetary Market, a division of the CME, Chicago Mercantile Exchange, where futures and options on currencies, interest rates equities and commodities are traded).

Commodity The basis of the contract is ¥12.5 million.

Delivery It is possible for the ¥12.5 million to be delivered (if the contract is not reversed before maturity) against an equivalent value in USD.

Delivery date The third Wednesday in March, June, September and December, with six delivery months available.

Trading It is possible to trade the contract until 09:16 a.m. two business days before the delivery date. Trading is either electronic or via "open outcry" (i.e. face-to-face dealing between individuals standing in the exchange).

Price The price is expressed as the dollar value of ¥1.

Price movement Prices are generally quoted to six decimal places, with a minimum movement (one tick) of $0.000001. A one-tick movement is equivalent to a profit or loss of $12.50.

Settlement price At the close of trading, the EDSP is the closing spot JPY/USD rate as determined by the IMM.

EXCHANGE STRUCTURE AND MARGINS

Market participants

The users of an exchange are its members and their customers. An exchange also has "locals" – private traders dealing for their own account only.

Dealing

There are two methods of dealing. The first, traditional, method is "open outcry", whereby the buyer and seller deal face to face in public in the exchange's "trading pit". This should ensure that a customer's order will always be transacted at the best possible rate. The second is screen-trading, designed to simulate the transparency of open outcry, and which is now far more usual.

Clearing

The futures exchange is responsible for administering the market, but all transactions are cleared through a clearing house, which may be separately owned. On LIFFE, for example, this function is performed by the London Clearing House (LCH.Clearnet). Following confirmation of a transaction, the clearing house substitutes itself as a counterparty to each user and becomes the seller to every buyer and the buyer to every seller.

Margin requirements

In order to protect the clearing house, clearing members are required to place collateral with it for each deal transacted in a "margin" account. This collateral is called "initial margin".

Members are then debited or credited each day with "variation margin" which reflects the day's loss or profit on contracts held. Customers, in turn, are required to pay initial margin and variation margin to the member through whom they have cleared their deal. The initial margin is intended to protect the clearing house for the short period until a position can be revalued and variation margin called for if necessary. As variation margin is paid each day, the initial margin is relatively small in relation to the potential price movements over a longer period.

The calculation of variation margin is equivalent to "marking to market" – that is, revaluing a futures contract each day at the current price. The variation margin required is the tick value multiplied by the number of ticks price movement. For example, if the tick value is €12.50 on each contract, and the price moves from 94.73 to 94.215 (a fall of 103 ticks), the loss on a long futures contract is €(12.50 × 103) = €1,287.50. On some exchanges, variation margin is not called for if it can be deducted from the margin account without reducing the account below a certain level known as the "maintenance margin", which is set by the clearing house at less than the initial margin.

Delivery

A futures position can be closed out by means of an exactly offsetting transaction. Depending on the specification of the particular futures contract, contracts which are not settled before maturity are required to be either "cash settled" – that is, reversed at maturity and the price difference paid – or (if delivery is permitted) delivered. The mechanics of the delivery process differ for each type of contract.

Limit up / down

Some markets impose limits on trading movements on certain contracts, in an attempt to prevent wild price fluctuations and hence limit risk to some extent. If the price reaches this limit, trading stops for a specified time.

FUTURES COMPARED WITH FRAs

An FRA is an OTC equivalent to an interest rate futures contract. Exactly the same forward-forward pricing mechanism is therefore used to calculate a futures price – although the futures price is then expressed as an index (100 – rate). In practice, an FRA trader will often take his price from the futures market (which may not be precisely in line with the theoretical calculations), rather than directly from the forward-forward calculation. This is because the FRA trader would use the futures market rather than a forward-forward to hedge his FRA book – because of both the balance sheet implications and the transaction costs. In practice therefore, the FRA rate for a period coinciding with a futures contract would be (100 – futures price).

An important practical difference between FRAs and futures is in the settlement mechanics. An FRA settlement is paid at the beginning of the notional borrowing period, and is discounted. The futures "settlement" – the profit or loss on the contract – is also all settled by the same date, via the margin payments made during the period from transaction until the futures delivery date. However, in most futures markets, this settlement is *not discounted*. A 90-day FRA is not therefore exactly matched by an offsetting futures contract even if the amounts and dates are the same.

It should also be noted that FRAs and futures are "in opposite directions". A *buyer* of an FRA will profit if interest rates rise. A *buyer* of a futures contract will profit if interest rates fall. If a trader sells an FRA to a counterparty, he must therefore also *sell* a futures contract to cover his position.

OTC vs. exchange-traded

It is worthwhile summarising the differences between over the counter contracts such as an FRA, and futures contracts.

> **Key Point**
>
> **Amount** The amount of a futures contract is standardised. The amount of an OTC deal is entirely flexible.
>
> **Delivery date** The delivery date of a futures contract is standardised. The delivery date of an OTC deal is entirely flexible.
>
> **Margin** Dealing in futures requires the payment of collateral (called "initial margin") as security. In addition, "variation margin" is paid or received each day to reflect the day's loss or profit on futures contracts held. When trading OTC, professional traders usually deal on the basis of credit lines, with no security required.
>
> **Settlement** Settlement on an instrument such as an FRA is discounted to a present value. Settlement on a futures contract, because it is paid through variation margin, is not discounted.
>
> **Credit risk** The margin system ensures that the exchange clearing house is generally fully protected against the risk of default. As the counterparty to each futures contract is the clearing house, there is therefore usually virtually no credit risk in dealing futures. OTC counterparties are generally not of the same creditworthiness.
>
> **Delivery** Some futures contracts are not deliverable and must be cash settled. It is usually possible to arrange an OTC deal to include delivery.
>
> **Liquidity and spread** For major currencies and interest rates, standardisation and transparency generally ensure a liquid market in futures contracts, together with narrower spreads between bid and offer than in OTC deals. For delivery dates far in the future, meanwhile, there may be insufficient liquidity in the futures market, where an OTC price may be available.
>
> **Underlying commodity** Futures contracts are not available in all underlying commodities. For example, there is no ringgit/rand futures contract but a ringgit/rand forward is available.

PRICING AND HEDGING FRAs WITH FUTURES

In Chapter 3 on forward-forwards and FRAs, we calculated FRA rates from cash market interest rates – for example, a 3 v 6 FRA from a 3-month interest rate and a 6-month interest rate. In practice however, a trader may well generate an FRA price from futures prices and also hedge the resulting position by buying or selling futures.

Example 4.4

Suppose we have the following prices on 17 March for USD and wish to sell a 3 v 6 FRA for $10 million. How should the FRA be priced (ignoring any buy/sell spread) and hedged, based on these prices?

June futures price (delivery 18 June): 91.75 (implied interest rate: 8.25%)
September futures price (delivery 17 Sept): 91.50 (implied interest rate: 8.50%)
December futures price (delivery 17 Dec): 91.25 (implied interest rate: 8.75%)

The FRA will be for the period 19 June to 19 September (92 days) and will settle against LIBOR fixed on 17 June. The June futures contract EDSP will also be LIBOR on 17 June. The FRA rate should therefore be the implied June futures rate of 8.25%.

The settlement amount for the FRA will be:

$$\frac{\$10 \text{ million} \times (0.0825 - \text{LIBOR}) \times \frac{92}{360}}{1 + \text{LIBOR} \times \frac{92}{360}}$$

The profit or loss on the futures contract (which is not discounted) is:

$$\text{Number of contracts} \times \$1 \text{ million} \times (0.0825 - \text{LIBOR}) \times \frac{90}{360}$$

In order for these to be equal, we need:

$$\text{Number of contracts} = 10 \times \frac{\frac{92}{90}}{\left(1 + \text{LIBOR} \times \frac{92}{360}\right)}$$

We do not know what LIBOR will be. Taking 8.25% as our best guess however, we have:

$$\text{Number of contracts} = 10 \times \frac{\frac{92}{90}}{\left(1 + 0.0825 \times \frac{92}{360}\right)} = 10.01$$

As futures contracts can only be traded in whole numbers, we hedge by selling 10 futures contracts.

In Chapter 3, we considered a strip of FRAs to create a rate for a longer period. The same theory applies just as well here.

Example 4.5

With the same prices as in Example 4.4, we wish to sell a 3 v 9 FRA and a 6 v 12 FRA. How should these be priced and hedged?

A 3 v 6 FRA can be priced at 8.25% and hedged exactly as in Example 4.4. A 6 v 9 FRA (91 days from 19 September to 19 December) can similarly be priced at the implied September futures rate of 8.50% and hedged by selling 10 September futures (although there is a slight discrepancy in the dates as the futures contract delivery is 17 September). The 3 v 9 FRA should be equivalent to a strip combining the 3 v 6 FRA and 6 v 9 FRA (because, if not, there would be an arbitrage opportunity). This gives the 3 v 9 FRA rate as:

$$\left[\left(1 + 0.0825 \times \frac{92}{360}\right) \times \left(1 + 0.085 \times \frac{91}{360}\right) - 1\right] \times \frac{360}{183} = 8.463\%$$

The hedge required is the combination of the hedges for each leg: sell 10 June futures and 10 September futures.

In the same way, we can build up the 6 v 12 FRA from a strip of the 6 v 9 FRA and 9 v 12 FRA (90 days, from 19 December to 19 March), and hedge it by selling 10 ·September futures and 10 December futures.

$$\left[\left(1 + 0.085 \times \frac{91}{360}\right) \times \left(1 + 0.875 \times \frac{90}{360}\right) - 1\right] \times \frac{360}{181} = 8.718\%$$

In Example 4.5, when we reach 17 June, we need to close out the June and September futures hedges against the 3 v 9 FRA. The June contract will be closed at the current 3-month LIBOR and the September contract at the current futures price which will approximate the current 3 v 6 FRA; combined in a strip, these two rates approximate to the current 6-month LIBOR against which the 3 v 9 FRA will settle at the same time. The hedge therefore works. The result of the hedge is not perfect however, for various reasons:

- In creating a strip of FRAs, we compounded, by increasing the notional amount for each leg to match the previous leg's maturing amount. With futures, we cannot do this – futures contracts are for standardised notional amounts only.

- Similarly, the futures profit / loss is based on a 90-day period rather than 91 or 92 days etc. as the FRA period.

- FRA settlements are discounted but futures settlements are not.

- There is a "convexity bias" (see the section on this later), which means that the theoretical FRA rate and theoretical implied futures rate are not quite the same, even if everything else is in line.

- The futures price when the September contract is closed out in June may not exactly match the rate which theoretically it should be at that time.

- Even if the September futures price does exactly match the theoretical rate, there is in fact a slight discrepancy in dates. On 17 June, the 3 v 6 FRA period is 19 September to 19 December (LIBOR is therefore fixed on 17 September) but the September futures delivery is 17 September (EDSP is therefore fixed on 16 September).

The result of these effects is considered later, in Example 4.10.

Pricing FRAs from futures in this way is not as theoretically straightforward as pricing FRAs from the cash market because in practice, the FRA period is unlikely to coincide exactly with a futures date. If we have only 3-month futures prices available, we know only what the market expects 3-month interest rates to be at certain times in the future. We do not know what 3-month rates are expected to be at any other time, or, for example, what 4-month or 5-month rates are expected to be at any time. We therefore need to interpolate between the prices we do have, to build up the rates we need.

There are various possible approaches to this interpolation. Typically, a bank might do the following:

- Build a curve of discount factors. The very short end of this curve – up to the nearest available STIR futures date – is built by deriving discount factors (as explained in Chapter 1) from cash interest rates. The discount factor for 3 months after the nearest futures date can then be derived by compounding the discount factor for the nearest futures date with the forward-forward discount factor implied by the price of that nearest futures contract. Compounding this again with the factor implied by the next available STIR contract produces the factor for 3 months later, and so on.

- Fit a curve to these discount factors, to produce a discount factor for any date.

- The implied forward-forward rate for any period can then be calculated directly from the ratio between the discount factors for those two dates.

Curve building in this way involves two problems. First, the beginning and end dates of the STIR contracts do not fit neatly together – there are gaps and overlaps. Second, the exact mathematical approach used to join any two dates by a curve is open to argument (and not discussed in this book).

Whatever the details chosen for building the curve, a forward-forward rate can be derived from it. This leaves however the problem of how to hedge an FRA quoted on the basis of this rate. In order to approach this, the following two examples derive an FRA rate from futures by interpolation without building a curve. This simpler approach might not be used in practice to derive the FRA rate quoted, but does give a methodology for calculating a reasonable hedge.

Example 4.6

With the same prices as in Example 4.4, we wish to sell a 3 v 8 FRA (153 days from 19 June to 19 November) and a 6 v 11 FRA (153 days from 19 September to 19 February). How do we price and hedge these?

For the 3 v 8 FRA, we are effectively asking what the market expects the 5-month rate to be in 3 months' time. The information available is what the market expects the 3-month rate to be in 3 months' time (8.25%, the 3 v 6 rate) and what it expects the 6-month rate to be at the same time (8.463%, the 3 v 9 rate from Example 4.5). An approach is therefore to interpolate, to give the 3 v 8 FRA as:

$$3 \text{ v } 6 + (3 \text{ v } 9 - 3 \text{ v } 6) \times \frac{(\text{days in } 3 \text{ v } 8 - \text{days in } 3 \text{ v } 6)}{(\text{days in } 3 \text{ v } 9 - \text{days in } 3 \text{ v } 6)}$$

$$= 8.25\% + (8.463\% - 8.25\%) \times \frac{153 - 92}{183 - 92} = 8.393\%$$

The hedge can similarly be considered as the sale of the following futures contracts:

$$10 \text{ June} + (10 \text{ June} + 10 \text{ September} - 10 \text{ June}) \times \frac{153 - 92}{183 - 92}$$

$$= 10 \text{ June} + 6.7 \text{ September}$$

We therefore sell 10 June futures and 7 September futures.

In the same way, we can interpolate between the 6 v 9 rate and the 6 v 12 rate for the 6 v 11 rate:

$$6 \text{ v } 9 + (6 \text{ v } 12 - 6 \text{ v } 9) \times \frac{(\text{days in 6 v 11} - \text{days in 6 v 9})}{(\text{days in 6 v 12} - \text{days in 6 v 9})}$$

$$= 8.50\% + (8.718\% - 8.50\%) \times \frac{153 - 91}{181 - 91} = 8.650\%$$

This is hedged by selling 10 September futures and 7 December futures.

So far, we have considered FRAs where the start of the FRA period coincides with a futures contract. In practice, we need to be able to price an FRA which starts between two futures dates. Again, interpolation is necessary.

Example 4.7 With the same prices as before, we wish to sell and hedge a 5 v 10 FRA.

From the previous example, we have the following prices:

> 3 v 8 FRA (153 days from 19 June to 19 November): 8.393%, hedged by selling 10 June futures and 7 September futures

> 6 v 11 FRA (153 days from 19 September to 19 February): 8.650%, hedged by selling 10 September futures and 7 December futures

We are now asking what the market expects the 5-month rate to be in 5 months' time. The information available is what the market expects this rate to be in 3 months' time and in 6 months' time. An approach is therefore to interpolate again, to give the 5 v 10 FRA as:

$$3 \text{ v } 8 + (6 \text{ v } 11 - 3 \text{ v } 8) \times \frac{(\text{days to fixing 5 v 10} - \text{days to fixing 3 v 8})}{(\text{days to fixing 6 v 11} - \text{days to fixing 3 v 8})}$$

$$= 8.393\% + (8.650\% - 8.393\%) \times \frac{153 - 92}{184 - 92} = 8.563\%$$

The hedge for this would follow the same approach, as a sale of the following futures contracts:

$$(10 \text{ June} + 6.7 \text{ Sept}) + (10 \text{ Sept} + 6.7 \text{ Dec} - 10 \text{ June} - 6.7 \text{ Sept}) \times \frac{153 - 92}{184 - 92}$$

$$= 3.4 \text{ June} + 8.9 \text{ September} + 4.4 \text{ December}$$

We would really like to sell 16.7 contracts. As before, we need to approximate by selling 17 contracts. We could therefore for example sell 3 June futures, 10 September futures and 4 December futures. (The extra September contract is an approximation for 0.4 June and 0.4 December.)

In these examples we have built up a 5 v 10 FRA by interpolating in two stages:

1. Interpolate between known rates for different standard forward periods but starting from the same time:

    3 v 8 from 3 v 6 and 3 v 9
    6 v 11 from 6 v 9 and 6 v 12

2. Interpolate between rates for the same non-standard period but starting from different times:

    5 v 10 from 3 v 8 and 6 v 11

An alternative would be to approach these operations in reverse:

1. Interpolate between known rates for the same standard forward periods but starting from different times:

    5 v 8 from 3 v 6 and 6 v 9
    5 v 11 from 3 v 9 and 6 v 12

2. Interpolate between rates for different standard periods but starting from the same non-standard time:

    5 v 10 from 5 v 8 and 5 v 11

The result of this approach would be slightly different but generally not significantly. Neither approach is perfect. However the 5 v 10 rate is calculated, it is an estimate for a particular forward period, from a particular time, neither of which can actually be known from the current futures prices.

Hedging the basis risk

In Example 4.7, the hedge put in place in March for selling the 5 v 10 FRA was to sell 3 June futures, 10 September futures and 4 December futures. When the June futures contract closes on 17 June, there are still two months before the FRA settles. The hedge needs to be maintained but if we replace the sale of 3 now non-existent June contracts by the nearest available – that is, the sale of 3 September contracts – there is a risk. Suppose that interest rates rise. We will make a loss on the 5 v 10 FRA we have sold and a corresponding gain on the futures hedge. If, however, the yield curve flattens somewhat at the same time (shorter-term rates rise more than longer-term rates), we will make less of a profit on the 3 new September contracts than we would have made on the 3 June contracts. The hedge will not therefore be as effective. This is a form of basis risk – that the movement in the instrument used as a hedge does not match the movement in the instrument being hedged.

An attempt to hedge against this basis risk is as follows. If there is a flattening or steepening of the yield curve while the June contract does still exist, any change in the September futures price is assumed to be approximately equal to the average of the change in the June futures price and the December futures price. For example, if the June price falls 10 ticks and the December price rises 10 ticks (yield curve flattening), the September price is assumed not to change. On this assumption, the following two positions would give the same profit or loss as each other:

> sell 6 September futures
>
> or
>
> sell 3 June futures and sell 3 December futures.

It follows that the following two positions would also give the same profit or loss as each other:

> sell 6 September futures and buy 3 December futures
>
> or
>
> sell 3 June futures.

In this way, if we must replace the sale of 3 June futures contracts (because they no longer exist) by the sale of 3 September contracts, we should then additionally sell a further 3 September contracts and buy 3 December contracts in an attempt to hedge the basis risk.

In Example 4.7 therefore, when the 3 June contracts expire, we replace them by a further sale of 6 September futures and a purchase of 3 December futures, to leave a net hedge then of short 16 September futures and 1 December futures.

TRADING WITH INTEREST RATE FUTURES

Basis

In practice, the actual futures price trading in the market is unlikely to be exactly the same as the "fair" theoretical value which can be calculated according to the underlying cash market prices. The difference between the actual price and the theoretical "fair" price is termed the "basis".

Suppose the following prices for a 3-month interest rate futures contract:

> Actual futures price 94.40
> Fair futures price 94.31 (based on a 5.69% forward-forward rate)
> Implied cash price 93.90 (based on cash 3-month LIBOR of 6.10%)

"Basis" or "simple basis" is the difference between the price based on the current cash rate and the actual price (93.90 − 94.40 = −0.50). This difference will tend towards zero on the last trading day for the futures contract.

"Theoretical basis" is the difference between the price based on the current cash rate and the fair price (93.90 − 94.31 = −0.41). This difference depends on the calculation of the fair price and will also tend towards zero on the last trading day for the futures contract.

"Value basis" is the difference between the fair and actual prices (94.31 – 94.40 = –0.09). If the value basis is temporarily large, arbitrageurs will trade in such a way as to reduce it.

Clearly:

Basis = theoretical basis + value basis

"Basis risk" is the risk arising from the basis on a futures position. Suppose for example that on 1 April a futures trader sells a 1 v 4 FRA to a customer which will settle on 4 May and that he hedges this by selling futures contracts for the nearest futures contract – say for delivery on 18 June. The trader cannot be perfectly hedged because on 4 May the cash market 3-month LIBOR against which the FRA will be settled will not necessarily have moved since 1 May to the same extent as the futures price. He thus has a basis risk.

Basis = implied cash price – actual futures price
Theoretical basis = implied cash price – theoretical futures price
Value basis = theoretical futures price – actual futures price

Calculation summary

Volume and open interest

"Open interest" in a particular futures contract represents the number of purchases of that contract which have not yet been reversed or "closed out". It is thus a measure of the extent to which traders are maintaining their positions. The daily volume in a particular contract represents the total number of contracts traded during the day. In both cases, contracts are not double-counted; either all the long positions or all the short positions are counted, but not both.

The development of volume and open interest are useful in assessing how a futures price might move. If the futures price is rising, for example, and volume and open interest are also rising, this may suggest that the rising price trend will continue for the immediate future, as there is currently enthusiasm for opening new contracts and maintaining them. If the open interest is falling however, this may suggest that traders are taking profits and not maintaining their positions. Analogous interpretations are possible with a falling futures price.

Speculation

As with an FRA, the most basic trading strategy is to use a futures contract to speculate on the cash interest rate on maturity of the futures contract being higher or lower than the interest rate implied in the futures price now. If the trader expects interest rates to rise, he sells the futures contract; if he expects rates to fall, he buys the futures contract.

As noted earlier, the profit or loss for a futures buyer is:

$$\text{Contract size} \times \frac{\text{increase in price}}{100} \times \frac{\text{length of contract in months}}{12}$$

Arbitrage

Example 4.8

Market prices are currently as follows. The futures delivery date is in 2 months' time:

2 v 5 FRA:	7.22 / 7.27%
3-month futures:	92.67 / 92.68

A trader can arbitrage between these two prices by dealing at 7.27% in the FRA and at 92.68 in the futures market. He buys the FRA and is therefore effectively paying an agreed 7.27% in 2 months' time. He also buys the futures contract and is therefore effectively receiving (100 − 92.68)% = 7.32%. He has therefore locked in a profit of 5 basis points.

In practice, Example 4.8 will be complicated by several factors in the same way as in the previous section on hedging FRAs.

First, there is the problem that the FRA settlement is discounted but the futures settlement generally is not. The trader needs to decrease slightly the number of futures contracts traded to adjust for this. As we do not know the discount factor in advance, we need to estimate it − for example, by using the FRA rate itself.

Second, the period of the 2 v 5 FRA might be, for example, 92 days, while the futures contract specification is effectively 90 days (for a currency where the money market convention is ACT/360) and the two settlements will reflect this. The trader needs to increase slightly the number of futures contracts traded to adjust for this.

Combining these last two points, we could make an adjustment as follows:

$$\text{Notional amount of FRA} \times \frac{1}{\left(1 + \text{FRA rate} \times \frac{92}{360}\right)} \times \frac{92}{90}$$

Third, the futures delivery date is unlikely to coincide with the start date of the 2 v 5 FRA period, which gives rise to a basis risk. The trader therefore also needs to adjust for this. If the nearest futures date is earlier than 2 months, the trader could buy some futures for the nearest futures date and some for the following date, in a ratio dependent on the time between the two futures dates and the 2-month date. If the nearest futures date is later than 2 months, the trader could buy all the futures for that date and then superimpose another futures trade as an approximate hedge against the basis risk. As before, this hedge involves buying more futures for the nearest date and selling futures for the following date.

Calendar spread

Just as with FRAs, a spread is a strategy whereby the trader buys one futures contract and sells another, because he expects the difference between them to change but does not necessarily have any expectation about the whole yield curve moving in one direction or the other. A calendar spread, for example, is used when the trader expects the yield curve to change shape – that is, become more or less positive – but does not have a view on rates overall rising or falling. This is similar to the basis risk hedge already described, but using the spread to speculate rather than to hedge.

On 19 June, USD rates are as follows and a trader expects that the yield curve will become even more negative:

Example 4.9

3-month LIBOR:	6.375%
6-month LIBOR:	6.0625%
9-month LIBOR:	5.75%
September futures price:	94.34
December futures price:	95.03

If longer-term rates fall relative to shorter-term ones as expected, the December futures price will rise relative to the September futures price. The trader therefore sells September and buys December futures. In this case, he is "selling" the spread. Suppose after one month the prices are as follows:

2-month LIBOR:	6.75%
5-month LIBOR:	6.35%
8-month LIBOR:	5.87%
September futures price:	93.98
December futures price:	95.05

The trader can now reverse his position, having made the following profit and loss on the two trades:

September contract:	+ 36 ticks (94.34 – 93.98)
December contract:	+ 2 ticks (95.05 – 95.03)
Total profit:	+ 38 ticks × $25 = $950

The spread was successful because there was a shift in the yield curve as expected.

A longer-term spread can be taken if a trader has a view on short-term yields compared with bond yields – for example, a spread between a 3-month Eurodollar futures and long-term USD bond futures. In this case an adjustment has to be made for the difference in maturity of the underlying instrument. Settlement on the short-term futures relates to a 90-day instrument, while settlement on the bond futures relates to a notional 15-year bond. For a given change in yield therefore, there will be a far greater profit or loss on the bond futures than on the short-term futures. To balance this, the trader would buy or sell a much smaller notional amount of the bond futures than of the short-term futures.

Cross-market spread

A spread can similarly be taken on the difference between two markets. For example, if sterling interest rates are above dollar rates and a trader believes that the spread between them will narrow, he could buy sterling futures and sell dollar futures.

Strip trading

Just as we used a strip of futures to hedge an FRA in the last section, we could use a strip to hedge an interest rate risk directly. If a trader, for example, buys a June futures and a September futures at the same time, he has hedged against interest rates for six months rather than just for three months.

Example 4.10   A dealer expects to borrow €10 million for six months from 19 June and wishes to lock in a future borrowing rate.

Date:	17 March
Amount:	€10 million
June futures price:	91.75 (implied interest rate: 8.25%)
September futures price:	91.50 (implied interest rate: 8.50%)

To hedge the borrowing, the dealer sells 10 June and 10 September EUR futures. Three months later, the rates are as follows:

Date:	17 June
3-month LIBOR:	9.00%
6-month LIBOR:	9.50%
June futures EDSP:	91.00
September futures price:	90.22

The dealer now reverses the futures contracts and has the following profits:

June contract:	75 ticks (91.75 – 91.00)
September contract:	128 ticks (91.50 – 90.22)
Total profit:	203 ticks

The total profit on the June/September strip is 203 ticks, in *3-month interest rate terms*. This is equivalent to 1.015% in *6-month interest rate terms*. This profit is received in June, but could be invested (say at LIBOR) until December when the borrowing matures. This would give a profit of:

$$1.015\% \times \left(1 + 0.095 \times \tfrac{183}{360}\right) = 1.064\%$$

Therefore:

Effective borrowing rate = 6-month LIBOR – futures profit

= 9.50% – 1.064%

= 8.436%

The rate of 8.436% achieved in Example 4.10 comes from the same prices as we used in Example 4.5. In that example, however, we calculated the FRA rate slightly differently, as:

$$\left[\left(1 + 0.0825 \times \tfrac{92}{360}\right) \times \left(1 + 0.085 \times \tfrac{91}{360}\right) - 1\right] \times \tfrac{360}{183} = 8.463\%$$

This demonstrates the effect of the various discrepancies mentioned after Example 4.5.

The strip in Example 4.10 is a rather short strip. It is possible to buy or sell a longer series of contracts to make a longer strip, which can be used, for example, to hedge or arbitrage against a longer-term instrument. Another strategy, known as a "boomerang", involves buying a strip and simultaneously selling the same number of contracts all in the nearest date. This is a type of spread and, traded this way round, will make a profit, for example if a negative yield curve becomes more negative.

The convexity bias

A 90-day FRA is not exactly matched by an offsetting futures contract even if the amounts and dates are the same. This creates a pricing and hedging problem.

On 15 April, a bank sells a $1 million FRA at 5.00% for the period 17 June to 15 September (a 90-day period). The bank simultaneously sells a June futures contract at 95.00. The third Wednesday of June is 17 June. The two positions appear to be equal and opposite. **Example 4.11**

Suppose that LIBOR on 15 June is fixed at 6%. The bank will have a loss on the FRA of $2,463.05:

$$1,000,000 \times \frac{(0.05 - 0.06) \times \dfrac{90}{360}}{\left(1 + \left(0.06 \times \dfrac{90}{360}\right)\right)} = 2,463.05$$

The futures EDSP will be 100.00 – 6.00 = 94.00. The bank will therefore have a profit of 100 basis points on the futures position, giving $2,500.00:

100 × $25 = $2,500

The bank therefore makes an overall profit of $36.95 because the FRA loss is discounted to a present value but the futures profit is not. The higher LIBOR is fixed, the greater the profit.

Suppose however that LIBOR is fixed at 4.00%. In this case, the FRA position will show a profit of $2,475.25:

$$1,000,000 \times \frac{(0.05 - 0.04) \times \dfrac{90}{360}}{\left(1 + \left(0.04 \times \dfrac{90}{360}\right)\right)} = 2,475.25$$

The futures position will this time show a loss of $2,500, giving an overall loss of $24.75. The lower the LIBOR fixing, the lower the loss.

The effect of the FRA settlement discounting is to create a greater profit as the LIBOR fixing rises but a smaller loss as the LIBOR fixing falls. The result of the combined strategy (short FRA and short futures) is therefore not "linear" – i.e. the following profit/loss profile is not a straight line but is instead "convex".

Profit/loss on short futures/short FRA strategy

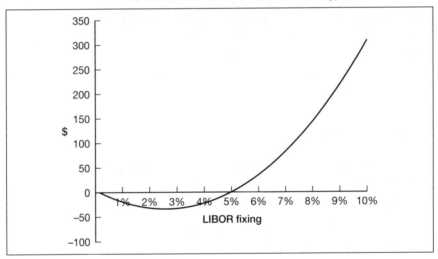

The convexity implies that the result of taking the above strategy many times should be positive on average – the profits should be greater than the losses over time. The reverse strategy should be negative on average. Assuming that the market acts efficiently to remove this effect, the futures contract should therefore in practice be priced slightly lower in the market than the simple equivalent of the FRA.

The convexity creates a problem for hedging an FRA position with futures. If the relationship were linear (i.e. the graph above were a straight line), it would be possible to hedge the profit or loss described above by buying or selling a small amount of futures. Given the convexity however, the exact result of such a hedge cannot be known until the fixing rate is known.

EXERCISES

39. You sell a June futures contract (3-month USD) at 94.20. You subsequently close out the position at 94.35. In which direction did you expect US interest rates to move? What is your profit or loss?

40. Given the following 3-month euro futures prices, what is the implied 3 v 12 euro FRA rate? Assume that the June futures contract settlement date is exactly 3 months from spot settlement.

June:	95.45
September:	95.20
December:	95.05

41. Given the futures prices in the previous question, what is the implied 4 v 8 FRA rate? If you sell a 4 v 8 FRA to a customer, how would you hedge the position using futures?

42. It is now June. You are overlent by €10 million over the six-month period from September to March (i.e. you have lent out €10 million more over that period than you have borrowed and will need to borrow in due course to cover this mismatch). Given the rates quoted to you, what is the cheapest way to hedge your risk, assuming that all the dates match (i.e. the September futures settlement is in exactly three months' time from now, etc.)?

a.	**Cash market**	3 months (92 days):	4.50%/4.65%
		6 months (183 days):	4.60%/4.75%
		9 months (273 days):	4.75%/4.90%
b.	**FRAs**	3 v 6:	4.86%/4.96%
		6 v 9:	4.90%/5.00%
		3 v 9:	4.97%/5.07%
c.	**Futures**	September:	95.03
		December:	95.05

"The different conventions used in different markets to relate price and yield should not affect the economics of an instrument. The economics are determined by what the price actually is and what the future cashflows are. From these, the investor can use a consistent approach of his choice to calculate yields for comparison."

■ ■ ■

Bond Market Calculations

OVERVIEW OF CAPITAL MARKET INSTRUMENTS

We have already considered short-term securities issued by borrowers in the money market – treasury bills, CDs, commercial paper and bills of exchange. Longer-term securities are considered as "capital market" instruments rather than money market ones. Like commercial paper, capital market borrowing normally involves lending directly from the investor to the borrower without the intermediation of a bank. As a result of this disintermediation, only companies of high creditworthiness – or governments, quasi-governmental bodies and supranational bodies – can usually borrow from the capital markets. Those that do so however, may raise finance more cheaply than they could on the same terms from a bank.

A straightforward security issued as a medium-term borrowing, with a fixed coupon paid at regular intervals, is generally called a bond – although a medium-term CD issued by a bank is very similar. There is however a wide range of variations on this basic theme.

Domestic, foreign and Eurobonds

As with money market instruments, there is a distinction between domestic bonds (where the issuer sells the bond in its own country) and Eurobonds (where the issuer sells the bond internationally). A further distinction is drawn for foreign bonds, where a company issues a bond in a foreign country. For example, a US company might issue a bond in the domestic Japanese market – a "Samurai" bond. Other examples of this are "Yankee" bonds (foreign issues in the US domestic market), "Bulldog" bonds (in the UK), and "Alpine" bonds (in Switzerland).

Eurobonds are issued in bearer form – investors do not have to be registered as in the domestic US bond markets, for example. Ownership is evidenced by physical possession and the interest is payable to the holder presenting the coupon, which is detachable from the bearer bond. This is clearly an advantage to an investor who wishes to remain anonymous. Accrued coupon on Eurobonds is calculated on an ACT/ACT basis or a 30/360 basis (see later for an explanation of the various day / year conventions) and paid gross of tax.

As in other markets, there is an important distinction between a "Eurobond" (a bond issued internationally) and a "euro bond" (a bond denominated in euros, whether issued "domestically" in the euro zone, or internationally). The term "international security" is therefore preferable sometimes to avoid confusion.

Government bond markets

Domestic debt markets are usually dominated by government debt for two reasons. First, government debt outstanding is usually large in relation to the market as a whole and therefore offers good liquidity. Second, government debt issued in the domestic currency is usually considered virtually riskless, because the government can always print its own money to redeem the issue. Its debt therefore provides a good benchmark for yields. The following are a few of the important markets.

USA

US government issues with an original maturity between one year and ten years are called "treasury notes". Issues with an original maturity longer than ten years (in practice up to 30 years) are called "treasury bonds". The difference in name does not affect calculations for these bonds. All pay semi-annual coupons and have both the accrued coupon and price calculated on an ACT/ACT basis (see later in this chapter for an explanation of the different calculation bases).

In addition to US treasury bonds, there is a large market in bonds issued by US federal agencies (generally supported by the US government), such as the Federal National Mortgage Association (FNMA or "Fannie Mae"), Student Loan Marketing Association (SLMA or "Sallie Mae"), Federal Home Loan Mortgage Corporation (FHMC or "Freddie Mac") and Government National Mortgage Association (GNMA or "Ginnie Mae"). Coupons and price are calculated on a 30/360 basis.

UK

UK government securities are called gilt-edged securities or "gilts". Conventional gilts are generally called "shorts" if they have a remaining maturity up to five years, "mediums" between five and fifteen years, and "longs" over fifteen years. Almost all gilts pay coupons semi-annually, although there are a few with quarterly coupons. Some are index-linked, where both the coupon and redemption amount paid depend on the inflation rate. Accrued coupon and price are both calculated on an ACT/ACT basis.

Most gilts are conventional bonds with a fixed maturity. Some may be redeemed by the government early, and some ("convertibles") may be converted by the holder into other specific issues. There are a few irredeemable gilts, although these are no longer issued.

Germany

German government bonds pay annual coupons, with accrued coupon and price both calculated on an ACT/ACT basis. Important bonds are Bunds (Bundesanleihen), normally with an original maturity of ten years, BOBLS or OBLs (Bundesobligationen), with maturities up to five years, and Schätze (federal treasury notes) with two-year maturities.

France

French government bonds pay annual coupons, with accrued coupon and price both calculated on an ACT/ACT basis. The most important bonds are BTANs (bons du trésor à taux fixe et intérêt annuel), with original maturities of between two and five years, and OATs (obligations assimilables du trésor) with original maturities of between seven and 30 years.

FEATURES AND VARIATIONS

What we have described so far are essentially straightforward bonds with a fixed coupon and a fixed maturity date when all the bond is redeemed (that is, repaid). There are several variations available.

Floating rate note (FRN)

An FRN is a bond whose coupon is not fixed in advance, but rather is refixed periodically on a "refix date" by reference to some floating interest rate index. In the Euromarkets, this is often some fixed margin over six-month LIBOR.

Essentially, investing in an FRN is equivalent to investing in a short-term money market instrument such as a six-month CD and then reinvesting the principal in a new CD on a rolling basis as the CD matures.

Index-linked bonds

With an index-linked bond, the coupon, and possibly the redemption amount, are linked to a particular index rather than fixed. For example, some governments issue index-linked bonds where the coupon paid is a certain margin above the domestic inflation index. Index-linked bonds issued by companies are often linked to stock indexes or commodity price indexes.

Zero-coupon bonds

Zero-coupon bonds are bonds that make no interest payments. Similar to commercial paper or treasury bills in the money market, the price must be less than the face value, so that they are sold at a discount to their nominal value.

The only cashflows on a zero-coupon bond are the price paid and the principal amount received at maturity, so that the investor's return is represented by the relationship between these two amounts. With a "normal" coupon-bearing bond, the investor is vulnerable to the risk that, by the time he/she receives the coupons, interest rates have fallen so that he/she can only reinvest the coupons received at a lower rate. Whether the reinvestment rate has in fact fallen or risen, the final outcome for the investor is not known exactly at the beginning. With a zero-coupon bond however, the outcome is known exactly because there are no coupons to reinvest. Because of this certainty, investors may accept a slightly lower overall yield for a zero-coupon bond. Differences in tax treatment between capital gains/losses and coupon income may also affect the attractiveness of a zero-coupon bond compared with a coupon-bearing bond.

Strips

The process of stripping a bond is separating all the cashflows – generally a series of coupon payments and a redemption payment – and then trading each cashflow as a separate zero-coupon item. Various governments (US, UK, German and French, for example) facilitate the trading of their securities as strips in this way. Before government securities were officially strippable however, strips were created by investment banks. The bank sets up a special purpose vehicle (SPV) to purchase the government security, holds it in custody, and issues a new stripped security in its own name on the back of this collateral.

Amortisation

A straightforward bond has a "bullet" maturity, whereby all the bond is redeemed at maturity. An alternative is for the principal amount to be repaid in stages – "amortised" – over the bond's life.

Perpetual bonds

A perpetual bond is one with no redemption date. Most such bonds have been FRNs issued by banks, although there are some government perpetuals, such as the "War Loan" UK gilt.

Calls and puts

Bonds are often issued with options for the issuer to "call" (i.e. redeem) the bond prior to maturity. This often requires that the redemption amount is higher than it would be at maturity. This option is particularly helpful with fixed rate bonds, to protect the issuer from paying too much if market interest rates fall after the bond has been issued. This is because he can then redeem the bond early and issue a new one with a lower coupon.

Bonds can also be issued with an option for the investor to "put" (i.e. require redemption on) the bond before maturity.

Bond warrants

A warrant attached to a bond is an option to buy something – generally more of the same bond or a different bond.

Medium-term note (MTN)

An MTN is a hybrid between commercial paper and a bond. Like commercial paper, an MTN is issued continually rather than as a one-off. Like a bond, it has a maturity over one year and pays a coupon, either fixed- or floating-rate. The interest calculation may be either on a money market basis – for example ACT/360 for US domestic MTNs – or on a bond basis.

Securitisation

Asset-backed security

With a "normal" corporate bond, payments of coupon and principal to investors are made from cashflows derived from the issuer's overall operations. With an asset-backed security (ABS) however, specific assets both serve as security for the issue and also generate (directly or indirectly) the payment streams of interest and principal to the investors. This is known as "securitisation" – the process of issuing a security specifically backed by certain assets. A major sector of the ABS market is mortgage-backed securities (MBS), where the assets used to back the security are mortgages which the issuer has on its books.

The original lender sells the assets which are to back the securities to a trust or another form of SPV, which in turn issues securities to investors. The investors receive income and return of capital, derived from the assets over the life of the securities. The securities are guaranteed by the assets, and the assets themselves are also usually guaranteed.

■ In a "pass-through" security, the investors have a direct interest in a pool of assets. Payments of interest and principal are passed through directly to investors on a pro rata basis without restructuring of the cashflows. The pattern of principal repayments which the investor receives on a pass-through are unknown, as they depend on the principal repayments from the underlying assets. This uncertainty is known as "prepayment risk".

- In a "pay-through" security, the cashflows generated from a pool of assets are not passed directly to investors, but are restructured through the issue of multiple tranches of bonds backed by the same pool of assets, and are used to pay interest on the bond and redeem principal payments on the different tranches in a predetermined sequence.

Asset-covered security/covered bond

In a covered bond, the assets are not transferred to an SPV but remain on the issuer's balance sheet, rather than being placed in an SPV. The cashflows are not passed through directly to the investors and involve no prepayment risk, since the cashflows to the investors are structured in a predetermined way. The credit risk on the assets, and any prepayment risk, remain with the issuer, and the bondholders still have a credit exposure to the issuer.

INTRODUCTION TO BOND PRICING

We have already seen that for a given yield, any future cashflow C has a present value equal to:

$$\frac{C}{(1+i)^N}$$

where i is the annual yield and N is the number of years ahead that the cashflow occurs.

Given a series of cashflows – some of which could be negative and some positive – the net present value of the whole series is the sum of all the present values.

The principles of pricing in the bond market are the same as the principles of pricing in other financial markets – the total price paid for a bond now is the net present value now of all the future cashflows which arise from holding the bond. The price is expressed as the price for 100 units of the bond.

In general therefore, the theoretical all-in price P of a straightforward bond should be given by:

$$P = \sum_k \frac{C_k}{\left(1 + \dfrac{i}{n}\right)^{\frac{d_k \times n}{year}}}$$

Calculation summary

where: C_k = the kth cashflow arising

d_k = number of days until C_k

i   = yield on the basis of n payments per year

year = number of days in the conventional year

The important thing to note here is the concept that the all-in price of a bond equals the NPV of its future cashflows.

Key Point	All-in price of a bond = NPV of the bond's future cashflows.

Because the price is the net present value, the greater the yield used to discount the cashflows, the lower the price.

Key Point	A bond's price falls as the yield rises and vice versa.

There are four small but significant differences in practice between calculations for a bond price and the price of a money market instrument such as a medium-term CD. These differences are helpful in understanding the ideas behind bond pricing:

1. The coupon actually paid on a CD is calculated on the basis of the exact number of days between issue and maturity. With a bond, the coupons paid each year or half-year (or occasionally each quarter) are paid as fixed "round" amounts. For example, if a 10 percent coupon bond pays semi-annual coupons, exactly 5 percent will be paid each half-year regardless of the exact number of days involved (which will change according to weekends and leap years, for example).

Key Point	Bond coupons are paid in round amounts, unlike CD coupons which are calculated to the exact day.

2. When discounting to a present value, it is again assumed that the time periods between coupons are "round" amounts – 0.5 years, 1 year, etc. – rather than an odd number of days. For this purpose, the first outstanding coupon payment is usually assumed to be made on the regular scheduled date, regardless of whether this is a non-working day.

Key Point	For straightforward bonds, pricing conventionally assumes that periods between coupons are regular.

3. When discounting back to a present value from the first outstanding coupon payment date, the price calculation is made on the basis of compound interest rather than simple interest. Suppose, for example, there is a cashflow of 105 occurring 78 days in the future, the yield is 6 percent and

the year-count basis is 360. The present value calculation for a CD would be $\dfrac{105}{(1 + 0.06 \times \frac{78}{360})}$, which uses the 6 percent yield for 78 days on a simple basis. The corresponding calculation for a bond would be $\dfrac{105}{(1 + 0.06)^{\frac{78}{360}}}$ which compounds the 6 percent yield for $\frac{78}{360}$ of a year.

> **Bond pricing conventionally assumes compound discounting to NPV.**   **Key Point**

4. The day/year count basis for money market instruments and bonds is generally different. The first have been described earlier. The day/year counts for bonds are described later in this chapter.

Given these differences, it is possible to express the equation for a bond price given earlier as follows:

Calculation summary

$$P = \frac{100}{\left(1 + \frac{i}{n}\right)^{W}} \frac{R}{n} \left[\frac{\left(1 - \dfrac{1}{\left(1 + \frac{i}{n}\right)^{N}}\right)}{\left(1 - \dfrac{1}{\left(1 + \frac{i}{n}\right)}\right)} + \frac{1}{\left(1 + \frac{i}{n}\right)^{N-1}} \right]$$

where: R = the annual coupon rate paid n times per year
W = the fraction of a coupon period between purchase and the next coupon to be received
N = the number of coupon payments not yet paid
i = yield per annum based on n payments per year

Despite the simplifying assumptions behind this formula, it is important because it is the conventional approach used in the markets. Adjustments to the formula are of course necessary if there are different cashflows to be discounted – for example, an unusual first coupon period which gives an odd first coupon payment, early partial redemptions of the bond or changes in the coupon rate during the bond's life. Even with these adjustments, the market approach is still generally to calculate the total price as the NPV assuming precisely regular coupon periods and certain day/year conventions.

It is clearly possible to calculate a price without making these assumptions – that is, to use the formula:

$$P = \sum_{k} \frac{C_k}{\left(1 + \frac{i}{n}\right)^{\frac{d_k \times n}{year}}}$$

with the exact time periods between cashflows and a consistent day/year basis for all types of bonds. For bonds of short maturity, the result can be significantly different from the conventional formula and this approach is clearly more satisfactory when comparing different bonds. In the UK gilt market, for example, some market participants quote yields taking into account the exact number of days between the actual cashflows. Some also use a year basis of $ACT/365\frac{1}{4}$ to allow for the average effect of leap years.

Accrued interest

The price we have calculated so far is in fact known as the "dirty" price of the bond and represents the total amount of cash paid by the buyer. From the seller's point of view however, he expects to receive "accrued" coupon on the bond. The accrued coupon is the coupon which the seller of a bond has "earned" so far by holding the bond since the last coupon date. He feels he is entitled to this portion of the coupon and therefore insists on the bond buyer paying it to him. The buyer however, will pay no more than the NPV of all the future cashflows. Therefore the total price paid is the dirty price but this is effectively considered as two separate amounts – the "clean" price and the accrued coupon. The price quoted in the market is the "clean" price, which is equal to dirty price minus the accrued coupon. In the market generally, accrued coupon is often called accrued interest.

Example 5.1 A bond pays a 9% coupon annually. Maturity is on 12 August 2014. The current market yield for the bond is 8%. Interest is calculated on a 30/360 basis (see later in this section for an explanation of this convention). What are the accrued coupon, dirty price and clean price for settlement on 9 June 2009?

Time from 12 August 2008 (the last coupon date) to 9 June 2009 is 297 days on a 30/360 basis:

$$\text{Accrued coupon} = 9 \times \frac{297}{360} = 7.4250$$

Time from 9 June 2009 to 12 August 2009 is 63 days on a 30/360 basis:

$$\text{Dirty price} = \frac{100}{1.08^{\frac{63}{360}}} \times \left(0.09 \times \frac{\left(1 - \frac{1}{1.08^6}\right)}{\left(1 - \frac{1}{1.08}\right)} + \frac{1}{1.08^5}\right) = 111.4811$$

Clean price = 111.4811 – 7.4250 = 104.06

```
1.08 ENTER 6 ☐ ∧ ☐ ¹/x 1 ☐ x≷y −
1.08 ☐ ¹/x 1 ☐ x≷y − ÷
.09 ×
1.08 ENTER 5 ☐ ∧ ☐ ¹/x +
100 ×
1.08 ENTER 63 ENTER 360 ÷ ☐ ∧ ÷          (Dirty price)
9 ENTER 297 × 360 ÷                        (Accrued interest)
−                                          (Clean price)
```

> Dirty price = NPV of cashflows
>
> Accrued coupon = proportion of coupon since last coupon payment
>
> Clean price = dirty price − accrued coupon

Calculation summary

Clean bond prices are generally quoted in terms of the price per 100 units of the bond, often to two decimal places. US bonds are however generally quoted in units of $\frac{1}{32}$. Thus a price of 95–17 for a US treasury bond means $95\frac{17}{32}$ (= 95.53125) per \$100 face value, rather than \$95.17 per \$100 face value. This is sometimes refined further to units of $\frac{1}{64}$ by use of "+". Thus a price of 95–17+ means $95\frac{35}{64}$ = 95.546875. Option prices on US government bonds are quoted in units of $\frac{1}{64}$.

Coupon dates

Apart from the first coupon period or the last coupon period, which may be irregular, coupons are generally paid on regular dates – usually annual or semi-annual and sometimes quarterly. Thus semi-annual coupons on a bond maturing on 17 February 2015 would typically be paid on 17 August and 17 February each year. If a semi-annual bond pays one coupon on 30 April for example (that is, at month-end), the other coupon might be on 31 October (also month-end) as with a US treasury bond, or 30 October as with a UK gilt.

Even though the previous coupon may have been delayed – for example, the coupon date was a Sunday so the coupon was paid the following day – the accrual calculation is taken from the regular scheduled date, not the actual payment date. Also, the accrued interest is calculated up to a value date which in some markets can sometimes be slightly different from the settlement date for the transaction. This does not affect the total dirty price paid.

Ex-dividend

When a bond is bought or sold shortly before a coupon date, the issuer of the bond generally needs some days to change the records in order to make a note of the new owner. If there is not enough time to make this administrative change, the coupon will still be paid to the previous owner.

The length of time taken varies widely between different issuers. The issuer pays the coupon to the holder registered on a date known as the record date. This is therefore the last date on which a bond transaction can be settled in order for the new owner to be recorded in time as entitled to the coupon, and a bond sold up to this date is said to be "cum-dividend". A bond sold for settlement after this date is said to be sold "ex-dividend" or "ex-coupon". In some cases it is possible to sell a bond ex-dividend before the normal ex-dividend period.

If a bond sale is ex-dividend, the seller, rather than needing to receive accrued interest from the buyer, will need to pay it to the buyer – because the final days of the coupon period which "belong" to the buyer will in fact be paid to the seller. At the ex-dividend point therefore, the accrued interest becomes negative. In this case, the accrued interest is calculated from value date to the next scheduled coupon date (rather than the next actual coupon payment date if that is different because of a non-working day).

Example 5.2　Consider a bond with a coupon (annual) of 7.3% and maturity 14 August 2013, purchased for settlement on 10 August 2009 at a price of 98.45. Assume the record date is 7 working days before the coupon date.

The accrued interest is: $\frac{-4}{365} \times 7.3 = -0.08$

The all-in price is therefore $98.45 - 0.08 = 98.37$

Calculation summary

$$\text{Accrued coupon} = 100 \times \text{coupon rate} \times \frac{\text{days since last coupon}}{\text{year}}$$

For ex-dividend prices, accrued coupon is negative:

$$\text{Accrued coupon} = -100 \times \text{coupon rate} \times \frac{\text{days to next coupon}}{\text{year}}$$

Day / year conventions

Fractional periods of a year for price / yield calculations and accrued coupon are calculated according to different conventions in different markets. As in the money markets, these conventions are generally expressed in the form "days / year" where "days" is the conventional number of days in a particular period to be calculated and "year" is the conventional number of days in a year.

The following methods describe how to calculate the accrued coupon on a bond between two dates $d_1/m_1/y_1$ and $d_2/m_2/y_2$ according to some of the different conventions. Please note that this area is something of a minefield! One particular convention might be named differently by different people, and the same name might be used by different people for two different conventions. Also, the conventions do sometimes change and the list below is not exhaustive and not all bonds conform to the "expected" method!

These methods apply to "straightforward" situations. To calculate accrued coupon when there is an irregular (longer or shorter than normal) coupon period at the beginning or end of the bond's life, see "Irregular first or final coupon period" below.

The most common of the bond market methods below are probably the ones we have called "ACT/365", "ACT/ACT", "30/360", "30/360" and "30/360" (SIFMA).

For all the following "actual" methods except with Japanese bond yields:

days = actual number of calendar days in the period

ACT/360 year = 360

Used for many money markets, as discussed in Chapter 2 "The Money Markets", and FRNs but not used in the bond markets.

ACT/365 year = 365

Used for GBP and other money markets, as discussed in Chapter 2. Also used for Japanese (accrued coupon) and other government bonds.

In ISDA (International Swaps and Derivatives Association) documentation for interest rate swaps, this convention is also known as "ACT/365 (fixed)".

ACT/365 year = 365
(Japanese For calculating Japanese bond yields, 29 February is consid-
yield ered to be 28 February and ignored when counting "days".
method)

ACT/365L year = 366 if the next coupon falls in a leap year, but 365 otherwise

Used for some GBP FRNs.

ACT/ACT year = actual number of days in the current coupon period multiplied by the number of coupon periods per year.

With annual coupons, this results in a year of 365 or 366. With semi-annual coupons, it results in a year of 362, 364, 366 or 368 (twice the coupon period of 181, 182, 183 or 184).

Used for US and most European government bonds and also non-USD Eurobonds issued after 1998.

Also called the ICMA method. ICMA is the International Capital Markets Association.

ACT/ACT year = 366 if the coupon period (including the first day of the
(AFB) period but not the last) includes 29 February
year = 365 otherwise

Also called "ACT/365–366". AFB is the Association Française des Banques.

ACT/ACT If the days counted all fall in a non-leap year:
(ISDA) year = 365

Otherwise, divide the number of days which fall in a non-leap year by a year of 365, divide the number of days which fall in a leap year by a year of 366, and add the two results.

Importantly, when counting the days in each part, include the first day of the period and not the last.

Used for some interest rate swaps.

In ISDA documentation, this convention is also known (confusingly!) as "ACT/365".

For all the following 30/360 methods:

$$\text{days} = (y_2 - y_1) \times 360 + (m_2 - m_1) \times 30 + (d_2 - d_1) \quad \text{year} = 360$$

30(E)/360 (ICMA) First make the following adjustments:

If d_1 or d_2 is 31, change it to 30.

Used for all Eurobonds issued before 1999, USD Eurobonds issued after 1998, and also some European domestic markets.

Also called "30(E)/360" or "360/360".

30/360 (German/ Swiss) First make the following adjustments:

If d_1 or d_2 is 31 or the last day of February, change it to 30.

Used for Swiss government bonds and some German bonds.

For accrued coupon, d_1 is normally the last coupon date before settlement date (i.e. d_2). For Swiss bonds however, it is the last coupon date before trade date.

30/360 (ISDA) First make the following adjustments:

If d_1 is 31, change it to 30.
If d_2 is 31 and d_1 is 30 or 31, change d_2 to 30.

Used for some interest rate swaps and US municipal bonds.

Also called "30(A)/360" or "360/360", or in the US "municipal 30/360".

30(E)/360 (ISDA) The same as 30/360 (German / Swiss version) except that if d_2 is the termination date of the interst rate swap, and is also the last day of February, do not change d_2 to 30.

30/360 (SIFMA) If the security follows the "end-of-month rule" (if one coupon is at month end, then all coupons are at month end), then first make the following adjustments:

If d_1 is 31 or the last day of February, change it to 30.
If d_2 is 31 and d_1 is 30, 31 or the last day of February, change d_2 to 30.
If d_2 is the last day of February, and d_1 is the last day of February, change d_2 to 30.

If the security does not follow the "end-of-month rule", use the 30(A)/360 method instead.

Used for most US federal agency and corporate bonds. SIFMA is the Securities Industry and Financial Markets Association in the US (formerly the SIA).

In general, the convention for accrued interest in a particular market is the same as the convention used in that market for calculating the fraction of a year for the price/yield formula. This is not always so however.

Even when the same convention is used, there remain two methods for calculating the number of days from calculation date until next coupon date for the purpose of the price/yield calculation. One method is to count the days using the appropriate convention. The other is first to calculate the number of days accrued coupon and then to subtract this from the total days in the period. These two methods do not always agree.

Note that, because coupons are paid in "round" amounts, it is possible for the accrued coupon to be greater than the actual coupon payable for the period. For example, if coupons are paid semi-annually on an ACT/365 basis, the interest accrued from a 15 March coupon date to 14 September would be coupon $\times \frac{183}{365}$, which is greater than the coupon $\times \frac{1}{2}$ payable. This possibility depends on the ex-dividend period for the bond.

Example 5.3

Consider a bond whose previous coupon was due on 16 January 2012 and whose next coupon is due on 16 July 2012. The number of calendar days in the current coupon period is 182. The day/year calculation under the various conventions is shown below for accrued interest from 16 January up to 30 March, 31 March and 1 April respectively:

	30 March	31 March	1 April
ACT/360	74/360	75/360	76/360
ACT/365	74/365	75/365	76/365
ACT/ACT	74/364	75/364	76/364
ACT/ACT(AFB)	74/366	75/366	76/366
30/360 (ICMA)	74/360	74/360	75/360
30/360 (ISDA)	74/360	75/360	75/360
30/360 (SIFMA)	74/360	75/360	75/360

We have given a list, in Appendix 2, of the conventions used in some markets.

Irregular first or final coupon period

Sometimes the first or last coupon period of a bond is shorter or longer than the standard period (annual, semi-annual, etc.) for that bond. An adjustment is needed when calculating the "year" for accrued coupon and yield, for a date falling within such an irregular coupon period. The general approaches are as follows.

For a short first coupon period, calculate the date on which the bond "should have been" issued – the "quasi-issue date" – which is a full coupon period before the first actual coupon date. This gives the number of days there "should have been" in the first coupon period. Now calculate the accrued coupon (counting from the actual issue date) and yield (discounting back from the actual first coupon payment date) as usual on the basis of this quasi-coupon period.

For a short final coupon period, calculate the date on which the bond "should have" matured – the "quasi-maturity date" – which is a full coupon period after the previous actual coupon date before maturity. This gives the number of days there "should have been" in the final coupon period. Now calculate the accrued coupon (counting from the previous actual coupon date) and yield (discounting back from the actual maturity date) as usual on the basis of this final quasi-coupon period.

For a long first coupon period, calculate the first quasi-coupon date, when a first short coupon "should have been" paid, by going backwards one full period from the first actual coupon date, and also the quasi-issue date on which the bond "should have been" issued, which is two full periods before the first actual coupon date. This creates two first quasi-coupon periods.

For a date between issue and the quasi-coupon date, calculate the accrued coupon (counting from the actual issue date) as usual on the basis of the first quasi-coupon period. Calculate the yield by first discounting back one full coupon period from first actual coupon date to quasi-coupon date; then discount back again based on the period from the calculation date to quasi-coupon date divided by the first quasi-coupon period.

For a date between the quasi-coupon date and the first actual coupon date, first calculate accrued coupon from actual issue until quasi-coupon date on the basis of the first quasi-coupon period, and then add accrued coupon from the quasi-coupon date until the calculation date on the basis of the second quasi-coupon period. Calculate the yield by discounting back as usual from first actual coupon date on the basis of the second quasi-coupon period.

For a long final coupon period, calculate the final quasi-coupon date, which is a full coupon period after the final actual coupon date prior to maturity, and also the quasi-maturity date, which is two full coupon periods after the final actual coupon date prior to maturity. This creates two final quasi-coupon periods.

For a date between the final actual coupon date prior to maturity and the quasi-coupon date, calculate the accrued coupon as usual on the basis of the first quasi-coupon period. Calculate the yield by first discounting back from the actual maturity date to quasi-coupon date on the basis of the second quasi-coupon period; then discount back again from quasi-coupon date to calculation date on the basis of the first quasi-coupon period.

For a date between the quasi-coupon date and maturity, first calculate accrued coupon from the final actual coupon date prior to maturity until the quasi-coupon date on the basis of the first quasi-coupon period. Then add accrued coupon from the quasi-coupon date until calculation date on the basis of the second quasi-coupon period. Calculate the yield by discounting back as usual from actual maturity date on the basis of the second quasi-coupon period.

Using an HP calculator

The HP17 and HP19 calculators have inbuilt functions specifically for calculating clean bond prices and yields. They allow for coupons to be paid annually or semi-annually and also for the day/year counts to be 30(A)/360 or ACT/ACT. Provided that neither the settlement date nor the next coupon date is the 31st day of a month, 30(A)/360 is the same as 30(E)/360. Also, provided that the current coupon period does not include 29 February, ACT/ACT annual is the same as ACT/365 annual. The calculator cannot however calculate on an ACT/365 semi-annual basis.

HP calculator example

Example

We can repeat Example 5.1 using the HP bond function as follows:

HP19BII	
FIN BOND	
TYPE 360 ANN EXIT	(Set for 30/360, annual coupons)
9.062009 SETT	(Settlement date)
12.082014 MAT	(Maturity date)
9 CPN%	(Coupon)
MORE 8 YLD%	(Yield)
PRICE	(Clean price)
ACCRU	(Accrued interest)
+	(Dirty price)

Similarly to the TVM function of the calculator, it is possible to calculate the clean price from the yield or the yield from the clean price. It is also possible to allow for a redemption amount different from the normal 100 by entering the appropriate value as a "call" amount – i.e. the amount which the issuer must pay on redemption if he wishes to call the bond on the date entered as the maturity date.

HP calculator example

Example

A bond pays a 6.5% coupon semi-annually. Maturity is on 19 July 2023. The bond will be redeemed at a rate of 105 per 100. The current (clean) price for the bond for settlement on 24 March 2009 is 97.45. Interest and price/yield calculations are both on a semi-annual ACT/ACT basis. What is the yield of the bond?

Answer: 6.99%

HP19BII	
FIN BOND	
TYPE A/A SEMI EXIT	(Set for ACT/ACT, semi-annual)
24.032009 SETT	(Settlement date)
19.072023 MAT	(Maturity date)
6.5 CPN%	(Coupon)
105 CALL	(Redemption amount per 100)
MORE 97.45 PRICE	(Clean price)
YLD%	(Yield)
MORE 100 CALL	(Reset redemption to 100)

Note that it is probably useful to reset the call amount to 100 after such a calculation, to avoid forgetting this next time!

As already mentioned, some bonds calculate accrued interest on one day / year basis but calculate the dirty price from the future cashflows on a different day / year basis. The HP bond function is not able to calculate with a mixture in this way, and the numbers must be manipulated to get round the problem. The exercises at the end of the chapter include some examples of this. The procedures necessary are as follows:

To calculate the clean price from the yield

- Set the calculator for the day / year basis used for the price / yield calculation.
- Calculate the clean price and accrued interest as usual. Add together to give the true dirty price.
- Reset the calculator for the day / year basis used for the accrued interest.
- Calculate the conventional accrued interest and subtract from the dirty price to give the clean price.

To calculate the yield from the clean price

- Set the calculator for the day / year basis used for the accrued interest calculation.
- Calculate the accrued interest as usual. Add to the known clean price to give the true dirty price.
- Reset the calculator for the basis used for the price / yield calculation.
- Recalculate an adjusted accrued interest and subtract from the true dirty price to give an adjusted clean price.
- Use this adjusted clean price to calculate the yield.

DIFFERENT YIELD MEASURES AND PRICE CALCULATIONS

Yield to maturity

We have so far considered how to calculate a bond's price if we know its yield. This is the same as calculating an NPV given a rate of discount. Calculating the yield if we know the price is the same as calculating the internal rate of return of all the cashflows including the price paid. As noted in Chapter 1, there is no formula for this calculation. Instead, it is necessary to use the price formula and calculate the yield by iteration – estimate a yield, calculate the price based on this estimate, compare with the actual price, adjust the yield estimate, recalculate the price, etc.

The yield we have used is known as the yield to maturity (sometimes YTM). It is also known simply as "yield", "redemption yield" or "gross redemption yield" (GRY) because it is the yield to the redemption date assuming all cashflows are paid gross (without deduction of tax).

Some bonds make partial redemptions – that is, the principal is repaid in stages rather than all at maturity. Using the same approach as we have so far requires that all the cashflows, including the partial redemptions, are discounted at the yield to give the dirty price. In this case, the yield is sometimes known as "yield to equivalent life".

The yield to maturity has the same disadvantage that we considered in Chapter 1; it assumes that all cashflows can be reinvested at the same rate. Consider, for example, a 7-year bond with annual coupons of 10 percent, a price of 95.00 and an annual yield of 11.063 percent. This means that if all the cashflows are discounted at 11.063 percent, they have an NPV of 95. Equivalently, if all the cashflows received over the bond's life can be reinvested to maturity at 11.063 percent, the final internal rate of return will also be 11.063 percent.

In practice, reinvestment rates will be different. However, given that a bond does have a market price, an investor wishes to be told, in summary, what rate of return this implies. There are as many answers to the question as there are assumptions about reinvestment rates. One possibility would be to calculate the current market forward-forward rates at which all the coupon cashflows could be reinvested. In practice, the conventional summary answer given to the question is the internal rate of return – i.e. the yield to maturity.

Yield vs. coupon

It is intuitively reasonable that when a bond's yield is the same as its coupon, the bond's price should be par (that is, 100) – because the bond's future cashflows are created by applying an interest rate to the face value of 100 and discounting back again to an NPV at the same rate should arrive back at 100.

Similarly, as the yield rises above the coupon rate, the NPV will fall and vice versa. Therefore:

> **Generally, if a bond's price is greater than par, its yield is less than the coupon rate, and vice versa.**   **Key Point**

Although this intuitive result is almost true, the price is not in fact exactly 100 when the yield is equal to the coupon, except on a coupon date. This is because accrued interest is calculated on a simple interest basis and price on a compound interest basis.

Example 5.4 Consider the same bond as in Example 5.1, but assume the yield is now 9%. What is the clean price?

$$\text{As before, accrued coupon} = 9 \times \frac{297}{360} = 7.4250$$

$$\text{Dirty price} = \frac{100}{1.09^{\frac{63}{360}}} \times \left(0.09 \times \frac{\left(1 - \frac{1}{1.09^6}\right)}{\left(1 - \frac{1}{1.09}\right)} + \frac{1}{1.09^5} \right) = 107.3685$$

$$\text{Clean price} = 107.3685 - 7.4250 = 99.94$$

```
FIN BOND TYPE 360 ANN EXIT
9.062009 SETT
12.082014 MAT
9 CPN%
MORE 9 YLD%
PRICE
```

In Example 5.4, if the clean price were exactly 100, the yield would in fact be 8.986%.

This calculation is complicated further, of course, when the day / year basis for the price / yield calculation is different from the day / year convention for the accrued interest. In general, however:

Key Point On a non-coupon date, if a bond is priced at par, the yield is slightly lower than the coupon rate.

The effect increases as the settlement date moves away from the coupon dates and is greater for bonds of short maturity.

Current yield

A much more simple measure of yield, which can be calculated easily, is the current yield. This ignores any capital gain or loss arising from the difference between the price paid and the principal amount received at redemption. It also ignores the time value of money. Instead it considers only the coupon income as a proportion of the price paid for the bond – essentially considering the investment as an indefinite deposit:

Calculation summary

$$\text{Current yield} = \frac{\text{coupon}}{\text{clean price}}$$

Simple yield to maturity

Simple yield to maturity does take into account the capital gain or loss as well as the coupon but, like current yield, ignores the time value of money.

The capital gain or loss is amortised equally over the time left to maturity:

Calculation summary

$$\text{Simple yield to maturity} = \frac{\text{coupon} + \left(\dfrac{\text{redemption amount} - \text{clean price}}{\text{years to maturity}}\right)}{\text{clean price}}$$

The simple yield to maturity is used in the Japanese bond market.

Example 5.5

For a 7-year bond paying annual 10% coupons and with a price of 95.00, what are the yield to maturity, current yield and simple yield to maturity?

Yield to maturity = 11.06%

$$\text{Current yield} = \frac{10}{95.00} = 10.53\%$$

$$\text{Simple yield to maturity} = \frac{10 + \left(\frac{100 - 95}{7}\right)}{95.00} = 11.28\%$$

```
FIN TVM
7 N
95 +/– PV
10 PMT
100 FV
I %YR                                  (Yield to maturity)
10 ENTER 95 ÷                          (Current yield)
100 ENTER 95 – 7 ÷ 10 + 95 ÷          (Simple yield to maturity)
```

Figure 5.1 compares the different measures for the same bond at different prices.

Comparison of yield measures for a 7-year 10% coupon bond

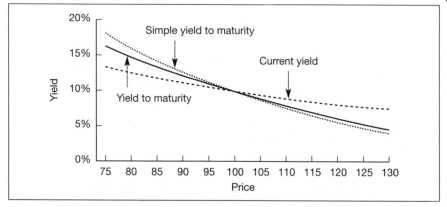

Figure 5.1

Yield in a final coupon period

When a bond has only one remaining coupon to be paid (at maturity), it looks very similar, in cashflow terms, to a short-term, money market instrument. For this reason, yields for such bonds are sometimes quoted on a basis comparable to money market yields. This means that the future cashflow is discounted to a present value (the price) at a simple rate rather than a compound rate – but still using the day/year basis conventional for that particular bond market.

Example 5.6

Consider the following bond:

Coupon:	8% semi-annual
Maturity date:	16 October 2009
Settlement date:	10 August 2009
Clean price:	100.26
Price/yield calculation basis:	ACT/ACT
Accrued interest calculation basis:	ACT/ACT

The current coupon period from 16 April to 16 October is 183 days.

Therefore the accrued interest is $8 \times \dfrac{116}{366} = 2.5355$

Therefore the dirty price is $100.26 + 2.5355 = 102.7955$

(a) Following the logic of usual bond pricing, the price/yield equation would be:

$$\text{Dirty price} = \frac{\text{final cashflow}}{(1 + \text{yield})^{\frac{\text{days}}{\text{year}}}}$$

This can be manipulated to become:

$$\text{Yield} = \left(\frac{\text{final cashflow}}{\text{dirty price}}\right)^{\frac{\text{year}}{\text{days}}} - 1$$

$$= \left(\frac{104}{102.7955}\right)^{\frac{366}{67}} - 1 = 6.57\%$$

(b) Using simple interest however, the result would be:

$$\text{Yield} = \left(\frac{\text{final cashflow}}{\text{dirty price}} - 1\right) \times \frac{\text{year}}{\text{days}}$$

$$= \left(\frac{104}{102.7955} - 1\right) \times \frac{366}{67} = 6.40\%$$

Method (b) is assumed by the HP calculator. It is often used in the market, for example, for US treasury bonds (on an ACT/ACT basis), but not generally for Eurobonds.

104 ENTER 102.7955 ÷ 366 ENTER 67 ÷ ☐ ∧ 1 –	(a)
104 ENTER 102.7955 ÷ 1 – 366 × 67 ÷	(b)

Calculation summary

Alternative yield calculation in a final coupon period

$$i = \left[\frac{\text{total final cashflow including coupon}}{\text{dirty price}} - 1\right] \times \frac{\text{year}}{\text{days to maturity}}$$

where days and year are measured on the relevant bond basis

Bond-equivalent yields for treasury bills

In the previous section we considered what is the yield of a bond in its last coupon period, calculated by a method which enables comparison with a money market instrument. In the US market, the reverse is also considered: what is the yield of a treasury bill calculated by a method which enables comparison with a bond which will shortly mature? The bond-equivalent yield of a treasury bill is therefore the coupon of a theoretical US treasury bond, trading at par, with the same maturity date, which would give the same return as the bill.

If the bill has 182 days or less until maturity, the calculation for this is the usual conversion from discount to yield, except that it is then quoted on a 365-day basis:

$$i = \frac{D}{\left(1 - D \times \frac{days}{360}\right)} \times \frac{365}{360}$$

where: D = discount rate (on a 360-day basis)
  days = number of days until maturity
  i = the bond-equivalent yield we are trying to calculate

If 29 February falls during the 12-month period starting on the purchase date, 365 is conventionally replaced by 366.

If the bill has more than 182 days until maturity however, the calculation must take account of the fact that the equivalent bond would pay a coupon during the period as well as at the end. The amount of the first coupon is taken to be the coupon accrued on the bond between purchase and coupon date (which is half a year before maturity). This coupon is:

$$P \times i \times \left(\frac{days - \frac{365}{2}}{365}\right)$$

$$= P \times i \times \left(\frac{days}{365} - \frac{1}{2}\right)$$

where: P = the price paid for the bond (= its par value)

If this coupon is reinvested at the same yield i, then at maturity it is worth:

$$P \times i \times \left(\frac{days}{365} - \frac{1}{2}\right) \times \left(1 + \frac{i}{2}\right)$$

The bond also returns at maturity the face value P and the final coupon – a total of:

$$P \times \left(1 + \frac{i}{2}\right)$$

Adding together these amounts, the total proceeds at maturity are:

$$P \times \left(1 + \frac{i}{2}\right) \times \left(1 + i \times \left(\frac{\text{days}}{365} - \frac{1}{2}\right)\right)$$

Since the return on this theoretical bond is the same as the return on the treasury bill, these total proceeds must be the face value F of the bill paid on maturity, and the price paid P must be the same as the discounted value paid for the bill. Thus:

$$F = P \times \left(1 + \frac{i}{2}\right) \times \left(1 + i \times \left(\frac{\text{days}}{365} - \frac{1}{2}\right)\right)$$

and $P = F \times \left(1 - D \times \frac{\text{days}}{360}\right)$

Therefore:

$$i^2 \times \left(\frac{\text{days}}{365} - \frac{1}{2}\right) + i \times \frac{2 \times \text{days}}{365} + 2 \times \left(1 - \frac{1}{\left(1 - D \times \frac{\text{days}}{360}\right)}\right) = 0$$

Solving for a quadratic equation, this gives the formula shown below. Again, if 29 February falls in the 12-month period starting on the purchase date, 365 is conventionally replaced by 366.

Calculation summary

Bond-equivalent yield for US treasury bill

If 182 days or less to maturity:

$$i = \frac{D}{1 - D \times \frac{\text{days}}{360}} \times \frac{365}{360}$$

If more than 182 days to maturity:

$$i = \frac{-\frac{\text{days}}{365} + \left(\left(\frac{\text{days}}{365}\right)^2 + 2 \times \left(\frac{\text{days}}{365} - \frac{1}{2}\right) \times \left(\frac{1}{\left(1 - D \times \frac{\text{days}}{360}\right)} - 1\right)\right)^{\frac{1}{2}}}{\left(\frac{\text{days}}{360} - \frac{1}{2}\right)}$$

If 29 February falls in the 12-month period starting on the purchase date, replace 365 by 366.

It should be noted that if there happen to be a treasury bill and a treasury bond maturing on the same day in less than 182 days, the bond-equivalent yield for the bill is not exactly the same as the yield quoted for a bond in its final coupon period, even though this is intended to take the same approach as money market instruments. Example 5.7 demonstrates this.

Consider a US treasury bill maturing on 16 October 2009 and quoted at a discount rate of 6.2229% for settlement 10 August 2009. (The discount rate would not normally be quoted to that level of precision, but we need this for a comparison with the previous example.)

Example 5.7

The bond-equivalent yield for this bill is:

$$\frac{6.2229\%}{\left(1 - 0.062229 \times \frac{67}{360}\right)} \times \frac{365}{360} = 6.38\%$$

Suppose that we purchase face value $10,400 of the bill. The price paid would be:

$$\$10,400 \times \left(1 - 0.062229 \times \frac{67}{360}\right) = \$10,279.55$$

The cashflows for this bill are exactly the same as if we buy face value $10,000 of the bond in the previous example; the final proceeds are principal plus a semi-annual coupon and the dirty price paid is 102.7955. The yield quoted for that bond however was 6.40%, because the year basis was 2 × 181 days.

0.062229 ENTER 67 × 360 ÷ 1 − +/− 6.2229 ☐ $x \gtrless y$ ÷ 365 × 360 ÷

Money market yield

The difference in price / yield conventions between instruments such as a long-term CD and a bond makes comparison between them difficult. An investor may therefore wish to bring them into line by calculating a money market yield for a bond.

From earlier, we saw that the differences between the two approaches (apart from the fact that coupons on bonds are paid in round amounts and those on CDs are not) are:

1. CD price calculations use exact day counts rather than assume regular time intervals between coupon payments.

2. CDs calculate the final discounting from the nearest coupon date back to the settlement date using simple interest rather than compound interest.

3. CDs and bonds generally also have different day / year count bases.

It is possible to calculate a money market yield for a bond, exactly as we did for a medium-term CD in Chapter 2. An alternative is to compromise between the two approaches by using the bond approach for (1) above and the CD approach for (2) and (3). The result is to adjust the basic bond dirty price formula to the following:

<table>
<tr><td>

Calculation summary

</td><td>

Money market yield for a bond

$$P = \frac{100}{\left(1 + \frac{i}{n} \times W\right)} \left|\frac{R}{n} \times \frac{\left(1 - \dfrac{1}{\left(1 + \frac{i}{n} \times \frac{365}{360}\right)^N}\right)}{\left(1 - \dfrac{1}{\left(1 + \frac{i}{n} \times \frac{365}{360}\right)}\right)} + \frac{1}{\left(1 + \frac{i}{n} \times \frac{365}{360}\right)^{N-1}}\right|$$

where i and W are the yield and fraction of a coupon period on a money market basis rather than a bond basis.

</td></tr>
</table>

<table>
<tr><td>

Example 5.8

</td><td>

What is the money market yield for the same bond as used in Example 5.1, assuming that the appropriate money market convention is ACT/360?

We know that the dirty price is 111.4811. On an ACT/360 basis, the fraction of a coupon period from settlement to the next coupon is $\frac{64}{360}$ rather than $\frac{63}{360}$. We therefore have:

$$111.4811 = \frac{100}{\left(1 + i \times \frac{64}{360}\right)} \times \left(0.09 \times \frac{\left(1 - \dfrac{1}{\left(1 + i \times \frac{365}{360}\right)^6}\right)}{\left(1 - \dfrac{1}{\left(1 + i \times \frac{365}{360}\right)}\right)} + \frac{1}{\left(1 + i \times \frac{365}{360}\right)^5}\right)$$

The solution to this is that the money market yield is 7.878%.

</td></tr>
</table>

This cannot be solved by the HP bond calculator. The HP does have an equation solver however (available only in algebraic mode rather than RPN mode) which can be used to solve the formula as follows. Note that the equation solver respects the normal mathematical conventions for the order of operations, whereas the HP used normally in algebraic mode does not (operating instead in the order in which operations are entered, thus requiring the use of extra parentheses).

```
SOLVE □ ↓
PRICE = 100 × (CPN × (1 – 1 ÷ (1 + YLD × 365 ÷ 360) □ ∧ N) ÷ (1 – 1÷ (1 +
YLD × 365 ÷ 360)) + 1 ÷ (1+ YLD × 365 ÷ 360) □ ∧ (N – 1)) ÷ (1 + YLD ×
DAYS ÷ 360)
CALC
111.4811 PRICE
.09 CPN
6 N
64 DAYS
YLD
```

Moosmüller yield

The Moosmüller method of yield calculation (Figure 5.2) is used in some German markets. The same method is also used by the US Treasury for yields

and prices on new issues. It is similar to the money market yield in the previous section, in that it calculates the final discounting for the next coupon date
to settlement using simple interest rather than compound interest. The
day / year convention however is not changed to a money market basis. The
result is the following formula, which can be seen to be a hybrid between the
formulas for yield to maturity and money market yield.

$$P = \frac{100}{(1 + \frac{i}{n} \times W)} \left[\frac{R}{n} \times \frac{\left(1 - \frac{1}{(1 + \frac{i}{n})^N}\right)}{\left(1 - \frac{1}{(1 + \frac{i}{n})}\right)} + \frac{1}{(1 + \frac{i}{n})^{N-1}} \right]$$

Calculation summary

Comparison of yield to maturity with Moosmüller yield for a 10% coupon bond priced at par

Figure 5.2

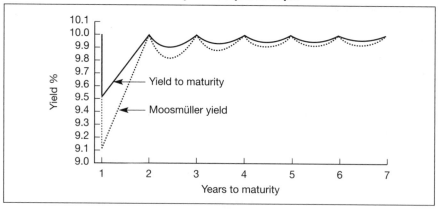

Zero-coupon and strip prices

Pricing a zero-coupon bond or a single component of a stripped bond is
similar in concept to pricing a coupon-bearing bond except that the fraction of an interest period used for discounting – generally taken as the time
to the next scheduled coupon date for a coupon-bearing bond – must be
determined. It is appropriate to use the date which would be the next
coupon date if it existed – known as a "quasi-coupon date". There remain
then the same choices as with coupon-bearing bonds: which day / year convention to use, whether to use simple interest for short maturities, and
whether to use a mixture of simple and compound interest for longer maturities. As there is no coupon, the clean price and dirty price are the same.

Example 5.9 What is the price of the following zero-coupon bond?

Maturity date:	21 September 2016
Settlement date:	8 January 2009
Yield:	8.520%
Price/yield calculation basis:	ACT/ACT (semi-annual)

As the quasi-coupon periods are semi-annual, the next quasi-coupon date is 21 March 2009 and the previous one was 21 September 2008 (despite the fact that these are Saturday and Sunday respectively). On an ACT/ACT basis therefore, the fraction of a quasi-coupon period from settlement to the next quasi-coupon date is $\frac{72}{181}$. The price is therefore:

$$\frac{100}{\left(1 + \frac{0.0852}{2}\right)^{\frac{72}{181}+15}} = 52.605014$$

This is exactly the same as the conventional general bond price formula given earlier, with R (coupon rate) = 0, n (coupon frequency) = 2 and ACT/ACT semi-annual as the day/year convention.

```
.0852 ENTER 2 ÷ 1 +
72 ENTER 181 ÷ 15 + ☐ ∧
100 ☐ x≷y ÷
```

or

```
FIN BOND TYPE A/A SEMI EXIT
8.012009 SETT
21.092016 MAT
0 CPN%
MORE 8.52 YLD%
PRICE
```

Because the quasi-coupon dates are used as reference points for discounting to a present value but do not reflect actual cashflows, two identical zero-coupon bonds stripped from different coupon-bearing bonds could appear to have inconsistent yields.

Example 5.10 Suppose that the bond in Example 5.9 is in fact a coupon stripped from a UK gilt (semi-annual coupons). Consider another zero-coupon bond in the same currency with the same maturity date and face value, but which is in fact a coupon stripped from a French government bond (annual coupons). What is the yield of this bond if the price is the same as the bond in Example 5.9?

The fraction of a period to the next quasi-coupon date (21 September 2009) is now $\frac{256}{365}$. The price is therefore given by:

$$52.605014 = \frac{100}{(1 + \text{yield})^{\frac{256}{365}+7}}$$

Solving for the yield gives 8.699%.

Continuing from the previous example:
MORE TYPE ANN EXIT
MORE YLD%

or

52.605014 ENTER 100 ÷
256 ENTER 365 ÷ 7 + □ ¹/ₓ □ ∧
□ ¹/ₓ 1 −

We would not expect the yields in Examples 5.9 and 5.10 to be the same, because one is semi-annual and the other is annual. However, the usual conversion from semi-annual to annual will not bring them in line:

$$\left(1 + \frac{0.0852}{2}\right)^2 - 1 = 8.701\%$$

In this case, the annual equivalent of the yield quoted for the gilt strip is greater than the yield quoted for the identical French strip. The reason is the uneven division of days between the semi-annual quasi-coupon periods (181 days, then 184 days, etc.).

A SUMMARY OF THE VARIOUS APPROACHES TO PRICE/YIELD

Beware! The different conventions used in different markets to relate price and yield are just that – different conventions. When quoting, comparing or discussing a yield you should always ensure that you are using the same approach as the other person. The conventions should not affect the economics of an instrument. If the market convention is to trade a particular instrument in terms of yield rather than price, the investor must first convert this yield to a price using the appropriate conventions. The economics of the investment are then determined by what the price actually is and what the future cashflows are. From these, to compare two investments, the investor can ignore the yield quoted by the market and use a single consistent approach of his choice to calculate yields for comparison. In Chapter 7 we shall see how, in reverse, the investor can calculate a price for each investment using zero-coupon yields; again, this can be done consistently, ignoring market conventions.

Summarising the issues we have already seen, the following factors need to be considered.

Day/year convention for accrued coupon

This is ACT/365 (for example, Norway), ACT/ACT (France), 30/360 (ICMA) (older Eurobonds) or 30/360 (SIFMA) (US federal agency) etc.

Day / year convention for discounting cashflows to the dirty price

This is often the same as for accrued coupon, but may not be. For a consistent calculation disregarding market convention, ACT/365.25 might be used to compensate on average for the distorting effect of leap years.

Adjustment for non-working days

Conventional bond calculations generally ignore the effect of non-working days, assuming coupons are always paid on the regular scheduled date (even if this is not a working day). This approach is not taken with medium-term CDs. The UK Stock Exchange calculations for gilt prices for example however, have in the past discounted to the dirty price using actual payment dates for the cashflows.

Simple interest vs. compound interest

In some markets, the yield for a bond in its final coupon period is calculated on the basis of simple interest (USA). For bonds with more than one coupon remaining, compound interest is usual, although it is possible, for example, to take simple interest for the first fractional coupon period compounded with periodic interest thereafter (the US Treasury's calculation method for new issues). For a medium-term CD, simple interest discount factors for each period are compounded together.

Compounding method

It is usual to discount bond cashflows by compounding in "round" years. Using the same notation as earlier in this chapter, the discount factor is $\left(\dfrac{1}{1 + \frac{i}{n}}\right)^{W\ +\ \text{a number of whole coupon periods}}$. A more precise approach is to use the total exact number of days to each cashflow rather than a round number of years: a factor of $\left(1 + \dfrac{i}{n}\right)^{\frac{\text{total days to cashflow}}{\text{year}} \times n}$. For medium-term CDs, the approach is to compound each exact time separately.

Other considerations

One basic question is whether a yield is quoted annually, semi-annually or quarterly. The usual convention is to quote an annual yield if the coupons are paid annually, a semi-annual yield if the coupons are paid semi-annually, etc. Care would need to be taken, for example, in comparing a semi-annual yield for a UK gilt paying semi-annual coupons with a quarterly yield for a gilt paying quarterly coupons.

The concept of a bond yield as an internal rate of return implies that all coupons are also reinvested at the yield. An alternative is to assume a particular reinvestment rate (or series of different reinvestment rates). The coupon cashflows are then all reinvested at this rate until maturity. The yield is then the zero-coupon yield implied by the total future value accumulated in this manner, and the initial bond price.

DURATION, MODIFIED DURATION AND CONVEXITY

Duration

The maturity of a bond is not generally a good indication of the timing of the cashflows arising from the bond, because a significant proportion of the cashflows may occur before maturity in the form of coupon payments and also possibly partial redemption payments.

One could calculate an average of the times to each cashflow, weighted by the size of the cashflows. Duration is very similar to such an average. Instead of taking each cashflow as a weighting however, duration takes the present value of each cashflow.

Example 5.11

Consider the same 7-year 10% coupon bond as in Example 5.5, with a price of 95.00 and a yield of 11.063%. The size and timing of the cashflows of the bond can be shown as follows:

The average time to the cashflows weighted by the cashflows themselves would be calculated as:

$$\frac{\sum (\text{cashflow} \times \text{time to cashflow})}{\text{sum of the cashflows}}$$

$$= \frac{(10 \times 1) + (10 \times 2) + (10 \times 3) + (10 \times 4) + (10 \times 5) + (10 \times 6) + (110 \times 7)}{10 + 10 + 10 + 10 + 10 + 10 + 110} \text{ years}$$

$$= \frac{980}{170} \text{ years} = 5.76 \text{ years}$$

If you consider the diagram above as a beam with weights of 10,10, . . ., 110 placed on it, the point 5.76 along the beam is the point at which the beam would be balanced.

Now consider the same averaging process but instead using the present value of each cashflow (discounted at the yield of 11.063%). These present values are as follows:

The weighted average is now:

$$\frac{(9.00 \times 1) + (8.11 \times 2) + (7.30 \times 3) + (6.57 \times 4) + (5.92 \times 5) + (5.33 \times 6) + (52.77 \times 7)}{(9.00 + 8.11 + 7.30 + 6.57 + 5.92 + 5.33 + 52.78)} \text{ years}$$

$$= \frac{504.37}{95.00} \text{ years} = 5.31 \text{ years}$$

The duration of the bond is thus 5.31 years.

Note that the lower half of the calculation (9.00 + 8.11 + . . . + 52.77) is simply the price of the bond, because it is the NPV of the cashflows.

```
10 ENTER 1.11063 ÷
10 ENTER 1.11063 ENTER 2 ☐ ∧ ÷ 2 × +
10 ENTER 1.11063 ENTER 3 ☐ ∧ ÷ 3 × +
10 ENTER 1.11063 ENTER 4 ☐ ∧ ÷ 4 × +
10 ENTER 1.11063 ENTER 5 ☐ ∧ ÷ 5 × +
10 ENTER 1.11063 ENTER 6 ☐ ∧ ÷ 6 × +
110 ENTER 1.11063 ENTER 7 ☐ ∧ ÷ 7 × +
95 ÷
```

Calculation summary	
	$$\text{Duration} = \frac{\sum (\text{present value of cashflow} \times \text{time to cashflow})}{\sum (\text{present value of cashflow})}$$

It is worth noting that for a zero-coupon bond, there is only one cash-flow, at maturity. The duration of a zero-coupon bond is therefore the same as its maturity.

The concept of duration can be extended to any series of cashflows and hence to a portfolio of investments.

Duration is useful partly because of its relationship with the price sensitiv-ity of a bond (see modified duration below) and partly because of the concept of investment "immunisation".

If I invest in a bond and there is a fall in yields (both short-term and long-term), there are two effects on my investment. First, I will not be able to earn as much as I had expected on reinvesting the coupons I receive. As a result, if I hold the bond to maturity, my total return will be less than anticipated. The price of the bond will however rise immediately (yield down, price up). If I hold the bond for only a very short time therefore, my total return will be more than anticipated because I will not have time to be affected by lower reinvestment rates. There must be some moment between now and the bond's maturity when these two effects – the capital gain from the higher bond price and the loss on reinvestment – are in balance and the total return is the same yield as originally anticipated. The same would be true if yields rise – there is some point at which the capital loss due to the higher bond price would be balanced by the reinvestment gains.

Suppose that an investor wishes to be sure of the total return on his port-folio between now and a particular time in the future, regardless of interest rate movements. It can be shown that, if he arranges the portfolio to have a duration equal to that period (rather than have a maturity equal to it), he will then not be vulnerable to yield movements up or down during that period – the portfolio will be "immunised".

There are practical problems with this concept. First, the idea assumes that short-term reinvestment rates and long-term bond yields move up or down together. Second, the portfolio's duration will change as its yield changes, because the calculation of duration depends on the yield. In order to keep the portfolio's duration equal to the time remaining up to his particular investment horizon, and so remain immunised, the investor therefore needs to adjust the portfolio continually by changing the investments.

Modified duration

It is useful to know the sensitivity of a bond price to yield changes – that is, if a yield rises by a certain amount, how much will the bond's price fall? The answer can be seen as depending on how steeply the price/yield curve slopes (see Figure 5.3).

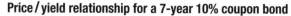

Price/yield relationship for a 7-year 10% coupon bond

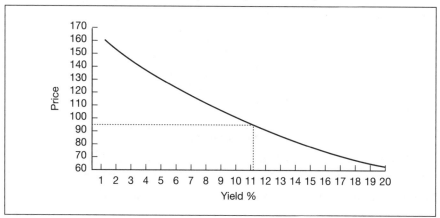

If the curve is very steeply sloped, then a given move up in the yield will cause a sharp fall in the price from 95.00. If the curve is not steeply sloped, the price fall will be small. This gives the following approximation:

Change in price = change in yield × slope of curve

We are probably more interested in how much the value of our investment changes relative to the size of the investment (rather than as an absolute amount) – that is, $\frac{\text{change in price}}{\text{dirty price}}$. This must therefore be equal to:

$$\text{Change in yield} \times \frac{\text{slope of curve}}{\text{dirty price}}$$

Mathematically, the slope of the curve is $\frac{dP}{di}$. By taking the general bond price formula:

$$P = \sum_k \frac{C_k}{\left(1 + \frac{i}{n}\right)^{\frac{d_k \times n}{year}}}$$

and differentiating, we get:

$$\frac{dP}{di} = - \frac{\sum \frac{C_k}{\left(1 + \frac{i}{n}\right)^{n \frac{d_k}{year}}} \times \frac{d_k}{year}}{\left(1 + \frac{i}{n}\right)}$$

Comparing this with the formula for duration in the previous section, it can be seen that:

$$\frac{\text{slope of curve}}{\text{dirty price}} = \frac{dP}{di} \Big/ \text{dirty price} = - \frac{\text{duration}}{\left(1 + \frac{i}{n}\right)}$$

Therefore it can be seen that the sensitivity factor relating $\frac{\text{change in price}}{\text{dirty price}}$ to $-$(change in yield) is $\frac{\text{duration}}{\left(1 + \frac{i}{n}\right)}$. Because this factor is so similar to duration, it is known as "modified duration".

Calculation summary	$$\text{Modified duration} = \frac{-\frac{dP}{di}}{\text{dirty price}} = \frac{\text{duration}}{\left(1 + \frac{i}{n}\right)}$$

So that we have:

Calculation summary	**Approximation** Change in price $\approx$ $-$ dirty price $\times$ change in yield $\times$ modified duration

In some markets, modified duration is known as "volatility".

Example 5.12 Consider the same bond as before, and assume a 1% rise in the yield from 11.063% to 12.063%.

As the duration is 5.31 years and n = 1 (coupons are annual), the modified duration is:

$$\frac{5.31}{(1 + 0.11063)} = 4.78 \text{ years}$$

Using the price sensitivity, we know:

Change in price $\approx$ $-$ dirty price $\times$ change in yield $\times$ modified duration
= $-95.00 \times 0.01 \times 4.78 = -4.54$

We should therefore expect the price to fall from 95.00 to 95.00 $-$ 4.54 = 90.46.

If now we check this by repricing at 12.063% (for example, by using the HP's TVM function), we find that the bond's price has actually fallen to 90.60.

Dollar value of an 01

A measure very closely related to modified duration is the "dollar value of an 01" (DV01) – or the "present value of an 01" (PV01), or "the value of a basis point". This is simply the change in price due to a 1 basis point change in yield – usually expressed as a positive number. From the above, it can be seen that:

DV01 = modified duration × dirty price × 0.0001

Calculation summary

Convexity

For small yield changes, the approximation above is fairly accurate. For larger changes, it becomes less accurate. The reason that the modified duration did not produce exactly the correct price change in the last example is that the slope of the curve changes as you move along the curve. The equation:

$$\text{Change in price} = \text{change in yield} \times \frac{dP}{di}$$

in fact calculates the change along the straight line shown in Figure 5.4 rather than along the curve.

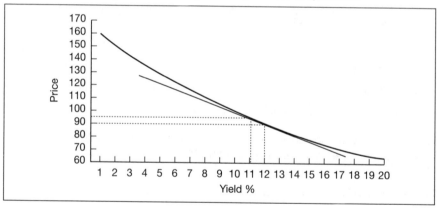

Price / yield relationship for a 7-year 10% coupon bond

Figure 5.4

As a result, using modified duration to calculate the change in price due to a particular change in yield will generally underestimate the price. When the yield rises, the price does not actually fall as far as the straight line suggests; when the yield falls, the price rises more than the straight line suggests. The difference between the actual price and the estimate depends on how curved the curve is. This amount of curvature is known as "convexity" – the more curved it is, the higher the convexity.

Mathematically, curvature is defined as:

Key Point

$$\text{Convexity} = \frac{\dfrac{d^2P}{di^2}}{\text{dirty price}}$$

By applying this to the bond price formula, we get:

Calculation summary

$$\text{Convexity} = \frac{\sum \left[\dfrac{C_k}{\left(1 + \frac{i}{n}\right)^{n\frac{d_k}{\text{year}}+2}} \times \dfrac{d_k}{\text{year}} \times \left(\dfrac{d_k}{\text{year}} + \dfrac{1}{n}\right) \right]}{\text{dirty price}}$$

Using convexity, it is possible to make a better approximation of the change in price due to a change in yield:

Calculation summary

Better approximation

Change in price $\approx$ – dirty price $\times$ modified duration $\times$ change in yield
$+ \frac{1}{2}$ dirty price $\times$ convexity $\times$ (change in yield)^2

Example 5.13 Using the same details again as in the last example, the bond's convexity can be calculated as:

$$\frac{\left(\frac{10}{(1.11063)^3} \times 2 + \frac{10}{(1.11063)^4} \times 6 + \frac{10}{(1.11063)^5} \times 12 + \frac{10}{(1.11063)^6} \times 20 \right.}{}$$

$$\frac{\left. + \frac{10}{(1.11063)^7} \times 30 + \frac{10}{(1.11063)^8} \times 42 + \frac{110}{(1.11063)^9} \times 56 \right)}{95.00}$$

$$= 31.08$$

A 1% rise in the yield would then give the following approximate change in price:

$$-95 \times 4.78 \times .01 + \tfrac{1}{2} \times 95 \times 31.08 \times (.01)^2 = -4.39$$

We should therefore now expect the price to fall from 95.00 to 95.00 – 4.39 = 90.61 – which is very close to the actual price of 90.60.

For bonds without calls, it can be shown in general that:

■ for a given yield and maturity, a higher coupon rate implies lower duration and convexity

■ for a given coupon rate and maturity, a higher yield implies lower duration and convexity.

In Example 5.11 convexity is a positive number. This is always true for a straightforward bond – that is, the shape of the price / yield curve is roughly as shown in Figure 5.4. It is possible however, for convexity to become negative at some point along the curve. Suppose, for example, that the bond issuer has the choice of redeeming the bond early if market yields fall below a certain level. In that case, the price will cease rising beyond a certain point as yields fall. The result is a reversal of the curvature at low yields. Mortgage-backed securities, where the homeowners are more likely to repay mortgages and refinance as yields fall, can provide a similar situation.

In general, high positive convexity is good from an investor's point of view. If two bonds have equal price, yield and duration but different convexities, the bond with higher convexity will perform relatively better if the yield changes. In practice, therefore, the two bonds should not be priced the same. In the same way, when hedging a portfolio, an investor should try to ensure higher convexity in his long positions and lower convexity in short positions.

Portfolio duration

As mentioned above, the concept of duration – and also modified duration and convexity – can be applied to any series of cashflows and hence to a whole portfolio of investments rather than to a single bond.

To calculate precisely a portfolio's duration, modified duration or convexity, the same concept should be used as for a single bond, using all the portfolio's cashflows and the portfolio's yield (calculated in the same way as for a single bond). In practice, a good approximation is achieved by taking a weighted average of the duration, etc. of each investment:

Approximations for a portfolio	Calculation summary

$$\text{Duration} = \frac{\sum (\text{duration of each investment} \times \text{value of each investment})}{\text{value of portfolio}}$$

$$\text{Modified duration} = \frac{\sum (\text{mod. dur. of each investment} \times \text{value of each investment})}{\text{value of portfolio}}$$

$$\text{Convexity} = \frac{\sum (\text{convexity of each investment} \times \text{value of each investment})}{\text{value of portfolio}}$$

A portfolio's modified duration, for example, gives the sensitivity of the whole portfolio's value to yield changes. Although this has the limitation that it assumes all yields move up or down in parallel along the yield curve, it can provide a useful quick measure of risk. With the same limitation, an organisation wishing to avoid any such risk can match the modified durations of its liabilities and its assets.

We own the following portfolio:

Example 5.14

	Face value	Dirty price	Modified duration
Bond A	10 million	107.50	5.35
Bond B	5 million	98.40	7.20
Bond C	7 million	95.25	3.45

How much of the following bond should we short to make the portfolio immune to small changes in yield, assuming parallel movements in the yield curve?

	Dirty price	Modified duration
Bond D	110.20	9.75

For any small change in yield, the change in value of our portfolio is approximately:

– change in yield ×

$$\left[\left(10 \text{ mln} \times \frac{107.50}{100} \times 5.35\right) + \left(5 \text{ mln} \times \frac{98.40}{100} \times 7.20\right) + \left(7 \text{ mln} \times \frac{95.25}{100} \times 3.45\right)\right]$$

We therefore need to short enough of bond D to have an offsetting effect. The above change in value therefore needs to equal:

$$- \text{change in yield} \times \left(\text{face value of bond D} \times \frac{110.20}{100} \times 9.75\right)$$

Therefore face value of bond D to be sold =

$$\frac{(10 \text{ mln} \times 1.075 \times 5.35) + (5 \text{ mln} \times 0.984 \times 7.2) + (7 \text{ mln} \times 0.9525 \times 3.45)}{1.102 \times 9.75}$$

$$= 10.8 \text{ million}$$

---

10 ENTER 1.075 × 5.35 ×
5 ENTER .984 × 7.2 × +
7 ENTER .9525 × 3.45 × +
1.102 ÷ 9.75 ÷

BOND FUTURES

A bond futures contract is generally an agreement whereby the seller must deliver to the buyer an agreed amount of a bond at an agreed time, for an agreed price. In practice, bond futures contracts are generally closed out before maturity in the same way that short-term futures contracts are, and the profit / loss is captured through variation margins. In the case of most bond futures contracts however, a bond futures buyer can in theory insist on delivery of a bond at maturity of the contract. There are several complications which do not arise in the case of short-term interest rate futures.

Bond specification

A bond futures contract must be based on a precisely specified bond, in the same way that a short-term interest rate futures contract is generally based precisely on a 3-month deposit. It may be preferable however, to allow any one of a range of existing bonds – which can change over time – to be delivered at maturity of the futures contract. Bond futures prices are therefore usually based on a *notional* bond index rather than any one of these particular bonds. In the case of a US treasury bond futures, for example, the bond specified is a fictional 6 percent bond of at least 15 years' maturity.

Deliverable bonds and conversion factors

The seller of the futures contract cannot of course deliver this fictional bond. Instead, he is usually entitled to deliver any one of a range of bonds which is defined in the specifications for the futures contract. In this case, it is the seller who chooses which bond to deliver to the buyer. In the case of US treasury bond futures, for example, the seller may deliver any bond maturing at least 15 years after the first day of the delivery month if the bond is not callable. If it is callable, the earliest call date must be at least 15 years after the first day of the delivery month.

Because the different deliverable bonds have different coupons and maturities, they need to be put on a common basis. The futures exchange therefore publishes a "price factor" or "conversion factor" for each deliverable bond. The amount paid by the buyer if the bond is delivered then depends on this conversion factor. In the case of a treasury bond, this is the price per $1 nominal value of the specific bond at which the bond has a gross redemption yield of 6 percent on the first day of the delivery month (i.e. it has the same yield as the coupon of the fictional bond underlying the contract). The maturity of the deliverable bond is found by measuring the time from the first day of the delivery month to the maturity of the bond (first call day if callable) and rounding down to the nearest quarter. Note that although the same general approach is used across different bond futures markets, the precise specification of this calculation for the conversion factor does vary.

> **Conversion factor =**
> clean price at delivery for one unit of the deliverable bond, at which that bond's yield equals the futures contract notional coupon rate.

Key Point

On the delivery day, the specific bond nominated by the seller will be delivered and the seller will receive from the buyer the relevant invoicing amount. The invoicing amount is based on the "Exchange Delivery Settlement Price" (EDSP – the futures price at the close of trading for that futures contract, as determined by the exchange) and the size of the futures contract ($100,000 in the case of a US treasury bond futures):

$$\text{Invoicing amount} = \text{face value} \times \left(\frac{\text{EDSP}}{100} \times \text{conversion factor} + \text{accrued coupon rate} \right)$$

This choice of deliverable bonds also gives rise to the concept of "cheapest to deliver": the seller will always choose to deliver whichever bond is the cheapest for him to do so – known as the "cheapest-to-deliver" or "CTD" bond.

> **Key Point** A bond futures contract is based on a notional bond. The real bonds deliverable into the contract are made comparable by their conversion factors.

Delivery date

Delivery specifications vary between futures contracts and exchanges. In the case of a US treasury bond futures, for example, the seller is entitled to deliver on any business day in the delivery month. Clearly he will deliver later if the coupon he is accruing is higher than the cost of funding the position and earlier if the coupon is lower.

Coupons

If there is an intervening coupon payment on the actual bond which the futures seller expects to deliver, he will take this into account in calculating the futures price.

Pricing

The theoretical futures price depends on the elimination of arbitrage. The seller of a futures contract, if he delivers a bond at maturity of the futures contract, will receive the invoicing amount on delivery. He will also receive any intervening coupon plus interest earned on this coupon between receipt of the coupon and delivery of the bond to the futures buyer.

In order to hedge themselves, the futures sellers must buy the bond in the cash market at the same time as they sell the futures contract. For this they must pay the current bond price plus accrued coupon. This total amount must be funded from the time they buy the bond until the time they deliver it to the futures buyer.

By delivery, the market futures price (which becomes the EDSP at the close of the contract) should converge to the cash market price of the CTD bond divided by the conversion factor. If this were not so, there would be an arbitrage difference between the invoicing amount for the CTD at delivery and the cost of buying the CTD bond in the cash market at the same time. During the period from selling the futures contract to delivery, the futures seller pays or receives variation margin (as with short-term interest rate futures) based on the notional amount of the futures contract. These variation margin cashflows represent the difference between the price at which he sold the futures contract and the EDSP.

It can be seen from the cashflows shown below that, in order to achieve a hedge which balances correctly, the nominal amount of cash bond sold should be $\frac{\text{notional size of futures contract}}{\text{conversion factor}}$. If the buyer requires delivery of the bond, the seller will need to buy or sell a small amount of the cash bond at maturity – the difference between the notional futures amount, which must be delivered, and the amount already bought as the hedge. This will be done at the price of the cash bond at maturity, which should converge to (EDSP × conversion factor), as noted above.

Assuming that the futures seller makes zero profit / loss, the cashflows received and paid by the futures seller should net to zero. For any given notional face value of futures, these cashflows are as follows:

Receive on delivery of the bond

$$\text{face value} \times \left(\frac{\text{EDSP}}{100} \times \text{conversion factor} + \text{accrued coupon rate at delivery} \right)$$

Receive as variation margin

$$\text{face value} \times \left(\frac{\text{futures price} - \text{EDSP}}{100} \right)$$

Receive any intervening coupon

$$\frac{\text{face value}}{\text{conversion factor}} \times (\text{coupon rate} + \text{reinvestment})$$

Pay the total cost of funding the cash bond purchase

$$\frac{\text{face value}}{\text{conversion factor}} \times \left(\frac{\text{cash bond price}}{100} + \text{accrued coupon rate at start} \right) \times$$

$$\left(1 + \text{funding rate} \times \frac{\text{days to delivery}}{\text{year}} \right)$$

Pay (or receive) the cost of the difference between the amount of bond hedged and the amount of the bond to be delivered to the buyer

$$\left(\text{face value} - \frac{\text{face value}}{\text{conversion factor}} \right) \times \left(\frac{\text{EDSP} \times \text{conversion factor}}{100} + \begin{array}{l} \text{accrued coupon} \\ \text{rate at delivery} \end{array} \right)$$

From this, it follows that:

Theoretical bond futures price

$$\frac{\left(\left[\text{bond price} + \text{accrued coupon now} \right] \times \left[1 + i \times \frac{\text{days}}{\text{year}} \right] \right) - (\text{accrued coupon at delivery}) - (\text{intervening coupon reinvested})}{\text{conversion factor}}$$

where i = short-term funding rate

Calculation summary

Example 5.15

What is the theoretical September T-bond futures price on 18 June if the cheapest-to-deliver bond is the Treasury $6\frac{1}{4}$% 2028, trading at 109–09 (i.e. $109\frac{9}{32}$)? The conversion factor for the 2028 is 1.0281. Coupon dates are 15 May and 15 November. Short-term funds can be borrowed at 5.45%.

Answer:

Payment for the bond purchased by the futures seller to hedge himself is made on 19 June. Coupon on the purchase of the bond is accrued for 35 days. The current coupon period is 184 days. Therefore:

$$\text{Accrued coupon now} = 6.25 \times \frac{35}{368} = 0.594429$$

Assume that delivery of the bond to the futures buyer requires payment to the futures seller on 30 September. The futures seller must then fund his position from 19 June to 30 September (103 actual days) and coupon on the sale of the bond will then be accrued for 138 days.

Therefore:

$$\text{Accrued coupon at delivery} = 6.25 \times \frac{138}{368} = 2.343750$$

$$\text{Theoretical futures price} = \frac{(109.281250 + 0.594429) \times (1 + 0.0545 \times \frac{103}{360}) - 2.343750}{1.0281}$$

$$= 106.2593$$

$$= 106\text{–}08 \ (\text{i.e. } 106\tfrac{8}{32})$$

6.25 ENTER 35 × 368 ÷	(Accrued interest at start)
109.28125 +	(Clean bond price at start)
.0545 ENTER 103 × 360 ÷ 1 + ×	
6.25 ENTER 138 × 368 ÷	(Accrued interest at end)
−	
1.0281 ÷	(Theoretical futures price)

The construction above of a theoretical futures price does not take account of the fact that the seller of a bond futures contract has a choice of which bond to deliver. This effectively gives the seller an option built into the futures contract. This optionality has a value, which should in general be reflected in a slightly lower theoretical futures price than the formula above suggests.

Forward bond prices

The arbitrage method used above to calculate a theoretical bond futures price could equally well be used to calculate a forward market price for a bond which is to be delivered on any date later than the normal convention – that is, a forward bond price. In this case, there is no conversion factor involved.

Calculation summary

Forward bond price

$$\left(\left[\text{bond price} + \text{accrued coupon now}\right] \times \left[1 + i \times \tfrac{\text{days}}{\text{year}}\right]\right)$$
$$- (\text{accrued coupon at delivery}) - (\text{intervening coupon reinvested})$$

Ignoring differences between the day/year conventions for the bond and the short-term financing, the formula above can be rewritten as:

(Forward price − cash price) =

$$\text{cash price} \times \left(i - \frac{\text{coupon rate}}{\frac{\text{cash price}}{100}}\right) \times \frac{\text{days to delivery}}{\text{year}}$$

$$+ \left[\text{accrued coupon now} \times i \times \frac{\text{days}}{\text{year}} - \text{interest earned on intervening coupon}\right]$$

The expression in square brackets is rather small, so that in general, the amount (forward price − cash price) is positive or negative − that is, the forward price is at a premium or a discount to the cash price − if $\left(i - \frac{\text{coupon rate}}{\frac{\text{cash price}}{100}}\right)$ is positive or negative. This is reasonable, because it reflects whether the cost of funding a long bond position is greater or less than the coupon accruing on the position.

> **Generally, a forward bond price is at a premium (discount) to the cash price if the short-term funding cost is greater than (less than) $\frac{\text{coupon rate}}{\frac{\text{cash price}}{100}}$.**   **Key Point**

Using futures to hedge a cash position

If a dealer takes a cash position in bonds, he can use bond futures to hedge his position in the same way that a cash position in short-term interest rates can be hedged by interest rate futures. The commodity traded in a bond futures contract − the notional bond − will however behave differently from any particular cash bond. As a result, the notional amount of the futures hedge needs to be different from the face value of the cash position.

Suppose that a dealer takes a position in the CTD bond. We know that the theoretical futures price is given by:

Futures price =

$$\frac{\left(\left[\text{bond price} + \text{accrued coupon now}\right] \times \left[1 + i \times \frac{\text{days}}{\text{year}}\right]\right) - (\text{accrued coupon at delivery}) - (\text{intervening coupon reinvested})}{\text{conversion factor}}$$

If the price of the CTD changes therefore, the instantaneous change in the futures price is found by differentiating the above formula:

$$\text{Change in futures price} = \frac{\text{change in CTD price} \times \left(1 + i \times \frac{\text{days}}{\text{year}}\right)}{\text{conversion factor}}$$

or, $\text{Change in CTD price} = \text{change in futures price} \times \left(\frac{\text{conversion factor}}{1 + i \times \frac{\text{days}}{\text{year}}}\right)$

In order to hedge a position in \$100 face value of the CTD bond therefore, the dealer should take an opposite position in $\$100 \times \left(\dfrac{\text{conversion factor}}{1 + i \times \frac{\text{days}}{\text{year}}} \right)$ nominal of the futures contract. This will still leave the risks that the actual futures price will not move exactly in line with the CTD bond and that the CTD bond will change, but it will provide an approximate hedge. The factor $\left(\dfrac{\text{conversion factor}}{1 + i \times \frac{\text{days}}{\text{year}}} \right)$ is known as a hedge ratio – the necessary ratio of the size of the futures hedge to the size of the underlying position.

We could reverse this concept to say that a dealer could hedge a futures position by an opposite position in the CTD bond. The amount of the CTD bond required is then:

$$\text{Notional amount of futures contract} \times \frac{\left(1 + i \times \frac{\text{days}}{\text{year}}\right)}{\text{conversion factor}}$$

Note that this is not exactly the same as the amount of CTD bond we used in establishing the theoretical futures price in the previous section: the amount there was simply $\frac{\text{notional amount of futures contract}}{\text{conversion factor}}$.

The difference arises because in establishing the theoretical futures price, we needed an arbitrage which we could hold to delivery – even though, in practice, futures contracts are rarely delivered. In this section, we are concerned about a hedge for an *instantaneous* change in price. If we held the hedge to delivery, the $(1 + i \times \frac{\text{days}}{\text{year}})$ factor would converge to 1.

Example 5.16

A dealer wishes to hedge his short position in \$15 million face value of the bond which is currently the CTD for the US treasury bond futures contract. The conversion factor for the CTD is 1.1482. Assume that delivery of the futures contract is in 73 days and that the cost of short-term funding is 5.2%. The size of a US treasury bond futures contract is \$100,000 nominal. How should the dealer hedge his position?

$$\text{Hedge ratio} = \left(\frac{\text{conversion factor}}{1 + i \times \frac{\text{days}}{\text{year}}} \right) = \left(\frac{1.1482}{1 + 0.052 \times \frac{73}{360}} \right) = 1.1362$$

The dealer should therefore buy \$15 million × 1.1362 = \$17,043,000 nominal of futures. As the nominal size of each futures contract is \$100,000, this involves buying $\frac{17,043,000}{100,000} = 170$ futures contracts.

If the dealer wishes to hedge a different bond, he will need to assess how that bond's price is likely to move compared with the CTD's price. For small yield changes, one approach is to use modified duration. Assuming that the yield on the actual bond purchased and the yield on the CTD move in parallel, we have:

Change in bond price =
     – dirty bond price × modified duration of bond × yield change

and:

> Change in price of CTD =
> − dirty price of CTD × modified duration of CTD × yield change

so that:

> Change in bond price =
>
> change in price of CTD × $\dfrac{\text{dirty bond price}}{\text{dirty price of CTD}}$ × $\dfrac{\text{modified duration of bond}}{\text{modified duration of CTD}}$

This gives a hedge ratio as follows:

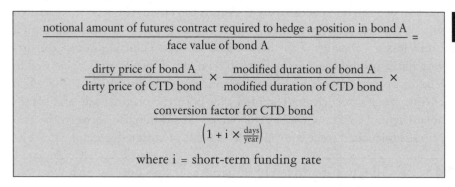

$$\frac{\text{notional amount of futures contract required to hedge a position in bond A}}{\text{face value of bond A}} =$$

$$\frac{\text{dirty price of bond A}}{\text{dirty price of CTD bond}} \times \frac{\text{modified duration of bond A}}{\text{modified duration of CTD bond}} \times$$

$$\frac{\text{conversion factor for CTD bond}}{\left(1 + i \times \frac{\text{days}}{\text{year}}\right)}$$

where i = short-term funding rate

Calculation summary

Note that this hedge assumes, as with all modified duration hedging, that the yield curve shift is the same for all bonds – that is, that the yields on bond A and the CTD bond respond in the same way to market changes. It might be that even for a yield curve shift which is parallel in general, bond A in particular responds more sluggishly or less sluggishly than the market in general. Any expectation of this would need to be taken into account in the size of the hedge.

CASH-AND-CARRY ARBITRAGE

This arbitrage involves repo as well as bond futures. Therefore, although there is a much more detailed discussion of repos elsewhere in the book, we have included a brief description here also, in order to understand the cash-and-carry arbitrage.

Overview of repos

"Repo" is short for "sale and repurchase agreement" and is essentially a transaction whereby the two parties involved agree to do two deals as a package. The first deal is a purchase or sale of a security – often a government bond – for delivery straight away (the exact settlement date will vary according to the market convention for the security involved). The second deal is a reversal of the first deal, for settlement on some future date.

Key Point	A repo is a purchase or sale of a security now, together with an opposite transaction later.

Because it is understood from the outset that the first deal will be reversed, it is clear that both parties intend the transfer of securities (in one direction) and the transfer of cash (in the other direction) to be temporary rather than permanent. The transaction is therefore exactly equivalent to a loan of securities in one direction and a loan of cash in the other. The repo is structured so that the economic benefit of owning the securities – income and capital gains / losses – remains with their original owner. These are in fact the driving forces behind the repo market; all repos are driven by either the need to lend or borrow cash, which is collateralised by securities, or the need to borrow specific securities. The prices for both the original sale and subsequent repurchase are agreed at the outset. The difference between the two prices is calculated to be equivalent to the cost of borrowing secured money.

Key Point	All repos are driven by either the need to borrow cash or the need to borrow a specific security.

A repo is defined as an initial sale of securities followed by a subsequent repurchase. A "reverse repo" is the opposite – an initial purchase of securities followed by a subsequent resale. Because the two parties involved are of course doing opposite transactions, a "repo" to one party is a "reverse" to the other.

Figure 5.5	A repo

Flows on the start date

Bond

Lender of bond (borrower of cash) ← Borrower of bond (lender of cash)

Cash

On maturity of the repo, the dealer will repay the cash with interest:

Flows on the end date

Same nominal amount of bond

Lender of bond (borrower of cash) → Borrower of bond (lender of cash)

Same amount of cash *plus* interest

Price calculation

The total price at which the first leg of the repo is transacted is the straightforward current market price for the security, plus accrued coupon, taking into account any margin (see below) if agreed. The total price for the second leg however, reflects only the repo interest rate and not the accrued coupon due on the security at that time. This is because the security is in reality only playing the part of collateral. The repo interest rate is calculated according to the normal convention in the relevant money market. On a repo in euros, for example, this would be calculated on an ACT/360 basis; this is unaffected by the fact that the coupon on the collateral might be calculated on an ACT/ACT basis.

> **The price on the first leg of a classic repo is the market price. The price on the second leg is the first price plus the repo interest.** **Key Point**

For our purposes here therefore, the cashflows in a repo can be seen as the same as those arising from a straightforward cash borrowing or lending.

Implied repo rate

When we constructed a theoretical bond futures price earlier, we did so by considering how the seller of a bond futures contract could hedge himself. This was by borrowing cash, using the cash to buy the bond and holding the bond until the futures contract matures and the bond is delivered against it. If the actual futures price is the same as the theoretical price, this "round trip" should give a zero result – no profit and no loss.

The same calculation can be considered in reverse: assuming that we already know the current futures price and the current bond price, what is the interest rate at which it is necessary to borrow the cash to ensure a zero result?

This interest rate is called the "implied repo rate" and is the break-even rate at which the futures sale can be hedged. The reason for the name "implied repo rate" is that in order to borrow the money to buy the bond, the dealer can repo the bond out. It is thus the "repo borrowing rate implied by the current futures price". The "cheapest-to-deliver" bond will generally be the one with the highest implied repo rate (because any other deliverable bond will require a lower repo rate to break even).

Taking our earlier formula and reversing it, we get:

> **Implied repo rate** **Calculation summary**
>
> $$\left[\frac{\text{(futures price} \times \text{conversion factor)} + \text{(accrued coupon at delivery of futures)} + \text{(intervening coupon reinvested)}}{\text{(bond price} + \text{accrued coupon now)}} - 1 \right] \times \frac{\text{year}}{\text{days}}$$

This can also be expressed as:

$$\left[\frac{\text{total cash received at delivery}}{\text{initial cash expenditure}} - 1 \right] \times \frac{\text{year}}{\text{days}}$$

Cheapest-to-deliver bond

The CTD bond will change according to coupon and yield. If the futures seller does hedge his position using one particular deliverable bond, his profit on delivery at maturity will be:

$$\text{Nominal value of futures contract} \times \frac{\text{dirty bond price}}{\text{conversion factor}} \times$$

$$(\text{implied repo rate} - \text{actual repo rate}) \times \frac{\text{days to delivery}}{\text{year}}$$

The CTD bond will be the one which maximises this profit. As yields fall, bonds with lower duration are likely to become cheaper to deliver (because the price of a bond with a low duration rises less, as yields fall, than the price of a bond with a high duration) and vice versa.

Key Point

The "implied repo rate" for any particular deliverable bond is the repo rate at which you would need to fund yourself, so that the cash-and-carry arbitrage gives zero profit or loss.

The CTD is generally the deliverable bond with the highest implied repo rate.

The arbitrage structure

If in fact the current futures price, bond price and actual repo rate are not all in line, an arbitrage opportunity will be available. Thus, if the actual repo rate is less than the implied repo rate, it will be possible to finance the hedge cheaply – that is, to buy the bond, repo it, sell the futures contract and deliver the bond at maturity of the futures contract, all at a locked-in profit. Such a round-trip is called "cash-and-carry arbitrage".

If the actual repo rate is higher than the implied repo rate, it is possible to effect a cash-and-carry arbitrage in reverse – that is, borrow a bond through a reverse repo, sell the bond, buy the futures contract and take delivery of a bond at maturity of the futures contract. A problem arises however, that the buyer of the futures contract has no control over which bond will be delivered. If the "cheapest-to-deliver" bond at maturity is not the same as the bond he has borrowed, arbitrage will not be complete; he must then sell the bond which has been delivered and buy the bond he has borrowed. In addition to the difference in value of the two bonds, this will involve extra transaction costs. Where the seller may choose the exact delivery date within the month (as in US treasury bond and UK gilt futures), there is a further uncertainty for the futures buyer.

Buying a bond and selling a futures contract is also known as "buying the basis". Selling a bond and buying a futures contract is "selling the basis".

> **Key Point**
>
> "Cash-and-carry arbitrage" means making a locked-in profit by selling the bond futures contract, buying the bond in the cash market, and funding the bond purchase until delivery of the futures contract.
>
> "Reverse cash-and-carry arbitrage" means the opposite: making a locked-in profit by buying the bond futures contract, selling the bond in the cash market, and borrowing the bond until delivery of the futures contract.

Example 5.17

CTD Bund 8 7/8% 22/02/2014 price:	105.24
Accrued coupon:	1.92089
Bund futures price:	93.75
Conversion factor for CTD:	1.1181
Repo rate:	3.29%
Days to futures delivery date:	31
Futures contract amount:	€100,000
Accrued coupon on CTD at futures delivery date:	2.67466

Depending on whether the implied repo rate (= the break-even funding rate implied by the current bond futures price and the current cash price of the "cheapest-to-deliver" bond) is higher or lower than the actual current repo rate, the cash-and-carry arbitrage is:

Either (A)

- Buy the cash CTD bond now.
- Fund this purchase by repoing the bond.
- Sell the bond futures contract.
- Deliver the bond at maturity of the futures contract

or (B) the opposite:

- Sell the cash CTD bond now.
- Borrow this bond (to deliver it now) through a reverse repo, using the cash raised by the bond sale.
- Buy the futures contract.
- Take delivery of the futures contract at maturity and use the bond to deliver on the second leg of the reverse repo.

(In practice, rather than deliver or take delivery of the bond at maturity of the futures contract, the cash bond purchase or sale and the futures contract can both be reversed at maturity. In (B) particularly, there would be no certainty that the bond delivered to us by the futures seller would match the bond we are obliged to return under the reverse repo.)

Assume for the moment that the profitable arbitrage is (A). (If in fact the result is negative, the profitable arbitrage is (B) instead):

Sell the bond futures contract (notional €100,000)

Buy the cash CTD bond with nominal amount $\dfrac{€100,000}{1.1181}$

$= €89,437$

Cost of buying bond is nominal × (clean price + accrued coupon)

$= €89,437 \times \dfrac{(105.24 + 1.92089)}{100} = €95,841.49$

Total borrowing (principal + interest) to be repaid at the end

$= €95,841.49 \times \left(1 + 0.0329 \times \dfrac{31}{360}\right) = €96,113.01$

Anticipated receipt from delivering bond = notional amount of bond × (futures price × conversion factor + accrued coupon) ∕ 100

$= €89,437 \times \dfrac{(93.75 \times 1.1181 + 2.67466)}{100} = €96,141.68$

In fact, the futures contract requires that €100,000 nominal of the bond be delivered by the seller, rather than the €89,437 which has been purchased as the hedge. The balance of €10,563 would need to be purchased at the time of delivery for onward delivery to the counterparty. Apart from transaction costs, this should involve no significant profit or loss, as the futures exchange delivery settlement price should converge by delivery to (CTD cash price × conversion factor).

Profit = € (96,141.68 – 96,113.01) = €28.67
Therefore profit per futures contract = €28.67

In practice, the profit in Example 5.17 cannot be calculated precisely for several reasons:

■ The CTD bond may not be the same at maturity of the futures contract as it is when the arbitrage is established. This provides an advantage to the futures seller, who can profit by switching his hedge from the original CTD bond to a new one during the life of the arbitrage.

■ The futures price and the CTD bond cash price may not converge exactly by maturity of the futures contract (that is, the basis may not move exactly to zero).

■ The profit or loss on the futures contract is realised through variation margin payments; because the timing of these payments is unknown in advance, it is impossible to calculate their exact value.

Cash-and-carry arbitrage

Assume the arbitrage is achieved by buying the cash bond and selling the futures:

Cash cost at start = nominal bond amount × (cash bond price + accrued coupon at start) / 100

Total payments = (cash cost at start) × $\left(1 + \text{repo rate} \times \dfrac{\text{days to futures delivery}}{\text{year}}\right)$

Total receipts = nominal bond amount × (futures price × conversion factor + accrued coupon at delivery of futures) / 100

Profit = total receipts – total payments

For each futures contract sold, the nominal bond amount above is:

$$\frac{\text{notional size of contract}}{\text{conversion factor}}$$

Basis, net cost of carry and net basis

The concept of "basis" is similar to that for a short-term interest rate futures contract, but using the conversion factor to adjust for the difference between the actual bond and the notional futures bond. Therefore for any deliverable bond:

$$\text{Basis} = \text{bond price} - \text{futures price} \times \text{conversion factor}$$

Using the formula we derived earlier for the implied repo rate, this can also be expressed as:

$$\text{Basis} = \text{coupon} \times \frac{\text{days to delivery}}{\text{year}}$$

$$- \text{dirty bond price} \times \text{implied repo rate} \times \frac{\text{days to delivery}}{\text{year}}$$

where "days to delivery" and "year" are calculated by the appropriate method in each case.

Buying a bond and selling a futures contract is known as "buying the basis". Selling a bond and buying a futures contract is "selling the basis".

The "net cost of carry" in holding any position is the difference between the financing cost of holding it and the interest income from the position.

If we define this as negative when there is a net cost and positive when there is a net income, we have:

Calculation summary

$$\text{Net cost of carry} = \text{coupon income} - \text{financing cost}$$

In the case of 100 units of a bond purchased to hedge a futures sale, this can be expressed as:

$$\text{Net cost of carry} = \text{coupon} \times \frac{\text{days to delivery}}{\text{year}}$$

$$- \text{ dirty bond price} \times \text{actual repo rate} \times \frac{\text{days to delivery}}{\text{year}}$$

The concept of "net basis" is similar to value basis for a short-term interest rate futures contract and is defined as the difference between basis and cost of carry:

Calculation summary

$$\text{Net basis} = \text{basis} - \text{net cost of carry}$$

From the above, it can be seen that:

$$\text{Net basis} = \text{dirty bond price} \times (\text{actual repo rate} - \text{implied repo rate})$$

$$\times \frac{\text{days to delivery}}{\text{year}}$$

If the actual repo rate is equal to the implied repo rate, the basis and net cost of carry are equal and the net basis is zero. The net basis shows whether there is potentially a profit in a cash-and-carry arbitrage (net basis is negative) or a reverse cash-and-carry arbitrage (net basis is positive).

"Basis risk" in general is the risk that the prices of any two instruments will not move exactly in line. If a long position in bond A is being hedged by a short position in bond B for example, there is a risk that any loss on the long position will not be fully offset by a gain on the short position. Similarly, there is a basis risk involved in hedging a bond position by an offsetting futures position because the two positions again may not move exactly in line. This point arose earlier in "Using futures to hedge a cash position" and also in Chapter 4, Interest Rate Futures.

EXERCISES

43. What is the yield of a 15-year bond paying an annual coupon of 7.5% and priced at 102.45?

44. You buy the following bond for settlement on a coupon-payment date. What is the cost of the bond? Make the calculation *without* using the built-in bond function or time value of money function on a calculator.

Amount:	€100,000,000.00
Remaining maturity:	3 years
Coupon:	8.0%
Yield:	7.0%

What are the current yield and simple yield to maturity of the bond? What is the duration of the bond?

45. What is the clean price and accrued coupon of the following bond? Show the structure of a formula you would use to calculate the clean price as an NPV from first principles, but then use a calculator bond function for the answer.

Nominal amount:	5 million
Coupon:	6.8% (semi-annual)
Maturity date:	20 March 2017
Settlement date:	6 November 2009
Yield:	7.4% (semi-annual)
Price/yield calculation basis:	ACT/ACT (semi-annual)
Accrued interest calculation basis:	30/360

46. What is the yield of the following bond?

Coupon:	8.3% (annual)
Maturity date:	12 June 2015
Settlement date:	29 October 2009
Price:	102.48
Price/yield calculation basis:	30/360 (annual)
Accrued interest calculation basis:	ACT/365

47. What is the yield of the following zero-coupon bond? Try calculating this first without using the HP bond functions.

Maturity date:	26 March 2018
Settlement date:	19 July 2010
Price:	65.48
Price/yield calculation basis:	ACT/ACT (semi-annual)

48. You buy a US treasury bill at a discount rate of 8% with 97 days left to maturity. What is the bond-equivalent yield?

49. What would the bond-equivalent yield be in the previous question if the T-bill had 205 days left to maturity?

50. If the bond-equivalent yield which you want to achieve in the previous question is 9%, at what discount rate must you buy?

51. What is the price of the following bond?

Coupon:	4.5% in the first year of issue, increasing by 0.25% each year to 5.75% in the final year. All coupons paid annually
Issue date:	2 March 2009
Maturity date:	2 March 2015
Settlement date:	10 November 2009
Yield:	5.24%
Price/yield calculation basis:	30/360 (annual)
Accrued interest calculation basis:	30/360

52. What is the yield of the following bond?

Coupon:	3.3% (annual)
Maturity date:	19 September 2019
Settlement date:	7 December 2009
Redemption amount:	110 per 100 face value
Price:	98.00 per 100 face value
Price/yield calculation basis:	30/360 (annual)
Accrued interest calculation basis:	30/360

You buy the above bond on 7 December 2009 and then sell it on 14 December at 98.50. What is your simple rate of return over the week on an ACT/360 basis? What is your effective rate of return (ACT/365)?

53. What is the accrued coupon on 27 July 2009 on the following bonds?

a.	7.5% gilt	Maturity 6 December 2017
b.	5.625% US treasury bond	Maturity 14 August 2017
c.	6.25% bond (30/360 annual coupons)	Maturity 25 October 2017
d.	7.25% OAT	Maturity 24 October 2017
e.	3.00% JGB	Maturity 19 September 2017

54. Would the following bond futures contract trade at a discount or a premium to 100?

Date:	27 March 2009
Futures maturity:	December 2009
CTD bond:	clean price 100 coupon 7% annual
CTD conversion factor:	1.0000
9-month money market interest rate:	5% p.a.

55. What is the theoretical September Bund futures price on 22 April 2008 if the cheapest-to-deliver bond is the 7.375% Bund of 2017, trading at 106.13? The conversion factor for that bond is 1.1247. The last coupon date was 3 January. Short-term funds can be borrowed at 3.35%. Futures delivery would be on 10 September. Assume that spot settlement for a Bund traded on 22 April would be 25 April and the coupon is accrued on an ACT/ACT basis.

56. With the same details as in the previous question but supposing that the actual futures price is 93.10, what is the implied repo rate?

57. Given the following information, there is a cash-and-carry arbitrage opportunity. What trades are necessary to exploit it and how much profit can be made?

CTD Bund 8 7/8% 20/12/2011 price:	102.71
Accrued coupon:	3.599 per 100
Bund futures price:	85.31
Conversion factor for CTD:	1.2030
Repo rate:	6.80%
Days to futures delivery date:	24
Futures contract amount:	€100,000
Accrued coupon on CTD at futures delivery date:	4.182 per 100

58. You own the following portfolio on 7 August 2009:

	Face value	Price	Coupon	Maturity	Duration
Bond A	10 million	88.50	5.0% (annual)	1/7/2014	4.41 years
Bond B	5 million	111.00	12.0% (annual)	13/3/2012	2.31 years
Bond C	15 million	94.70	6.0% (annual)	7/10/2013	3.61 years

What is the approximate modified duration of the portfolio? How do you expect the value of the portfolio to change if yields all rise by 10 basis points? Assume that all the bond calculations are on an ACT/ACT basis.

59.

	Price	Coupon	Maturity	Duration
Bond A	88.50	5.0% (annual)	1/7/2014	4.41 years
Bond B	107.50	10.0% (annual)	1/4/2021	7.56 years

You own 10 million face value of bond A. You wish to hedge this position by selling bond futures. Bond B is currently the CTD for the futures contract and has a conversion factor of 1.2754. The notional size of the futures contract is 100,000. Short-term interest rates are 10%. Settlement date is 7 August 2009 and the futures contract delivery date is 8 September 2009. How many futures contracts should you sell? Assume that all the bond calculations are on an ACT/ACT basis.

"Although the legal benefit of the collateral passes from seller to buyer for the period of the repo, the economic benefit remains with the seller."

■ ■ ■

Repos, Buy/Sell-backs and Securities Lending

INTRODUCTION

"Repo" is short for "sale and repurchase agreement" and is essentially a transaction whereby the two parties involved agree to do two deals as a package. The first deal is a purchase or sale of something – usually a government bond or other security – for delivery straight away (the exact settlement date will vary according to the market convention for the security involved). The second deal is a reversal of the first deal, for settlement on some future date.

> **Key Point**
> A repo is a purchase or sale of a security now,
> together with an opposite transaction later.

Because it is understood from the outset that the first settlement in a repo will be reversed later, it is clear that both parties intend the transfer of the asset in one direction and the transfer of cash in the other to be temporary rather than permanent. The transaction is therefore exactly equivalent to a loan of assets in one direction and a loan of cash in the other. These are the driving forces behind the transaction: all repos are driven by either the need to lend or borrow cash, which is collateralised by assets, or the need to borrow a specific asset. The prices for both the original sale and subsequent repurchase are agreed at the outset. The difference between the two prices is calculated to be equivalent to the cost of borrowing secured money. The asset involved is therefore referred to as the "collateral".

> **Key Point**
> All repos are driven by either the need to borrow cash
> or the need to borrow a specific security.

A repo is defined as an initial sale of an asset followed by a subsequent repurchase. A "reverse repo" is the opposite – an initial purchase of the asset followed by a subsequent resale. Because the two parties involved are of course doing opposite transactions, a "repo" to one party is a "reverse" to the other. In a repo, the "seller" (or "lender") is the party selling securities at the outset and repurchasing them later. The "buyer" (or "borrower" or "investor") is the other party. It is important to note that the terminology is taken from the viewpoint of the bond market, not the money market: the party borrowing cash is usually known as the lender in the repo (see Figure 6.1).

In the same way, "bid" and "offer" are used in most repo markets according to the same convention. Thus if a rate of 5.30/5.20% is quoted in the interbank deposit market, 5.30% is the offered rate (the dealer offers cash at 5.30%) and 5.20% is the bid rate (the dealer bids for cash at 5.20%). In

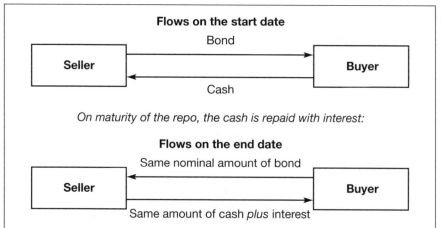

Figure 6.1

Flows on the start date

Bond

Seller → Buyer

Cash

On maturity of the repo, the cash is repaid with interest:

Flows on the end date

Same nominal amount of bond

Seller ← Buyer

Same amount of cash *plus* interest

the repo market however, although the rates still mean the same to each party in *cash* terms, the terminology is generally reversed: 5.30% is the bid rate (the dealer bids for securities against cash at 5.30%) and 5.20% is the offered rate (the dealer offers securities against cash at 5.20%).

> **Repo terminology is based on the security side of the deal, not the cash side.** **Key Point**

Legal title to the collateral passes to the buyer for the period of the repo. The effect of this is that if the seller defaults on the cash repayment, the buyer should not (depending on the legal jurisdiction) need to establish his right to the collateral. For the lender of cash, a repo therefore has the advantage of double security – if the counterparty defaults, he can rely on the collateral. He can therefore look to the creditworthiness of both the counterparty and the issuer of the collateral. This does not mean that the buyer does not need to have a credit line for the seller, but it does increase the security of the cash loan, particularly if the collateral is a government bond, as is often the case.

In other words, there is still counterparty risk, but it is much reduced as long as the repo is set up properly. This in itself creates legal risk (is the repo set up properly?). A repo also carries market risk – both in the same way that any cash borrowing or lending carries market risk and in that the collateral's value might fall suddenly.

For the borrower of cash, the advantage is that he can make use of an investment in his portfolio to borrow cash either more cheaply or which he might not otherwise be able to borrow at all.

It is important to note that we are not using the word "collateral" in its usual sense here. Collateral normally means something which is given temporarily as a guarantee, but which does not actually change ownership. In a repo however, ownership of the securities *does* pass from one party to the other. The securities are nevertheless generally referred to as collateral, both in the market and in the standard legal agreements for repos.

The repo market involves three very similar types of transaction – the classic repo, the buy/sell-back and securities lending.

CLASSIC REPO

Price calculation

The total cash amount at which the first leg of the repo is transacted (known as the "purchase price") is the current market value of the security (including accrued coupon), plus any haircut (see below) if agreed. In practice, a slightly different price might be agreed, or the amount of collateral rounded up. This would not affect the economics of the deal, which is determined by the cash amounts. In all the examples in this chapter we use exact amounts to make the calculations clear, even though in practice this would sometimes be unrealistic.

The total cash amount for the second leg at the end of a repo (known as the "repurchase price") reflects only the repo interest rate and not the accrued coupon due on the security at that time. This is because the security is in reality only playing the part of collateral. The repo interest rate is calculated according to the normal convention in the relevant money market. On a repo in EUR for example, this would be calculated on an ACT/360 basis; this is unaffected by the fact that the coupon on the collateral would probably (depending on the bond used) be calculated in a different way, such as ACT/ACT.

The security returned at the end of the repo is the same amount of the same security delivered at the beginning of the repo. Note that this means the same *face value* of that security. It is very likely that this security will not have the same *market value* as it did at the beginning. This does not matter, as the economic ownership of the bond remains with the seller throughout.

> **Key Point**
>
> The cash amount on the first leg of a classic repo is the market price of the security.
>
> The cash amount on the second leg is the starting cash amount plus the repo interest.

> **Key Point**
>
> Interest on the cash in a repo is calculated using the appropriate money market basis for the period of the cash loan.

Note that, in the examples that follow in this chapter, we have generally used eight decimal places when calculating accrued coupon and dirty prices, in order to avoid rounding discrepancies. In practice, dealers would often agree a less precise number than this with counterparties.

We transact a repo as follows:

Example 6.1

Currency:	EUR
Start date:	14 July 2008
Term:	28 days (11 August 2008)
Repo rate:	4.0% (ACT/360 basis)
Collateral:	€60,000,000 nominal 8.5% bond maturity 23 March 2013 annual coupons (ACT/ACT basis)
Clean bond price:	108.95

Clean price of bond for value 14 July 2008 is 108.95

Accrued coupon on bond on 14 July 2008 $= \dfrac{113}{365} \times 8.5 = 2.63150685$

Dirty price = 111.58150685

Purchase amount

$$= €60,000,000 \times \frac{111.58150685}{100} = €66,948,904.11$$

Flows on 14 July 2008

€60,000,000 bond

Seller	→	Buyer
	←	

€66,948,904.11 cash

On maturity of the repo, the seller will repay the cash with interest calculated at 4.0%:

Principal = €66,948,904.11

Interest $= €66,948,904.11 \times 0.04 \times \dfrac{28}{360} = €208,285.48$

Total repayment = €67,157,189.59

Flows on 11 August 2008

€60,000,000 bond

Seller	←	Buyer
	→	

€67,157,189.59 cash

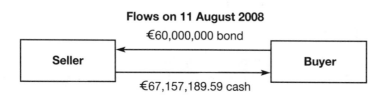

In the example above, we started with a given nominal amount of bond that we had available and calculated how much cash we could borrow, using this bond as collateral. It might be the other way round – we might need to borrow a specific amount of cash and need to calculate what nominal amount of a particular bond we need to provide as collateral. In this case, the first part of the example would have been instead:

$$\text{Nominal amount of security} = \frac{\text{cash amount at start}}{(\text{dirty price at start} \times 100)}$$

We can summarise these calculations as follows:

<table>
<tr>
<td>

Calculation summary

</td>
<td>

The cashflows in a classic repo

Cash amount at the start =

$$\text{nominal bond amount} \times \frac{(\text{clean price} + \text{accrued coupon})}{100}$$

or:

$$\text{Nominal bond amount} = \frac{\text{cash amount at the start}}{\left(\dfrac{(\text{clean price} + \text{accrued coupon})}{100} \right)}$$

and:

Cash amount at the end =

$$\text{cash amount at the beginning} \times \left(1 + \left(\text{repo rate} \times \frac{\text{repo days}}{\text{repo year}} \right) \right)$$

</td>
</tr>
</table>

<table>
<tr>
<td>

Beware!

</td>
<td>

Be very careful with the day/year basis throughout all the calculations in this chapter

</td>
</tr>
</table>

Whenever you are calculating accrued interest on a bond, you must use the appropriate bond basis, calculated from the last coupon date.

Whenever you are calculating cash interest, you must use the appropriate money market basis for the period of the cash loan.

Coupon payments

Although the legal benefit of the collateral passes from seller to buyer for the period of the repo, the economic benefit remains with the seller. Although the buyer has legal title to the collateral, it is not intended that the asset used should form part of the economics of the deal. The buyer's financial reward from the transaction comes from the interest on the cash loan, which he is effectively receiving through the difference between the cash amounts on the first and second legs of the repo. If the asset increases in value during the repo, it is the seller, not the buyer, who benefits because the asset is returned to him at the end. Similarly, if the asset loses value, it is the seller who suffers because the asset is returned to him at the end. The seller therefore keeps the asset on his balance sheet and the buyer does not put it on his balance sheet.

> **During the repo, the legal benefit of the collateral passes to the buyer but the economic benefit remains with the seller.** **Key Point**

If a coupon is payable on the security during the term of the repo, the buyer, who is the legal owner of the security, will receive the coupon. However because he should not have the economic benefit of this, the coupon is passed immediately back to the seller. This payment back to the seller, due on the same date as the buyer receives the coupon, is known as a "manufactured dividend" or "manufactured payment".

> **Any coupon during a classic repo is received by the borrower, but he must make a matching payment to the lender.** **Key Point**

It is assumed that the seller has arranged his own affairs so that he normally receives his coupons gross (i.e., without deduction of withholding tax). So that he remains in the same economic position, the buyer, when he receives the coupon, must pay the manufactured dividend gross, even if he (the buyer) has in fact received the coupon net of withholding tax.

> **The buyer pays the manufactured dividend to the seller gross, regardless of whether the buyer himself has received the coupon gross or net of withholding tax.** **Key Point**

MARGIN CALLS

In order for the collateral in a repo or similar transaction to be of adequate value, it is important for the buyer to recalculate its value continually and ensure that it is at least equal to the cash lent. This "marking to market" is customarily done at least daily. If the transactions are to qualify for favourable treatment under capital adequacy guidelines for example, this must be done. If the value of the collateral falls, the buyer may make a "margin call", requiring the seller to transfer more collateral. This can be either in cash or in more securities acceptable to the buyer, to make up the correct value. If cash collateral is used, the buyer would normally pay the seller interest on it at call money rate, or some other agreed rate. Such cash collateral does not affect the cash loan underlying the repo transaction.

It is normal in the European market to have two days' grace for transferring the margin.

When revaluing the collateral, it is the dirty price including accrued coupon interest which is considered, because this is the amount of money which could be realised by the buyer by selling the collateral if necessary. Similarly, interest accrued on the cash lent, at the repo interest rate originally transacted, is added to the cash principal amount when valuing the cash loan.

> **Key Point**
>
> Marking to market includes both accrued coupon on the security and accrued interest on the cash.

If the value of the collateral rises rather than falls, the seller can similarly make a margin call, requiring the buyer to return some of the collateral. If the seller has previously transferred cash to the buyer as collateral, then in any subsequent margin transfer from the buyer, the seller is entitled to ask for cash back first, rather than securities.

Because collateral prices are constantly changing, there would be small transfers of collateral every day if the collateral value were always maintained precisely equal to the cash value. To avoid the costs and administrative burden of this, the parties agree a "margin threshold", below which differences in value do not trigger a margin call. If the margin call is calculated to be less than this threshold, no margin is called for. If the margin call is calculated to be greater than the threshold, the margin call is made in full. This margin threshold is therefore the minimum transfer amount.

A repo dealer might possibly prefer to use collateral of shorter maturity because its value will fluctuate less (shorter maturity implies shorter modified duration), thereby reducing the need for margin calls.

The term "variation margin" generally means the same as a margin transfer. In the UK gilt repo market however, variation margin is used to mean the threshold below which a margin call is not made.

Under standard repo documentation (the GMRA – Global Master Repo Agreement), it is usual to calculate margin calls based on a net current valuation of all the repos and reverses outstanding between the two parties – rather than make margin calls on a deal-by-deal basis.

> **Key Point**
>
> Margin calls are made to keep the value of the collateral in line with the value of the cash loan.

Haircut

The buyer sometimes requires that the collateral value is always slightly higher – by say 2% – than the cash loan. This extra collateral is called a "haircut" or "initial margin".

A common reason for the buyer requiring a haircut is illiquidity of the collateral. This is because, if the seller defaults and the buyer then needs to sell the collateral in order to recover his money, the buyer has an extra risk with illiquid collateral that the value of the collateral might fall by the time he has been able to sell it. Haircuts are also common in repos using junk bonds as collateral, and if the seller is of poor creditworthiness.

Another reason is that the value of the collateral might fall significantly before there is time to ensure that the seller has increased it in response to a margin call. Whether a haircut is applied depends on the relative credit-worthiness of the two parties. If the seller is of a greater creditworthiness than the buyer, he may insist on having no haircut, or even the opposite – that the cash loan is a few percent greater than the collateral. If there is no haircut, the repo is sometimes said to be transacted "flat".

> **Initial margin protects against adverse movements in the value of the collateral in the event of illiquidity or before a margin call can be paid.**
>
> **Key Point**

It is important to apply the haircut the right way round. If there is a 2% haircut for example, this means that the collateral should always be 2% greater than the cash amount – i.e. it should be the cash amount multiplied by 1.02. Similarly, if we are starting with a known value of collateral, the cash amount should be the value of collateral divided by 1.02 (*not* multiplied by 0.98). In other words, the ratio

$$\frac{\text{market value of collateral}}{\text{amount of cash loan plus accrued interest}}$$

(which is called the "margin ratio") should in this case always be 1.02.

> **The following should be maintained throughout the repo**
>
> **Calculation summary**
>
> Current market value of collateral =
>
> cash amount plus interest accrued so far × (1 + haircut)
>
> *or:*
>
> Cash amount plus interest accrued so far =
>
> $$\frac{\text{current market value of collateral}}{(1 + \text{haircut})}$$

Example 6.2   We transact a repo, with the same information as before, but also with a 2% hair-cut:

Currency:	EUR
Start date:	14 July 2008
Term:	28 days (11 August 2008)
Repo rate:	4.0% (ACT/360 basis)
Collateral:	€60,000,000 nominal 8.5% bond maturity 23 March 2013 annual coupons (ACT/ACT basis)
Clean bond price:	108.95
Haircut:	2%

Clean price of bond for value 14 July 2008 is 108.95

$$\text{Accrued coupon on bond on 14 July 2008} = \frac{113}{365} \times 8.5 = 2.63150685$$

Market dirty price = 111.58150685

$$\text{Dirty price adjusted for 2\% haircut} = \frac{111.58150685}{1.02} = 109.39363417$$

$$\text{Purchase amount} = €60,000,000 \times \frac{109.39363417}{100} = €65,636,180.50$$

Flows on 14 July 2008

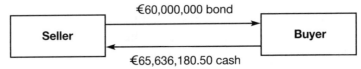

On maturity of the repo, the seller still repays the cash with interest calculated at 4.0%:

Principal = €65,636,180.50

$$\text{Interest} = €65,636,180.50 \times 0.04 \times \frac{28}{360} €204,201.45$$

Total repayment = €65,840,381.95

Flows on 11 August 2008

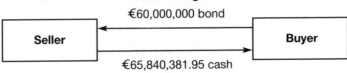

Suppose that, in the same transaction as in the previous example, the bond price falls to 107.15 on 21 July and a margin call is made. **Example 6.3**

Collateral value required:

Cash originally lent plus interest accrued so far at 4.0%

$$= €65,636,180.50 \times \left(1 + \left(0.04 \times \frac{7}{360}\right)\right) = €65,687,230.86$$

Allowing for the 2% haircut, the buyer will require that the collateral is now worth:

$$€65,687,230.86 \times 1.02 = €67,000,975.48$$

Existing collateral:

Accrued coupon on the bond on 21 July $= \dfrac{120}{365} \times 8.5 = 2.79452055$

New dirty price = 107.15 + 2.79452055 = 109.94452055

Value of existing collateral

$$= €60,000,000 \times \frac{109.94452055}{100} = €65,966,712.33$$

Margin call

The buyer will therefore call for the shortfall of €67,000,975.48 − €65,966,712.33 = €1,034,263.15 to be made up, either in cash or in securities worth this amount.

Haircut calculation

Calculation summary

Cash amount at the start =

$$\frac{\text{nominal bond amount} \times \dfrac{(\text{clean price} + \text{accrued coupon})}{100}}{(1 + \text{haircut rate})}$$

Cash amount at the end =

$$\text{cash amount at the short} \times \left(1 + \left(\text{repo rate} \times \frac{\text{repo days}}{\text{year}}\right)\right)$$

Variation margin calls

Calculate the value of collateral required by buyer:

- Add the accrued interest to the amount of the cash loan
- Add any haircut required to this total

Calculate the current value of the collateral held by the buyer:

- Value each security held as collateral in the usual way, including accrued coupon as appropriate

Calculate the margin call:

- The difference between the two amounts above is the value of transfer required
- Either transfer this amount of cash, or securities which have the same market value

GENERAL COLLATERAL (GC) AND SPECIALS

Where a repo is driven by the buyer's need – or at least willingness – to invest cash, the exact nature of the collateral is not important. Clearly it needs to be of adequate quality, and government or quasi-government securities are by far the most widely used, but the precise security is not important.

In such a situation, a repo can in general be transacted using any security or type of security (for example, junk bonds as well as government bonds) agreed between the two parties. The legal agreement already in place between the buyer and seller will generally state what categories of collateral are acceptable between them. It is not however important to the buyer exactly which bond is received as collateral. For each deal therefore, he does not specify which bond he is prepared to accept as collateral, as long as it falls within these categories. He can agree a repo rate for the trade, without knowing the precise maturity or coupon of the bond, or possibly even the issuer. In some markets however, the buyer is not obliged to accept the collateral if there is a coupon falling due during the repo, even if it is otherwise acceptable as collateral.

The collateral in such a case is known as "general collateral" or "GC". In the market in general, GC is usually defined in most markets as securities issued by the government of that currency – although, as already mentioned, the two parties might agree on something of lower quality.

ICMA (International Capital Markets Association, formerly ISMA) is the professional body covering the bond and repo markets. ICMA maintains a list of securities considered to be acceptable GC in various currencies, as follows:

ICMA GC list		
Country	Currency	Securities
Austria	EUR	Government guaranteed bonds and bills
Belgium	EUR	Government guaranteed bonds and bills
Finland	EUR	Government guaranteed bonds and bills
France	EUR	OAT, BTAN, BTF, Strips
Germany	EUR	Unity bond, Bund/DBR, Bobl/OBL, Treuhand, Schatz, Bubill
Greece	EUR	Government guaranteed bonds and bills
Ireland	EUR	Government guaranteed bonds and bills
Italy	EUR	CCT, BTP, BOT, CTZ
Luxembourg	EUR	Government guaranteed bonds and bills
Netherlands	EUR	Government guaranteed bonds and bills
Portugal	EUR	Government guaranteed bonds and bills
Spain	EUR	Government guaranteed bonds and bills (Note: the seller must specify if the securities go over record date 30 days prior to the trades being consummated)
UK	GBP	UK Treasury stock, UK Conversion stock
Denmark	DKK	Government guaranteed bonds and bills (Danish mortgages are excluded)
Sweden	SEK	Government guaranteed bonds and bills (Swedish mortgages are excluded)
Norway	NOK	Government guaranteed bonds and bills
Switzerland	CHF	Government guaranteed bonds and bills

In some cases a repo is driven by the buyer's need to borrow a bond, rather than his desire to lend cash. For example, the buyer in a repo could be a bond dealer who has deliberately taken a short bond position (because he believes that the market is falling) by selling a particular bond. Because he has sold the bond, he must deliver it to his counterparty. In order to maintain his short position for a time however, he cannot immediately buy the bond back from someone else. Instead, he must borrow it. He can do this with a reverse repo. In this case, the collateral delivered in the repo must be the specific security of which he has gone short, rather than any other.

If the security the buyer wishes to borrow is in short supply in the bond lending market, it is called "special", as opposed to "general collateral".

The extent to which any particular security becomes special depends on the supply of, and demand for, that security in the market generally.

If the seller is aware that the security being requested by the buyer is in particularly short supply, he is able to negotiate a lower interest rate for the cash he is taking through the repo. The more special the security, the lower the repo interest rate. Thus if a particular security is "expensive" for the buyer to borrow, this implies a lower rather than a higher repo rate.

Key Point	General collateral (GC) is usually defined as securities issued by the government of that currency.
	A "special" is a specific security in demand by borrowers.
	The more special the security, the lower the repo rate.

The most common reason for a bond going special is dealers in bond futures shorting the cheapest-to-deliver bond deliverable into a bond futures contract, in order to hedge a long position in the futures contract. Another reason is simply that the bond is overpriced and bond dealers therefore take significant short positions in it. Another reason is that dealers are using that bond as a hedge against other positions. For example, dealers tend to go short of the "on-the-run" government bond (the most recently issued one) as a hedge against an existing long position in bonds or an interest rate swap position where the dealer is receiving fixed (see Chapter 9 on interest rate and currency swaps).

OTHER FEATURES

Substitution

In the case of general collateral, the repo might include the right for the seller to change the exact security used as collateral during the period of the repo – a right of "substitution" – as long as the new collateral is equally acceptable. The maximum number of such substitutions is agreed in advance. If the buyer originally requested a specific security as collateral, such a right of substitution would clearly not have been agreed, as this would negate the purpose of the repo for the buyer.

In calculating the nominal amount of the new collateral in a substitution, the same approach is taken as with making a margin call – the cash amount is marked-to-market, any haircut added and then new collateral is transferred with this value.

We transact a repo, with the same information as before, with a 2% haircut:

Example 6.4

Currency:	EUR
Start date:	14 July 2008
Term:	28 days (11 August 2008)
Repo rate:	4.0% (ACT/360 basis)
Collateral:	€60,000,000 nominal 8.5% bond maturity 23 March 2013 annual coupons (ACT/ACT basis)
Clean bond price:	108.95
Haircut:	2%

Flows on 14 July 2008

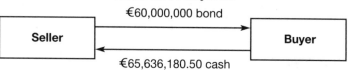

€60,000,000 bond

Seller → Buyer

€65,636,180.50 cash

On 21 July, we wish to make a substitution. This time, we are not concerned with the current market price of the existing collateral. This is simply returned and new collateral transferred in its place. The new collateral we use is as follows:

Collateral:	6.2% bond maturity 13 August 2018 annual coupons (ACT/ACT basis)
Clean bond price:	97.85

New collateral price:

The previous coupon date on the new collateral was 13/8/2007. The accrued coupon on the new collateral on 21 July is therefore:

$$\frac{343}{366} \times 6.2 = 5.81038251$$

Dirty price of new collateral = 97.85 + 5.81038251 = 103.66038251

New collateral value required:

Cash originally lent plus interest accrued so far at 4.0%

$$= €65,636,180.50 \times \left(1 + \left(0.04 \times \frac{7}{360}\right)\right) = €65,687,230.86$$

Allowing for the 2% haircut, the buyer will require that the new collateral is worth:

$$€65,687,230.86 \times 1.02 = €67,000,975.48$$

New collateral face value required:

The face value of the new collateral required is therefore:

$$\frac{€67,000,975.48}{\left(\frac{103.66038251}{100}\right)} = €64,635,084.16$$

On maturity of the repo, the seller still repays the cash with interest calculated at 4.0% as before:

Principal = €65,636,180.50

$$\text{Interest} = €65,636,180.50 \times 0.04 \times \frac{28}{360} \; €204,201.45$$

Total repayment = €65,840,381.95

Flows on 11 August 2008

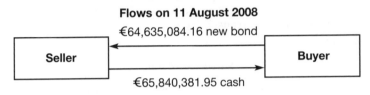

€64,635,084.16 new bond

| Seller | | Buyer |

€65,840,381.95 cash

Cross-currency repo

It might be that the seller in the repo wishes to borrow cash in one currency but has a security to offer in a different currency. This is acceptable in principle because the security is being offered essentially as collateral, and is known as a cross-currency repo. In this case however, the buyer is exposed to greater potential volatility in the value of the collateral – it is vulnerable to changes in both yields and exchange rates. The buyer may therefore require a larger haircut for a cross-currency repo. In general, because of the greater flexibility given to the seller, the buyer can also expect a slightly higher repo rate for cross-currency repo than for single currency repo.

Example 6.5 We transact a repo as follows:

Cash borrowing:	£50 million
Start date:	14 July 2008
Term:	28 days (11 August 2008)
Repo rate:	4.0% (ACT/365 basis)
Collateral:	EUR government bond
	maturity 23 March 2013
	8.5% annual coupons (ACT/ACT basis)
Clean bond price:	108.95
Haircut:	3%
EUR/GBP spot:	0.6523

Clean price of bond for value 14 July 2008 is 108.95

$$\text{Accrued coupon on bond on 14 July 2008} = \frac{113}{365} \times 8.5 = 2.63150685$$

Market dirty price = 111.58150685

$$\text{Dirty price adjusted for 3\% haircut} = \frac{111.58150685}{1.03} = 108.33156005$$

Amount of cash to be borrowed is £50 million. This is equivalent to €76,651,847.31 (converted at 0.6523). The nominal amount of collateral required is therefore:

$$\frac{€76,651,847.31}{\left(\dfrac{108.33156005}{100}\right)} = €70,756,709.56$$

Flows on 14 July 2008

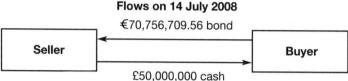

€70,756,709.56 bond

£50,000,000 cash

On maturity of the repo, the seller repays the cash with interest calculated at 4.0%:

Principal = £50,000,000

$$\text{Interest} = £50,000,000 \times 0.04 \times \frac{28}{365} = £153,424.66$$

Total repayment = £150,153,424.66

Flows on 14 August 2008

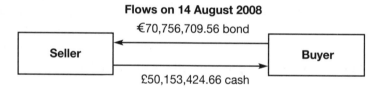

€70,756,709.56 bond

£50,153,424.66 cash

Maturity

Repos can in theory be transacted for any length of time. In practice, the period (or "term") is usually short – generally from one day (an "overnight" repo) to several months – because the market is driven largely by bond dealers' positions, which tend not to be established with a long time horizon. If the period is fixed and agreed in advance, it is a "term repo". The alternative is an "open repo", where either party may call for the repo to be terminated at any time, although often requiring two days' notice. In an open repo, the repo interest rate changes each day – effectively the repo is rolled over each day. Another name for an open repo is a "day-to-day" repo.

Other possibilities

Flex repo

In a "flex repo", the cash is repaid to the buyer in stages. This is useful, for example, when the seller is using the repo to finance the purchase of an amortising asset such as a mortgage-backed security.

Repo to maturity

In a "repo to maturity", the maturity date of the repo is the same as the maturity date of the security used as collateral.

Dollar repo

In a "dollar repo", the buyer is permitted, within agreed parameters, to return different securities from those originally purchased, provided that they have the same all-in value.

Forward-start repo

The first leg of a repo is normally settled on the usual settlement date for the security involved, or earlier. It is possible to deal a repo where the first leg settles on a different date – a "forward-start repo" – equivalent to a forward-forward borrowing or deposit.

Floating-rate repo

In this, the repo interest rate is reset at predetermined intervals according to some benchmark such as LIBOR. When the reset is a fixing such as 3-month LIBOR for example, the repo would often be a longer-term one. However repos are also dealt for short periods based on an overnight index such as EONIA. Such overnight-indexed floating-rate repos are common in France, for example.

Bilateral, triparty and hold-in-custody repos

When the delivery arrangements in a repo are as we have already described them, the repo is said to be a "bilateral repo". The cash is paid to the lender and the security is delivered to the borrower.

A "triparty" or "third party" repo involves another organisation (the "triparty agent") to act as custodian for the collateral. In this case, the collateral is delivered by the seller to the agent and held by that agent in a segregated account owned by the buyer. The custodian's duties include:

- Arranging the delivery versus payment (DVP) settlement at each end of the repo.
- Ensuring that the collateral satisfies the buyer's criteria regarding haircut, credit rating, tradeability/liquidity and currency.
- Marking to market daily to ensure that the collateral is adequate.
- Overseeing any substitutions.
- Providing daily reports to both parties confirming the value of the collateral.

Such an arrangement requires a separate agreement called the "triparty agreement" to be signed by all three parties, regarding the custody arrangements. This is separate from, and in addition to, the repo agreement (typically the GMRA) signed by the two counterparties. The third party's fees are paid by the seller. Major international triparty custodians include Euroclear, Clearstream, Bank of New York and Chase.

An advantage for the seller in a triparty repo is the ability to effect multiple substitutions. He can request the triparty agent to return the collateral to his account and take another – which can be automatically assigned by the agent from the seller's account in accordance with the triparty agreement – in substitution. The corresponding disadvantage for the buyer is that he cannot normally sell or repo out the collateral himself on the other side. He is also unlikely anyway to receive a special as collateral, because the seller is likely to make a substitution if the existing collateral becomes special.

Advantages for the buyer are:

- The administrative simplicity and lack of administrative and legal costs, particularly for corporates, which can avoid the systems needed by banks dealing regularly in repos.

- The ability to adjust daily the amount of cash lent through a triparty open reverse repo; the settlement costs involved in daily changes where delivery is involved could make it uneconomic for the seller to enter such a transaction on a bilateral basis.

- The seller should typically be prepared to pay a slightly higher repo rate because a triparty repo facilitates substitutions.

If a repo is of very short duration, or if the seller wishes to effect many substitutions, the administrative burden of transferring the collateral, either to the counterparty or to a third party, becomes increasingly costly in relative terms and could make a repo uneconomic. One solution is a "hold-in-custody" ("HIC") repo (also known as a "due-bill repo"), where the seller continues to hold the collateral, but on the buyer's behalf, in a segregated account. For the buyer, the main concern is that the seller's custodial arrangements are safe. This clearly entails a significantly greater credit risk, in return for which the buyer expects a higher return on his cash. As with a triparty repo, the buyer is unable to use the collateral in a repo himself. For the seller, a HIC repo offers reduced costs and administration, and ease of substitution. The seller in a HIC repo is of course not permitted to use the same collateral in more than one repo. This illegal practice is called "double-dipping". See Figures 6.2–6.4.

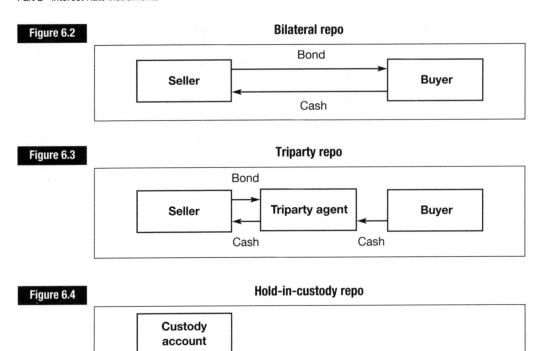

Figure 6.2

Bilateral repo

Seller → Bond → Buyer
Buyer → Cash → Seller

Figure 6.3

Triparty repo

Seller → Bond → Triparty agent
Triparty agent → Cash → Seller
Buyer → Cash → Triparty agent

Figure 6.4

Hold-in-custody repo

Custody account
Seller → Bond → Custody account
Buyer → Cash → Seller

The repo rate

In general, the rate at which it is possible to borrow through a repo is lower than for an unsecured (or "clean") interbank loan for the same term, and lower than issuing a CD. This is because the credit risk on which the buyer is relying is improved. First, there is a second line of defence in that if the buyer defaults, the seller can look to the collateral to recover his money. Second, the credit quality of the collateral – usually but not always government bonds – is often higher than the credit quality of the seller.

The repo rate should not however generally be as low as the treasury bill rate, because that would mean that banks could, by repoing government bonds, borrow more cheaply than the government.

Various factors affect the repo rate:

■ To the extent that the collateral quality is reduced by using lesser credits, the repo rate will be relatively higher.

■ A right of collateral substitution provides a convenience for the seller and an administrative burden and loss of flexibility for the buyer, for which the seller must be willing to pay.

- A hold-in-custody repo is more expensive than a triparty or bilateral repo, because of the greater credit risk to the buyer. The rate for a bilateral repo is typically lower than for a triparty, because the borrower is able to use the collateral.

- Willingness on the buyer's part to accept a lower haircut and/or a cross-currency repo will tend to increase the repo rate.

- The most dramatic effect on repo rates can arise when the collateral is special. In this case, the price is driven by the buyer's need for that specific security. If the security is in very short supply in the market, the repo rate can be several percentage points below the normal cost of funds and possibly even negative.

Eurepo

Eurepo is a reference fixing rate for repos transacted in EUR, analogous to EURIBOR for unsecured cash transactions. It is the rate at which, at 11:00 a.m. Brussels time, one prime bank offers cash in EUR to another prime bank in a repo against "eurepo GC". The list of eligible eurepo GC is the same as the ICMA GC list, but limited to collateral in EUR. Note that this rate is the "bid" for the collateral (equivalent to the "offer" for cash).

As with EURIBOR, quotes are taken from a panel of banks and each quote rounded to two decimal places. As with EURIBOR, the highest and lowest 15% of quotes are discarded and the remainder then averaged. The result is rounded to two decimal places and published.

Eurepo is quoted for spot value (T+2) for 1-, 2- and 3-week and 1-, 2-, 3-, 6-, 9- and 12-month maturities, and also for T/N. It is quoted on an ACT/360 day basis, as normal. Eurepo is available on each day that TARGET (the clearing system for EUR) is open.

The eurepo calculation is performed, on behalf of the European Banking Federation (FBE).

BUY/SELL-BACK

The repo market involves two very similar types of transaction – a "repo" and a "sell/buy-back". As the name suggests, a sell/buy-back is an agreement to sell first and then buy back in the future – which is equivalent to a repo. The other way round, a "buy/sell-back", is equivalent to a reverse repo. Confusingly, while repos and reverse repos in general are described as "repo", buy/sell-backs and sell/buy-backs in general are more often described as "buy/sell-back" (which is the opposite way round!).

A third type of transaction, which is also similar but not quite as close as these first two, is "securities lending" (or "securities borrowing" the other way round).

A repo, as we have already described it, is also known as a "repurchase agreement" or "RP" or "US-style repo" or "classic repo", to distinguish it from a sell/buy-back.

A sell/buy-back is essentially the same as a repo but the two legs of the deal, although dealt simultaneously, are treated as two separate transactions rather than one. The reasons for the transactions are the same as for a repo, the economics are the same and the amounts of cash which pass at the beginning and the end are often the same.

Confusing or what?	The term "repo" is used on three levels:
	1. As a general name for this market (repo, reverse repo, buy/sell-back, sell/buy-back).
	2. To distinguish the repo (or reverse repo) structure from the sell/buy-back (or buy /sell-back) structure.
	3. To specify that we are the lender in the repo (i.e. we are doing a repo, not a reverse repo).

In the examples given above of a classic repo, the cash amount passing in the second leg of the repo was calculated as "principal plus interest" on the cash loan and expressed as a single amount. In a straightforward buy/sell-back, the same total amount of cash passes on the second leg as in a repo. The difference is that this amount is then expressed as a forward clean price for the security. As with a repo, a buy/sell-back may incorporate a haircut.

In a "sell/buy-back", the first leg of the transaction is the sale of a bond or other asset and the second is the purchase of the same asset back again from the same counterparty for settlement on a later date. This is equivalent to a repo. A "buy/sell-back" is the same transaction viewed from the counterparty's point of view. This is equivalent to a reverse repo.

Key Point	A sell/buy-back is economically the same as a classic repo but treats the two legs as separate transactions.

An important reason for structuring a deal as a buy/sell-back is sometimes that in certain jurisdictions it is legally stronger than a reverse repo, because it is structured as two normal securities transactions. Also, no special documentation (such as the GMRA used for repos) is required – although the GMRA is nevertheless generally recommended internationally.

Another reason is tradition – in Italy and Spain for example, the domestic markets are historically more accustomed to buy/sell-backs than repos.

Also, although a haircut is possible, there is generally no provision for daily marking to market and making margin transfers, which some parties might see as an advantage and others as a disadvantage. It is however possi-

ble to take account of a change in collateral value, using a different procedure (see "close-out and repricing" later).

Price calculation

Because the two legs of the deal are booked separately in a buy/sell-back, a
forward clean price must be calculated in order to book the transaction for
the second leg of the deal.

We transact a buy/sell-back with the same information as before (no haircut):
Example 6.6

Currency:	EUR
Start date:	14 July 2008
Term:	28 days (11 August 2008)
Repo rate:	4.0% (ACT/360 basis)
Collateral:	€60,000,000 nominal 8.5% bond
	maturity 23 March 2013
	annual coupons (ACT/ACT basis)

Clean bond price: 108.95

Clean price of bond for value 14 July 2008 is 108.95

Accrued coupon on bond on 14 July 2008 $= \dfrac{113}{365} \times 8.5 = 2.63150685$

Total purchase price = 111.58150685

Purchase amount $= €60,000,000 \times \dfrac{111.58150685}{100} = €66,948,904.11$

Flows on 14 July 2008

€60,000,000 bond

Seller → **Buyer**

€66,948,904.11 cash

On maturity of the repo, the seller will repay the cash with interest calculated at 4.0%:

Principal = €66,948,904.11

Interest $= €66,948,904.11 \times 0.04 \times \dfrac{28}{360} = €208,285.48$

Total repayment = €67,157,189.59

Note that so far, the calculations are identical to a classic repo.

Now the total repayment must be converted to a forward price for the bond:

Forward dirty price $= \dfrac{\text{total cash repayment}}{\text{nominal bond amount}} \times 100$

$$= \dfrac{€67,157,189.59}{€60,000,000} \times 100 = 111.92864932$$

$$\text{Accrued interest on the bond on 11 August 2008} = \frac{141}{365} \times 8.5 = 3.28356164$$

Therefore the dirty forward price is split into accrued interest of 3.28356164 and a clean forward price of 111.92864932 – 3.28356164 = 108.64508768

Flows on 11 August 2008

€60,000,000 bond

Repurchased at a price of 108.64508768

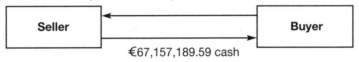

€67,157,189.59 cash

In Chapter 5 on bond market calculations, we saw that a forward bond price is lower than the price for normal delivery, if the coupon rate is higher than the cash funding rate. The same is true here, because the forward price in a buy/sell-back is simply a forward bond price. In other words:

> **Key Point**   The forward price in a buy/sell-back is lower than the spot price if the coupon rate is higher than the repo rate.

Coupon payments

If there is a coupon payment on the security during the term of the buy/sell-back, it is received by the buyer in the same way as in a classic repo. Unlike in a classic repo however, it is typically not then paid over to the counterparty. Clearly this affects the economics of the deal, as the counterparty needs to be compensated.

In order to restore the economics of the deal, the value of the coupon payment is deducted from the cash amount repaid by the seller at maturity. Furthermore, as the buyer is also able to invest the coupon payment itself, we also deduct the investment income he can earn on it from coupon date until maturity of the repo. A usual assumption is that the coupon can be invested at the original repo rate; although unlikely to be correct, the effect of using a different rate would generally be very small.

> **Key Point**   Coupon payments during a buy/sell-back are received by the borrower but he does *not* make a matching payment to the lender (unlike in a classic repo). The forward price is adjusted to reflect this.

We transact another buy/sell-back, but this time the example includes a haircut **Example 6.7**
and also a coupon in the middle of the repo:

Currency:	EUR
Start date:	14 July 2008
Term:	28 days (11 August 2008)
Repo rate:	4.0% (ACT/360 basis)
Collateral:	€60,000,000 nominal 8.5% bond
	maturity 26 July 2013
	annual coupons (ACT/ACT basis)
Clean bond price:	108.95
Haircut:	2%

Accrued coupon on bond on 14 July 2008 $= \dfrac{354}{366} \times 8.5 = 8.22131148$

Dirty price $= 108.95 + 8.22131148 = 117.17131148$

Purchase price without haircut $= €60,000,000 \times \dfrac{117.17131148}{100}$

$$= €70,302,786.89$$

Purchase price adjusting for haircut $= \dfrac{€70,302,786.89}{1.02} = €68,924,300.87$

Flows on 14 July 2008

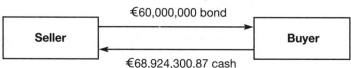

On maturity of the buy/sell-back, the seller owes the cash with interest calculated
at 4.0%:

Principal $= €68,924,300.87$

Interest $= €68,924,300.87 \times 0.04 \times \dfrac{28}{360} = €214,431.16$

Total due $= €68,924,300.87 + €214,431.16 = €69,138,732.03$

However the buyer has had the benefit of a coupon paid on 26 July 2008 which
amounted to: $€60,000,000 \times 8.5\% = €5,100,000$

He has also earned interest on this – say at the repo rate of 4% – for the 16 days
from 26 July to 11 August, to give a total of:

$$€5,100,000 \times \left(1 + \left(0.04 \, \dfrac{16}{360}\right)\right) = €5,109,066.67$$

This will therefore be deducted from the amount due at maturity of the repo, to
give:

$$€69,138,732.03 - €5,109,066.67 = €64,029,665.36$$

Flows on 11 August 2008

€60,000,000 bond

| Seller | | Buyer |

€64,029,665.36 cash

The dirty price for settlement on 11 August is therefore:

$$\frac{64{,}029{,}665.36}{60{,}000{,}000} \times 100 = 106.71610893$$

We need to calculate a clean price. We must therefore calculate the accrued coupon on the end date in the normal way, and subtract it from the dirty price. There are 16 days from the last coupon on 26 July to the end date of 11 August. Therefore:

$$\text{Accrued coupon on 11 August 2008} = \frac{16}{365} \times 8.5 = 0.37260274$$

Clean forward price for 11 August = dirty price – accrued coupon
$$= 106.71610893 - 0.37260274 = 106.34350619$$

Key Point

The **cash amount** on the second leg of a buy/sell-back (where a coupon is payable during the deal) is:

Spot amount + repo interest – coupon – interest on coupon

The **forward price** on the second leg of a buy/sell-back (where a coupon is payable during the deal) is:

**Spot amount + repo interest – coupon – interest on coupon
– accrued coupon**

Calculation summary

The cashflows in a buy/sell-back

1. Calculate the cash amount at the start (the same as for a classic repo):

$$\frac{\text{nominal bond amount} \times \left(\dfrac{\text{clean price} \times \text{accrued coupon}}{100} \right)}{(1 + \text{haircut})}$$

2. Calculate a final cash amount (the same as for a classic repo):

$$\text{Cash amount at the start} \times \left(1 + \left(\text{repo rate} \times \frac{\text{repo days}}{\text{year}} \right) \right)$$

3. Subtract the value of any intervening coupon payment to give the actual cash amount at the end (this is the "repurchase price"):

Cash coupon payment $\times$

$$\left(1 + \left(\text{repo rate} \times \frac{\text{days from coupon payment to end}}{\text{year}}\right)\right)$$

4. Calculate the dirty forward price:

$$\text{Dirty forward price} = \frac{\text{cash amount at the end}}{\text{nominal bond amount}} \times 100$$

5. Calculate the accrued coupon at the end date as usual
6. Calculate the clean forward price as usual:

Clean forward price = dirty forward price − accrued coupon at end

CLOSE-OUT AND REPRICING

Because a buy/sell-back is booked as two separate transactions, making a margin call at some time between the start date and the end date does not make sense in the same way that it does in a repo, which is booked as a single transaction. Margin calls are therefore not possible with a buy/sell-back.

There is however an alternative procedure for keeping the value of the collateral and the value of the cash in line with each other, called "close-out and repricing". The two parties can include this as part of the agreement if they choose to.

Close-out and repricing means that, if the two sides do move out of line, the original forward transaction is terminated early. A new pair of transactions is simultaneously put in place. The new spot transaction offsets the closing transaction, and the new forward transaction has the same date as the original forward transaction and replaces it. The new pair of transactions uses the same original repo rate but the new current price of the security (hence "repricing"). The balance between the cash and collateral values is thus restored. At the moment of early termination and start of the new transaction, only the net cash difference and the net collateral difference are transferred.

There are two methods of structuring this rebalancing. Under the first method, the new transactions use the same face value of collateral as the original transactions; in this case, there is no net movement of collateral, but there is a change in the amount of cash borrowed. Under the second method, the new transactions use the same cash amount as in the original transactions; in this case, there is a net change in the face value of collateral, and a payment of the interest amount so far.

Close-out and repricing with adjustment of the cash amount

In this method, the original cash amount is repaid together with accrued interest so far, and a new deal transacted with the same maturity date and based on the same repo rate but valuing the collateral at current prices. The amount of collateral remains the same but the cash is adjusted. The calculations are as follows:

Calculation summary

- Calculate the new dirty market value of the existing collateral
- Calculate the new cash loan (A) which can now be made based on this collateral value, adjusted for the haircut
- Add the accrued interest on the original cash loan to the amount of the original cash loan to give what must now be repaid (B) to close it out
- Settle the difference (A − B) in cash

Example 6.8

We transact the following buy/sell-back (similar to a previous example):

Currency:	EUR
Start date:	14 July 2008
Term:	28 days (11 August 2008)
Repo rate:	4.0% (ACT/360 basis)
Collateral:	€60,000,000 nominal 8.5% bond maturity 23 March 2013 annual coupons (ACT/ACT basis)
Clean bond price:	108.95
Haircut:	2%

Clean price of bond for value 14 July 2008 is 108.95

$$\text{Accrued coupon on bond on 14 July 2008} = \frac{113}{365} \times 8.5 = 2.63150685$$

Market dirty price = 111.58150685

$$\text{Dirty price adjusted for 2\% haircut} = \frac{111.58150685}{1.02} = 109.39363417$$

$$\text{Purchase amount} = €60,000,000 \times \frac{109.39368417}{100} = €65,636,180.50$$

Flows on 14 July 2008

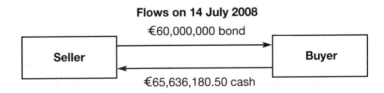

€60,000,000 bond

Seller → Buyer

€65,636,180.50 cash

Suppose that the bond price falls to 107.15 on 21 July and we agree to close out and reprice the original deal:

Cash

Cash originally lent plus interest accrued so far at 4.0% =

$$€65,636,180.50 \times \left(1 + \left(0.04 \times \frac{7}{360}\right)\right) = €65,687,230.86$$

This cash amount is repaid.

Close out original deal:

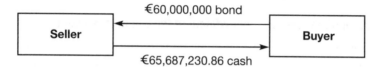

Collateral:

$$\text{Accrued coupon on the bond on 21 July} = \frac{120}{365} \times 8.5 = 2.97452055$$

New dirty price = 107.15 + 2.79452055 = 109.94452055

Establish a new repriced deal:

A new deal is established at the same repo rate based on the same collateral but reducing the amount of the cash loan to equate to the new value of the collateral after adjustment for the haircut – which is:

$$€ \frac{60,000,000 \times \frac{109.94452055}{100}}{1.02} = €64,673,247.38$$

As the transactions are settled on a net basis, there is only a single cash transfer:

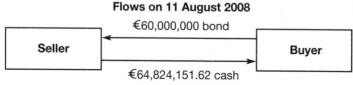

At the maturity of the new repriced deal, the new cash amount will be repaid plus interest:

$$€64,673,247.38 \times \left(1 + \left(0.04 \times \frac{21}{360}\right)\right) = €64,824,151.62$$

Flows on 11 August 2008

The net effect of this method is slightly less beneficial to the seller than variation margin. Because the seller has closed out the deal and re-established it at the same rate for a shorter period, he is effectively paying some interest early on the cash without any compensation – that is, he is paying compound interest on the cash he has borrowed instead of simple interest. In order not to change the economics of the deal in this way, it would be necessary to agree to defer the interest payment of €51,045.48 until 14 August, to avoid the compounding effect.

Close-out and repricing with adjustment of the collateral amount

In this method, the cash loan amount remains the same but the collateral is adjusted to reflect the current price. The calculations are as follows:

Calculation summary

- Pay to the buyer the accrued interest on the cash loan
- Establish a new cash loan of exactly the same amount as the original loan at the same repo rate, to the same maturity date
- Calculate the nominal amount of collateral needed (C) for the cash loan amount at the new dirty market price, adjusted for the haircut
- Settle the difference between C and the original nominal collateral amount, in securities

---

Example 6.9 With the same information as in the last example, we agree to close out the original deal on 21 July with the seller repaying the cash plus accrued interest to the buyer:

Close out original deal:

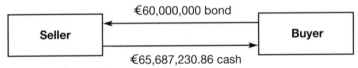

€60,000,000 bond

| Seller | Buyer |

€65,687,230.86 cash

At the same time, a new deal is established at the same repo rate based on the same original amount for the cash loan, €65,636,180.50.

Adjusting for the haircut, the collateral value must be (as it was originally):

€65,636,180.50 × 1.02 = €66,948,904.11

At the new dirty market price of 109.94452055, the nominal amount of collateral must be:

$$\frac{66,948,904.11}{\left(\dfrac{109.94452055}{100}\right)} = 60,893,352.19$$

Establish a new repriced deal:

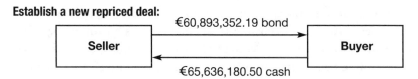

€60,893,352.19 bond

Seller → Buyer

€65,636,180.50 cash

As the transactions are settled on a net basis, the transfers are as follows:

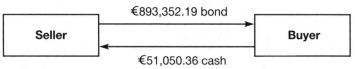

€893,352.19 bond

Seller → Buyer

€51,050.36 cash

At the maturity of the new repriced deal, the cash amount will be repaid plus interest:

$$€65,636,180.50 \times \left(1 + \left(0.04 \times \frac{21}{360}\right)\right) = €65,789,331.59$$

Flows on 11 August 2008

€60,893,352.19 bond

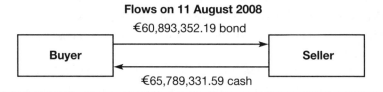

Buyer → Seller

€65,789,331.59 cash

The economics of this method are the same as the previous method – that is, slightly less beneficial for the seller – for the same reason that the seller is effectively paying some interest early.

Substitution and maturity

Again, because a buy/sell-back is booked as two separate transactions rather than one, substitution cannot usually be included. The forward leg of buy/sell-back would need to be unwound before a substitution could be made.

Similarly, a buy/sell-back has a fixed term and cannot normally be an open transaction.

SECURITIES LENDING

When a repo is driven by the need of one party to borrow a particular security because he is short of it, it might be that the lender of the security does not wish to borrow cash in return; if he is already cash-rich, then borrowing more cash which he would then need to place on deposit would probably cost him the bid-offer spread. Nevertheless, he wishes to take advantage of the fact that he owns a security in demand. In this case, he simply lends the securities for a fee. However because he wishes to be secured against default by the borrower, he also takes collateral from the borrower, possibly also in the form of securities. The exchange therefore becomes a loan of a specific security against a loan of other collateral, with the lender of the specific security earning a fee. This is known as "securities lending" or "securities borrowing" (or "stock lending" or "stock borrowing").

Key Point

Securities lending is the loan of a specific security against collateral.

A securities lending transaction is a temporary transfer of legal title in a security from one party to another. Securities borrowing is the same transaction viewed from the counterparty's point of view.

In securities lending, the term "collateral" is not used for the same side of the transaction as in a reverse repo. Suppose that I need to borrow bond A and that I do so through a reverse repo. In this case, it is bond A that is referred to as the collateral. However if instead I borrow bond A through securities borrowing, it is whatever I lend in return that is referred to as the collateral.

Similarly, in securities lending the "lender" is the party lending the specific security (not the party lending the "collateral") and the borrower is the party borrowing the specific security.

The lender in a securities lending transaction is paid a fee by the borrower. The fee is quoted in terms of basis points per annum (on a money market basis) and is calculated on the market value of the securities lent, and paid at the end of the transaction. See Figure 6.5.

Key Point

The lender in securities lending is paid a fee based on the market value of the security.

Figure 6.5

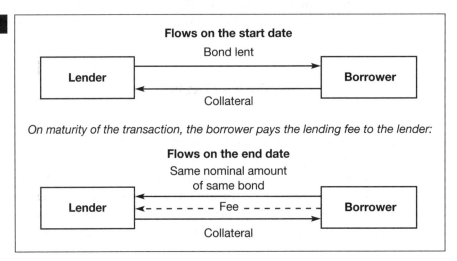

Flows on the start date

Bond lent

Lender → Borrower

Collateral

On maturity of the transaction, the borrower pays the lending fee to the lender:

Flows on the end date

Same nominal amount of same bond

Lender ← Borrower

← – – – – – – – Fee – – – – – – – –

Collateral

Collateral

The collateral used in securities lending may be general collateral of a similar nature to the special. There is however no need for the collateral to be similar, and in fact securities lending can be transacted against any collateral acceptable to the lender, such as equities, treasury bills, CDs, banker's acceptances or bank letters of credit. A letter of credit has the disadvantage that the bank providing it will charge the borrower for issuing it as a guarantee for him, but the borrower may still be willing to provide this collateral if he has no other available.

Cash can also be used as collateral. In this case, the transaction is very similar in all respects to a reverse repo and the lender (that is, the lender of the securities) pays the borrower interest on the cash collateral at an agreed rate.

Coupon payments and other rights

If a coupon, or other payment such as a partial redemption, is payable on the security lent during the transaction, the treatment under the GMSLA (Global Master Securities Lending Agreement) is the same as in a classic repo, not as in a buy/sell-back – that is, the borrower is obliged to make a matching payment ("manufactured payment") to the lender to compensate him for the loss of the income. Similarly, if there is a payment on the collateral, the lender is obliged to make a matching payment to the borrower. The situation is not however the same everywhere. In securities lending transactions in some domestic markets, the collateral is only pledged with no transfer of ownership, so the coupon continues to be paid to the original owner, and no compensating payment is required.

Depending on the nature of the security lent, there may also be other rights attached to ownership, such as voting rights, rights to convert the security to a different security (for example from a bond to equity), or rights to purchase more of the security (a "rights issue"). As far as the issuer of the security is concerned, it is the current registered owner of the security or, in the case of a bearer security, the current holder of the security, who can exercise these rights – that is, the borrower. The treatment of such rights under the securities lending transaction also varies according to the documentation used.

Coupon payments on the security lent are received by the borrower, **Key Point** who must make matching payments to the lender.

Payments on the collateral (assuming ownership is transferred) are received by the lender, who must make matching payments to the borrower.

Margin

A haircut may be taken, as in a classic repo or a buy/sell-back. In the case of securities lending however, it is the lender who would request the initial margin, not the borrower as would typically be the case in a classic repo, because in this case it is the securities being lent which are driving the deal and the lender who is receiving the collateral. Variation margin may also be paid in the same way as in a classic repo, but again this is by adjusting the amount of collateral rather than the amount of the security lent, because the deal has been driven by the borrower's need for that particular amount of that security.

Key Point	When initial margin is required, it is generally in favour of the lender, not the borrower.

Other features

A securities lending transaction is similar to a classic repo in other respects, such as the possibility of including the following features in the transaction:

- Substitution. Note that it is the collateral which can be substituted by the borrower (not the security lent which can be substituted by the lender as in a repo).
- Cross-currency lending (the ability to supply collateral in a different currency from the security lent, if acceptable to the lender).
- An open transaction rather than a fixed-term transaction.

In addition to borrowing a security in the market, it is often possible to borrow from the clearing house through which it is settled (such as Clearstream, Euroclear or a domestic securities clearing system) if this facility is available. Although this can be expensive, it has the advantage that the clearer can arrange automatic borrowing from another user of the clearer in the event that the account is short at the end of the day.

Example 6.10 A dealer borrows €60,000,000 face value of a bond as follows:

Start date:	14 July 2008
Term:	28 days (11 August 2008)
Lending fee:	50 basis points per annum (ACT/360 basis)
Bond borrowed:	€60,000,000 nominal 8.5% bond
	maturity 23 March 2013
	annual coupons (ACT/ACT basis)
Clean bond price:	108.95
Haircut:	2%

The bond used as collateral is as follows:

Coupon:	6.5% (annual, ACT/ACT basis)
Coupon dates:	18 September
Clean price:	99.26

The bond borrowed

Accrued coupon on 14 July 2008 $= \dfrac{113}{365} \times 8.5 = 2.63150685$

Dirty price $= 108.95 + 2.63150685 = 111.58150685$

Value of bond $= €60,000,000 \times \dfrac{111.58150685}{100} = €66,948,904.11$

Value of collateral required, including haircut $= €66,948,904.11 \times 1.02$
$= €68,287,882.19$

The collateral

Accrued coupon on 14 July 2008 $= \dfrac{300}{366} \times 6.5 = 5.32786885$

Dirty price $= 99.26 + 5.32786885 = 104.58786885$

Face value of collateral required $= \dfrac{€68,287,882.19}{\left(\dfrac{104.58786885}{100}\right)} = €65,292,354.59$

Flows on 14 July 2008

€60,000,000 face value
security

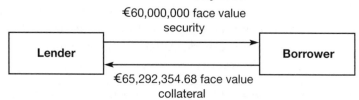

€65,292,354.68 face value
collateral

Lending fee $= €66,948,904.11 \times 0.005 \times \dfrac{28}{360} = €26,035.68$

Flows on 11 August 2008

€60,000,000 face value security

€65,292,354.68 face value
collateral

In practice, the face value of the collateral used is often a rounded amount.

Calculation method for securities lending	Calculation summary

1. Value the security lent at its current market price, including accrued coupon.

2. Increase this market value by any haircut agreed.

3. Calculate the current market price of the collateral, including accrued coupon.

4. The face value of collateral needs to be the right amount so that the market value of the collateral is equal to (2) above.

5. Lending fee =

$$\text{market value of security borrowed} \times \text{fee rate} \times \frac{\text{period of loan in days}}{\text{days in year}}$$

Note that "days in year" is on a money market basis and can mean 365 (for example with sterling) or 360 (for example with US dollars).

The lending fee

If you are asked to lend out a specific security, you will charge a fee – even if the security is not special – because you are in the fortunate position of having something that someone else wants to borrow. The same is true in a repo: if you use a repo to lend out a specific security requested by the borrower, rather than GC, you expect to borrow the cash slightly cheaper even if the security is not special.

When the security borrowed is a special, you can demand a higher fee, in the same way that the lender in a repo can force a lower interest on the cash.

The fee is equivalent in practice to the difference between the market rate for a classic repo using general collateral and the market rate for a classic repo using a specific security.

Example 6.11   You are asked to lend bond A. The GC repo rate is 5.6%, but bond A is special so that you can lend it out in a repo at 5.2%. You therefore do this. However you do not need the cash, so you simultaneously lend out the cash to another party in a GC reverse repo at 5.6%. You are secured and your net profit is 40 basis points.

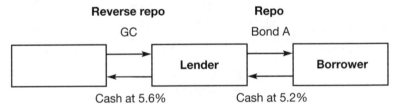

An alternative way of achieving the same result is to lend out bond A in a securities lending transaction. In this case what lending fee should you require? The answer is 40 basis points, because you are again secured by GC:

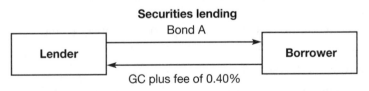

The fee paid by the borrower of the specific security to the lender is quoted in terms of basis points per annum (on a money market basis) and is calculated on the market value of the securities lent, and paid at the end of the transaction.

The fee is equivalent in practice to the difference between the market rate for a classic repo using general collateral and the market rate for a classic repo using a specific security.

> **The lender in securities lending is paid a fee based on the market value of the security.**   **Key Point**

COMPARISON BETWEEN THE DIFFERENT TRANSACTIONS

The table below compares a classic repo, buy/sell-back and securities lending.

	Classic repo	Buy/sell-back	Securities lending
Basis of transaction	Cash vs. securities	Cash vs. securities	Securities vs. other securities, letter of credit, cash or any other acceptable collateral
Maturity	Fixed-term or open	Fixed-term only	Fixed-term or open
Fee/cost	Quoted as repo rate; paid as interest rate on cash amount	Quoted as repo rate; paid through price differential between initial price and forward price	Quoted as fee (% per annum on the cash value); paid at maturity. Interest paid on collateral if it is cash
Margin rights	Initial margin (usually in favour of borrower) and variation margin both possible	Initial margin possible. Variation margin possible only through close-out and repricing	Initial margin (usually in favour of lender) and variation margin both possible
Coupon payment	Returned to seller as manufactured payment	Kept by buyer and forward price is adjusted	Returned to lender. Other rights depend on documentation
Substitution	Lender can substitute collateral	Not normal	Borrower can substitute collateral
Documentation (see later)	Single agreement such as the GMRA; full rights of offset in case of default	Two separate transactions with no specific rights of offset in case of default (although can be under the GMRA, which does include offset)	Single lending agreement such as the GMSLA; full rights of offset in case of default

USES OF REPO AND SECURITIES LENDING

We have brought together here various uses of the repo markets. Some of the comments here will therefore repeat some of the things we have already said.

Cash borrowing

A repo provides the ability to borrow cash cheaper than using a straight cash loan, because of the additional security provided by the collateral. If the borrower has collateral which has become special, the borrowing will be even cheaper. It might be that the borrower is so uncreditworthy that he could in fact not borrow at all without collateral.

Funding a long bond position

Assuming that he is starting from a square position, with no surplus funds, a bond dealer needs to borrow cash to fund a long position. In order to borrow the cash easily and relatively cheaply, he repos out the security he is buying (or another he already has) as collateral against the cash.

Covering a short bond position

Conversely, a bond dealer may acquire a short position in a particular security. If he is not already long in that security, he cannot deliver on the sale. If he does not deliver the security however, the deal is not cancelled and he is still liable for delivery. Any delay can be very expensive for the defaulting dealer. Assuming that settlement is DVP, he will not receive his cash until he does deliver, so that the counterparty continues to earn interest on the cash. On the other side however, no adjustment will be made to the accrued coupon included in the sale price – when the security is finally delivered, the seller has not earned extra coupon on the security but he has lost interest on the cash. In addition, dealers in some markets are charged a penalty for failed trades.

The dealer must therefore borrow the security in order to deliver it on time. One possibility is to borrow the security from the exchange or clearing house through which it is settled (such as Clearstream or Euroclear for example) if this facility is available. There are several disadvantages with this. First, the particular security may not be available, although this should not often be a problem as these clearing houses have access to large volumes of the security. Second, the cost is usually high. Third, the dealer does not know when the security he has borrowed will be demanded back by the seller.

An alternative is to reverse in the security against the cash which has been generated by the security sale. In this case, the security is a special, because only that specific security, and no other, is of use to the dealer in this situation.

Even if a dealer does not have a short position on his book, he may still be short of a security on delivery because an offsetting purchase which he has made has failed on settlement. Suppose for example that a dealer has both bought and sold the same security; if the purchase settlement has failed, he cannot deliver on the sale. An automatic borrowing facility at the clearing organisation can overcome this.

It may also be that a transfer of a security between a domestic clearing system and Euroclear or Clearstream cannot take place on the same day, so that the dealer knows he will be short for a day or longer. It is therefore worthwhile borrowing the security to deliver on his sale, until such time as his purchase is delivered.

Secured cash investment

An investor with cash to deposit in the money market has various choices – a clean deposit, a certificate of deposit, a bill of exchange, a treasury bill, commercial paper or a repo. With a repo, the investor can look to the credit standing of both the counterparty and the issuer of the collateral. It also has the advantage that the investor can determine both the exact maturity and exact amount of the investment – features not shared by some of the other instruments. A repo also offers a range of risk/reward profiles. For example, a bilateral repo secured against government T-bills offers very little risk, and a correspondingly low return (often below LIBID, although if the seller is not of top creditworthiness, the return will often be above LIBID and can be above LIBOR, particularly with a triparty or HIC repo). A hold-in-custody repo, or a repo based on low quality collateral on the other hand, offers a higher return but higher risk – because of the possibility of default of either the counterparty or the collateral issuer, or both.

Matched book dealing – taking a view on interest rates

A "matched book" dealer is not in fact a dealer who always keeps his trading book completely matched, but rather a dealer who trades repos and might take a position on repo interest rates.

Matched book dealing is trading in repos.	**Key Point**

If a dealer has a view on interest rates – for example that short-term rates will rise – he can borrow cash through a longer-term repo and lend it through a shorter-term reverse. If he is correct, he can then lend out the cash again through a new reverse repo when the first one matures. This is equivalent to selling short-term futures or buying an FRA. Having taken such a view, the position can in fact later be hedged through FRAs or futures if the dealer changes his mind.

Matched book dealing – taking a view on specials

A dealer may reverse in a bond which he believes will become special in due course, repoing it out on the other side for only a short period. If he is correct, he will be able to roll over the repo at a lower rate later.

Fund management – yield enhancement

If a fund manager does not need funds, but owns a security in demand, he can use this special to repo in cash which he can then reverse out again against general collateral. Because the general collateral can be of the same credit-worthiness as the special, he is using his existing portfolio to make an extra yield without sacrificing anything with regard to credit risk. The profit made is simply the difference between the two repo rates, for the period of the repo.

Fund managers – leverage

The manager of a "hedge fund" (generally a leveraged fund) can leverage his portfolio through repo, by using his existing holdings as collateral to repo in more cash, which he then invests in new securities. The process can be repeated to leverage as far as prudence and margin requirements allow. Similarly, he can short securities in a leveraged way by reversing them in against cash, selling them and then repeating the cycle.

Cash and carry arbitrage

In Chapter 5 on bond market calculations, we saw that a theoretical bond futures price comes from the following: if you sell a bond futures contract, buy a deliverable bond for cash and fund the bond purchase until delivery of the bond futures contract, this should result in zero profit or loss. Financing the bond purchase is likely to be done through the repo market, so the funding rate concerned is the repo rate.

As in all markets however, the actual futures market price is sometimes slightly out of line with what it should be theoretically. If the current futures price is theoretically too high relative to the bond price and repo rate, there will be an arbitrage opportunity available as follows: sell the futures contract, buy the bond and do a repo. This is called a "cash-and-carry arbitrage".

If the current futures price is theoretically too low relative to the bond price and repo rate, there will again be an arbitrage opportunity available, the other way round: buy the futures contract, sell the bond and do a reverse repo. This is called a "reverse cash-and-carry arbitrage".

Hedging derivatives positions

When an interest rate swap (IRS) dealer establishes a position, he is imme-diately vulnerable to a change in long-term interest rates. One way of reducing this risk is to buy or sell a bond with similar modified duration to the swap. Similarly, when a bond option dealer buys or sells bond options for example, he is exposed to the risk that the price of the underlying bond will change. He can delta hedge by buying or selling an appropriate amount of the bond. These points are covered in more detail in other chapters. The important point here however is that, in either case, in order to finance the bond purchase or cover the short bond position, the dealer can then repo or reverse the bond.

Central banks

The development of a healthy domestic repo market is important to a central bank partly because it reduces risk in the banking system (secured lending is safer than unsecured lending) and partly because it facilitates derivatives hedging as mentioned above. The development of a healthy domestic repo market also encourages the development of a strong bond market. A more efficient and liquid bond market in turn helps to facilitate the government's issuance of bonds when it needs to borrow, and should also reduce the government's cost of borrowing slightly, as a greater demand for the bonds should tend to lower yields. Repo also provides a mechanism for the central bank's intervention in the money market. When there is a shortage of liquidity in the market due to temporary cashflow fluctuations, a central bank can add cash to the banking system by lending cash to the banks against collateral, and when it wishes to drain liquidity from the banking system it can borrow cash against collateral. Many central banks also use repos as the mechanism through which changes in interest rate levels are signalled to the market.

It is important to be careful about the terminology here however, as these operations are generally viewed from the commercial banking system's viewpoint rather than the central bank's viewpoint. Thus when we say "the Bank of England is doing repos", it is in fact the banking system that is doing repos and the Bank of England that is doing reverse repos – and thereby putting liquidity *into* the market. Similarly, when we say "the central bank is doing reverse repos", we mean that the central bank is doing repos and is *draining* liquidity from the system.

In the USA in particular, even more care is needed because another way of saying "the Federal Reserve ("Fed") is doing reverse repos" is "the Fed is doing matched sale-purchases" (MSPs).

In operations of the European Central Bank system, the general term "reverse transactions" or "reverse operations" can refer to either lending or borrowing cash. "Refinancing operations" refers to the central bank lending cash to the banking system.

The following is known as a "system repo" or a "central bank repo", despite the fact that strictly, the central bank is doing a reverse repo.

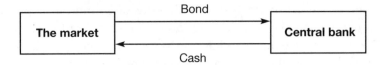

The following is known as a "system reverse" or a "central bank reverse", despite the fact that strictly, the central bank is doing a repo. In the USA, it is also known as an MSP.

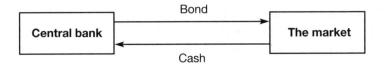

When the Fed or another central bank undertakes these transactions for liquidity management or reasons of interest rate policy, they are called "system repos" or "system reverses" because they are for the purpose of deliberate adjustment to the banking system. However the Fed also undertakes "customer repos", when it lends money to the banking system on behalf of the Fed's own clients – generally major foreign central banks and supranational bodies investing surplus funds – and normally announces the size of these transactions in advance in order not to disturb the market.

EXERCISES

60. You repo out €40 million face value of a 28-day French treasury bill. The treasury bill is trading at 5.2%. The repo is for 7 days at 5.3%. There is a 2% haircut. How much cash do you receive (rounded to the nearest €1,000)?

61. You borrow $30 million via a repo, using the US T-bond 5.75% of 17/8/2020. The repo is transacted at 3.97% from 13/3/2009 to 13/4/2009, with a 2.5% haircut. The current price of the bond is 97.32.

   a. What nominal amount of bond do you deliver at the beginning of the repo?

   b. What is the cash amount you repay at the end of the repo?

62. With the same information as in the previous question, the bond price rises to 99.14 on 28 March and there is a margin call. What is the cash value of the margin call and in which direction is it transferred?

63. A treasurer wants to borrow USD for 2 months, using his holding of CHF 20 million bonds in a cross-currency repo as follows:

Term:	5 July (spot) to 5 September
2-month USD repo rate:	4.80%
Haircut:	5%
Clean price of bond:	98.00
Coupon rate on bond:	5%
Previous coupon date:	21 March
Accrual basis:	30/360
Spot USD/CHF:	1.4735

a. How many USD does the treasurer receive on 5 July?

b. How many USD does he repay on 5 September?

64. You have borrowed £40,000,000 at 5.9% on 21/3/2008 via a repo using the 5.7% gilt of 15/4/2013. On 4/4/2008, you want to substitute the BTP 4.8% of 14/7/2019 for the gilt. How much nominal of the BTP do you need to deliver? The haircuts agreed are 3% for a cross-currency repo and 2% for a same currency repo. The spot EUR/GBP rate is 0.6540. The price of the gilt is 98.93. The price of the BTP is 101.24.

65. A coupon is paid during a buy/sell-back, 15 calendar days before maturity. The collateral is a gilt. The face value of the security is £20,000,000. The repo rate of the trade is 4.63%. The coupon rate is 5.75%. The current repo rate on coupon date is 4.37%. By what amount is the cash settlement on the forward date adjusted because of the coupon?

66. A dealer does the following buy/sell-back. What is the forward price (to six decimal places)?

Start date:	18 April 2009
Maturity date:	18 July 2009
Repo rate:	5.52%
Security:	€200 million 8% BTAN
Previous coupon date:	6 June 2008
Clean price of bond at start:	103.42
Haircut:	2.5%

67. You borrow a Bono (nominal €50 million) in a securities borrowing deal from 16 June 2009 to 23 June 2009. You provide an OLO as collateral. There is a 1% haircut. The lending fee is 35 basis points.

Bono lent:	5.45% of 21/3/2013
Price:	98.73

OLO collateral:	5.85% of 9/10/2029
Price:	100.34

a. What is the minimum face value of collateral required?

b. What is the amount of the lending fee?

68. The repo rate for GC is 6.37%. The current securities lending fee for a particular bond which has gone special is 60 bp. Approximately what would be the repo rate for that bond?

69. In the following securities lending transaction, you lend a bond against a CD.

a. What is the minimum face value of collateral required?

b. What is the amount of the lending fee?

Start date:	18 April 2008
Maturity date:	18 July 2008
Lending fee:	45 bp per annum
Security lent:	€50 million 6% Eurobond (30/360 basis)
Previous coupon date:	6 June 2007
Clean price of bond at start:	105.23
Collateral:	EUR CD with 4% coupon issue date: 14 March 2008; maturity: 14 September 2008 current market yield 5.85%
Initial margin:	3.0%

70. It is July 2008. A fund manager owns €50 million nominal of a 9% coupon (annual, ACT/ACT) government bond which is currently on special. He can repo this at 2.15% for 30 days and invest in 30-day euro treasury bills at a yield of 4.1%. The bond currently has a clean price of 110.54 and 45 days' accrued coupon. Assuming no haircut, how much profit in EUR can he make?

"A zero-coupon yield is unambiguous: it is simply a measure of the relationship between a single future value and its present value."

■ ■ ■

7

Zero-coupon Rates and Yield Curves

ZERO-COUPON YIELDS AND PAR YIELDS

Constructing par yields from zero-coupon yields

A zero-coupon instrument is one which pays no coupon. For example, a company might issue a 5-year bond with a face value of 100 but no coupon. Clearly investors would not pay 100 for this; they would pay considerably less to allow for the fact that alternative investments would earn them interest. A zero-coupon yield is the yield earned on such an instrument, taking into account the fact that it is purchased for less than its face value. It is the (annual) interest rate which it is necessary to use to discount the future value of the instrument (i.e. its face value) to the price paid for it now. This interest rate is always given as the decompounded rate, not the simple annual rate (i.e. in this example, it is not sufficient just to divide the difference between face value and purchase price by 5).

In many markets and periods, there may be no zero-coupon instrument available. There must nevertheless be a theoretical zero-coupon rate which is consistent with the "usual" interest rates available in the market – that is, the yields on coupon-bearing instruments. A clear advantage of zero-coupon yields over these "usual" yields to maturity is that they avoid the question of reinvestment risk.

A par yield is the yield to maturity of a coupon-bearing bond priced at par. The reason for considering par yields in particular rather than coupon-bearing bond yields in general is that anything else would be arbitrary. We could, for example, consider a range of existing five-year bonds – one with a 3 percent coupon, one with a 7 percent coupon and one with a 12 percent coupon. Even assuming the same issuer for all the bonds and no tax or other "hidden" effects, we would not expect the market yield to be exactly the same for the three bonds. The cashflows are on average rather further in the future in the case of the 3 percent coupon bond, than in the case of the 12 percent coupon bond; if longer-term yields are higher than shorter-term yields, for example, the later cashflows should be worth relatively more than the early cashflows, so that the 3 percent coupon bond should have a slightly higher yield than the 12 percent coupon bond. The 7 percent coupon bond's yield should lie between the other two. Rather than choose one of these (or even a different one) arbitrarily, we choose a bond priced at par to be "representative" of coupon-bearing yields for that particular maturity. On a coupon date, this is a bond whose coupon is the same as the yield.

Clearly however it is very unlikely at any one time that there will be a bond priced exactly at par for any particular maturity. Therefore we probably need to use actual non-par, coupon-bearing bond yields available in the market to construct the equivalent zero-coupon yields. From there, we can go on to construct what the par yields would be if there were any par bonds. It should be noted of course that there is not only one par yield curve or one zero-coupon yield curve. Rather, there are as many par yield curves as there are issuers. Government bond yields will generally be lower than corporate bond yields or interest rate swap yields, for example. Associated with each par yield curve is a separate zero-coupon yield curve – also known as a spot yield curve.

It is probably clearest to begin constructing these relationships from the zero-coupon yield curve. A zero-coupon yield or spot yield is unambiguous: it is simply a measure of the relationship between a single future value and its present value. If we then know the market's view of what zero-coupon yields are for all periods, we can calculate precisely the NPV of a series of bond cashflows by discounting each cashflow at the zero-coupon rate for that particular period. The result will be the price for that bond exactly consistent with the zero-coupon curve. A single yield – the internal rate of return – can then be calculated which would arrive at this same price; this single yield is the usual "yield to maturity" quoted for the bond. If we can then construct a bond where the NPV calculated in this way using the zero-coupon rates is 100, the coupon of this bond is the par yield.

Suppose that we have the following zero-coupon yield structure:

Example 7.1

1-year:	10.000%
2-year:	10.526%
3-year:	11.076%
4-year:	11.655%

What are the zero-coupon discount factors? What would be the prices and yields to maturity of:

a. a 4-year, 5% coupon bond?
b. a 4-year, 11.5% coupon bond?
c. a 4-year, 13% coupon bond?

The zero-coupon discount factors are:

1-year: $\dfrac{1}{(1.1)} = 0.90909$

2-year: $\dfrac{1}{(1.10526)^2} = 0.81860$

3-year: $\dfrac{1}{(1.11076)^3} = 0.72969$

4-year: $\dfrac{1}{(1.11655)^4} = 0.64341$

(a) Price = $(5 \times 0.90909) + (5 \times 0.81860) + (5 \times 0.72969) + (105 \times 0.64341) = 79.84$

Yield to maturity = 11.58% (using TVM function of HP calculator)

(b) Price = (11.5 × 0.90909) + (11.5 × 0.81860) + (11.5 × 0.72969) +
            (111.5 × 0.64341) = 100.00

Yield to maturity = 11.50% (the par yield is the same as the coupon because the bond is priced at par)

(c) Price = (13 × 0.90909) + (13 × 0.81860) + (13 × 0.72969) +
            (113 × 0.64341) = 104.65

Yield to maturity = 11.49% (using TVM function of HP calculator)

1.1 ☐ $^1/_x$	(1-year discount factor)
1.10526 ENTER 2 ☐ ∧ ☐ $^1/_x$	(2-year discount factor)
1.11076 ENTER 3 ☐ ∧ ☐ $^1/_x$	(3-year discount factor)
1.11655 ENTER 4 ☐ ∧ ☐ $^1/_x$	(4-year discount factor)
.90909 ENTER .8186 + .72969 + 5 ×	
105 ENTER .64341 × +	(Price of (a))
FIN TVM $^+/_-$ PV	
4 N 5 PMT 100 FV I %YR	(Yield to maturity of (a))
.90909 ENTER .8186 + .72969 + 11.5 ×	
111.5 ENTER .64341 × +	(Price of (b))
.90909 ENTER .8186 + .72969 + 13 ×	
113 ENTER .64341 × +	(Price of (c))
$^+/_-$ PV 13 PMT I %YR	(Yield to maturity of (c))

It can be seen from (b) above that if the zero-coupon discount factor for k years is df_k, and the par yield for N years is i, it will always be the case that:

$$(i \times df_1) + (i \times df_2) + ... + (i \times df_N) + (1 \times df_N) = 1$$

This gives: $i \times (df_1 + df_2 + ... + df_N) = 1 - df_N$

Therefore: $i = \dfrac{1 - df_N}{\sum\limits_{k=1}^{N} df_k}$

Calculation summary

$$\text{Par yield for N years} = \frac{1 - df_N}{\sum\limits_{k=1}^{N} df_k}$$

where: df_k = zero-coupon discount factor for k years

Zero-coupon yields from coupon-bearing yields

In Example 7.1, we effectively calculated the 4-year par yield (11.50%) from the series of zero-coupon yields. We can similarly calculate a zero-coupon yield from a series of coupon-bearing yields. A method to do this is to build up synthetic zero-coupon structures by combining a series of instruments such that all the cashflows net to zero except for the first and the last.

Suppose that the 1-year interest rate is 10% and that a series of bonds is currently priced as follows:

Example 7.2

	Price	Coupon	Maturity
Bond A	97.409	9	2 years
Bond B	85.256	5	3 years
Bond C	104.651	13	4 years

Consider a 2-year investment of 97.409 to purchase 100 face value of bond A and a 1-year borrowing of 8.182 at 10.0%. The cashflows are:

Year			Net cashflows
0	– 97.409	+ 8.182	– 89.227
1	+ 9.000	– 9.000	
2	– 109.000		+ 109.000

In this way, we have constructed what is in effect a synthetic 2-year zero-coupon instrument, because there are no cashflows between now and maturity. The amount of 8.182 was calculated as the amount necessary to achieve 9.00 after 1 year – that is, the present value of 9.00 after 1 year.

The 2-year zero-coupon rate is therefore $\left(\dfrac{109.00}{89.227}\right)^{\frac{1}{2}} - 1 = 10.526\%$

Next, consider a 3-year investment of 85.256 to purchase 100 face value of bond B, a 1-year borrowing of 4.545 at 10.0% and a 2-year zero-coupon borrowing of 4.093 at 10.526%. The cashflows are:

Year				Net cashflows
0	– 85.256	+ 4.545	+ 4.093	– 76.618
1	+ 5.000	– 5.000		
2	+ 5.000		– 5.000	
3	– 105.000			+ 105.000

The 3-year zero-coupon rate is $\left(\dfrac{105.00}{76.618}\right)^{\frac{1}{3}} - 1 = 11.076\%$

Again, 4.545 is the present value of 5.00 after 1 year; 4.093 is the present value of 5.00 after 2 years.

Finally, consider a 4-year investment of 104.651 to purchase 100 face value of bond C, a 1-year borrowing of 11.818 at 10%, a 2-year zero-coupon borrowing of 10.642 at 10.526% and a 3-year zero-coupon borrowing of 9.486 at 11.076%. The cashflows are:

Year					Net cashflows
0	– 104.651	+ 11.818	+ 10.642	+ 9.486	– 72.705
1	+ 13.000	– 13.000			
2	+ 13.000			– 13.000	
3	+ 13.000		– 13.000		
4	+ 113.000				+ 113.000

The 4-year zero-coupon rate is $\left(\dfrac{113.000}{72.705}\right)^{\frac{1}{4}} - 1 = 11.655\%$

This process of building up a series of zero-coupon yields from coupon-bearing yields is known as "bootstrapping". In Example 7.2, we used three bonds as our starting point, none of which was priced at par. We could instead have used bonds priced at par, or time deposits (which also return the same original principal amount at maturity). In the case of interest rate swaps, for example, we would indeed expect to have par swap rates as our starting point. The bootstrapping process is exactly the same, with initial cashflows of 100 each instead of the non-par bond prices (97.409, 85.256 and 104.651) in Example 7.2. As long as we have four different investments, it is possible to build a synthetic zero-coupon structure and hence calculate the four-year, zero-coupon yield.

The zero-coupon rates calculated in Example 7.2 are in fact the same ones as used in Example 7.1. We can see that the rates are consistent, in that in Example 7.1 we have already used these zero-coupon rates to value the 4-year 13% coupon bond and arrived at the same price. The process is circular.

If all market prices and yields are consistent, it will not matter which existing bonds we use to construct the zero-coupon yields. In practice however, they will not be exactly consistent and it is generally preferable to use bonds priced as closely as possible to par.

There are two more very important practical issues which we shall mention, but which are beyond the scope of this book. First, it is not generally possible in practice to find a series of existing bonds with the most convenient maturities – say 1 year, 2 years, 3 years, 4 years, etc. – from which we can construct the zero-coupon rates. Instead, we must use what are actually available. Second, we need to interpolate between existing yields in order to establish rates for all possible maturities. To do this, we must somehow fit a curve along all the points. This requires assumptions to be made about the mathematical nature of the curve, and some degree of compromise in order to make the curve smooth.

FORWARD-FORWARD YIELDS

Constructing forward-forward yields from zero-coupon yields

In Chapter 3, we constructed short-term forward-forward rates from a series of "normal" rates for periods beginning now. Exactly the same approach can be used for constructing long-term, forward-forward yields from long-term, zero-coupon yields.

Example 7.3 Suppose the same zero-coupon curve as in Example 7.1. What are the 1-year v 2-year forward-forward yield, the 2-year v 3-year forward-forward yield and the 1-year v 3-year forward-forward zero-coupon yield?

Using the 1-year zero-coupon rate of 10.000%, an amount of 1 now has a future value after 1 year of 1.10000.

Using the 2-year zero coupon rate of 10.526%, an amount of 1 now has a future value after 2 years of $(1.10526)^2$.

It follows that an amount worth 1.1000 after 1 year is worth $(1.10526)^2$ after 2 years. The yield linking these two amounts over that 1-year forward-forward period is:

$$\frac{(1.10526)^2}{(1.10000)} - 1 = 11.055\%$$

This is therefore the 1-year v 2-year forward-forward yield.

Using the 3-year zero-coupon rate of 11.076%, an amount of 1 now has a future value after 3 years of $(1.11076)^3$.

The 2-year v 3-year forward-forward rate is therefore:

$$\frac{(1.11076)^3}{(1.10526)^2} - 1 = 12.184\%$$

The relationship between an amount after 1 year and an amount after 3 years is:

$$\frac{(1.11076)^3}{(1.10000)} = 1.2459$$

The 1-year v 3-year zero-coupon forward-forward is therefore:

$$(1.2459)^{1/2} - 1 = 11.618\%$$

In general, if z_k and z_m are the zero-coupon yields for k years and m years respectively, we have the following:

Forward-forward zero-coupon yield from k years to m years is:

$$\left[\frac{(1 + z_m)^m}{(1 + z_k)^k} \right]^{\frac{1}{(m-k)}} - 1$$

Calculation summary

In particular, the forward-forward yield from k years to (k + 1) years is:

$$\frac{(1 + z_{k+1})^{k+1}}{(1 + z_k)^k} - 1$$

Zero-coupon yields from forward-forward yields

In Chapter 3, we first used "normal" interest rates to calculate forward-forward rates. We then said that this approach could be reversed. It may make more sense to begin with the question: what does the market expect interest rates to be in the future? From this, we can construct a series of "normal" rates.

Exactly the same question arises with long-term, forward-forward yields and zero-coupon yields.

Example 7.4

The 1-year interest rate is now 10%. The market expects 1-year rates to rise to 11.05% after one year and to 12.18% after a further year. What would you expect the current 2-year and 3-year zero-coupon yields to be, consistent with these expectations?

An amount of 1 now will be worth $(1 + 10\%) = 1.10$ after one year. This is expected to increase by a further 11.05% and 12.18% in the following two years. We can therefore construct a strip of rates for the expected value at the end of three years:

$$1.10 \times 1.1105 \times 1.1218 = 1.3703$$

The 3-year zero-coupon rate should therefore be:

$$\left(\frac{1.3703}{1}\right)^{\frac{1}{3}} - 1 = 11.07\%$$

The result of Example 7.4 is consistent with our earlier examples, demonstrating that we could begin with a forward-forward yield curve (that is, a series of 1-year, forward-forward rates), create from them a consistent zero-coupon yield curve, and then create a consistent par yield curve.

Calculation summary

$$z_k = [(1 + i_1) \times (1 + i_2) \times (1 + i_3) \times \ldots \times (1 + i_k)]^{\frac{1}{k}} - 1$$

where: $i_1, i_2, i_3 \ldots i_k$ are the 1-year cash interest rate and the 1-year v 2-year, 2-year v 3-year, ..., (k −1)-year v k-year forward-forward rates

SUMMARY

Although all the yields we have considered should in theory be consistent, actual market yields might not be. This is important for bond valuation. A bond trading in the market has an actual known market price at which traders are willing to sell it. An investor can calculate the yield to maturity implied by this price and decide whether he considers the bond a good investment. However he can also calculate what the theoretical price should be if all the bond's cashflows are individually valued to an NPV using a series of separate zero-coupon rates. The result may in practice be different from the actual market price. The investor then needs to decide whether, if the theoretical price is lower, he considers the bond overpriced.

Generally, there is no exact arbitrage to bring the market price precisely in line with this theoretical price, because there are no corresponding zero-coupon instruments. The zero-coupon yields are themselves often theoretical. It is therefore often more a question of using zero-coupon yields to compare different bonds, to see which is better value at current market prices. In the case of government securities where the bonds themselves can be stripped however, a direct comparison can be made between the price of the bond and the prices of its stripped components, so that the arbitrage is possible.

Conversion between yield curves

- To create a zero-coupon yield from coupon-bearing yields: **bootstrap**

- To calculate the yield to maturity on a non-par coupon-bearing bond from zero-coupon yields: **calculate the NPV of the bond using the zero-coupon yields, then calculate the yield to maturity of the bond from this dirty price**

- To create a par yield from zero-coupon yields: **use the formula above**

- To create a forward-forward yield from zero-coupon yields: **use the formula above**

- To create a zero-coupon yield from forward-forward yields: **create a strip of the first cash leg with a series of forward-forwards**

A par yield curve tends to be exaggerated by the corresponding zero-coupon curve. That is, a positive par yield curve is reflected by a more positive zero-coupon curve and a negative par yield curve by a more negative zero-coupon curve. The forward-forward curve tends to exaggerate further a change in shape of the zero-coupon curve (see Figure 7.1).

Comparison between par, zero-coupon and forward-forward yields

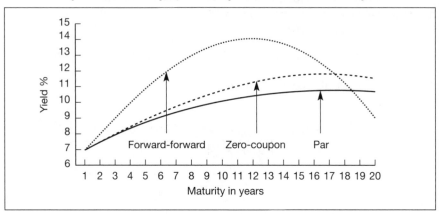

LONGER-DATED FRAs

In Chapter 3, we considered FRAs up to one year. For FRAs beyond a year, the calculation of a theoretical FRA price is complicated by the fact that deposits over one year generally pay some interest at the end of the first year or each six months. There are two approaches to this. The first is to consider all the cashflows involved; the second is to calculate zero-coupon discount factors and then use these to calculate an FRA rate.

Example 7.5 Given the following interest rates, what is the theoretical 15 v 18 FRA rate? All rates are on an ACT/360 basis.

12 months (365 days): 8.5%
15 months (456 days): 8.6% (interest paid after 12 months and 15 months)
18 months (548 days): 8.7% (interest paid after 12 months and 18 months)

First approach

Consider an amount of 1 deposited for 12 months, rolled over at the 12 v 18 FRA rate. The result after 18 months will be:

$$\left(1 + 0.085 \times \frac{365}{360}\right) \times \left(1 + [12 \text{ v } 18 \text{ FRA}] \times \frac{183}{360}\right)$$

The same result should be achieved by depositing for 18 months and rolling over the interim interest payment (received after 12 months) at the 12 v 18 FRA rate:

$$1 + \left[0.087 \times \frac{365}{360} \times \left(1 + [12 \text{ v } 18 \text{ FRA}] \times \frac{183}{360}\right)\right] + \left[0.087 \times \frac{183}{360}\right]$$

If these two are equal, we can calculate the 12 v 18 FRA as:

$$12 \text{ v } 18 \text{ FRA} = \left[\frac{\left(1 + 0.087 \times \frac{183}{360}\right)}{\left(1 + 0.085 \times \frac{365}{360} - 0.087 \times \frac{365}{360}\right)} - 1\right] \times \frac{360}{183} = 9.1174\%$$

The same result should *also* be achieved by depositing for 15 months and rolling over at the 15 v 18 FRA rate, with the interim interest payment (received after 12 months) rolled over from 12 months to 18 months at the 12 v 18 FRA rate. The result after 18 months will be:

$$\left[0.086 \times \frac{365}{360} \times \left(1 + 0.091174 \times \frac{183}{360}\right)\right] + \left[\left(1 + 0.086 \times \frac{91}{360}\right) + \left(1 + [15 \text{ v } 18 \text{ FRA}] \times \frac{92}{360}\right)\right]$$

If this is equal to the first result, we have:

15 v 18 FRA =

$$\left[\frac{\left(1 + 0.085 \times \frac{365}{360}\right) \times \left(1 + 0.091174 \times \frac{183}{360}\right) - \left[0.086 \times \frac{365}{360} \times \left(1 + 0.091174 \times \frac{183}{360}\right)\right]}{\left(1 + 0.086 \times \frac{91}{360}\right)} - 1\right] \times \frac{360}{92}$$

= 9.02%

Second approach

The 12-month discount factor is $\dfrac{1}{\left(1 + 0.085 \times \frac{365}{360}\right)} = 0.92066$

Consider the following cashflows (a 15-month deposit and a 12-month borrowing):

Months			Net
0	−100	+(8.6 × $\frac{365}{360}$ × 0.92066)	− 91.9724
12	+(8.6 × $\frac{365}{360}$)	−(8.6 × $\frac{365}{360}$)	
15	+(100 + 8.6 × $\frac{91}{360}$)		+102.1739

The 15-month discount factor is $\dfrac{91.9724}{102.1739} = 0.90016$

Now consider the following cashflows (an 18-month deposit and a 12-month borrowing):

Months			Net
0	-100	$+(8.7 \times \frac{365}{360} \times 0.92066)$	-91.8790
12	$+(8.7 \times \frac{365}{360})$	$-(8.7 \times \frac{365}{360})$	
18	$+(100 + 8.7 \times \frac{183}{360})$		$+104.4225$

The 18-month discount factor is $\dfrac{91.8790}{104.4225} = 0.87988$

The 15 v 18 FRA is therefore $\left[\dfrac{\frac{1}{0.87988}}{\frac{1}{0.90016}} - 1 \right] \times \dfrac{360}{92} = 9.02\ \%$

The two approaches are effectively the same; the second is rather more structured.

EXERCISES

71. Calculate the 2-year, 3-year and 4-year zero-coupon yields and discount factors consistent with the following bonds. The 1-year yield is 10.00%.

Maturity	Coupon		Price
2 years	9.0%	(annual)	97.70
3 years	7.0%	(annual)	90.90
4 years	11.0%	(annual)	99.40

What are the 1-year v 2-year, 2-year v 3-year and 3-year v 4-year forward-forward yields?

72. The forward-forward curve is as follows:

1-year yield:	8.00%
1-year v 2-year:	8.24%
2-year v 3-year:	9.00%
3-year v 4-year:	9.50%

a. Calculate the 2-year, 3-year and 4-year zero-coupon yields and par yields.

b. What is the yield to maturity of a 4-year 12% annual coupon bond, consistent with the rates above?

73. What is the 18 v 24 FRA rate based on the following? All rates are ACT/360.

6 months (182 days):	8.60% / 8.70%
12 months (365 days):	8.70% / 8.80%
18 months (548 days):	8.80% / 8.90% (interest paid 6-monthly)
24 months (730 days):	8.90% / 9.00% (interest paid 6-monthly)

Part 3

Foreign Exchange

"A forward foreign exchange swap is a temporary purchase or sale of one currency against another. An equivalent effect could be achieved by borrowing one currency, while lending the other."

■ ■ ■

8

Foreign Exchange

Throughout this book, we have mostly used ISO codes (also used by the SWIFT system) to abbreviate currency names. You can find a list of the codes in Appendix 5 for reference.

INTRODUCTION

A convention has been used that, for example, the US dollar/Japanese yen exchange rate is written as USD/JPY if it refers to the number of yen equal to 1 US dollar and JPY/USD if it refers to the number of US dollars equal to 1 yen. The currency code written on the left is the "base" currency; there is always 1 of the base unit. The currency code written on the right is the "variable" currency (or "counter" currency or "quoted" currency). The number of units of this currency equal to 1 of the base currency varies according to the exchange rate. Although some people do use the precisely opposite convention, the one we use here is the more common. The important point to remember is to be consistent.

SPOT EXCHANGE RATES

A "spot" transaction is an outright purchase or sale of one currency for another currency, for delivery two working days after the dealing date (the date on which the contract is made). This allows time for the necessary paperwork and cash transfers to be arranged. Normally, therefore, if a spot deal is contracted on Monday, Tuesday or Wednesday, delivery will be two days after (i.e. Wednesday, Thursday or Friday respectively). If a spot deal is contracted on a Thursday or Friday, the delivery date is on Monday or Tuesday respectively, as neither Saturday nor Sunday are working days in the major markets.

There are however some exceptions. For example, a price for USD/CAD without qualification generally implies delivery on the next working day after the dealing day. Outside Canada, this is often referred to as "funds". A "spot" price (value two working days after the dealing day, as usual) can generally be requested as an alternative. Another problem arises in trading Middle East currencies where the relevant markets are closed on Friday but open on Saturday. A USD/SAR spot deal on Wednesday would need to have a split settlement date: the USD would be settled on Friday, but the SAR on Saturday.

If the spot date falls on a public holiday in one or both of the centres of the two currencies involved, the next working day is taken as the value date. For example, if a spot GBP/USD deal is transacted on Thursday 31 August, it would normally be for value Monday 4 September. If this date is a holiday in the UK or the USA however, all spot transactions on Thursday 31 August are for value Tuesday 5 September. If the intervening day (between today and spot) is a holiday in one only of the two centres, the spot value date is usually also delayed by one day.

How spot rates are quoted

In the foreign exchange market, a variable number of units of one currency is quoted per one unit of another currency. When quoting against the euro, it is the practice in the interbank market to quote all currencies in terms of a varying number of units of currency per 1 euro. In other words, the euro is, by convention, always the base currency if it is one of the two currencies involved. Similarly, apart from the euro, it is the interbank convention to quote most currencies against the US dollar using the dollar as the base currency.

There are however some currencies which are conventionally quoted as the base currency against the USD. Apart from the euro, the major ones are sterling, Australian dollar and New Zealand dollar.

The Canadian dollar is generally quoted as the variable currency against USD (this is sometimes known as "Canada Funds"), although the other way round is possible (sometimes known as "Canada cross").

In the currency futures markets, as opposed to the interbank market, quotations against the US dollar usually have USD as the variable currency.

Although dealing is possible between any two convertible currencies – for example, New Zealand dollars against euros or Swiss francs against Japanese yen – the interbank market historically quoted mostly against US dollars, so reducing the number of individual rates that needed to be quoted. The exchange rate between any two non-US dollar currencies could then be calculated from the rate for each currency against US dollars. A rate between any two currencies, neither of which is the dollar, is known as a cross-rate. The cross-rates themselves (for example, euro/sterling, euro/yen, euro/Swiss franc) have however increasingly been traded between banks in addition to the dollar-based rates. This sometimes reflects the importance of the relationship between the pair of currencies. The economic relationship between the Swiss franc and the euro, for example, is closer than the relationship between the Swiss franc and the dollar. It is therefore more true nowadays to say that the dollar/franc exchange rate is a function of the euro/dollar rate and the euro/franc rate, rather than that the euro/franc rate is a function of the euro/dollar rate and the dollar/franc rate. However, the principle of calculating cross-rates remains the same.

As in other markets, a bank normally quotes a two-way price, whereby it indicates at what level it is prepared to buy the base currency against the variable currency (the "bid" for the base currency – a cheaper rate), and at what level it is prepared to sell the base currency against the variable currency (the "offer" of the base currency – a more expensive rate). For example, if a bank is prepared to buy dollars for 1.2375 Swiss francs, and sell dollars for 1.2385 Swiss francs, the USD/CHF rate would be quoted as: 1.2375 / 1.2385.

The quoting bank buys the base currency (in this case, dollars) on the left and sells the base currency on the right. If the bank quotes such a rate to a company or other counterparty, the counterparty would sell the base currency on the left, and buy the base currency on the right – the opposite of how the bank sees the deal.

In the money markets, the order of quotation is not important and it does differ between markets. From a quotation of either "5.80% / 5.85%" or "5.85% / 5.80%", it is always clear to the customer that the higher rate is the offered rate and the lower rate is the bid rate. In foreign exchange however, the market-maker's bid for the base currency (the lower number in a spot price) is always on the left. This is particularly important in forward prices.

The difference between the two sides of the quotation is known as the "spread". Historically, a two-way price in a cross-rate would have a wider spread than a two-way price in a dollar-based rate, because the cross-rate constructed from the dollar-based rates would combine both the spreads. Now however the spread in the cross-rate could be narrower than the spread in the dollar-based exchange rate, if it is the cross-rate that is "driving" the market, as noted above.

Any quotation with a particular currency as the base currency can be converted into the equivalent quotation with that currency as the variable currency, by taking its reciprocal. Thus, a USD/CHF quotation of 1.2375 / 1.2385 can be converted to a CHF/USD quotation of $(1 \div 1.2375)/(1 \div 1.2385)$. However this would still be quoted with a smaller number on the left, so that the two sides of the quotation are reversed: 0.8074/0.8081. In either case, the bank buys the base currency against the variable currency on the left, sells the base currency against the variable currency on the right.

Rates are normally quoted to $\frac{1}{100}$ th of a cent, etc. (known as a "point" or a "pip"). Thus the US dollar/Swiss franc rate would usually be quoted as 1.2375 / 1.2385, for example. This depends on the size of the number however, and in the case of USD/JPY for example, which might be quoted say "105.05 / 15", "15 points" means 0.15 yen.

As the first three digits of the exchange rate (known as the "big figure") do not change in the short term, dealers generally do not mention them when dealing in the interbank market. In the example above (1.2375 / 1.2385), the quotation would therefore be given as simply 75 / 85. However when dealers are quoting a rate to a corporate client, they will often mention the big figure also. In this case, the quotation would be 1.2375 / 85.

As the market moves very quickly, dealers need to deal with great speed and therefore abbreviate when dealing. For example, if one dealer wishes to buy USD 5 million from another who is quoting him a USD/CHF price, he will say simply "5 mine"; this means "I wish to buy from you 5 million of the base currency and sell the other currency, at your offered price". Similarly, if he wishes to sell USD 5 million, he will say simply "5 yours", meaning "I wish to sell you 5 million of the base currency and buy the other currency, at your bid price".

To earn profit from dealing, the bank's objective is clearly to sell the base currency at the highest rate it can against the variable currency and buy the base currency at the lowest rate.

Example 8.1

| Deal 1: | Bank buys USD 1,000,000 against CHF at 1.2830 |
| Deal 2: | Bank sells USD 1,000,000 against CHF at 1.2855 |

	Inflows	*Outflows*
Deal 1:	USD 1,000,000	CHF 1,283,000
Deal 2:	CHF 1,285,500	USD 1,000,000
Net result:	CHF 2,500	

Dealers generally operate on the basis of small percentage profits but large turnover. These rates will be good for large, round amounts. For very large amounts, or for smaller amounts, a bank would normally quote a wider spread. The amount for which a quotation is "good" (that is, a valid quote on which the dealer will deal) will vary to some extent with the currency concerned and market conditions.

Cross-rates

As indicated above, if the euro is involved in an exchange rate, it is generally the base currency. Apart from that, if sterling, Australian dollar, New Zealand dollar or US dollar are included, they would generally be the base currency. In other cases, there is not a universal convention for which way round to quote a cross-rate – that is, which is the base currency and which the variable currency. If a rate between CHF and NOK is requested "in NOK terms", for example, this would generally mean that NOK is the base and CHF the variable.

Example 8.2

Suppose that we need to quote to a counterparty a spot rate between the Canadian dollar and the Singapore dollar, and that our bank does not have a CAD/SGD trading book. The rate must therefore be constructed from the prices quoted by our bank's USD/CAD dealer and our bank's USD/SGD dealer as follows:

| Spot USD/CAD: | 1.1474 / 1.1479 |
| Spot USD/SGD: | 1.5782 / 1.5792 |

Consider first the left side of the final CAD/SGD price we are constructing. This is the price at which our bank will buy CAD (the base currency) and sell SGD. We must therefore ask: at which price (1.1474 or 1.1479) does our USD/CAD dealer buy CAD against USD, and at which price (1.5782 or 1.5792) does our USD/SGD dealer sell SGD against USD? The answers are 1.1479 (on the right) and 1.5782 (on the left) respectively. Effectively, by dealing at these prices, our bank is both selling USD (against CAD) and buying USD (against SGD) simultaneously, with a net zero effect in USD. If we now consider the right side of the final CAD/SGD price we are constructing, this will come from selling CAD against USD (on the left at 1.1474) and buying SGD against USD (on the right at 1.5792). Finally, since each 1 dollar is worth 1.14 Canadian dollars and also 1.57 Singapore dollars, the CAD/SGD exchange rate must be the ratio between these two:

> 1.5782 ÷ 1.1479 = 1.3749 is how the bank sells SGD and buys CAD
> 1.5792 ÷ 1.1474 = 1.3763 is how the bank buys SGD and sells CAD

Therefore the spot CAD/SGD rate is: 1.3749 / 1.3763.

In summary, therefore, to calculate a spot cross-rate from two other rates which share the same base currency (in our example USD), divide opposite sides of the exchange rates. Following the same logic shows that to calculate a spot cross-rate from two other rates which share the same variable currency (also USD in the following example), we again need to divide opposite sides of the exchange rates.

Example 8.3

Spot EUR/USD: 1.2166 / 1.2171
Spot AUD/USD: 0.6834 / 0.6839

The EUR/USD dealer buys EUR and sells USD at 1.2166 (on the left).

The AUD/USD dealer sells AUD and buys USD at 0.6839 (on the right).

Therefore:

> 1.2166 ÷ 0.6839 = 1.7789 is how the bank buys EUR and sells AUD

Similarly:

> 1.2171 ÷ 0.6834 = 1.7809 is how the bank sells EUR and buys AUD

Therefore the spot EUR/AUD rate is: 1.7789 / 1.7809.

Finally, to calculate a cross-rate from two rates where the common currency is the base currency in one quotation but the variable currency in the other, following the same logic through again shows that we multiply the same sides of the exchange rates.

Example 8.4

Spot EUR/USD: 1.2166 / 1.2171
Spot USD/SGD: 1.6782 / 1.6792

The EUR/USD dealer buys EUR and sells USD at 1.2166 (on the left).

The USD/SGD dealer buys USD and sells SGD at 1.6782 (on the left).

Also, since each 1 euro is worth 1.21 US dollars, and each of these US dollars is worth 1.67 Singapore dollars, the EUR/SGD exchange rate must be the product of these two numbers. Therefore:

$1.2166 \times 1.6782 = 2.0417$ is how the bank buys EUR and sells SGD

Similarly:

$1.2171 \times 1.6792 = 2.0438$ is how the bank sells EUR and buys SGD

Therefore the spot EUR/SGD rate is: 2.0417 / 2.0438.

To calculate cross-rates	**Calculation summary**

■ From two rates with the same base currency or the same variable currency: divide opposite sides of the exchange rates

■ From two rates where the base currency in one is the same as the variable currency in the other: multiply the same sides of the exchange rates

---

The examples above all construct cross-rates from exchange rates involving the US dollar (which is often the case). The same approach applies when constructing other rates: considering the way in which each of the two separate dealers will deal to create the cross-rate gives the construction:

Example 8.5

Spot EUR/GBP: 0.7374 / 0.7379
Spot GBP/CHF: 2.1702 / 2.1707
Spot GBP/JPY: 192.70 / 193.00

1 To construct spot CHF/JPY:

$192.70 \div 2.1707 = 88.77$ is how the bank buys CHF and sells JPY
$193.00 \div 2.1702 = 88.93$ is how the bank sells CHF and buys JPY

Therefore the spot CHF/JPY rate is: 88.77/88.93.

2 To construct spot JPY/CHF:

$2.1702 \div 193.00 = 0.011245$ is how the bank buys JPY and sells CHF
$2.1707 \div 192.70 = 0.011265$ is how the bank sells JPY and buys CHF

Therefore the spot JPY/CHF is 0.011245/0.011265.

3 To construct spot EUR/CHF:

$0.7374 \times 2.1702 = 1.6003$ is how the bank buys EUR and sells CHF
$0.7379 \times 2.1707 = 1.6018$ is how the bank sells EUR and buys CHF

Therefore the spot EUR/CHF rate is: 1.6003/1.6018.

4 To construct spot CHF/EUR, take the reciprocal of the EUR/CHF:

$1 \div (0.7379 \times 2.1707) = 0.6243$ is how the bank buys CHF and sells EUR
$1 \div (0.7374 \times 2.1702) = 0.6249$ is how the bank sells CHF and buys EUR

Therefore the spot CHF/EUR rate is 0.6243 / 0.6249.

The construction of one exchange rate from two others in this way can be seen "algebraically":

> Given two exchange rates A/B and A/C, the cross-rates are:
>
> $$B/C = A/C \div A/B$$
> $$\text{and } C/B = A/B \div A/C$$
>
> Given two exchange rates B/A and A/C, the cross-rates are:
>
> $$B/C = B/A \times A/C$$
> $$\text{and } C/B = 1 \div (B/A \times A/C)$$
>
> When dividing, use opposite sides. When multiplying, use the same sides.

FORWARD EXCHANGE RATES

Forward outrights

Although "spot" is settled two working days in the future, it is not considered in the foreign exchange market as "future" or "forward", but as the baseline from which all other dates (earlier or later) are considered.

A "forward outright" is an outright purchase or sale of one currency in exchange for another currency for settlement on a fixed date in the future other than the spot value date. Rates are quoted in a similar way to those in the spot market, with the bank buying the base currency "low" (on the left side) and selling it "high" (on the right side). In some emerging markets, forward outrights are non-deliverable and are settled in cash against the spot rate at maturity as a contract for differences.

Example 8.6 The spot EUR/USD rate is 1.2166 / 1.2171, but the rate for value one month after the spot value date is 1.2186 / 1.2193.

The "spread" (the difference between the bank's buying price and the bank's selling price) is wider in the forward quotation than in the spot quotation. Also, in this example, the euro is worth more in the future than at the spot date. EUR 1 buys USD 1.2186 in one month's time as opposed to 1.2166 at present. In a different example, the euro might be worth less in the future than at the spot date.

The forward outright rate may be seen both as the market's assessment of where the spot rate will be in the future and as a reflection of current interest rates in the two currencies concerned.

Consider, for example, the following "round trip" transactions, all undertaken simultaneously:

1. Borrow dollars for 3 months starting from spot value date.
2. Sell dollars and buy euros for value spot.

3. Deposit the purchased euros for 3 months starting from spot value date.

4. Sell forward now the euro principal and interest which mature in 3 months' time, into dollars.

In general, the market will adjust the forward price for (4) so that these simultaneous transactions generate neither a profit nor a loss. When the four rates involved are not in line (USD interest rate, EUR/USD spot rate, EUR interest rate and EUR/USD forward rate), there is in fact opportunity for arbitrage – making a profit by round-tripping. That is, either the transactions as shown above will produce a profit or exactly the reverse transactions (borrow EUR, sell EUR spot, deposit USD, sell USD forward) will produce a profit. The supply and demand effect of this arbitrage activity is such as to move the rates back into line. If in fact this results in a forward rate which is out of line with the market's "average" view, supply and demand pressure will tend to move the spot rate or the interest rates until this is no longer the case.

In more detail, the transactions might be as follows:

1. Borrow USD 100 at an interest rate of v per annum. The principal and interest payment at maturity will be:

$$100 \times \left(1 + v \times \frac{days}{360}\right)$$

2. Sell USD 100 for EUR at spot rate to give EUR (100 ÷ spot).

3. Invest EUR (100 ÷ spot) at an interest rate of b per annum. The principal and interest returned at maturity will be:

$$(100 \div spot) \times \left(1 + b \times \frac{days}{360}\right)$$

4. Sell forward this last amount at the forward exchange rate to give:

$$USD\ (100 \div spot) \times \left(1 + b \times \frac{days}{360}\right) \times forward\ outright$$

Arbitrage activity will tend to make this the same amount as that in (1), so that:

$$Forward\ outright = spot \times \frac{\left(1 + v \times \frac{days}{360}\right)}{\left(1 + b \times \frac{days}{360}\right)}$$

$$Forward\ outright = spot \times \frac{\left(1 + variable\ currency\ interest\ rate \times \frac{days}{year}\right)}{\left(1 + base\ currency\ interest\ rate \times \frac{days}{year}\right)}$$

Calculation summary

Notice that the length of the year may be 360 or 365, depending on each currency.

Example 8.7

31-day USD interest rate: 5%
31-day EUR interest rate: 3%
Spot EUR/USD rate: 1.2168

$$\text{Then forward outright} = 1.2168 \times \frac{\left(1 + 0.05 \times \frac{31}{360}\right)}{\left(1 + 0.03 \times \frac{31}{360}\right)} = 1.2189$$

.05 ENTER 31 × 360 ÷ 1 +
.03 ENTER 31 × 360 ÷ 1 + ÷
1.2168 ×

Forward swaps

Although forward outrights are an important instrument, banks do not in practice deal between themselves in forward outrights, but rather in forward "swaps", where a forward swap is the difference between the spot and the forward outright. The reason for not dealing in outrights will become clear later. The forward outright rate can therefore be seen as a combination of the current spot rate and the forward swap rate (which may be positive or negative) added together.

Key Point

Forward outright = spot + forward swap

Example 8.8

Spot EUR/USD: 1.2166 / 1.2171
Forward swap: 0.0145 / 0.0150
Forward outright: 1.2311 / 1.2321

Forward outright = spot + swap

In this case: 1.2311 = 1.2166 + 0.0145
                1.2321 = 1.2171 + 0.0150

In the previous section, we saw that:

$$\text{Forward outright} = \text{spot} \times \frac{\left(1 + \text{variable currency interest rate} \times \frac{days}{year}\right)}{\left(1 + \text{base currency interest rate} \times \frac{days}{year}\right)}$$

Since we know that:

$$\text{Forward swap} = \text{forward outright} - \text{spot}$$

it follows that:

$$\text{Forward swap} =$$

$$\text{spot} \times \frac{\left(\text{variable currency interest rate} \times \frac{\text{days}}{\text{year}} - \text{base currency interest rate} \times \frac{\text{days}}{\text{year}}\right)}{\left(1 + \text{base currency interest rate} \times \frac{\text{days}}{\text{year}}\right)}$$

As before, the length of each year may be 360 or 365 days. If the year basis is the same for the two currencies and the number of days is sufficiently small, so that the denominator in the last equation is close to 1, the following approximation holds:

Approximation

$$\text{Forward swap} \approx \text{spot} \times \text{interest rate differential} \times \frac{\text{days}}{\text{year}}$$

In reverse, one can calculate an approximate interest rate differential from the swap rate as follows:

Approximation

$$\text{Interest rate differential} \approx \frac{\text{forward swap}}{\text{spot}} \times \frac{\text{year}}{\text{days}}$$

Example 8.9

31-day USD interest rate: 5%
31-day EUR interest rate: 3%
Spot EUR/USD rate: 1.2168

$$\text{Forward swap} = 1.2168 \times \frac{0.05 \times \frac{31}{360} - 0.03 \times \frac{31}{360}}{1 + 0.03 \times \frac{31}{360}}$$

$$= 0.0021 \text{ or } +21 \text{ points}$$

$$\textit{Approximate} \text{ swap} = 1.2168 \times (+0.02) \times \left(\frac{31}{360}\right) = +21 \text{ points}$$

Example 8.10 shows that the approximation is generally not accurate enough for longer periods. It also becomes less accurate as the base currency interest rate increases.

Example 8.10

1-year USD interest rate: 5%
1-year EUR interest rate: 3%
Spot EUR/USD rate: 1.2168

$$\text{Forward swap} = 1.2168 \times \frac{0.05 \times \frac{365}{360} - 0.03 \times \frac{365}{360}}{1 + 0.03 \times \frac{365}{360}}$$

$$= 0.0239 \text{ or } +239 \text{ points}$$

$$\textit{Approximate} \text{ swap} = 1.2168 \times (+0.02) \times \frac{365}{360} = +247 \text{ points}$$

Swap prices are quoted as two-way prices in the same way as other prices. In theory, one could use a borrowing rate for dollars and a deposit rate for euros in Example 8.10, to calculate the swap price where the bank buys euros from the customer against dollars for spot value and simultaneously sells euros to the customer against dollars for value one month forward. One could then use the deposit rate for dollars and the borrowing rate for euros to determine the other side of the price. However, this would produce a rather large spread. It is more realistic to use middle prices throughout, to calculate a middle price for the swap, and then to spread the two-way swap price around this middle price. In practice, a dealer does not recalculate swap prices continually in any case, but takes them from the market just as the spot dealer takes spot prices.

Discounts and premiums

It can be seen from the formulas given above that when the base currency interest rate is lower than the variable currency rate, the forward outright exchange rate is always greater than the spot rate. That is, the base currency is worth more forward units of the variable currency forward than it is spot. This can be seen as compensating for the lower interest rate: if I deposit money in the base currency rather than the variable currency, I will receive less interest. However if I sell forward the maturing deposit amount, the forward exchange rate is correspondingly better. In this case, the base currency is said to be at a "premium" to the variable currency, and the forward swap price must be positive.

The reverse also follows. In general, given two currencies, the currency with the higher interest rate is at a "discount" (worth fewer units of the other currency forward than spot) and the currency with the lower interest rate is at a "premium" (worth more units of the other currency forward than spot). When the variable currency is at a premium to the base currency, the forward swap points are negative; when the variable currency is at a discount to the base currency, the forward swap points are positive.

When the swap points are positive, and the forward dealer applies a bid/offer spread to make a two-way swap price, the left price is smaller than the right price as usual. When the swap points are negative, he must similarly quote a "more negative" number on the left and a "more positive" number on the right in order to make a profit. However, the minus sign " − " is generally not shown. The result is that the larger number appears to be on the left. As a result, whenever the swap price *appears* larger on the left than the right, it is in fact negative and must be subtracted from the spot rate rather than added.

Example 8.11

EUR interest rate:	3%
USD interest rate:	5%

EUR is at a premium to USD
USD is at a discount to EUR
Forward swap points are positive.

Swap prices are generally quoted so that the last digit of the price coincides with the same decimal place as the last digit of the spot price. For example, if the spot price is quoted to four decimal places (1.216<u>6</u>) and the swap price is "2<u>0</u> points", this means "0.002<u>0</u>".

Example 8.12

The euro is at a premium to the US dollar, and the swap rate is quoted as 20 / 22.

Spot EUR/USD:	1.2166 /	71
1-month swap:	20 /	22
1-month outright:	1.2186 /	1.2193

The spot euro will purchase USD 1.2166; the forward euro will purchase USD 1.2186. The euro is therefore worth more in the future and is thus at a forward premium.

Example 8.13

Spot EUR/JPY:	144.25 /	144.30
1-month swap:	2.30 /	2.20
1-month outright:	141.95 /	142.10

The spot euro will purchase JPY 144.25; the forward euro will purchase JPY 141.95. The euro is therefore worth less in the future and is thus at a forward discount.

If a forward swap price includes the word "par" it means that the spot rate and the forward outright rate are the same: "par" in this case represents zero. A/P is "around par", meaning that the left-hand side of the swap must be subtracted from spot and the right-hand side added. This happens when the two interest rates are the same or very similar.

Example 8.14

Spot USD/CAD:	1.1695 /	00
Swap:	6 /	4 A/P
Forward outright:	1.1689 /	1.1704

This is often written −6 / +4, which means the same as 6 / 4 A/P but indicates more clearly how the outrights are calculated.

Terminology

It is important to be careful about the terminology regarding premiums and discounts. The clearest terminology, for example, is to say that "the EUR is at a premium to the USD" or that "the USD is at a discount to the EUR"; then there is no ambiguity. If however a dealer says that "the EUR/USD is at a discount", he generally means that the *variable* currency, USD, is at a discount and that the swap points are to be added to the spot. Similarly, if he says that "the GBP/JPY is at a premium", he means that the *variable* currency, JPY, is at a premium and that the points are to be subtracted from the spot. If there is no qualification, he is generally referring to the variable currency, not the base currency. This is not the same in all countries however.

A forward swap position

In order to see why a bank trades in forward swaps rather than forward outrights, consider how the following swap and outright rates change as the spot rate and interest rates move:

Spot rate	EUR interest rate	USD interest rate	31-day forward outright	31-day forward swap
1.2168	3.0%	5.0%	1.2189	+ 0.0021
1.2268	3.0%	5.0%	1.2289	+ 0.0021
1.2268	3.5%	5.0%	1.2284	+ 0.0016

A movement of 100 points in the exchange rate from 1.2168 to 1.2268 has not affected the forward swap price (to four decimal places). However a change in the interest rate differential from 2.0 percent to 1.5 percent has changed it significantly. Essentially, a forward swap is an interest rate instrument rather than a currency instrument; when banks take forward positions, they are taking an interest rate view rather than a currency view. If bank dealers traded outrights, they would be combining two related but different markets in one deal, which is less satisfactory.

When a bank quotes a swap rate, it quotes in a similar manner to a spot rate. The bank buys the base currency *forward* on the left and sells the base currency *forward* on the right.

The forward swap deal itself is an exchange of one currency for another currency on one date, to be reversed on a given future date. Thus, for example, when the bank sells EUR outright to a counterparty, it may be seen as doing the following:

Bank's spot dealer sells EUR spot   spot deal

$$\left. \frac{\text{Bank's forward dealer buys EUR spot}}{\text{Bank's forward dealer sells EUR forward}} \right\}$$ forward swap deal

Bank sells EUR forward outright   net effect

Therefore on a EUR/USD 1-month forward swap quote of 20/22, the bank quoting the price does the following:

20	/	22
sells EUR spot		buys EUR spot
buys EUR forward		sells EUR forward

A forward foreign exchange swap is therefore a temporary purchase or sale of one currency against another. An equivalent effect could be achieved by borrowing one currency for a given period, while lending the other currency for the same period. This is why the swap rate formula reflects the interest rate differential (generally based on Eurocurrency interest rates rather than domestic interest rates) between the two currencies, converted into foreign exchange terms.

If a forward dealer has undertaken a similar deal to the one above – bought and sold EUR (in that order) as a speculative position – what interest rate view has he taken? He has effectively borrowed euros and lent dollars for the period. He probably expects EUR interest rates to rise (so that he can relend them at a higher rate) and/or USD rates to fall (so that he can reborrow them at a lower rate). In fact, the important point is that the interest differential should move in the EUR's favour. For example, even if EUR interest rates fall rather than rise, the dealer will still make a profit as long as USD rates fall even further.

Although only one single price is dealt (the swap price), the transaction has two separate settlements:

- a settlement on the spot value date
- a settlement on the forward value date.

There is no net outright position taken, and the spot dealer's spread will not be involved, but some benchmark spot rate will nevertheless be needed in order to arrive at the settlement rates. As the swap is a representation of the interest rate differential between the two currencies quoted, as long as the "near" and "far" sides of the swap quotation preserve this differential, it does not generally make a significant difference which exact spot rate is used as a base for adding or subtracting the swap points. The rate must however generally be a current rate. This is discussed further below: see "Historic rate rollovers" and "Discounting future foreign exchange risk".

Example 8.15

Spot EUR/USD:	1.2166 / 1.2171
31-day USD interest rate:	5.0%
31-day EUR interest rate:	3.0%
31-day forward swap:	20 / 22

Our bank's dealer expects EUR interest rates to rise. He therefore asks another bank for its price, which is quoted as 20/22. Our dealer buys and sells EUR 10 million at a swap price of 20 (that is, +0.0020). The spot rate is set at 1.2168 and the forward rate at 1.2188. The cashflows are therefore:

Spot	*31 days forward*
buy EUR 10,000,000	sell EUR 10,000,000
sell USD 12,168,000	buy USD 12,188,000

Immediately after dealing, EUR rates in fact fall rather than rise, but USD rates also fall, as follows:

Spot EUR/USD:	1.2166 / 1.2171
31-day USD interest rate:	4.5%
31-day EUR interest rate:	2.75%
31-day forward swap:	17 / 19

Our dealer now asks another counterparty for a price, is quoted 17 / 19, and deals to close out his position. Thus he now sells and buys EUR at a swap price of 19 (that is, +0.0019). The spot rate is set at 1.2168 again and the forward rate at 1.2187. The new cashflows are:

Spot		*31 days forward*	
sell EUR	10,000,000	buy EUR	10,000,000
buy USD	12,168,000	sell USD	12,187,000

The net result is a profit of USD 1,000, 31 days forward. The dealer has made a profit because the interest differential between EUR and USD has narrowed from 2.0% to 1.75%, even though it did not narrow in the way he expected.

In general:

> **Key Point**   A forward dealer expecting the interest rate differential to move in favour of the base currency (for example, base currency interest rates rise or variable currency interest rates fall) will "buy and sell" the base currency. This is equivalent to borrowing the base currency and depositing in the variable currency.
>
> And vice versa.

Historic rate rollovers

We have mentioned above that the settlement rates (spot and forward) for a forward swap deal must generally be based on a current market spot rate. This is because many central banks require that banks under their supervision use only current rates. Example 8.16 illustrates why a corporate customer might wish to use an historic rate rather than a current rate, and the effect.

Example 8.16   In June, a German company sells EUR 10 million forward outright for value 15 August against USD, at a forward outright rate of 1.1250. This deal is done to cover the cost the company expects to pay for US imports. On 13 August, the company realises that it will not need to pay the dollars until a month later. It therefore rolls over the foreign exchange cover by using a forward swap – buying EUR spot and selling one month forward.

On 13 August, the exchange rates are as follows:

Spot EUR/USD:	1.2166 / 71
31-day forward swap:	20 / 22

The company therefore buys and sells EUR at 1.2168 (spot) and 1.2168 + 0.0020 = 1.2188 (forward).

The company's cashflows will then be:

	15 August	15 September
	sell EUR 1,000,000	
	buy USD 1,125,000	
	buy EUR 1,000,000	sell EUR 1,000,000
	sell USD 1,216,800	buy USD 1,218,800
Net:		sell EUR 1,000,000
	sell USD 91,800	buy USD 1,218,800

The overall net result is that the company sells EUR 1 million against USD 1,127,000 (= USD 1,218,800 − USD 91,800) − an all-in rate of 1.1270 which is effectively the original rate dealt of 1.1250 adjusted by the swap price of 20 points. The company may however have a cashflow problem on 15 August, because there is a cash outflow of USD 91,800. The company might therefore prefer to request the bank to base the swap on the "historic" rate of 1.1250 − dealing instead at 1.1250 spot and 1.1270 forward.

The cashflows would then be:

	15 August	15 September
	sell EUR 1,000,000	
	buy USD 1,125,000	
	buy EUR 1,000,000	sell EUR 1,000,000
	sell USD 1,125,000	buy USD 1,127,000
Net:		sell EUR 1,000,000
		buy USD 1,127,000

The overall net result is the same as before but there is no cashflow problem. Underlying this arrangement however, is an effective loan from the bank to the company of USD 91,800 for 31 days. If the bank is, exceptionally, prepared to base the swap on an historic rate, it needs to charge the company interest on this hidden loan. This interest would normally be incorporated into a less favourable swap price.

The reason many central banks discourage historic rate rollovers is that they may help a bank's customer to conceal foreign exchange losses. If a customer has taken a speculative position which has made a loss, an historic rate rollover enables him to roll the loss over to a later date rather than realise it.

Covered interest arbitrage

The link between interest rates and forward swaps allows banks and others to take advantage of different opportunities in different markets. This can be seen in either of two ways. First, suppose that a bank needs to fund itself in one currency but can borrow *relatively* cheaply in another. It can choose deliberately to borrow in the second currency and use a forward swap to convert the borrowing to the first currency. The reason for doing this would be that the resulting all-in cost of borrowing is slightly less than the cost of borrowing the first currency directly.

Second, even if the bank does not need to borrow, it can still borrow in the second currency, use a forward swap to convert the borrowing to the first currency and then make a deposit directly in the first currency. The reason for doing this would be that a profit can be locked in because the swap price is slightly out of line with the interest rates.

Taking advantage of such a strategy is known as "covered interest arbitrage".

Example 8.17

EUR/CHF	spot:	1.4810 / 1.4815
	3-month swap:	116 / 111

EUR	3-month interest rates:	7.43% / 7.56%
CHF	3-month interest rates:	4.50% / 4.62%

Suppose that the 3-month period is 92 days and the bank needs to borrow CHF 10 million. It deals on rates quoted to it as above by another bank.

(a) Bank borrows EUR 6,749,915.63 for 92 days from spot at 7.56%.

(b) At the end of 92 days, bank repays principal plus interest calculated as:

Principal EUR 6,749,915.63 plus interest EUR 6,749, 915.63 $\times$ 0.0756 $\times \frac{92}{360}$ = EUR 6,880,324.00

(c) Bank "sells and buys" EUR against CHF at a swap price of 111, based on a spot of 1.4815:

Bank sells EUR 6,749,915.63 / buys CHF 10,000,000.00 spot at 1.4815
Bank buys EUR 6,880,324.00 / sells CHF 10,116,828.41 3 months forward at 1.4704

The net EUR flows balance to zero.

The effective cost of borrowing is therefore interest of CHF 116,828.41 on a principal sum of CHF 10,000,000 for 92 days:

$$\frac{116,828.41}{10,000,000} \times \frac{360}{92} = 4.57\%$$

The net effect is thus a CHF 10 million borrowing at 4.57% – 5 basis points cheaper than the 4.62% at which the bank could borrow directly.

If the bank is in fact not looking for funds but is able to deposit CHF at higher than 4.57%, it can instead "round-trip", locking in a profit.

Three points to notice in Example 8.17 are:

1. The example assumes that we are not the bank quoting the price; we are taking another bank's rates to borrow at 7.56 percent and swap at 111 points. If we were able to trade on our own prices, the result would be even better.

2. When a swap is dealt, the amount of the deal (e.g. EUR 6,749,915.63) is usually the same at both ends of the deal, spot and forward. In the example above, the amounts are mismatched, with EUR 6,880,324.00 at the far end in order to match the cashflows exactly with the underlying flows arising from the borrowing. It is generally acceptable in the market to use mismatched amounts in this way as long as the mismatch is not great.

3. When dealing on a forward swap rather than a forward outright, it is the swap price that is dealt rather than the spot price; the spot price is needed only for settlement. The spot dealer is not involved and the spot spread is not involved. In general therefore, the spot and forward settlement prices could be 1.4815 and 1.4704 (as in Example 8.17) or 1.4810 and 1.4699 or something between. The spot rate must be a current market rate and the difference between the spot and forward settlement prices must be the correct swap price of 111 points. Conventionally, an approximate mid-price is taken for the spot.

However, in Example 8.17, because the amounts are mismatched, it is usual to use for the *whole* deal whichever side of the spot price would normally be used for the mismatch amount. The size of the mismatch in this example is a forward sale by the quoting bank of EUR 130,408.37 (= 6,880,324.00 − 6,749,915.63). The quoting bank will wish to deal on the right for this, based on a spot of 1.4815. This is therefore usually the spot rate used for the deal. Although this approach is common, it does not in fact necessarily benefit the quoting bank. In Example 8.17, for instance, the quoting bank is actually slightly worse off using a spot of 1.4815 and would instead benefit from using 1.4810. In general, this depends on which of the two currencies' interest rates are higher; the effect is in any case generally not great.

The formula we saw earlier for calculating a forward outright from interest rates was:

$$\text{Forward swap} = \text{spot} \times \frac{\left(1 + \text{variable currency interest rate} \times \frac{\text{days}}{\text{year}}\right)}{\left(1 + \text{base currency interest rate} \times \frac{\text{days}}{\text{year}}\right)}$$

This can be turned round to give the result of the covered interest arbitrage from the swap price:

Covered interest arbitrage   **Calculation summary**

Creating the variable currency interest rate:

Variable currency rate =

$$\left[\left(1 + \text{base currency rate} \times \frac{\text{days}}{\text{base year}}\right) \times \frac{\text{outright}}{\text{spot}} - 1\right] \times \frac{\text{variable year}}{\text{days}}$$

or

Creating the base currency interest rate:

Base currency rate =

$$\left[\left(1 + \text{variable currency rate} \times \frac{\text{days}}{\text{variable year}}\right) \times \frac{\text{spot}}{\text{outright}} - 1\right] \times \frac{\text{base year}}{\text{days}}$$

Example 8.18 Using the same data as in Example 8.17, we have:

Variable currency interest rate created

$$= \left[\left(1 + 7.56\% \times \frac{92}{360} \right) \times \frac{1.4704}{1.4815} - 1 \right] \times \frac{360}{92} = 4.57\%$$

.0756 ENTER 92 × 360 ÷ 1 + 1.4704 × 1.4815 ÷ 1 – 360 x 92 ÷

CROSS-RATE FORWARDS

Outrights

A forward cross-rate is calculated in a similar way to spot cross-rates. To calculate a forward outright cross-rate from two exchange rates with the same base currency (e.g. USD), divide opposite sides of the individual forward outright rates.

Example 8.19

Spot USD/SGD:	1.5782 /	92
6-month swap:	90 /	95
6-month outright:	1.5872 /	1.5887

Spot USD/CAD:	1.1474 /	79
6-month swap:	155 /	150
6-month outright:	1.1319 /	1.1329

Therefore 6-month CAD/SGD is:

$$\frac{1.5872}{1.1329} = 1.4010:\ \text{how the quoting bank buys CAD, sells SGD}$$

$$\frac{1.5887}{1.1319} = 1.4036:\ \text{how the quoting bank sells CAD, buys SGD}$$

The forward outright cross-rate is therefore 1.4010 / 1.4036.

To calculate a forward outright cross-rate from two exchange rates with the same variable currency, again divide opposite sides of the forward rates. Similarly, to calculate a forward outright cross-rate from two rates where the common currency is the base for one but the variable for the other, multiply the same sides.

Example 8.20

Spot EUR/USD:	1.2166 /	71
1-month swap:	14 /	9
1-month outright:	1.2152 /	1.2162

Spot AUD/USD:	0.6834 /	39
1-month swap:	60 /	55
1-month outright:	0.6774 /	0.6784

Therefore 1-month EUR/AUD is:

$$\frac{1.2152}{0.6784} = 1.7913:$$ how the quoting bank buys EUR, sells AUD

$$\frac{1.2162}{0.6774} = 1.7954:$$ how the quoting bank sells EUR, buys AUD

The forward outright cross-rate is therefore 1.7913 / 1.7954.

Swaps

To calculate cross-rate forward swaps, the process above must be taken a step further:

1. Calculate the spot cross-rate.

2. Calculate the two individual forward outrights.

3. From (2) calculate the forward outright cross-rate.

4. From (1) and (3) calculate the cross-rate swap.

Example 8.21

Using the same details as in Example 8.19, the CAD/SGD cross-rate swap can be calculated as follows:

From Example 8.19, the forward outright rate is:	1.4010 / 1.4036
From Example 8.2, the spot rate is:	1.3749 / 1.3763
Therefore the forward swap is (outright – spot):	0.0261 / 0.0273

That is, 261 / 273.

SHORT DATES

Value dates earlier than one month are referred to as "short dates". There are certain "regular" dates usually quoted, and the terminology used is the same as in the deposit market, as follows:

Terminology

Overnight	A deposit or foreign exchange swap from today until "tomorrow".
Tom-next	A deposit or foreign exchange swap from "tomorrow" to the "next" day (spot).
Spot-next	A deposit or foreign exchange swap from spot until the "next" day.
Spot-a-week	A deposit or foreign exchange swap from spot until a week later.

Tomorrow means "the next working day after today" and **next** means "the next working day following".

When referring to outright deals rather than swaps, one refers to **value today, value tomorrow, value spot-next, value a week over spot.**

In considering swaps and outright forwards for short dates later than the spot date, exactly the same rules apply as in calculating longer dates. However confusion can arise in considering the prices for dates earlier than spot – that is, value today and tomorrow. The rules are still the same in that the bank buys the base currency on the far date on the left and sells the base currency on the far date on the right. In other words, the bank always "sells and buys" (in that order) the base currency on the left and "buys and sells" the base currency on the right – regardless of whether it is before or after spot. The confusion can arise because the spot value date – effectively the baseline date for calculation of the outright rate – is the near date when calculating most forward prices. For value today and tomorrow, the spot date becomes the far date and the outright date is the near date.

Example 8.22

Spot EUR/USD: 1.2505 / 10
Overnight swap: 1 / ¾
Tom-next swap: ½ / ¼
1-week swap: 7 / 5

(a) Suppose a customer wishes to buy USD for outright value one week after spot. The bank spot dealer sells USD for value spot on the left at 1.2505. The bank forward dealer sells USD for value on the "far" date (= one week after spot) also on the left at a swap difference of 7 points. Therefore the bank sells USD outright one week after spot at 1.2505 – 0.0007 = 1.2498. The other side of the one week outright price is 1.2510 – 0.0005 = 1.2505.

(b) Suppose the customer wishes to buy USD for outright value tomorrow. This is equivalent to *buying* USD for value spot and, at the time, undertaking a swap to *buy* USD for value tomorrow and *sell* USD back for value spot.

Again, the bank spot dealer buys EUR for value spot on the left at 1.2505. However the bank forward dealer sells EUR for value on the "far" date (= spot this time) on the right at a swap difference of ¼ point. Furthermore (because USD interest rates are lower than EUR rates) the EUR is at a discount to the USD: the "bigger number" ½ is on the left. The EUR is therefore worth less on the "far" date and more on the "near" date. The swap difference is therefore *added* to the spot rate to give an outright value tomorrow price of 1.2505 + ¼ = 1.250525. The other side of the value tomorrow outright price is 1.2510 + ½ = 1.25105.

A simple rule to remember for the calculation of dates *earlier* than spot is "*reverse* the swap points and proceed exactly as for a forward later than spot". In Example 8.22, this would mean reversing ½/¼ to ¼ / ½. The outright value tomorrow price is then (1.2505 + ¼)/(1.2510 + ½), obtained by adding the swap points to the spot rate because the "bigger" swap number is now on the right. **However, it is important always to remember to make this reversal in your head only! Never actually quote the price in reverse!**

"Overnight" prices are the only regular swap prices not involving the spot value date. To calculate an outright value today price, it is therefore necessary to combine the "overnight" price with the "tom-next" price.

(c) Suppose the customer wishes to buy USD for outright value today. This is equivalent to three separate transactions: *buying* USD for value spot, under-taking a swap to *buy* USD for value tomorrow and *sell* USD back for value spot ("tom-next") and undertaking another swap to *buy* USD for value today and *sell* USD back for value tomorrow ("overnight"). The price is therefore 1.2505 + ¼ + ¾ = 1.2506.

Example

The "rules" can be thought of in terms of premiums and discounts, which apply in the same way as in forwards after spot. The swaps in the previous example show a EUR discount because USD interest rates are lower than EUR interest rates. Consequently, if the customer buys USD value today and not value spot, he will receive the currency with the lower interest rate two days early. The extra point which he receives from the bank reflects this.

Deals cannot always be done for value today. For example, when London and European markets are open, the Japanese banks have already closed their books for today, so deals in yen can only be done for value tomorrow. Similarly, in London, most European currencies can only be dealt early in the morning for value today, because of the time difference and the mechanical difficulties of ensuring good value. Even the market for value "tomorrow" generally closes during the morning.

Some further examples follow. "Overnight", "tom-next", "spot-next" and "spot-a-week" are often abbreviated as O/N, T/N, S/N and S/W respectively.

EUR/CHF spot rate:	1.5103 / 13
O/N:	¼ / ½
T/N:	¼ / ½
S/N:	¼ / ½

Example 8.23

The bank's customers can make purchases and sales as follows:

Value S/N: Outright purchase of CHF and sale of EUR:
1.5103 + 0.000025 = 1.510325

Outright sale of CHF and purchase of EUR:
1.5113 + 0.00005 = 1.51135

Value tomorrow: Outright purchase of CHF and sale of EUR:
1.5103 − 0.00005 = 1.51025

Outright sale of CHF and purchase of EUR:
1.5113 − 0.000025 = 1.511275

Value today: Outright purchase of CHF and sale of EUR:
1.5103 − 0.0001 = 1.5102

Outright sale of CHF and purchase of EUR:
1.5113 − 0.00005 = 1.51125

CALCULATION SUMMARY

It may be helpful to collect together here various "rules" which apply to calculating forwards:

1. The currency with higher interest rates (= the currency at a "discount") is worth less in the future.

   The currency with lower interest rates (= the currency at a "premium") is worth more in the future.

2. The bank quoting the price buys the base currency / sells the variable currency on the far date on the left.

   The bank quoting the price sells the base currency / buys the variable currency on the far date on the right.

For outright forwards later than spot

3. The right swap price is added to (or subtracted from) the right spot price.

   The left swap price is added to (or subtracted from) the left spot price.

4. If the swap price is larger on the right than the left, add it to the spot price.

   If the swap price is larger on the left than the right, subtract it from the spot price.

For outright deals earlier than spot

5. Calculate as if the swap price were reversed and then follow (3) and (4).

In general

6. Of the two prices available, the customer gets the worse one. Thus if the swap price is 3 / 2 and the customer knows that the points are "in his favour" (the outright will be better than the spot), the price will be 2. If he knows that the points are "against him" (the outright will be worse than the spot), the price will be 3.

7. The effect of combining the swap points with the spot price will always be to widen the spread, never to narrow it.

VALUE DATES

Swap rates are normally quoted for "regular" dates – for example 1, 2, 3, 6 and 12 months forward. They are quoted over the spot date. This means that the one-month swap rates are calculated for one calendar month after the present spot date. If the current spot date is 21 April, the one month forward date will be 21 May. If the forward delivery date falls on a weekend or holiday, the value date becomes the next working day. No adjustment in the forward value date is made for any weekends or public holiday *between* the spot date and the forward delivery date.

An exception to these rules is when the spot value date is at or close to the end of the month. If the spot value date is the last working day of a month, the forward value date is the last working day of the corresponding forward month; if necessary, the forward value date is brought *back* to the nearest previous business day in order to stay in the same calendar month, rather than moved forward to the beginning of the next month. This is referred to as dealing "end/end".

Ordinary run   Example 8.24

Dealing date:	Friday 14 April
Spot date:	Tuesday 18 April (2 working days forward)
1 month:	Thursday 18 May
2 months:	Monday 19 June (18 June is a Sunday)
3 months:	Tuesday 18 July
4 months:	Friday 18 August

End/End

Dealing date:	Wednesday 26 June
Spot date:	Friday 28 June (last working day of June)
1 month:	Wednesday 31 July (last working day of July)
2 months:	Friday 30 August (last working day of August)
etc.	

Similarly, even if the spot value date is earlier than the last working day of the month, but the forward value date would fall on a non-working day, this is still brought back rather than moved later if necessary to keep it in the appropriate month.

		Example 8.25
Dealing date:	Monday 28 August	
Spot date:	Wednesday 30 August (not the last working day)	
1 month:	Friday 29 September (30 September is a Saturday)	
2 months:	Monday 30 October	
etc.		

If a bank deals in any month that is not a regularly quoted date, for example, for four or five months' maturity, this is called an "in-between" month because it is between the regular dates. A forward deal may in fact be arranged for value on *any* day which is a working day in both currencies. Dates which do not fit in with calendar month dates are called "broken dates" or "odd dates". The forward swap points are generally calculated by straight-line interpolation between the nearest whole month dates either side.

FORWARD-FORWARDS

A forward-forward swap is a swap deal between two forward dates rather than from spot to a forward date – for example, to sell US dollars one month forward and buy them back in three months' time. In this case, the swap is for the two-month period between the one-month date and the three-month date. A company might undertake such a swap because it has previously bought dollars forward but wishes now to defer the transaction by a further two months, as it will not need the dollars as soon as it thought.

From the bank's point of view, a forward-forward swap can be seen as two separate swaps, each based on spot.

Example 8.26

EUR/CHF spot rate:	1.5325 / 35
1-month swap:	65 / 61
3-month swap:	160 / 155

If our bank's counterparty wishes to sell EUR one month forward and buy them three months forward, this is the same as undertaking one swap to buy EUR spot and sell EUR one month forward and another swap to sell EUR spot and buy EUR three months forward.

As swaps are always quoted as how the quoting bank buys the base currency forward on the left and sells the base currency forward on the right, the counterparty can "buy and sell" EUR "spot against one month" at a swap price of –65, with settlement rates of spot and (spot – 0.0065). He can "sell and buy" EUR "spot against three months" at a swap price of –155 with settlement rates of spot and (spot – 0.0155). He can therefore do both simultaneously – "sell and buy" EUR "one month against three months" – at settlement rates of (spot – 0.0065) and (spot – 0.0155), which implies a difference between the two forward prices of (–155) – (–65) = –90 points.

Conversely, the counterparty can "buy and sell" EUR "one month against three months" at a swap price of (–160) – (–61) = –99 points. The two-way price is therefore –99 / –90, quoted as usual without the "–" signs, as 99 / 90.

As with a swap from spot to a forward date, the two settlement prices in a forward-forward must be based on a current market rate. In Example 8.26, using the middle spot rate, the settlement rates could be 1.5265 (= 1.5330 – 0.0065) for 1 month forward and 1.5175 (= 1.5330 – 0.0155) for 3 months forward.

These settlement rates would enable our forward dealer to cover his position exactly with another bank. We could, for example, ask another bank for a 1-month swap price to cover the first leg of the forward-forward. Assuming prices have not moved, we could deal at –65 points with settlement rates of 1.5330 (spot) and 1.5265 (1 month). We could then cover the second leg with a 3-month swap at another bank's price of –155, with settlement rates of 1.5330 (spot) and 1.5175 (3 months). The spot settlements would offset each other and the forward settlements would exactly offset the settlements with our own counterparty.

In practice however, forward dealers often base the settlement rate for the first leg on a middle rate for spot and a middle rate for the near forward date. In the example above, this would give a settlement rate of 1.5330 (middle) – 0.0063 (middle) = 1.5267. The settlement rate for the second leg would then be 1.5267 – 0.0090 = 1.5177. The difference between the two settlement rates is still the –90 points agreed, but the settlement rates are slightly different.

The calculation rule to create the forward-forward price after spot is as follows:

Calculation summary

> **Forward-forward price after spot**
>
> Left side = (left side of far-date swap) – (right side of near-date swap)
>
> Right side = (right side of far-date swap) – (left side of near-date swap)

Note that the bid-offer spread of the resulting price is the sum of the two separate bid-offer spreads.

Care needs to be taken with swaps from before spot to after spot:

Example 8.27

EUR/CHF spot rate:	1.5325 /	35
T/N swap:	3 /	2
3-month swap:	160 /	155

If a counterparty requests a price to sell and buy EUR tomorrow against 3 months after spot, this can be seen as a price to sell tomorrow and buy spot at (–2) points with settlement rates of (spot + 0.0002) and spot, and a price to sell spot and buy 3 months later at (–155) points with settlement rates of spot and (spot – 0.0155). The total price is therefore the difference between (spot – 0.0155) and (spot + 0.0002), which is (–155) 2 (+2) = –157. The other side of the price is (–160) – (+3) = –163. The two-sided price is therefore 163 / 157.

TIME OPTIONS

When a bank makes a forward outright deal with a company, it will quote a rate for a fixed date, which means the company must deliver one currency and receive another on that date.

If the company has a commitment in the future but does not know the exact delivery date, it has an alternative means of covering this exposure in the traditional foreign exchange market, using "time options". These allow the company to deal now, but to choose the maturity date later, within a specified period. Delivery must take place at some point during that period, however, for the amount and rate agreed.

It is important not to confuse "time options" in this sense with "currency options" which are covered later. "Currency options" entail the up-front payments of an "insurance premium", in return for which the customer has the right to choose whether or not to deal at all.

In pricing a time option, the bank will always assume that the company will take delivery of the currency at the worst possible time for the bank. Therefore the company will always be charged the worst possible forward rate within the period of the time option.

Example 8.28	USD/CHF spot rate:	1.2950 / 60
	6-month swap:	485 / 475
	7-month swap	560 / 550

If a customer wants to buy CHF with an option for delivery between six and seven months, the bank will assume in pricing the option that delivery will be after seven months (560 points against the customer). However if the customer wants to sell CHF with an option for delivery between six and seven months, the bank will assume that delivery will be after six months (only 475 points in the customer's favour). The time option price will therefore be (1.2950 – 0.0560) / (1.2960 – 0.0475) = 1.2390 / 1.2485.

The advantage of a time option to a company is its flexibility. The company can lock in a fixed exchange rate at which it knows it can deal. There is no exposure to interest rate changes which would affect it if commitments were covered with a forward outright which subsequently needed to be adjusted by means of forward swaps. The disadvantage is the cost, given the wide bid/offer spread involved, particularly if the time period of the option is wide.

> **Key Point**   A time option price is the best for the bank / worst for the customer over the time option period.

LONG-DATED FORWARDS

The formula we have already seen for a forward outright less than one year is: This is derived from the fact that the interest on a Eurocurrency deposit or

$$\text{Forward outright} = \text{spot} \times \frac{\left(1 + \text{variable interest rate} \times \frac{\text{days}}{\text{year}}\right)}{\left(1 + \text{base interest rate} \times \frac{\text{days}}{\text{year}}\right)}$$

loan is paid on a simple basis. For deposits and loans over one year, the interest must be compounded. The formula for a forward over one year will be, correspondingly:

$$\text{Forward outright} = \text{spot} \times \frac{(1 + \text{variable interest rate})^N}{(1 + \text{base interest rate})^N}$$

where N is the number of years, and the interest rates are quoted on the basis of a true calendar year rather than a 360-day year. This theoretical formula is not precise in practice for two reasons. First, this compounding does not take account of reinvestment risk. This problem could be overcome by using zero-coupon yields for the interest rates. More importantly, the market in long-dated forwards is not very liquid and spreads are very wide. The prices available in practice therefore depend partly on banks' individual positions and hence their interest in quoting a price.

Calculation summary

For long-dated forwards

$$\text{Forward outright} = \text{spot} \times \frac{(1 + \text{variable interest rate})^N}{(1 + \text{base interest rate})^N}$$

ARBITRAGING AND CREATING FRAs

Foreign exchange forward-forwards can be used to arbitrage between FRAs in different currencies, or to create synthetic FRAs. Because theoretical forward swap prices and FRAs are both linked mathematically to the current Eurointerest rates, it should be possible to round-trip between FRAs and forward-forwards at zero cost – or, if prices are out of line, to make an arbitrage profit.

Example 8.29

Rate structure at the start:

	USD/NOK	USD%	NOK%
Spot:	6.0000		
3 months (91 days):	6.0598	6.00	10.00
6 months (182 days):	6.1178	6.00	10.00

The 3 v 6 USD FRA rate is:

$$\left[\frac{\left(1 + 0.06 \times \frac{182}{360}\right)}{\left(1 + 0.06 \times \frac{91}{360}\right)} - 1\right] \times \frac{360}{(182 - 91)} = 5.91\%$$

The theoretical 3 v 6 NOK FRA rate is:

$$\left[\frac{\left(1 + 0.10 \times \frac{182}{360}\right)}{\left(1 + 0.10 \times \frac{91}{360}\right)} - 1\right] \times \frac{360}{(182 - 91)} = 9.753\%$$

Outline structure

Assuming that it is not possible to obtain satisfactory FRA prices in NOK from a bank, we will create a synthetic NOK FRA by combining a USD FRA with various forward foreign exchange deals. This is structured as follows:

1 Assume a borrowing in USD for 3 months, starting in 3 months' time. Arrange now a USD FRA 3 v 6 on this USD borrowing.

2 Convert the resulting fixed-cost USD borrowing to a fixed-cost NOK borrowing by a forward-forward swap:
   selling USD/buying NOK now for value in 3 months' time
   buying USD/selling NOK now for value in 6 months' time.

3 After 3 months, instead of the dollar borrowing which has been assumed, this borrowing is synthesised from a 3-month NOK borrowing and more forward deals. To achieve this, it is necessary after 3 months to:

4 Convert the NOK borrowing to a USD borrowing by:
buying USD/selling NOK for value spot
selling USD/buying NOK for value 3 months forward.

Detailed structure

1 Assume a borrowing of USD $\dfrac{1,000,000}{6.0598}$ = USD 165,021.95 in 3 months' time.

This will achieve NOK 1,000,000 if it is converted forward now.

Arrange a 3 v 6 FRA at 5.91% on USD 165,021.95. Although the FRA settlement will in fact be after 3 months on a discounted basis, the economic effect will be as if we had borrowed at 5.91% for the period, with the following total repayment at the end of 6 months (we can in fact achieve exactly this result by investing or borrowing the FRA settlement amount from 3 months to 6 months at LIBOR):

$$\text{USD } 165,021.95 \times \left(1 + 0.0591 \times \frac{91}{360}\right) = \text{USD } 167,487.24$$

2 3 months forward: sell USD 165,021.95/buy NOK 1,000,000.00 (at 6.0598)
6 months forward: buy USD 167,487.24/sell NOK 1,024,653.44 (at 6.1178)

After 3 months from the start, suppose the following new rate structure:

	USD/NOK	USD%	NOK%
Spot:	7.0000		
3 months (91 days):	7.1223	5.00	12.0

1 The discounted FRA settlement amount is

$$\frac{\text{USD } 165,021.95 \times (0.0591 - 0.05) \times \frac{91}{360}}{\left(1 + 0.05 \times \frac{91}{360}\right)} = \text{USD } 374.86$$

2 We borrow this settlement amount (which is to be paid by us because interest rates have fallen) for 3 months at 5.00% to give an all-in settlement cost to be paid at the end of:

$$\text{USD } 374.86 \times \left(1 + 0.05 \times \frac{91}{360}\right) = \text{USD } 379.60$$

3 Borrow NOK (165,021.95 × 7.0000) = NOK 1,155,153.65 for 3 months

Total repayment after 3 months would be:

$$\text{NOK } 1,155,153.65 \times \left(1 + 0.12 \times \frac{91}{360}\right) = \text{NOK } 1,190,193.31$$

4 Spot: sell NOK 1,155,153.65/buy USD 165,021.95 (at 7.0000)
3 months forward: buy NOK 1,190,193.31/sell USD 167,108.00 (at 7.1223)

Resulting cashflows

	NOK		USD
After 3 months:	+ 1,000,000.00	(2) First hedge	– 165,021.95
	+ 1,155,153.65	(3) NOK loan	
	– 1,155,153.65	(4) Second hedge	+ 165,021.95
	+ 1,000,000.00		–

After 6 months:			
		(1) FRA settlement	− 379.60
	− 1,024,653.44	(2) First hedge	+ 167,487.24
	− 1,190,193.31	(3) Loan repayment	
	+ 1,190,193.31	(4) Second hedge	− 167,108.00
	− 1,024,653.44		−

The resulting effective cost of borrowing the NOK 1,000,000 is:

The final step

$\dfrac{24,653.44}{1,000,000} \times \dfrac{360}{91} = 9.753\%$, which is the theoretical SEK FRA cost.

So far, we have created a forward cash borrowing in NOK at 9.75%, rather than an FRA. The final step is to remove the cash element, by subtracting from step (3) in the structure the originally intended notional principal cash amount of NOK 1,000,000. This reduces the amount in step (3) to NOK 155,153.65. The repayment on this amount is:

$$\text{NOK } 155,153.65 \times \left(1 + 0.12 \times \tfrac{91}{360}\right) = \text{NOK } 159,859.98$$

This leaves the following cashflows:

	NOK			USD
After 3 months:	+1,000,000.00	(2) First hedge		− 165,021.95
	+ 155,153.65	(3) NOK loan		
	− 1,155,153.65	(4) Second hedge		+ 165,021.95
	−			−

	NOK			USD
After 6 months:		(1) FRA settlement	−	379.60
	− 1,024,653.44	(2) First hedge	+	167,487.24
	− 159,859.98	(3) Loan repayment		
	+ 1,190,193.31	(4) Second hedge	−	167,108.00
	+ 5,679.89			−

If we discount this resulting net inflow back 3 months at 12.00%, we have:

$$\frac{\text{NOK } 5,679.89}{\left(1 + 0.12 \times \tfrac{91}{360}\right)} = \text{NOK } 5,513$$

This is the same settlement amount as if we had been able to buy a NOK FRA at 9.753%:

$$\frac{\text{NOK } 1,000,000 \times (0.12 - 0.09753) \times \tfrac{91}{360}}{\left(1 + 0.12 \times \tfrac{91}{360}\right)} = \text{NOK } 5,513$$

In practice, because of the various bid/offer spreads involved, the effective cost would be higher than this – although the spreads on the FX forward deals are reduced slightly because they are swap deals rather than forward outright deals, so that the bid/offer spread is not paid on the spot price as well as on the forward swaps. The question would therefore be whether this synthetic FRA rate is more attractive than a straightforward FRA in NOK.

In an earlier section on covered interest arbitrage, we gave a formula for creating one interest rate from another:

Variable currency interest rate created =

$$\left[\left(1 + \text{base currency interest rate} \times \tfrac{\text{days}}{\text{base year}}\right) \times \frac{\text{outright}}{\text{spot}} - 1\right] \times \frac{\text{variable year}}{\text{days}}$$

This formula can be adapted for forward periods as follows:

<table>
<tr><td>Calculation summary</td><td>

Variable currency FRA rate =

$$\left[\left(1 + \text{base currency FRA rate} \times \tfrac{\text{days}}{\text{base year}}\right) \times \frac{\text{outright to far date}}{\text{outright to near date}} - 1\right] \times \frac{\text{variable year}}{\text{days}}$$

</td></tr>
</table>

In the example above, this would give the NOK FRA rate created as:

$$\left[\left(1 + 0.0591 \times \frac{91}{360}\right) \times \frac{6.1178}{6.0598} - 1\right] \times \frac{360}{91} = 9.75\%$$

Expressing this for the base currency gives:

<table>
<tr><td>Calculation summary</td><td>

Base currency FRA rate =

$$\left[\left(1 + \text{variable currency FRA rate} \times \tfrac{\text{days}}{\text{variable year}}\right) \times \frac{\text{outright to near date}}{\text{outright to far date}} - 1\right] \times \frac{\text{base year}}{\text{days}}$$

</td></tr>
</table>

In the same way, we can reverse the arbitrage process and create a forward-forward foreign exchange swap from two FRAs (or forward-forwards or futures). Again, the formula given in the section on forward swaps for a normal foreign exchange swap can be adapted directly for forward periods:

<table>
<tr><td>Calculation summary</td><td>

Forward-forward swap =

$$\text{outright to near date} \times \frac{\left(\text{variable currency FRA} \times \tfrac{\text{days}}{\text{year}} - \text{base currency FRA} \times \tfrac{\text{days}}{\text{year}}\right)}{\left(1 + \text{base currency FRA} \times \tfrac{\text{days}}{\text{year}}\right)}$$

</td></tr>
</table>

DISCOUNTING FUTURE FOREIGN EXCHANGE RISK

We have suggested on several occasions that there is a risk for a forward foreign exchange position which arises out of potential spot exchange rate movements rather than just the movements in the forward swap price.

Example 8.30 Our forward dealer sells and buys USD 1 million against SGD, 3 months against 6 months, at the following rates, because he expects the SGD's forward discount to increase (a fall in USD interest rates relative to SGD rates).

	USD/SGD	USD%	SGD%
Spot:	2.0000		
3 months (90 days):	2.0098	8.0	10.0
6 months (180 days):	2.0172	8.8	10.6

The cashflows arising from the deal are as follows:

90 days	180 days
– USD 1,000,000	+USD 1,000,000
+SGD 2,009,800	– SGD 2,017,200

Now consider an immediate move in rates to the following:

	USD/SGD	USD%	SGD%
Spot:	2.1000		
3 months:	2.1103	8.0	10.0
6 months:	2.1181	8.8	10.6

Even though interest rates have not moved, the SGD's forward discount has increased slightly, because the change in the spot rate from 2.0000 to 2.1000 has "magnified" the forward points. The dealer therefore expects to have made a profit.

In fact however the bank as a whole has made a loss. Suppose that the deal is now closed out at current rates. The cashflows become:

Spot	90 days	180 days
–	– USD 1,000,000	+USD 1,000,000
–	+SGD 2,009,800	– SGD 2,017,200
–	+USD 1,000,000	– USD 1,000,000
–	– SGD 2,110,300	+SGD 2,118,100
	– SGD 100,500	+SGD 100,900

The net effect appears to be a profit of SGD 400 (= SGD 100,900 – SGD 100,500). However, the outflow of SGD 100,500 after 90 days must be financed for 3 months before the inflow of SGD 100,900. The forward-forward rate for this financing is:

$$\left(\frac{1 + 0.106 \times \frac{180}{360}}{1 + 0.10 \times \frac{90}{360}} - 1 \right) \times \frac{360}{(180 - 90)} = 10.9268\%$$

The cost of funding is therefore:

$$SGD\ 100,500 \times 10.9268\% \times \tfrac{90}{360} = SGD\ 2,745$$

This financing cost is a real loss, which has arisen because of the spot rate movement. It is therefore possible for the dealer to make a profit by correctly anticipating interest rate movements, but for this profit to be more than offset by the spot rate movements.

The exposure – known as the forward "tail" – arises because of the time difference between the cashflows. It is possible to compensate for this effect by hedging the NPV of the original cashflows.

The NPV of the USD cashflows is:

$$\frac{USD\ 1,000,000}{\left(1 + 0.08 \times \tfrac{90}{360}\right)} + \frac{USD\ 1,000,000}{\left(1 + 0.088 \times \tfrac{180}{360}\right)} = -\ USD\ 22,538$$

On an NPV basis, the dealer is therefore short of USD 22,538.

A possible hedge is therefore to buy USD 22,538 for value spot at the same time as the original deal. The cashflows if the deal and the hedge were closed out would then be:

Spot	90 days	180 days
+USD 22,538	– USD 1,000,000	+USD 1,000,000
– SGD 45,076	+SGD 2,009,800	– SGD 2,017,200
– USD 22,538	+USD 1,000,000	– USD 1,000,000
+SGD 47,330	– SGD 2,110,300	+SGD 2,118,100
+SGD 2,254	– SGD 100,500	+SGD 100,900

It is possible to deposit the SGD 2,254 profit from spot until 3 months at 10%, for total proceeds of:

$$\text{SGD } 2,254 \times \left(1 + 0.10 \times \tfrac{90}{360}\right) = \text{SGD } 2,310$$

This gives a net cashflow after 3 months of:

$$\text{SGD } 2,310 - \text{SGD } 100,500 = -\text{SGD } 98,190$$

At the forward-forward SGD rate of 10.9268%, it is possible to fund this net SGD 98,190 from 3 months until 6 months for a total repayment of:

$$\text{SGD } 98,190 \times \left(1 + 0.109268 \times \tfrac{90}{360}\right) = \text{SGD } 100,872$$

This amount is offset by the SGD 100,900 profit after 6 months (the difference is due to rounding).

Discounting in this way is effective because forward swap deals are equivalent to deposits and loans in the two currencies. Clearly deposits and loans in the domestic currency (SGD in this case) are unaffected by exchange rate movements. Deposits and loans in a foreign currency (USD in this case) are however equivalent to their net present value, which is directly affected by the exchange rate. On the other hand, the hedge will be exact only to the extent that the interest rates used to discount the cashflows reflect the interest rates implicit in the forward exchange rates. The amount of the hedge required will also change as interest rates change, so that a hedged position will not remain hedged. In practice the exposure might, for example, be reassessed daily.

In forward transaction exposures, other elements, such as interest to be paid and received (rather than only interest already accrued), and the principal of a loan or deposit itself, should also be hedged.

EXERCISES

74. The Eurosterling interest rate for one year (exactly 365 days) is 6%. The EuroSwiss Franc interest rate for the same period is 3%. The spot rate today is GBP/CHF 2.1580 / 90.

What would you expect the GBP/CHF swap price to be for one year forward? (Ignore the buy–sell spread and calculate the middle price only.)

75.

	Spot	3-month forward swap
USD/CHF	1.5140 / 45	29 / 32
USD/NOK	7.1020 / 40	246 / 259
GBP/USD	1.6490 / 00	268 / 265

Based on the prices above, what are the two-way prices for:

a. CHF/NOK spot? Which side does the customer buy NOK?

b. GBP/NOK spot? Which side does the customer sell GBP?

c. USD/NOK 3 months forward outright?

d. GBP/USD 3 months forward outright?

e. GBP/NOK 3 months forward outright? Which currency has higher interest rates?

f. CHF/NOK 3 months forward outright? Which currency has higher interest rates?

g. CHF/NOK 3 months forward swap?

76.

	Spot	O/N	T/N	S/W	1 month
USD/NOK	7.1020 / 40	2.0 / 2.5	2.3 / 2.9	18 / 20	
EUR/USD	1.2490 / 00	10.6 / 10.1	3.5 / 3.3	23 / 22	96 / 94

Based on the prices above, what are the two-way prices for:

a. USD/NOK forward outright value one week after spot?

b. USD/NOK forward outright value tomorrow?

c. USD/NOK forward outright value today? Which side does the customer buy NOK?

d. EUR/USD forward outright value today? Which side does the customer buy EUR?

e. EUR/USD forward-forward swap from one week after spot to one month after spot? Which side does the customer buy and sell EUR (in that order)?

f. EUR/USD forward-forward swap from tomorrow to one month after spot? Which side does the customer buy and sell EUR (in that order)?

77. You are a bank FX dealer. Looking at the Reuters screen, you see the following rates:

USD/JPY spot:	126.95 / 15
T/N:	2.5 / 1.5
3 months:	310 / 290
6 months:	550 / 510
USD/NOK spot:	6.7620 / 40
T/N:	0.2 / 0.5
3 months:	15 / 15 A/P
6 months:	50 / 100

a. Some time ago, your customer sold NOK receivables forward into JPY, and that deal matures on the date which is now the 3-month forward date. However he now discovers that these receivables will be delayed by three months because of late delivery of the goods. He therefore needs to adjust the forward deal. What forward-forward swap price do you quote him? He asks for a two-way price and prefers to have it quoted in terms of number of JPY per 1 NOK. Which side of the price do you deal on?

b. Your customer has another deal to sell NOK and buy JPY, also previously undertaken, also maturing on the 3-month forward date. He discovers first thing in the morning that he needs the JPY by tomorrow and that he will have enough NOK in his account tomorrow to cover this. He therefore uses another forward-forward deal to adjust this second deal in order to take delivery of it tomorrow. Again, what two-way price do you quote, and on which side do you deal?

78. Today is Friday 19 April. You are a bank FX dealer. You look at your Reuters screen and see the following rates quoted:

USD/NOK	Spot:	7.2580 / 00
	S/W:	25 / 23
	1 month:	100 / 90
	2 months:	195 / 175
GBP/USD	Spot:	1.6157 / 67
	O/N:	– 0.4 / +0.1
	T/N:	1.5 / 1
	S/W:	11 / 9
	1 month:	50 / 45
	2 months:	105 / 95

a. Some time ago, your customer sold GBP forward against NOK for delivery on 3 June. He now discovers that he will need the NOK on 30 April instead. He therefore asks you for a swap price to adjust the deal's maturity date. What price do you quote (in terms of NOK per 1 GBP)?

b. Some time ago, you bought GBP from your customer against USD, and the deal matures today. He discovers (early enough) that he does not have the GBP in his account, and will not have them until 30 April. He asks you for a two-way price to swap the deal from today until 30 April. What price do you quote? On which side of the price do you deal?

c. He has discovered that he is not in fact going to receive the GBP in (b) at all, and decides to reverse the contract he made some time ago. He therefore asks you for a two-way outright value today price. What price do you quote? On which side of the price do you deal?

79. You are a bank FX dealer. You look at your Reuters screen and see the following rates quoted:

EUR/USD	spot:	1.2012 / 22
USD/JPY	spot:	127.30 / 35
USD/JPY	6-month swap:	266 / 260
USD	6-month interest rates:	5.25 / 5.375%
JPY	6-month interest rates:	1.00 / 1.25%

The 6-month value date is 182 days after spot value date.

a. Your customer needs to convert his JPY receivables into USD in six months' time. What two-way forward outright price would you quote for this? Is the JPY at a discount or a premium to the USD? On which side of the price would you deal?

b. He is not necessarily in a hurry to do this transaction, because he thinks that the spot exchange rate will get better for him. He expects the EUR/USD to move to 1.1900 over the next two days, but believes that the JPY is likely to move from its present level of 153 against the EUR to 151.

He also believes that USD interest rates will fall tomorrow by 0.5% but that JPY rates will probably rise 1.0% at the same time.

Should he sell the JPY forward now, or wait two days?

80. An investor has USD 15 million to invest for three months. He has a choice between two possible investments – either a USD deposit or EUR commercial paper which could be hedged back into USD (covered interest arbitrage). The commercial paper would yield EURIBOR + 4 basis points. If he invests via the commercial paper, what is his absolute all-in rate of return, and what is this relative to dollar LIBOR?

Spot EUR/USD:	1.2730 / 40
3-month swap:	132 / 128
3-month EUR%:	$8\frac{1}{4} / 8\frac{3}{8}\%$
3-month USD%:	$4\frac{1}{8} / 4\frac{1}{4}\%$

Assume that a mismatch of principal amounts is possible in the foreign exchange swap, and that the 3-month period has 91 days.

81. Market rates now are as follows for USD and NOK:

	USD/NOK	USD%	NOK%
Spot:	6.0000 / 10		
3 months (91 days):	590 / 605	5.87 / 6.00	9.87 / 10.00
6 months (182 days):	1274 / 1304	5.75 / 5.87	10.12 / 10.25
9 months (273 days):	1832 / 1872	5.75 / 5.87	10.00 / 10.12
FRA 3 v 9:		5.70 / 5.75	

Market rates three months later are as follows:

	USD/NOK	USD%	NOK%
Spot:	6.2060 / 65		
3 months (91 days):	649 / 664	6.00 / 6.12	10.25 / 10.37
6 months (182 days):	1394 / 1424	5.87 / 6.00	10.50 / 10.62
9 months (274 days):	2014 / 2054	5.87 / 6.00	10.37 / 10.50

What would be the effective synthetic forward-forward 3 v 9 cost for NOK for a borrower, created from an FRA 3 v 9 for USD, and all necessary forward foreign exchange deals, taking into account all the relevant bid / offer spreads? Show all the deals necessary based on an amount of NOK 1 million and assume that you are a price-taker.

82. You undertake the following two GBP/USD forward swap deals for value spot against 6 months (182 days):

a. You buy and sell GBP 10 million at 1.6510 and 1.6350.

b. You sell and buy GBP 10 million at 1.6495 and 1.6325.

6-month interest rates are as follows:

GBP: 6.5%
USD: 4.5%

What is the NPV of your position?

83. You are EUR-based and have the following transactions on your books:

■ A 6-month (182 days) forward purchase of USD 10 million.

■ A 12-month (365 days) forward sale of USD 10 million.

■ A borrowing from a counterparty of USD 10 million at 7% for 12 months (365 days; all the interest paid at maturity).

■ A deposit placed with a counterparty of USD 10 million at 6.5% for 3 months (91 days).

Rates are currently as follows:

	EUR/USD	EUR%	USD%
Spot:	1.2000		
3 months:	1.2027	6.5	7.4
6 months:	1.2059	6.5	7.5
12 months:	1.2114	7.0	8.0

a. Suppose that the spot exchange rate moves to 1.3000 but interest rates are unchanged. What is the effect on the profit and loss account, not considering discounting?

b. What is the effect considering discounting, and what spot EUR/USD deal would provide a hedge against this risk?

Part 4

Swaps and Options

"Any swap is effectively an exchange of one set of cashflows for another, considered to be of equal value. The concept of a basic interest rate swap is similar to an FRA, but is applied to a series of cashflows over a longer period of time rather than to a single period."

■ ■ ■

9

Interest Rate and Currency Swaps

BASIC CONCEPTS AND APPLICATIONS

Any swap is effectively the exchange of one set of cashflows for another considered to be of equal value. The concept of a basic interest rate swap in particular is very similar to an FRA, but is applied to a series of cashflows over a longer period of time, rather than to a single borrowing period.

Hedging borrowing costs

Consider, for example, the case we examined in Chapter 3 on FRAs, of a borrower who uses an FRA to hedge the cost of a single three-month borrowing due to begin in two months' time, by buying a 2 v 5 FRA (see Figure 9.1).

Figure 9.1

Hedging with an FRA

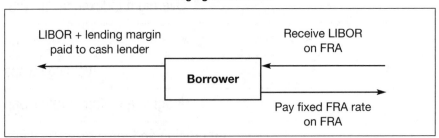

In this case, the borrower's *net* cost is (fixed FRA rate + lending margin).

Now consider the case of a borrower who takes a 5-year borrowing now and on which he will pay LIBOR refixed at 3-monthly intervals throughout the life of the borrowing. The cost of the first 3-month period is already fixed at the current LIBOR. The borrower could fix the cost of the second 3-month period of the borrowing with a 3 v 6 FRA. He could also fix the cost of the third 3-month period with a 6 v 9 FRA, and so on. However, if he wishes to hedge the cost of all the 3-month LIBOR settings throughout the 5 years, he would use an interest rate swap, which achieves exactly this (see Figure 9.2).

Figure 9.2

Hedging with an interest rate swap

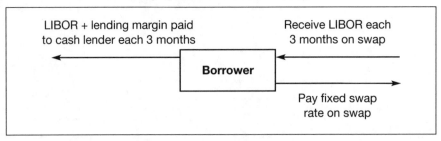

In this case, the borrower's net cost is (fixed swap rate + lending margin). The fixed rate quoted to the borrower by the swap dealer applies throughout the 5-year period of the swap. The fixed rate may be paid for example 3-monthly, 6-monthly or annually, depending on the exact terms of the swap. The floating rate may be 1-month LIBOR, 3-month LIBOR, 6-month LIBOR, etc. A basic interest rate swap is quoted as a fixed interest rate on one side and LIBOR exactly on the other (rather than, say, LIBOR + margin or LIBOR − margin). The fixed and floating payments may not have the same frequency. For example the fixed rate may be paid annually, but the floating rate may be based on 6-month LIBOR and paid semi-annually.

As with an FRA, an interest rate swap involves no exchange of principal. Only the interest flows are exchanged and, in practice, again as with an FRA, these are netted rather than transferred gross in both directions. An important mechanical difference is that the settlement amount in a swap is generally paid at the end of the relevant period (rather than at the beginning on a discounted basis as in an FRA).

The motivation for the borrower in the example above may be that he formerly expected interest rates to fall (and therefore took a floating rate borrowing), but now expects interest rates to rise − that is, he has changed his view. An alternative motivation could be that, regardless of his view, he has existing floating-rate funding but for commercial purposes needs fixed-rate funding (for example, a company funding a long-term project).

> **An interest rate swap is an exchange of one set of interest flows for another, with no exchange of principal.**　　**Key Point**

Relative advantage in borrowing

One particular driving force behind the swap market is the existence of cost discrepancies between different funding methods, as shown by the following example.

Example 9.1

Each of the following two companies wishes to borrow for 5 years and each has access to both fixed-rate borrowing and floating-rate borrowing.

Company AAA has access to floating-rate borrowing at LIBOR + 0.1% and also has access to fixed-rate borrowing at 8.0%. Company AAA would prefer floating-rate borrowing.

Company BBB has access to floating-rate borrowing at LIBOR + 0.8% and also has access to fixed-rate borrowing at 9.5%. Company BBB would prefer fixed-rate borrowing.

If AAA borrows at LIBOR + 0.1% and BBB borrows at 9.5%, each company achieves what it requires. There is however a structure which achieves the same result at a lower cost. This is for AAA to take a fixed-rate borrowing at 8.0%, BBB

to take a floating-rate borrowing at LIBOR + 0.8% and for AAA and BBB to transact a swap at 8.3% (which we will assume to be the current market rate for a swap)
against LIBOR as follows:

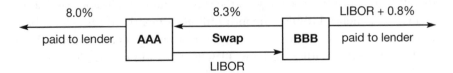

	8.0%		8.3%		LIBOR + 0.8%
	paid to lender	**AAA**	**Swap**	**BBB**	paid to lender

LIBOR

The net cost for AAA is: (8.0% – 8.3% + LIBOR) = LIBOR – 0.3%

The net cost for BBB is: (LIBOR + 0.8% + 8.3% – LIBOR) = 9.1%

In this way, each company achieves what it requires, but at a cost which is 0.4%
lower than it would achieve by the "straightforward" route.

In the example above, BBB's borrowing costs are higher than AAA's
whether we are comparing fixed-rate or floating-rate borrowing. However
the difference between their costs is greater in the fixed-rate market (9.5%
compared with 8.0%) than in the floating-rate market (LIBOR + 0.8%
compared with LIBOR + 0.1%). It is this discrepancy – which does arise in
practice – which makes the structure of the example possible. Company
BBB has an absolute cost disadvantage compared with company AAA in
either market. However BBB's *relative* advantage is in the floating-rate
market and AAA's *relative* advantage is in the fixed-rate market. It is therefore more cost-efficient for each company to borrow where it has a relative
advantage and then swap.

In practice, each company is likely to deal with a bank rather than
another company. The bank, whose role is to make a market in swaps, is
unlikely to deal with two offsetting counterparties in this way at the same
moment for the same period and the same amount. Nevertheless, the
simplified example above demonstrates what is an important force behind
the existence of the swap market.

Typically, the structure described above might involve company AAA in
issuing a fixed-rate bond and simultaneously arranging the swap. The bond
issue would give rise to various costs – issuing fees, underwriting fees, etc.
– which would not arise in a straightforward floating-rate borrowing, and
these need to be taken into account by AAA in calculating its all-in net
floating-rate cost after the swap.

This "arbitrage" between different borrowing markets can be extended.
Suppose that a company arranges to borrow at a floating rate based on
something other than LIBOR. For example, the company might be in a
position to issue commercial paper. If it believes that its cost of borrowing
through CP will average less than its cost would be based on a margin over
LIBOR over 5 years, it could use a rolling CP borrowing programme

instead. Clearly this leaves the company vulnerable to the risk that its CP costs may increase relative to LIBOR because the market's perception of the company's credit rating worsens, or because investors' demand for CP falls. The company may nevertheless be prepared to take this risk in return for a possible advantage – see Figure 9.3.

Seeking an advantage from CP funding Figure 9.3

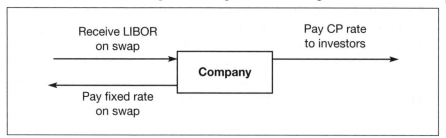

The net result of such an arrangement will be a borrowing cost of (fixed swap rate – (LIBOR – CP rate)). As long as the CP rate is below LIBOR, the borrowing cost will be less than the fixed swap rate. If the CP rate rises relative to LIBOR however, so will the all-in cost.

Asset swap

The examples we have used so far have been based on an underlying borrowing. That is, the "end-user" undertaking the swap has an underlying borrowing and wishes to change the character of the borrowing from fixed-rate to floating-rate or vice versa.

A swap can however be used by an investor just as well as by a borrower. An investor might, for example, buy an FRN and also transact a swap to receive a fixed interest rate and pay LIBOR. The result would be a synthetic fixed rate investment. A swap with an underlying asset like this is called an asset swap (Figure 9.4), while a swap with an underlying liability is called a liability swap. The swap itself is the same in both cases; the "asset" or "liabil-

Asset swap Figure 9.4

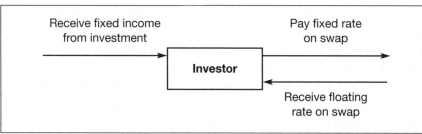

ity" tag refers to the package of which it forms a part. Often, the expression "asset swap" is used to describe the whole package – the swap **plus** the asset.

Speculation

As with any instrument, a swap may be used for speculation as well as hedging.

A dealer deliberately taking a position with a swap is speculating that long-term yields will move up or down. If he expects yields to rise, for example, he will undertake a swap where he is paying out the fixed interest rate and receiving LIBOR. If he is correct, he can later offset this with a swap, for the same period, where he is paying LIBOR and receiving the fixed interest rate – which will then be at a higher level, giving him a profit – see Figure 9.5.

Figure 9.5

Closing out an interest rate swap position

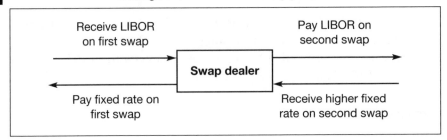

Basis swap

As described so far, an interest rate swap involves the payment of a fixed interest rate in one direction and a floating interest rate in the other direction. This is known as a "coupon swap". A swap can alternatively involve two differently defined floating rates – for example, the payment of LIBOR and the receipt of a rate based on commercial paper rates. Such a floating-floating swap is called a "basis swap". "Index swaps" can also be constructed, where the flows in one or other direction are based on an index (such as a stock index, for example).

OVERNIGHT INDEXED SWAP (OIS)

In Chapter 2, on the Money Market, we discussed overnight indexes such as EONIA, SONIA and Fed funds effective. An "overnight indexed swap" ("OIS") is a swap where one leg is based on an overnight index. As usual with such an index, settlement is made at the end of the period, based on compounding a series of daily tom/next fixings rather than a series of overnight indexes. Although "OIS" means "overnight indexed swap" in general, it usually refers to a USD OIS in particular. Similarly, although

"TOIS" means "tom/next indexed swap" in general, it usually refers to a CHF TOIS in particular. In the case of the CHF TOIS, the TOIS is fixed at a particular time of day, rather than being an average over the day.

An OIS is a swap against an overnight indexed rate.

Key Point

Settlement of the overnight index on an OIS is made at the end of the period, on a compound basis, in the same way as when a strip is calculated:

On Tuesday 14 March, I transact to pay 4.5% fixed in a 1-week OIS for USD 10 million. The swap is from Thursday 16 March to Thursday 23 March. The O/N fixings are as follows:

Example 9.2

Thursday fixing for Thursday/Friday:	4.6%
Friday fixing for Friday/Monday:	4.5%
Monday fixing for Monday/Tuesday:	4.7%
Tuesday fixing for Tuesday/Wednesday:	4.4%
Wednesday fixing for Wednesday/Thursday:	4.3%

I receive the following:

USD 10 million × (1 + (0.046 × 1/360)) × (1 + (0.045 × 3/360))
    × (1 + (0.047 × 1/360)) × (1 × (0.044 × 1/360))
    × (1 + (0.043 × 1/360)) − 1) = USD 8,752.81

I pay the following:

USD 10 million × 0.045 × 7/360 = USD 8,750.00

Net settlement:

I receive USD 8,752.81 − USD 8,750.00 = USD 2.81

The exact timing of the settlement on such a swap is often shortly after the maturity of the swap, rather than on the maturity date itself as would normally be the case with a swap. For example, a USD OIS is usually settled two days after maturity. The timing of an OIS or TOIS is as shown in the table.

Currency	Swap known as	O/N or T/N index	Deal date	Swap period start maturity	First index fixing	Settle -ment
USD	"OIS"	Fed funds effective	15 April	17 April – 17 May	17 April	19 May
GBP	"SONIA"	SONIA	15 April	15 April – 15 May	15 April	15 May
EUR	"EONIA"	EONIA	15 April	17 April – 17 May	17 April	18 May
CHF	"TOIS"	T/N	15 April	17 April – 17 May	16 April	19 May

Trading and hedging with an OIS

The OIS market has grown dramatically in volume because of the instrument's various advantages and uses:

- Liquidity requirements and interest rate risk can be managed separately. Suppose, for example, that a bank wishes to borrow for 1 year to ensure liquidity, but would prefer to fund itself overnight from the point of view of interest rate risk. It can take in a 1-year borrowing and transact a 1-year OIS to pay the OI and receive 1-year fixed.

- Because there is an advantage to the dealer in being able to lock in funding at an overnight cost in this way without needing to roll over each day, the OIS rate for a given period tends to trade slightly below the cash interest rate for the same period, and the difference between the two tends to widen in times whenever funding might be harder to find.

- An OIS can be used in arbitrage strategies. For example, a dealer might borrow funds repeatedly in the overnight market, lend for say a 3-month term, and pay fixed / receive the OI in an OIS.

- An OIS can help with collateral risk management. Rather than transact a term repo, a dealer can transact a series of overnight repos (so that the collateral is returned and replaced each day), but effectively fix the repo rate for a longer period by using an OIS. Conversely, if a dealer wishes to borrow for a longer term in order to secure the funds, but wishes to borrow at an overnight interest cost, he can transact a term repo and receive fixed / pay OI in an OIS.

- Credit risk can be reduced significantly. Rather than lend money for 1 year, a dealer can transact an OIS to pay the OI and receive 1-year fixed, and at the same time lend money for only 1 day in the overnight market and then roll over this overnight cash loan repeatedly for a year. The credit risk on the rolling overnight loan is far smaller than the credit risk would be on a 1-year loan. This separates the interest rate decision from the balance sheet decision. The same could be done with a traditional term swap, say for 1 year against 3-month LIBOR, but an overnight credit risk is clearly less than a 3-month one and leaves the dealer with greater flexibility in his lending decisions.

- Conversely, an investor can use an OIS for an asset swap, whereby he invests in an attractively-priced long-term investment but swaps the income to the overnight rate (receive the OI and pay the fixed in the OIS).

- Capital charges can be reduced. Traditionally, a bank money market dealer has taken a position on the yield curve by, for example, lending out long-term and funding himself in the overnight market. Such a strategy is profitable as long as the yield curve is more than slightly positive, but incurs capital charges because of the loan. The credit risk and capital charge are dramatically reduced by taking the same position using an OIS (for example paying the OI and receiving the fixed in the OIS in this example). Another way of seeing this is that, because of the reduced credit risk and capital charge, a bank can take a much greater position – i.e. increase its gearing. Using the swap also incurs lower transaction costs, because the bid/offer spread on an OIS is significantly lower than the spread in the cash market. The same is true in any situation where a dealer uses an interest rate swap instead of the cash market to take a position. An OIS however is closer to the strategy of a money market dealer, in maturity and characteristics, than a traditional longer-term IRS.

- Because of the reduced credit risk involved in using an OIS, the OIS fixed rate can be seen as a proxy for the government bond yield for the same period. Suppose that a dealer wishes to take a position on the IRS spread (i.e. the spread between the IRS rate for a particular period and the government bond yield for that period) because he expects that spread to widen or narrow. He might instead take a position in the spread between the IRS for that period against LIBOR, and an OIS for the same period. For example, if he expects the swap spread to narrow, he would receive the fixed/pay LIBOR in the traditional IRS and pay the fixed/receive OI in the OIS.

- The overnight interest rate responds immediately to any change in central bank interest rates. Therefore if a dealer wishes to take a position speculating on a change in central bank rates, he can instead take a position in an OIS.

- Two offsetting OISs can create a swap for a short period. Suppose that a dealer receives fixed in a 6-month OIS and pays fixed in a 1-week OIS; he rolls over the 1-week OIS when it matures, and repeats this each week until the end of the 6 months. The effect is to receive fixed at the end of 6 months and pay a floating 1-week rate each week during the 6 months.

- A dealer can create a short-term forward-forward interest rate with two OISs. Suppose, for example, that the dealer has sold an FRA to a customer for a 1-month period, starting in 1 week (1 week v 5 weeks). The dealer can hedge himself by paying the fixed in a 5-week OIS and receiving fixed in a 1-week OIS. Over the first week, the OI payment and receipt offset each other. At the end of the 1 week, when the FRA settles against LIBOR, the dealer transacts a 1-month OIS to receive the fixed (in line with LIBOR at the time, which will be used to settle the FRA), thereby reversing the original 5-week OIS.

- Similarly, a dealer with an existing IRS position on which LIBOR will be refixed soon has the risk that LIBOR might change against him, and might wish to cover this risk, effectively with a forward-forward constructed from OISs in the same way.

PRICING

Day / year conventions

The day / year conventions for calculating interest payments on swaps are largely the same as we have already seen for money market and bond calculations – that is, ACT/360, ACT/365, ACT/ACT, 30(E)/360 or 30(A)/360. There are a few points to mention, however.

Modified following

In the bond market, we have already seen that if a regular coupon date falls on a weekend or holiday, the payment is generally delayed until the next working day but the amount of the payment is not changed.

In the money market, in the same circumstances, the payment is delayed until the next working day unless this would move into the following calendar month, in which case the payment is made on the previous working day. In either case, the amount of the payment is calculated to the actual payment date, not the regular date.

The usual convention in the swap market is the same as in the money market and is called the "modified following" method. This can mean that the cashflows in a swap and a bond, which are intended to match precisely, are in fact slightly different in timing and amount.

ACT/ACT

In a swap, calculation of an interest payment on an ACT/ACT basis is split between that part of the interest period falling in a leap year, which is divided by 366, and the remainder, which is divided by 365.

Example 9.3 The fixed leg of a swap is based on 10% ACT/ACT (annual). What is the amount of the fixed payment for the period 15 October 2011 to 15 October 2012?

15 October 2011 to 31 December 2012 (inclusive):	78 days
1 January 2012 to 14 October 2012 (inclusive):	288 days

Interest amount is therefore $\left(10\% \times \dfrac{78}{365}\right) + \left(10\% \times \dfrac{288}{366}\right)$

ACT/365

In swap documentation (as in standard ISDA [International Swaps and Derivatives Association] documentation, for example), the expression "ACT/365" is sometimes used as an alternative for ACT/ACT, and the expression "ACT/365 (fixed)" is sometimes used instead for what we have defined in this book as ACT/365.

30/360

In Chapter 5 we discussed various 30/360 methods, including the ISDA versions.

Converting between different quotation bases

The basis for quoting the rate on the fixed leg of a swap might be annual, or semi-annual, quarterly, monthly, etc. As we have seen above, it may also be on a bond basis or a money market basis. We need to be able to convert between these different bases.

In this context, the market uses the expression "money market basis" to mean ACT/360. The term "bond basis" is used to mean ACT/365, ACT/ACT or 30/360. Over a non-leap year, these three are equivalent over a whole year (because $\frac{365}{365} = \frac{360}{360} = 1$).

Convert a USD interest rate of 10.3% SABB (semi-annual bond basis) to the AMM (annual money market) equivalent. **Example 9.4**

$$\left[\left(1 + \frac{0.103}{2}\right)^2 - 1\right] = 10.565\% \text{ ABB}$$

$$10.565\% \times \frac{360}{365} = 10.420\% \text{ AMM}$$

Answer: 10.42% AMM

Convert a EUR interest rate of 6.40% ABB (annual bond basis) to the SAMM (semi-annual money market) equivalent. **Example 9.5**

(1) $\left[(1.064)^{\frac{1}{4}} - 1\right] \times 2 = 6.301\% \text{ SABB}$

(2) $6.301\% \times \frac{360}{365} = 6.214\% \text{ SAMM}$

Answer: 6.21% SAMM

The conversions between annual and semi-annual in Examples 9.4 and 9.5 are the conversions we saw in Chapter 1, "Financial Arithmetic Basics", between effective and nominal rates. When we discussed effective rates on a 360-day basis in Chapter 2, "The Money Market", however, we saw that it is not possible to make this conversion precisely for rates on a money market basis (ACT/360).

Suppose that in Example 9.5, we try to compound the 6.214% SAMM directly to AMM:

(3) $\left(1 + \frac{0.06214}{2}\right)^2 - 1 = 6.311\% \text{ AMM}$

If we now finally try to convert back to ABB again, we have:

(4) $6.311\% \times \dfrac{365}{360} = 6.399\%$ ABB

This is almost the same as the 6.40% ABB with which we began in Example 9.5, but not quite. This is because step (3) above is not valid. Essentially, we can convert between the various bases but completing the square in Figure 9.6 below between SAMM and AMM is only approximate because it would be compounding on a 360-day basis rather than an annual basis.

Conversion between different quotation bases

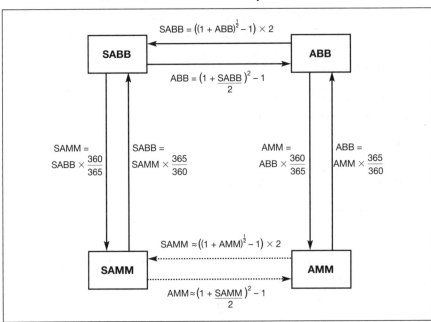

The following example uses the conversions we have seen above to calculate the approximate net result of an asset swap. We have repeated the example later (see Example 9.12) using exact cashflows and zero-coupon discount factors to calculate a slightly different result.

An investor purchases a 3-year bond yielding 10.686% (annual bond basis). He transacts a swap to pay 10.3% (annual bond basis) against 6-month LIBOR (semi-annual money market basis). What is the net yield to the investor of this asset swap?

Income from bond: 10.686% (ABB) = 10.415% (SABB) = 10.272% (SAMM)
Payment in swap: 10.300% (ABB) = 10.048% (SABB) = 9.910% (SAMM)
Receipt in swap: LIBOR (SAMM)
Net yield: •   LIBOR + 0.362% (SAMM)

The investor can therefore achieve an all-in yield on the asset swap of around 36 basis points over LIBOR.

Prices quoted as a spread over government bonds

Swap rates are sometimes quoted as a "spread" over government bond yields – particularly for example in the USD swap market, where there is a good series of government bonds available. In this case, the market is taking the current yield for the government bond of the nearest maturity which is "on the run" – that is, the benchmark bond which has been issued recently and will generally be trading near par. The two-sided swap price quoted is the difference between this yield and the swap rate.

Example 9.7

The 5-year USD swap is quoted as 33/37 over treasuries. The current 5-year treasury note yield is 7.43%. What is the swap rate on an AMM basis?

US treasuries always pay semi-annual coupons. The 7.43% yield and spread are therefore SABB. Therefore the swap rate is:

$$(7.43 + 0.33)\% / (7.43 + 0.37)\% = 7.76\% / 7.80\% \text{ SABB}$$

$$\left[\left(1 + \frac{0.0776}{2}\right)^2 - 1\right] \times \frac{360}{365} = 7.802\%$$

$$\left[\left(1 + \frac{0.0780}{2}\right)^2 - 1\right] \times \frac{360}{365} = 7.843\%$$

The AMM equivalent is therefore 7.80% / 7.84%.

The pricing link between FRAs and interest rate swaps

Since it is possible to fix in advance the cost of borrowing from 3 months to 6 months (an FRA 3 v 6), from 6 months to 9 months, from 9 months to 12 months, etc., it must be possible to fix the cost for all these at once, giving a fixed cost for the whole period. This is the same process as when we constructed strips in Chapters 3 and 4 on Forward-forwards and FRAs, and Futures. There should theoretically be no arbitrage between the result of doing this and the result of a single interest rate swap for the whole period. This is because borrowing on a rolling 3-month basis at LIBOR and at the same time transacting a swap to receive 3-month LIBOR quarterly against a fixed payment is an alternative to borrowing on a rolling 3-month basis at LIBOR and fixing the cost with a series of rolling FRAs. It is possible to arbitrage between the swap and the futures contracts if they are out of line. For example, if the swap rate is too high, a dealer could transact a swap to receive the fixed rate and pay LIBOR; at the same time, he would sell a strip of futures (or buy a strip of FRAs) to offset this. This therefore gives a method of arriving at a swap price derived from FRA rates (or equivalently, short-term futures prices).

Example 9.8

Suppose the following rates are available for borrowing dollars:

3-month	LIBOR:	14.0625%	(91 days)
FRA	3 v 6:	12.42%	(91 days)
	6 v 9:	11.57%	(91 days)
	9 v 12:	11.25%	(92 days)

It is possible to do the following:

■ Borrow USD 1 now for 3 months. At end of 3 months, repay:

$$USD \left(1 + 0.140625 \times \frac{91}{360}\right) = USD\ 1.03555$$

■ Arrange an FRA 3 v 6 at 12.42 on an amount of USD 1.03555. Considering the FRA settlement as made after 6 months rather than made on a discounted basis after 3 months, this gives a total repayment at the end of 6 months of:

$$USD\ 1.03555 \times \left(1 + 0.1242 \times \frac{91}{360}\right) = USD\ 1.06806$$

■ Similarly, after 6 months, borrow USD 1.06806 for 3 months, fixed at an FRA 6 v 9 cost of 11.57%, and at the end of 9 months repay:

$$USD\ 1.06806 \times \left(1 + 0.1157 \times \frac{91}{360}\right) = USD\ 1.09929$$

■ Similarly, after 9 months, borrow USD 1.09929 for 3 months, fixed at an FRA 9 v 12 cost of 11.25%, and at the end of 12 months repay:

$$USD\ 1.09929 \times \left(1 + 0.1125 \times \frac{92}{360}\right) = USD\ 1.13090$$

The effect of this is a fixed cost at the end of 12 months of 13.09%. This should therefore be the rate for a 12-month interest rate swap on an annual basis against quarterly LIBOR payments.

The rate of 13.090% is on a bond basis, not a money market basis, even though the FRA rates from which it has been constructed are quoted on a money market basis. This is because "bond basis" represents the cash interest amount paid by the end of 365 days – which is what we have calculated – while "money market basis" represents the cash interest amount paid by the end of 360 days.

To convert from this annual bond basis to an equivalent quarterly bond basis, we could decompound as before to give:

$$\left((1 + 0.13090)^{\frac{1}{4}} - 1\right) \times 4 = 12.49\%\ (QBB)$$

The equivalent quarterly money market swap rate for 1 year against 3-month LIBOR would then be calculated as:

$$12.49\% \times \frac{360}{365} = 12.32\%\ (QMM)$$

Note however that following Example 9.9, we calculate a slightly different result for this.

Example 9.8 gave a 1-year swap rate of 13.090% on a bond basis. We can use the same process to construct swap rates for other maturities: 3 months, 6 months, 9 months, 15 months, 18 months, etc. As long as forward-forward prices are available (either as FRAs or futures) for the periods leading up to the swap maturity, we can construct a strip. The result in each case is a zero-coupon swap rate, as the strip process rolls all the interest to an accumulated total at the end maturity.

If we calculate a series of zero-coupon swap rates in this way, we then have a set of discount factors for valuing cashflows. In Chapter 7 on Zero-coupon Rates and Yield Curves, we used zero-coupon discount factors to calculate the theoretical par bond yield. In exactly the same way, we can use the zero-coupon swap rates to calculate a swap rate.

The swap rates so constructed are called "par" swap rates. This refers to the market rate on the fixed side of a swap, which is conventionally quoted so as to be paid or received against LIBOR exactly on the other side. It may be (as in Example 9.12 below) that the final swap structure agreed involves the payment or receipt of an off-market fixed swap rate, in return for an amount which represents LIBOR plus or minus some compensating spread. Such an off-market swap structure may result in more convenient cashflows for one of the parties.

Suppose we have the following rates (the first four are the same as in Example 9.8). What is the 2-year par swap rate on a quarterly money market basis?

Example 9.9

3-month	LIBOR:	14.0625%	(91 days)
FRA	3 v 6:	12.42%	(91 days)
	6 v 9:	11.57%	(91 days)
	9 v 12:	11.25%	(92 days)
	12 v 15:	11.00%	(91 days)
	15 v 18:	10.90%	(91 days)
	18 v 21:	10.80%	(91 days)
	21 v 24:	10.70%	(92 days)

From Example 9.8, we know that if we borrow USD 1 now for 3 months, we repay USD 1.03555 at the end of the period. Therefore the 3-month discount factor is:

$$\frac{1}{1.03555} = 0.9657$$

Using the other results from Example 9.8, we have the discount factor for 6 months as:

$$\frac{1}{1.06806} = 0.9363$$

and for 9 months as: $\dfrac{1}{1.09929} = 0.9097$

and for 12 months as: $\dfrac{1}{1.13090} = 0.8843$

We can now extend the strip process for the next year:

for 15 months: USD $1.13090 \times \left(1 + 0.1100 \times \dfrac{91}{360}\right) =$ USD 1.16235

$$\text{Discount factor} = \frac{1}{1.16235} = 0.8603$$

for 18 months: USD $1.16235 \times \left(1 + 0.1090 \times \dfrac{91}{360}\right) =$ USD 1.19438

$$\text{Discount factor} = \frac{1}{1.19438} = 0.8373$$

for 21 months: USD $1.19438 \times \left(1 + 0.1080 \times \dfrac{91}{360}\right) =$ USD 1.22699

$$\text{Discount factor} = \frac{1}{1.22699} = 0.8150$$

for 24 months: USD $1.22699 \times \left(1 + 0.1070 \times \dfrac{92}{360}\right) =$ USD 1.26054

$$\text{Discount factor} = \frac{1}{1.26054} = 0.7933$$

We can now use these discount factors to calculate the 2-year par swap rate, exactly as in the first example in Chapter 7. If i is the 2-year swap rate on a quarterly money market basis, then we have:

$$1 = \left(i \times \frac{91}{360} \times 0.9657\right) + \left(i \times \frac{91}{360} \times 0.9363\right) + \left(i \times \frac{91}{360} \times 0.9097\right)$$

$$+ \left(i \times \frac{92}{360} \times 0.8843\right) + \left(i \times \frac{91}{360} \times 0.8603\right) + \left(i \times \frac{91}{360} \times 0.8373\right)$$

$$+ \left(i \times \frac{91}{360} \times 0.8150\right) + \left(\left(1 + i \times \frac{92}{360}\right) \times 0.7933\right)$$

The solution to this is i = 11.65%.

The same approach of valuing the cashflows in a par swap can be applied to the simpler case of a 1-year par swap on a quarterly money market basis. If this rate is i, then using the same discount factors as above, we have:

$$1 = \left(i \times \frac{91}{360} \times 0.9657\right) + \left(i \times \frac{91}{360} \times 0.9363\right) + \left(i \times \frac{91}{360} \times 0.9097\right) +$$

$$\left(\left(1 + i \times \frac{92}{360}\right) \times 0.8843\right)$$

The solution to this is i = 12.35%.

This is not the same result as the 12.32% calculated in Example 9.8. The reason is that we have now discounted each cashflow precisely using an appropriate discount rate. In Example 9.8, however, we decompounded from an annual rate to a quarterly rate. This decompounding process is circular – the interest rate used for discounting is the same as the decompounded result itself. The answer we now have of 12.35% is a more accurate answer based on the data available.

Pricing interest rate swaps from futures or FRAs	Calculation summary
■ For each successive futures maturity, create a strip to generate a discount factor ■ Use the series of discount factors to calculate the yield of a par swap	

Pricing longer-term swaps

The last two examples provide a pricing method for interest rate swaps for as far forward in maturity as there are futures contracts available. If futures or FRAs are not available up to the maturity of an interest rate swap however, there is not such a precise arbitrage structure to calculate a swap rate. Longer-term swap rates must however be linked to capital market yields. In Example 9.1, we considered how company AAA achieved a lower LIBOR-based borrowing cost than it could otherwise have done, by combining a fixed-rate bond issue with a swap. In that example, where we ignored any fees associated with issuing a bond and any cost of intermediation by a bank, a swap rate of 7.9% would have given company AAA an all-in borrowing cost of (8.0% − 7.9% + LIBOR) = LIBOR + 0.1% − which is exactly the same as the cost achieved through a straightforward LIBOR-based borrowing. It was therefore necessary for the swap rate to be higher than around 7.9% in order for AAA to achieve a lower cost through the liability swap structure (we are ignoring here any differences between annual and semi-annual, or money market and bond basis).

On the other hand, a swap rate of 8.7% would have given company BBB an all-in borrowing cost of (LIBOR + 0.8% + 8.7% − LIBOR) = 9.5% − which is exactly the same as the cost achieved through a straightforward fixed-rate borrowing. It was therefore necessary for the swap rate to be less than around 8.7% in order for BBB to achieve a lower cost through the swap structure.

Although the available borrowing costs in Example 9.1 are hypothetical, this shows the type of considerations which generate the swap rate available in the market. As in other markets, it is the rate at which supply and demand balance. Supply and demand will be affected by borrowing and investment rates available to a wide range of market participants, with a range of different opportunities and fee structures.

VALUING SWAPS

Marking-to-market a swap

To value an interest rate swap, we calculate its NPV, exactly as we value other instruments. The most appropriate rates to use for discounting the cashflows to present values are zero-coupon swap yields. A less satisfactory alternative is to use the current par swap rate for the maturity of the swap we are valuing. In the section above on "The pricing link between FRAs and interest rate swaps", we created shorter-term zero-coupon swap rates from strips of FRAs. Longer-term zero-coupon swap yields can be created by bootstrapping from the par swap yield curve. This is done in exactly the same way as we constructed zero-coupon bond yields in Chapter 7. Instead of using a series of existing bonds for the bootstrapping process, we use a series of fictitious bonds, each of which has an initial cost of 100 and a coupon equal to the par swap rate.

One complication is the valuation of the floating-rate side of the swap, as the cashflows are not yet known. One approach is first to calculate, for each period, the forward-forward interest rates consistent with the current yield structure, and then to calculate each floating-rate cashflow assuming this forward-forward rate. Another approach – mathematically equivalent – is to add to the schedule of actual swap cashflows a further set of fictitious cashflows which exactly offsets the unknown amounts. If the additional fictitious cashflows can be arranged so that they have a zero NPV, the NPV that we are trying to calculate will be unaffected. As we have offset the unknown cashflows, we are left with an NPV which we can calculate.

The additional series of fictitious cashflows to be added is effectively a par FRN. Assuming no change in credit risk, an FRN should be priced at par on a coupon date. For example, issuing 100 of an FRN with a 6-monthly coupon of LIBOR is equivalent to borrowing 100 at LIBOR for only six months, and then repeatedly rolling the borrowing over at the end of each six months. It follows that on a coupon date, 100 is the NPV of the future FRN flows. Therefore a series of cashflows consisting of 100 in one direction at the beginning, offset by future FRN flows in the other direction, has a zero NPV. If these cashflows have a zero NPV on a future coupon date, they must also have a zero NPV now. We can therefore add these flows to the swap structure, beginning at the next swap interest payment date, without changing the total NPV.

Example 9.10   Value the following interest rate swap on 27 March 2010:

Notional amount of swap:	10 million
Start of swap:	23 July 2009
Maturity of swap:	23 July 2012
Receive:	7.4% (annual 30/360)
Pay:	LIBOR (semi-annual ACT/360)
Previous LIBOR fixing:	9.3% from 23 January 2010 to 23 July 2010

The zero-coupon discount factors from 27 March 2010 are:

23 July 2010:	0.9703
23 January 2011:	0.9249
23 July 2011:	0.8825
23 January 2012:	0.8415
23 July 2012:	0.8010

The cashflows are as follows:

Date	Swap	
23 July 2010:	$+ 10\,m \times 7.4\%$	$- 10\,m \times 9.3\% \times \frac{181}{360}$
23 Jan 2011:		$- 10\,m \times L_1 \times \frac{184}{360}$
23 July 2011:	$+ 10\,m \times 7.4\%$	$- 10\,m \times L_2 \times \frac{181}{360}$
23 Jan 2012		$- 10\,m \times L_3 \times \frac{184}{360}$
23 July 2012:	$+ 10\,m \times 7.4\%$	$- 10\,m \times L_4 \times \frac{182}{360}$

where: L_1 is LIBOR from 23 July 2010 to 23 January 2011
L_2 is LIBOR from 23 January 2011 to 23 July 2011
L_3 is LIBOR from 23 July 2011 to 23 January 2012
L_4 is LIBOR from 23 January 2012 to 23 July 2012

Method 1

From the discount factors, we can calculate forward-forward rates to substitute for the unknown LIBOR fixings as follows:

L_1: $\left(\dfrac{0.9703}{0.9249} - 1\right) \times \dfrac{360}{184} = 9.6039\%$

L_2: $\left(\dfrac{0.9249}{0.8825} - 1\right) \times \dfrac{360}{181} = 9.5560\%$

L_3: $\left(\dfrac{0.8825}{0.8415} - 1\right) \times \dfrac{360}{184} = 9.5327\%$

L_4: $\left(\dfrac{0.8415}{0.8010} - 1\right) \times \dfrac{360}{182} = 10.0012\%$

Using these rates, we have the following cashflows:

Date	Swap	Net cashflows
23 July 2010:	$+10\,m \times 7.4\% - 10\,m \times 9.3\% \times \frac{181}{360}$	+ 272,417
23 Jan 2011:	$- 10\,m \times 9.6039\% \times \frac{184}{360}$	− 490,866
23 July 2011:	$+10\,m \times 7.4\% - 10\,m \times 9.5560\% \times \frac{181}{360}$	+ 259,546
23 Jan 2012:	$- 10\,m \times 9.5327\% \times \frac{184}{360}$	− 487,227
23 July 2012:	$+10\,m \times 7.4\% - 10\,m \times 10.0012\% \times \frac{182}{360}$	+ 234,384

We can now value these net cashflows using the discount factors, to give:

$(272,417 \times 0.9703) + (-490,866 \times 0.9249) + (259,546 \times 0.8825) +$
$(-487,227 \times 0.8415) + (234,384 \times 0.8010) = -182,886$

The swap is therefore showing a mark-to-market valuation of −182,886.

Method 2

Without upsetting the NPV valuation, we can add the cashflows for a fictitious "FRN investment" of 10 million which starts on 23 July 2010, matures on 23 July 2012 and pays LIBOR, because the NPV of these cashflows will be zero on 23 July 2010 (and hence zero on 27 March 2010). The resulting cashflows will then be:

Date	Swap	"FRN"	Net cashflows
23 July 2010:	$+10\text{ m} \times 7.4\% - 10\text{ m} \times 9.3\% \times \frac{181}{360}$	-10 m	$+10\text{ m} \times 7.4\%$ $-10\text{ m} \times 9.3\% \times \frac{181}{360}$ -10 m
23 Jan 2011:	$-10\text{ m} \times L_1 \times \frac{184}{360}$	$+10\text{ m} \times L_1 \times \frac{184}{360}$	
23 July 2011:	$+10\text{ m} \times 7.4\% - 10\text{ m} \times L_2 \times \frac{181}{360}$	$+10\text{ m} \times L_2 \times \frac{181}{360}$	$+10\text{ m} \times 7.4\%$
23 Jan 2012:	$-10\text{ m} \times L_3 \times \frac{184}{360}$	$+10\text{ m} \times L_3 \times \frac{184}{360}$	
23 July 2012:	$+10\text{ m} \times 7.4\% - 10\text{ m} \times L_4 \times \frac{182}{360}$	$+10\text{ m} \times L_4 \times \frac{182}{360}$ $+10\text{ m}$	$+10\text{ m} \times 7.4\%$ $+10\text{ m}$

We can now value these cashflows using the discount factors to give:

$$(-9{,}727{,}583 \times 0.9703) + (740{,}000 \times 0.8825) + (10{,}740{,}000 \times 0.8010) = -182{,}884$$

Reversing a swap transaction

Suppose that a dealer or customer, who has previously entered into a swap transaction, now wishes to close out this position. He can transact another swap in the opposite direction for the remaining term of the existing swap. If he has previously dealt a swap to pay a fixed rate and receive LIBOR, for example, he can now deal instead to receive a fixed rate and pay LIBOR. The LIBOR cashflows will balance but, because the fixed rate on the new swap is unlikely to be the same as the fixed rate on the old swap, there will be a net difference in the fixed amount on each future payment date. This difference may be a net receipt or a net payment.

Rather than put a new swap on the books however, if the counterparty in the new swap is the same as the counterparty in the original swap, it may well be preferable for both parties to settle immediately the difference between the original swap rate and the new swap rate. This would reduce both credit line utilisation and capital adequacy requirements. In order to settle immediately, the potential future cashflows – the difference between the two fixed rates – need to be valued. This is done, as usual, by calculating the NPV of these net cashflows. This NPV is then paid by one party to the other, the original swap is cancelled and no new swap is transacted.

Example 9.11 We have on our books the swap already described in Example 9.10. For value on 23 July 2010, we decide to reverse the swap. The same counterparty quotes a swap rate of 8.25% then for the remaining 2 years. What should the settlement amount be to close out the swap position, using the following discount factors?

23 July 2011:	0.9250
23 July 2012:	0.8530

The LIBOR-based flows on the two swaps offset each other exactly. The remaining flows are then:

Date	Original swap	Reverse swap	Net cashflows
23 July 2011	+10 m × 7.4%	– 10 m × 8.25%	– 85,000
23 July 2012	+10 m × 7.4%	– 10 m × 8.25%	– 85,000

The NPV of the net cashflows is:

$$(-85{,}000 \times 0.9250) + (-85{,}000 \times 0.8530) = -151{,}130$$

We therefore pay the counterparty 151,130 to close out the existing swap.

Constructing an asset swap

The following example considers essentially the same asset swap as Example 9.6. In this case however, we construct a par / par swap – that is, a package with an initial principal amount invested, the same "par" principal amount returned at maturity, and an income stream calculated as a constant spread above or below LIBOR based on this same par amount. This is an asset swap to create a synthetic FRN, priced at par and redeemed at par.

An investor purchases the following bond and wishes to convert it to a synthetic FRN with an asset swap: **Example 9.12**

Settlement date:	18 August 2010
Maturity date:	18 August 2013
Coupon:	11.5% (annual)
Price:	102.00
Yield:	10.686%

The 3-year par swap rate from 18 August 2010 is quoted at 10.2% / 10.3% (annual 30/360) against LIBOR (semi-annual, ACT/360). The investor would like a par / par asset swap structure.

The discount factors from 18 August 2010 are given as follows:

18 February 2011:	0.9525
18 August 2011:	0.9080
18 February 2012:	0.8648
18 August 2012:	0.8229
18 February 2013:	0.7835
18 August 2013:	0.7452

Suppose that the principal amount invested is 102, and that the investor transacts a "straightforward" swap based on a par amount of 100. The bond cashflows and swap cashflows would then be as follows:

Date	Bond	Swap	
18 Aug 2010:	– 102		
18 Feb 2011:			$+100 \times \text{LIBOR} \times \frac{184}{360}$
18 Aug 2011:	+ 11.5	$– 100 \times 10.3\%$	$+100 \times \text{LIBOR} \times \frac{181}{360}$
18 Feb 2012:			$+100 \times \text{LIBOR} \times \frac{184}{360}$
18 Aug 2012:	+ 11.5	$– 100 \times 10.3\%$	$+100 \times \text{LIBOR} \times \frac{182}{360}$
18 Feb 2013:			$+100 \times \text{LIBOR} \times \frac{184}{360}$
18 Aug 2013:	+ 100 +11.5	$– 100 \times 10.3\%$	$+100 \times \text{LIBOR} \times \frac{181}{360}$

These cashflows will clearly not provide a "clean" result in terms of a spread relative to LIBOR based on a principal of 100, for two reasons. First, the difference between the 11.5% coupon on the bond and the 10.3% swap rate is an annual cashflow, but LIBOR is semi-annual. Second, the principal invested is 102 rather than 100. These differences have an NPV of:

$$(11.5 – 100 \times 10.3\%) \times 0.9080 + (11.5 – 100 \times 10.3\%) \times 0.8229 +$$
$$(11.5 – 100 \times 10.3\ \%) \times 0.7452 + (100 – 102) = 0.9713$$

What interest rate i (ACT/360, semi-annual) is necessary so that a series of cashflows at i based on a principal of 100 would have the same NPV?

$$(100 \times i \times \tfrac{184}{360} \times .9525) + (100 \times i \times \tfrac{181}{360} \times .9080) + (100 \times i \times \tfrac{184}{360} \times .8648) +$$
$$(100 \times i \times \tfrac{182}{360} \times .8229) + (100 \times i \times \tfrac{184}{360} \times .7835) + (100 \times i \times \tfrac{181}{360} \times .7452)$$

$$= 0.9713$$

The solution to this is: i = 0.0038.

We can therefore replace the following fixed cashflows arising from a par swap:
annual 30/360 swap outflows of (100 × 10.3%)
plus an initial "odd" investment of 2,

by the following fixed cashflows – effectively an off-market swap:
annual 30/360 swap outflows of (100 × 11.5%)
plus semi-annual ACT/360 inflows of (100 × 0.38%).

This 0.38% can then be added to the semi-annual swap inflows of (100 × LIBOR) which we already have. We have therefore replaced the par swap by one with the same NPV as follows:

Receive: LIBOR + 0.38% (ACT/360, semi-annual)
Pay: 11.5% (30/360, annual)

The net effect is therefore a par/par asset swap giving the investor LIBOR plus 38 basis points.

It is worth noting that the result of the last example is around 2 basis points worse than the approximate result calculated in Example 9.6. This is because in Example 9.6, the bond yield and swap rate are converted to semi-annual rates by decompounding at their own respective semi-annual rates. In Example 9.12, all cashflows are discounted by the discount factors.

- To value a swap, calculate the NPV of the cashflows, preferably using zero-coupon swap yields or the equivalent discount factors
- To value floating-rate cashflows, superimpose offsetting floating-rate cashflows known to have an NPV of zero – effectively an FRN
- A swap at current rates has an NPV of zero
- If a current swap involves an off-market fixed rate, this is compensated by an adjustment to the other side of the swap, or by a one-off payment, so as to maintain the NPV at zero

HEDGING AN INTEREST RATE SWAP

As with every instrument, a dealer may find he has a position which he does not want – either because he has changed his mind about the direction of interest rates, or because he has made a two-way price and been taken up on it. He is therefore exposed to movements in the swap rate and will want to hedge himself. This he can do in any of several ways:

1. Deal an exactly offsetting swap.

2. Deal in a different instrument which will give him offsetting flows. Suppose, for example, that under the swap, the dealer is paying out a fixed interest rate for 5 years. As a hedge, he might buy a 5-year bond – or a bond with a modified duration the same as that of a bond with coupons equal to the fixed swap rate. This will give him a fixed income to offset the fixed payment on the swap. In order to buy the bond, he can fund himself at LIBOR or a rate linked to LIBOR.

Hedging an interest rate swap

Figure 9.7

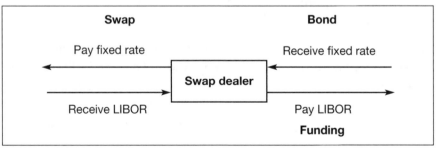

In this way, he is hedged for as long as he holds the bond. If the dealer does subsequently deal a second swap which offsets the first one, but 5-year rates have fallen, he will make a loss. However, the bond will have increased in value correspondingly. Clearly the hedge is not perfect, as the swap dealer is exposed during this period to the risk that the swap market does not move exactly in line with the bond he has used as a hedge – a basis risk.

3. Deal in bond futures or options. These may provide a liquid hedge, but the hedge could be less perfect, as the specifications of the futures or options contracts may imply a rather different maturity from the swap, so that the hedge value does not respond to yield changes in the same way as the swap.

AMORTISING AND FORWARD-START SWAPS

Amortising swap

In practice, a company often needs an interest rate swap on a borrowing which is amortising rather than one which has a bullet maturity – that is, the principal is repaid in instalments over the life of the borrowing rather than all at maturity. The borrowing may also be going to start at some time in the future, or already have begun so that the next interest payment is at some period ahead.

Consider a 2-year borrowing of 200 beginning now, with floating rate interest payments each 6 months and amortisations of 50 each 6 months. A single interest rate swap for 200 over 2 years would not match the borrowing profile, while four separate swaps of 50 each at different rates (one for 6 months, one for 1 year, one for 18 months and one for 2 years) would result in irregular interest flows. We therefore wish to create a single swap rate for the amortising structure.

Suppose that the swap rates (semi-annual bond basis against 6-month LIBOR) are as follows:

6 months:	6.00% (this is equivalent to current 6-month LIBOR)
1 year:	6.50%
18 months:	7.00%
2 years:	7.50%

We can calculate from these rates a set of zero-coupon discount factors by bootstrapping in the same way as we did in Chapter 7. These can be calculated to be:

6 months:	0.9709
1 year:	0.9380
18 months:	0.9016
2 years:	0.8623

If the single amortising swap rate is i, the cashflows on the borrowing plus swap would be as follows:

Time	Cashflow
Now:	$+200$
6 months:	$-50 - \left(200 \times \dfrac{i}{2}\right)$
1 year:	$-50 - \left(150 \times \dfrac{i}{2}\right)$
18 months:	$-50 - \left(100 \times \dfrac{i}{2}\right)$
2 years:	$-50 - \left(50 \times \dfrac{i}{2}\right)$

If the single rate i is consistent with the swap yield curve, the NPV of these flows will be zero:

$$\left(-50 - \left(200 \times \frac{i}{2}\right)\right) \times 0.9709 + \left(-50 - \left(150 \times \frac{i}{2}\right)\right) \times 0.9380 +$$

$$\left(-50 - \left(100 \times \frac{i}{2}\right)\right) \times 0.9016 + \left(-50 - \left(50 \times \frac{i}{2}\right)\right) \times 0.8623 + 200 = 0$$

The solution for this is i = 6.99%.

Forward-start swap

Consider now an 18-month borrowing of 150 which will not start for 6 months and which will amortise at the rate of 50 each 6 months again. It is possible to calculate the appropriate swap rate for this forward-start borrowing in exactly the same way. In this case, the cashflows are as follows:

Time	Cashflow
6 months:	$+150$
1 year:	$-50 - \left(150 \times \dfrac{i}{2}\right)$
18 months:	$-50 - \left(100 \times \dfrac{i}{2}\right)$
2 years:	$-50 - \left(50 \times \dfrac{i}{2}\right)$

Again, the NPV of these flows will be zero:

$$\left(-50 - \left(150 \times \frac{i}{2}\right)\right) \times 0.9380 + \left(-50 - \left(100 \times \frac{i}{2}\right)\right) \times 0.9016 +$$

$$\left(-50 - \left(50 \times \frac{i}{2}\right)\right) \times 0.8623 + 150 \times 0.9709 = 0$$

The solution for this is i = 7.69%.

The forward-start amortising swap rate is therefore 7.69% (semi-annual bond basis).

Calculation summary

> The current swap rate for a swap based on an irregular or forward-start notional principal is again the rate which gives the swap an NPV of zero.

Delayed-start swap

A swap may be transacted to start only a short time in the future, in which case the analysis in the last section cannot conveniently be used. An alternative approach is to consider that the dealer will hedge himself in the same way that he might when transacting a swap for immediate value – by buying or selling a bond. In this case however, the bond hedge will be immediate but the swap will not. The dealer will therefore incur a positive or negative net cost of carry – for example, the difference between the income on the bond and the funding cost of buying the bond, if the hedge is a bond purchase. This will be incurred for the period until the swap begins, at which time the hedge can be reversed and the dealer can cover his position with an offsetting swap.

An adjustment should therefore be made to the fixed rate quoted for the delayed-start swap. The NPV of this adjustment over the life of the swap should be equal to the net cost of carry for the hedging period.

CURRENCY SWAPS

Currency swaps involve an exchange of cashflows largely analogous to those in an interest rate swap, but in two different currencies. Thus one company might establish – or have already established – a borrowing in one currency, which it wishes to convert into a borrowing in another currency. One example would be where the existing borrowing, and the effective borrowing arrangement after the swap, are both fixed rate – a fixed-fixed currency swap. Currency swaps can also be fixed-floating or floating-floating. The transaction is the conversion of a stream of cashflows in one currency into a stream of cashflows in another currency.

It is important to note that, unlike an interest rate swap, a currency swap which is based on a borrowing or an asset generally involves exchange of the principal amount as well as the interest amounts. In a single-currency interest rate swap, nothing would be achieved by this – each party would simply be required to pay and receive the same principal amount, which would net to zero. In a currency swap however, the value of the principal amount at maturity depends on the exchange rate. If this is not included in the swap, the all-in result will not be known.

In order to exchange one cashflow stream for another, the two streams must have the same value at the time of the transaction. The appropriate value of each stream, as with other market instruments, is its NPV. To equate the two NPVs which are in different currencies, we use the current spot exchange rate.

> To value cashflows in a different currency,
> convert the resulting NPV at the spot exchange rate.

Calculation summary

Example 9.13

You purchase a 5-year USD bond with an annual coupon of 6.7%, at a price of 95.00. You convert this investment to a synthetic ZAR investment on a par amount, with an asset swap. The swap rate you achieve is 7.85% for USD against 8.35%, for ZAR (both annual bond basis). The current exchange rate is 6.00. What all-in ZAR yield do you achieve?

The future USD cashflows are as follows for each USD 100 face value:

Year 1 +   6.70
Year 2 +   6.70
Year 3 +   6.70
Year 4 +   6.70
Year 5 + 106.70

Discounting at a rate of 7.85%, the NPV of these flows is USD 95.390. At an exchange rate of 6.00, this is equivalent to ZAR 572.341.

For each USD 100 face value of the bond, you invested USD 95.00. This is equivalent to ZAR 570. You therefore wish to receive a series of ZAR cashflows, such that there is a regular ZAR cashflow in years 1 to 5, with an additional cashflow of ZAR 570 in year 5. The NPV of these cashflows, discounting at 8.35%, must be ZAR 572.341. This can be solved using the TVM function on an HP calculator to give the regular cashflow as ZAR 48.187. Other profiles for the ZAR cashflows could be chosen which also have an NPV of ZAR 572.341. This profile however provides the par structure at which we are aiming.

The yield on the asset swap is therefore the yield derived from an investment of ZAR 570, a principal amount of ZAR 570 returned at the end of 5 years and an income stream of ZAR 48.187 per year. This can be seen to be a yield of:

$$\frac{48.187}{570} = 8.454\%$$

Date	Bond USD	Swap USD	ZAR	Net cashflows ZAR
Now	– 95.00			– 570.000
Year 1	+ 6.70	– 6.70	+ 48.187	+ 48.187
Year 2	+ 6.70	– 6.70	+ 48.187	+ 48.187
Year 3	+ 6.70	– 6.70	+ 48.187	+ 48.187
Year 4	+ 6.70	– 6.70	+ 48.187	+ 48.187
Year 5	+ 106.70	– 106.70	+ 618.187	+ 618.187
NPV =		– 95.39	+ 572.341	

Cross-currency basis swaps

A cross-currency basis swap involves the payment of cashflows based on a floating rate index in one currency and the receipt of cashflows based on a floating rate index in another currency. Typically, the flows are based on LIBOR or EURIBOR. However it is unlikely that the flows would be, for example, exactly LIBOR in one currency against LIBOR in the other currency. Rather, there is likely to be a premium or discount paid in one direction.

When the swap involves the USD as one of the two currencies, the swap rate quotation implies that the USD LIBOR is paid without adjustment and that the other LIBOR is adjusted. A quotation of "5 / 7" for a USD/EUR basis swap, for example, would mean that the USD leg is USD LIBOR flat, but that the EUR leg is EUR LIBOR plus 5 basis points or 7 basis points. The party quoting the price is willing to receive LIBOR in USD and pay LIBOR + 5 basis points in EUR; he is also willing to pay LIBOR in USD and receive LIBOR + 7 basis points in EUR.

The spread could be negative. Suppose for example that a USD/JPY swap is quoted as –7 / –5. The party quoting the price is willing to receive LIBOR in USD and pay LIBOR –7 basis points in JPY; he is also willing to pay LIBOR in USD and receive LIBOR –5 basis points in JPY.

When the swap involves EUR against currencies other than USD, the swap rate quotation implies that the EUR LIBOR is paid without adjustment and that the other LIBOR is adjusted.

Key Point	In a cross-currency basis swap involving USD, the quotation implies USD LIBOR flat, against the other currency LIBOR adjusted by a few basis points. In a cross-currency basis swap involving EUR but not USD, the quotation implies EUR LIBOR flat, against the other currency LIBOR adjusted by a few basis points.

Cross-currency basis swaps can be used to build cross-currency fixed/fixed swaps and cross-currency fixed/floating swaps, as in the following example.

Example 9.14 You invest in a JPY bond yielding 1.5%. You swap this into floating rate USD. The JPY IRS is trading at 0.7 / 0.8%. The USD/JPY basis swap is trading at –12 / –9. What all-in yield do you achieve?

First, swap the fixed JPY income to floating JPY income. In the swap you receive JPY LIBOR and pay the fixed JPY, so this will be the higher rate (0.8%).

Second, swap the floating JPY income to floating USD income. In the swap you receive USD LIBOR exactly and pay JPY LIBOR less 9 basis points (if you had been receiving the JPY, this would have been JPY LIBOR less 12 basis points).

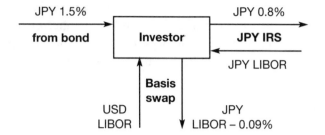

The net result is LIBOR plus 79 basis points:

Receive (JPY):	1.5%
Pay (JPY):	0.8%
Receive (JPY):	LIBOR
Pay (JPY):	(LIBOR – 0.09%)
Receive (USD):	LIBOR
Net income:	LIBOR + 0.79%

Clearly the example above gives only an approximate result, because we have combined the interest rates applying to two different currencies in a simplistic way, simply adding them together. The following approach is more rigorous, looking at the cashflows.

Example 9.15

Suppose that we have the same information as in the previous example, the bond and swaps are for 3 years, the USD/JPY exchange rate is 120, the amount involved is $100 (= ¥12,000) and the discount factors for the two currencies are as follows:

	USD	JPY
1-year:	0.9524	0.9862
2-year:	0.9070	0.9726
3-year:	0.8638	0.9591

The net interest cashflows arising from the bond and swaps described in the previous example are as follows (based on a net result of 0.79% each year on an amount ¥12,000):

Year 1:	+¥94.80	+ USD LIBOR
Year 2:	+¥94.80	+ USD LIBOR
Year 3:	+¥94.80	+ USD LIBOR

The NPV of the ¥ amounts is (¥94.80 × 0.9862) + (¥94.80 × 0.9726) + (¥94.80 × 0.9591) = ¥277 = $2.31.

What constant amount each year in USD would have this same NPV? The answer is 0.85:

($0.85 × 0.9524) + ($0.85 × 0.9070) +($0.85 × 0.8638) = $2.31

These USD amounts are equivalent to 0.85% each year on an amount of USD 100.

The all-in yield in USD is therefore LIBOR + 0.85%.

In the above example, the greater the difference between the level of interest rates between the two currencies – and hence the greater the difference between the two sets of discount factors – the greater the error produced by the approximate method shown in the previous example.

EXERCISES

84. You have a USD 10 million borrowing on which you are paying 8.9% fixed (annual money market basis) and which has exactly 5 years left to run. All the principal will be repaid at maturity.

The current 5-year dollar interest rate swap spread is quoted to you as 80/90 over treasuries. The current 5-year treasury yield is 9.0%. (*US treasuries are quoted on a semi-annual bond basis.*)

You believe that interest rates are going to fall and wish to swap the borrowing from fixed to floating. Without discounting all the cashflows precisely, what will the resulting net LIBOR-related cost of the swapped borrowing be approximately?

85. The 3-month USD cash rate and the futures prices for USD are as follows. The first futures contract period begins exactly 3 months after spot.

3-month cash:	(91 days)	6.25%
futures 3 v 6:	(91 days)	93.41
6 v 9:	(91 days)	92.84
9 v 12:	(92 days)	92.63
12 v 15:	(91 days)	92.38
15 v 18:	(91 days)	92.10

a. What are the zero-coupon swap rates (annual equivalent, bond basis) for each quarterly maturity from 3 months up to 18 months, based on these prices?

b. What should the 18-month par swap rate be on a quarterly money market basis?

86. A year ago your sterling-based company issued a USD 100 million 4-year bond with a 10% annual coupon and converted the proceeds to sterling at 1.80. The sterling/dollar exchange rate is now 1.55 and you wish to protect against any further currency loss by swapping the borrowing into sterling. A counterparty is prepared to pay the outstanding USD cashflows on your bond valued at 9% (annual bond basis) and receive equivalent sterling cashflows at 11%.

a. What will your future cashflows be if you enter into such a swap?

b. What would the cashflows be if, instead of using a swap, you used long-dated foreign exchange to convert all your dollar liabilities into sterling? To calculate the forward prices, assume that they are based on the following money market interest rates:

	USD	GBP
1 year	9.0%	14.0%
2 years	8.5%	12.0%
3 years	8.0%	10.0%

c. Which method would you prefer to use to hedge the dollar liabilities?

87. You issue a 5-year, 6.5% annual coupon bond for USD 10 million and swap it into floating-rate CHF. The spot USD/CHF exchange rate is 1.50 and the current swap rate is 6.8% fixed USD against 6-month CHF LIBOR. The swap matches your USD flows exactly and achieves a regular floating-rate cost based on the equivalent CHF amount borrowed with the same amount repaid at maturity.

Show the cashflows involved and calculate the all-in CHF floating-rate cost you achieve, assuming all CHF cashflows can be discounted at 4.5% (annual) and all USD cashflows at 6.8% (annual). Ignore all bond-issuing costs.

88. You have previously entered a currency swap to receive fixed-rate US dollars at 8% (annually, 30/360 basis) based on USD 10 million (with USD 10 million received at maturity) and pay floating-rate Swedish kronor at LIBOR (semi-annually, ACT/360 basis) based on SEK 75 million (with SEK 75 million paid at maturity). The swap terminates on 24 May 2011. It is now February 2010 and the spot USD/SEK exchange rate is 7.6500. The last krona LIBOR fixing was 5.3% for 24 November 2009. The discount factors to the remaining payment dates are as follows. What is the mark-to-market value of the swap now in dollars?

	USD	SEK
24 May 2010:	0.9850	0.9880
24 November 2010:	0.9580	0.9650
24 May 2011:	0.9300	0.9400

89. You issue a 3-year fixed-rate US dollar bond at 7% (annual) with a bullet maturity. After all costs, you receive 99.00 from the issue. You swap the bond to floating-rate dollars. You arrange the swap so that your net cashflows from the swapped bond issue give you a par amount at the beginning, a regular LIBOR-related cost based on this par amount for 3 years, and the same par amount to be repaid at maturity. The current par swap rate for 3 years is 7.5% (annual, 30/360 basis) against LIBOR (semi-annual, ACT/360). Assuming that this same rate of 7.5% (annual) can be used as a rate of discount throughout, what all-in floating-rate cost can you achieve above or below LIBOR?

"As with insurance premiums, assuming that option sellers can accurately assess the probability of each possible outcome, their total payments out on expiry of a portfolio of options sold should approximate to the premiums received. Option pricing theory therefore depends on assessing these probabilities."

■ ■ ■

10

Options

OVERVIEW

Two sections in this chapter include some mathematical equations which may seem rather more complex than those we have looked at so far – the sections on Black–Scholes and Greek letters. These have been included for completeness, and do not need to be considered in detail by most readers. We have kept to the aim of this book, which is to be practical rather than to frighten, and have therefore not shown here how to derive these formulas. The interested reader will find thorough mathematical treatments of the subject in some of the books mentioned in the Bibliography. The formulas given here should in any case be taken as a general theoretical introduction, not as a prescription for pricing any specific option, which would depend on the individual underlying instrument and any assumptions to be made.

An option is a contract whereby one party has the right to complete a transaction in the future (with a previously agreed amount, date and price) if he so chooses, but is not obliged to do so. The counterparty has no choice: they must transact if the first party wishes and cannot otherwise. For the first party, an option is therefore similar to a forward deal, with the difference that they can subsequently decide whether or not to fulfil the deal. For the second party, an option is similar to a forward deal with the difference that they do not know whether or not they will be required to fulfil it. Clearly, the contract will be fulfilled only if advantageous to the first party and disadvantageous to the second party. In return for this flexibility, the first party must pay a "premium" up-front to compensate the second party for the latter's additional risk.

For someone using an option as a hedge rather than as a trading instrument, it can be considered as a form of insurance. An insurance policy is not called upon if circumstances are satisfactory. The insured person is willing to pay an insurance premium however, in order to be able to claim on the insurance policy if circumstances are not satisfactory. An option as a hedge is similar. If an option enables a hedger to buy something at a certain rate but it turns out to be cheaper in the market than that rate, the hedger does not need the option. If however it turns out to be more expensive than the option rate, the hedger can "claim" on the option. The hedger thus has "insurance protection" at the option rate, for which a premium is paid.

For the trader selling the option, the situation is similar to that of the insurer – the trader is exposed to the risk of being obliged to deliver at the agreed rate but only being able to cover the position in the market at a much worse rate.

Options are available in a wide range of underlying instruments, including currencies, interest rates, bonds and commodities.

> An option is a deal for forward delivery, where the buyer of the option chooses whether the transaction will be consummated and pays a premium for this advantage.
>
> **Key Point**

Basic terminology

> The first party described above is the purchaser or **holder** of the option. The second party (the seller of the option who receives the premium) is called the **writer** of the option.
>
> **Terminology**
>
> To **exercise** an option is to use it, rather than allow it to **expire** unused at maturity.
>
> With a **European** option, the holder can only exercise the option at expiry. With a 3-month option, for example, the holder can only choose at the end of 3 months whether or not to exercise. With an **American** option however, the holder can choose to exercise at any time between the purchase of the option and expiry. European and American options are both available everywhere; the terms are technical rather than geographical.
>
> The price agreed in the transaction – the **strike price** or **strike rate** – is not necessarily the same as the forward rate for the same future date, but is chosen to suit the option buyer. If it is more advantageous than the forward rate to the option buyer, the option is referred to as **in-the-money**. If it is less advantageous than the forward rate to the option buyer, it is **out-of-the-money**. If the strike is the same as the forward rate, the option is **at-the-money** (ATM). As the market moves after the option has been written, the option will move in- and out-of-the-money.
>
> A **put** option is an option to sell something. A **call** option is an option to buy something. The "something" which is being bought or sold is referred to as the **underlying**. Thus in a bond option, the bond is the underlying. In a USD/CHF option, the exchange rate is the underlying. In a short-term interest rate option, the underlying is an FRA or an interest rate futures contract.
>
> It is always possible to exercise an in-the-money option at an immediate profit or, in the case of a European option, to lock in a profit immediately by reversing it with a forward deal and exercising it later. The locked-in profit – the difference between the strike price and the current market forward price – is known as the **intrinsic value** of the option. The intrinsic value of an out-of-the-money option is zero rather than negative. The remaining part of the premium paid for the option above this intrinsic value is known as the **time value**.

THE IDEAS BEHIND OPTION PRICING

The concepts

The pricing of an option depends on probability. In principle, ignoring bid offer spreads, the premium paid to the writer should represent the buyer's expected profit on the option. The profit arises from the fact that the option buyer is always entitled to exercise an option which expires in-the-money and simultaneously cover the position in the market at a better price. The buyer will never be obliged to exercise the option at a loss. As with insurance premiums, assuming that option sellers can accurately assess the probability of each possible outcome, the writer's total payments out on expiry of a portfolio of options sold should approximate to the premiums received. Option pricing theory therefore depends on assessing these probabilities and deriving from them an expected outcome, and hence a fair value for the premium.

The factors on which these probabilities depend are as follows:

■ **The strike price:** the more advantageous the strike is to the buyer at the time of pricing, the greater the probability of the option being exercised, at a loss to the writer, and hence the greater the option premium.

■ **Volatility:** volatility is a measure of how much the price fluctuates. The more volatile the price, the greater the probability that the option will become of value to the buyer at some time. This measurement is formalised in option pricing theory as the annualised standard deviation of the logarithm of relative price movements (see Chapter 1).

■ **The maturity:** the longer the maturity of the option, the greater the probability that it will become of value to the buyer at some time, because the price has a longer time in which to fluctuate.

■ **Interest rates:** the premium represents the buyer's expected profit when the option is exercised, but is payable up-front and is therefore discounted to a present value. The rate of discount therefore affects the premium to some extent. The forward price – and hence the relationship between the strike and the forward – is also affected by interest rate movements. Most importantly, in the case of an option on a bond or other interest rate instrument, the interest rate also directly affects the underlying price.

Because currency options involve two commodities (that is, each currency) rather than one, currency option prices can be expressed in various ways:

(a) As a percentage of the base currency amount.

(b) In terms of the base currency per unit of the base currency.

(c) As a percentage of the variable currency amount.

(d) In terms of the variable currency per unit of the variable currency.

(e) In terms of the base currency per unit of the variable currency.

(f) In terms of the variable currency per unit of the base currency.

A call option on USD 1 million against CHF (or alternatively, a CHF put option against USD) has a strike of 1.50, with a current spot rate of 1.40. The option premium in absolute terms is USD 10,000. This could be expressed as:

Example 10.1

(a) $1.00\% \left(= \dfrac{10{,}000}{1{,}000{,}000}\right)$

(b) 1 US cent per dollar

(c) $0.93\% \left(= \dfrac{10{,}000 \times 1.40}{1{,}000{,}000 \times 1.50}\right)$

(d) 0.93 Swiss centimes per Swiss franc

(e) 0.67 US cents per Swiss franc (= 0.93 ÷ 1.40)

(f) 1.4 Swiss centimes per dollar (= 1 cent × 1.40)

The most usual methods of quotation are (a) and (f).

PRICING MODELS

There are many option-pricing models. The suitability of any one depends on the assumptions made, and on the details of the underlying instrument. The comments in this chapter can be taken only as a general introduction, not as a prescription for pricing any specific option.

Black–Scholes

The most widely used pricing model for straightforward options was derived by Fischer Black and Myron Scholes and is known as the Black–Scholes formula. This model depends on various assumptions:

■ Future relative price changes are independent both of past changes and of the current price.

■ Volatility and interest rates both remain constant throughout the life of the option. In practice, volatility and interest rates are not constant throughout the option's life. In the case of a bond option, for example, this causes significant problems. First, volatility tends towards zero as the bond approaches maturity, because its price must tend to par. Second, the price of the bond itself is crucially dependent on interest rates, in a way that, say, an exchange rate is not.

■ The probability distribution of relative price changes is lognormal. The assumption of a lognormal distribution implies a smaller probability of significant deviations from the mean than is generally the case in practice. This is reflected in how fat or thin the "tails" of the bell-shaped probability curve are and affects the pricing of deep in-the-money and deep out-of-the-money options.

■ There are no transaction costs.

Based on these assumptions, the price of a European call option for one unit of an asset which does not pay a dividend is:

Calculation summary	**Black–Scholes option-pricing formula for a non-dividend-paying asset**

Call premium = spot price × $N(d_1)$ – strike price × $N(d_2)$ × e^{-rt}

Put premium = –spot price × $N(-d_1)$ + strike price × $N(-d_2)$ × e^{-rt}
= call premium + strike price × e^{-rt} – spot price

where: $d_1 = \dfrac{LN\left(\frac{\text{spot} \times e^{rt}}{\text{strike}}\right) + \frac{\sigma^2 t}{2}}{\sigma\sqrt{t}}$

$d_2 = \dfrac{LN\left(\frac{\text{spot} \times e^{rt}}{\text{strike}}\right) - \frac{\sigma^2 t}{2}}{\sigma\sqrt{t}}$

t = the time to expiry of the option expressed as a proportion of a year (365 days)

σ = the annualised volatility

r = the continuously compounded interest rate

$N(d)$ = the standardised normal cumulative probability distribution

One difficulty with the Black–Scholes formula is that the normal distribution function cannot be calculated precisely as a formula itself. Tables giving values of the function are however widely available. Alternatively, it can be very closely approximated – although the approximations are rather messy. One such approximation is:

$$N(d) = 1 - \frac{\dfrac{0.4361836}{1 + 0.33267d} - \dfrac{0.1201676}{(1 + 0.33267d)^2} + \dfrac{0.937298}{(1 + 0.33267d)^3}}{\sqrt{2\pi}\, e^{\frac{d^2}{2}}} \quad \text{when } d \geq 0$$

and $N(d) = 1 - N(-d)$ when $d < 0$

For options on exchange rates, the Black–Scholes formula was adjusted by Garman and Kohlhagen.

> ### Black–Scholes / Garman-Kohlhagen formula for currency option
>
> Call premium = (forward outright price $\times$ N(d$_1$) – strike price $\times$ N(d$_2$)) $\times$ e^{-rt}
>
> Put premium = (– forward outright price $\times$ N(–d$_1$) + strike price $\times$ N(–d$_2$)) $\times$ e^{-rt}
>
> = call premium + (strike price – forward price) $\times$ e^{-rt}
>
> where: the option is a call on a unit of the base currency (that is, a put on the variable currency) and the premium is expressed in units of the variable currency
>
> $$d_1 = \frac{LN\left(\frac{forward}{strike}\right) + \frac{\sigma^2 t}{2}}{\sigma\sqrt{t}}$$
>
> $$d_2 = \frac{LN\left(\frac{forward}{strike}\right) - \frac{\sigma^2 t}{2}}{\sigma\sqrt{t}}$$
>
> r = the continuously compounded interest rate for the variable currency

The expressions e^{rt} and e^{-rt} in the formulas above can be replaced by $(1 + i \times t)$ and $\frac{1}{(1 + i \times t)}$ respectively, where i is the simple interest rate for the period rather than the continuously compounded rate.

What is the cost (expressed as a percentage of the USD amount) of a 91-day USD call against EUR at a strike of 1.19? The spot rate is 1.20, the forward outright is 1.21, volatility is 9.0%, and the USD 3-month interest rate is 6.5%.

We are calculating the price of a EUR put. Using the Black–Scholes formula, with the same notation as above:

$$r = \frac{365}{91} \times LN\left(1 + 0.065 \times \frac{91}{360}\right) = 0.0654$$

$$d_1 = \frac{LN\left(\frac{1.21}{1.19}\right) + \frac{0.09^2 \times \frac{91}{365}}{2}}{0.09\sqrt{\frac{91}{365}}} = 0.3934$$

$$d_2 = \frac{LN\left(\frac{1.21}{1.19}\right) - \frac{0.09^2 \times \frac{91}{365}}{2}}{0.09\sqrt{\frac{91}{365}}} = 0.3484$$

$$\text{put premium} = (-1.21 \times N(-0.3934) + 1.19 \times N(-0.3484)) \times e^{-0.0654} \times \frac{91}{365}$$
$$= (-1.21 \times 0.3470 + 1.19 \times 0.3638) \times 0.9838$$
$$= 0.0128$$

The cost is therefore 0.0128 USD for each one euro underlying the option. As a percentage of the EUR amount, this is:

$$\frac{0.0128}{1.20} = 1.07\%$$

Binomial trees

One way of building a model for option pricing is to simplify the assumptions to the possibility that the price of something may move up a certain extent or down a certain extent in a particular time period. Suppose, for example, that the price of a particular asset is now 1, and that the price may rise by a multiplicative factor of 1.010000 or fall by a factor of $\frac{1.0000}{1.0100}$ = 0.990099 each month. After two months, the price may have moved along any of the following four routes, with three possible outcomes:

> from 1 to 1.010000 and then to (1.010000 × 1.010000) = 1.020100
> from 1 to 1.010000 and then to (1.010000 × 0.990099) = 1.000000
> from 1 to 0.990099 and then to (0.990099 × 1.010000) = 1.000000
> from 1 to 0.990099 and then to (0.990099 × 0.990099) = 0.980296

After three months, there are eight possible routes (up, up, up, or up, up, down, or up, down, up, etc.) and four possible outcomes. A lattice of possible paths for the price, known as a "binomial tree", can be built up in this way. Depending on the relative probabilities of an up movement or a down movement, we can calculate the expected outcome at the end. From this, we can assess the expected value of an option to buy or sell the asset at the end, at any given strike price. The first step therefore is to find the probabilities of up and down movements.

We can in fact calculate these probabilities if we know the rate of interest which would be earned on a cash deposit – the "risk-free" rate of return. We do this by equating the expected outcome of owning the asset to the known outcome of the deposit, as follows. See below ("Risk-free portfolio") for a justification for equating these two outcomes for this purpose.

Suppose that the probability of a move up in the asset price after one month is p, and that the probability of a move down is (1 – p). Suppose also that the current 1-month interest rate is 6 percent per annum.

Although we do not know what the asset price will be after one month, the expected price can be expressed as:

$$p \times 1.01 + (1 - p) \times 0.990099 = 0.990099 + 0.019901 \times p$$

As the interest rate is 6 percent, if we were to invest 1 in a risk-free deposit for one month, we would expect after one month to receive a total of:

$$1 + 6\% \times \tfrac{1}{12} = 1.005$$

If this outcome is the same as investing in the asset, we have:

$$0.990099 + 0.019901 \times p = 1.005$$

This gives:

$$p = \frac{1.005 - 0.990099}{0.019901} = 0.748756$$

We can thus calculate what is the probability of a move up or down, implied by the current expected rate of return (the interest rate) and the size of the possible movements up and down.

Now suppose that, based on this model, we wish to value a one-month call option on 1 unit of the asset with a strike of 1.004.

There is a probability p = 0.748756 that the price will end at 1.01, in which case the option will be worth 1.01 − 1.004 = 0.006. There is a probability (1 − p) = 0.251244 that the price will move down, in which case the option will expire worthless.

$$\begin{array}{l} 1 \times 1.01 = 1.01 \\ \text{with probability } p = 0.748756 \end{array}$$

$$1 \underset{(1-p)}{\overset{p}{\diagdown}}$$

$$\begin{array}{l} 1 \div 1.01 = 0.990099 \\ \text{with probability } (1-p) = 0.251244 \end{array}$$

The expected value of the option at maturity is therefore:

$$(0.748756 \times 0.006) + (0.251244 \times 0) = 0.004493$$

The present value of the option is therefore $\dfrac{0.004493}{(1 + 0.06 \times \frac{1}{12})} = 0.004470$

The price of the option is therefore 0.45%.

With the same details as above, what is the value of a 2-month call option and a 3-month call option with the same strike of 1.004?

Example 10.3

2 months

There is a probability of $p \times p = (0.748756)^2 = 0.560636$ that the price will be 1.01 × 1.01 = 1.020100 at maturity, in which case the option will be worth 1.020100 − 1.004 = 0.0161.

There are two routes along the tree to reach a price of 1 again at the end of two months – either up first then down again, or down first then up again. Therefore there is a probability of $2 \times p \times (1 - p) = 2 \times 0.748756 \times 0.251244 = 0.376241$ that the price will be 1.01 × 0.990099 = 1 at maturity, in which case the option will expire worthless.

There is a probability of $(1 - p)^2 = (0.251244)^2 = 0.063124$ that the price will be 0.990099 × 0.990099 = 0.980296 at maturity, in which case the option will expire worthless.

$$\begin{array}{l} 1 \times 1.01 \times 1.01 = 1.020100 \\ \text{with probability } p \times p = 0.560636 \end{array}$$

$$1 \underset{(1-p)}{\overset{p}{\diagdown}} \begin{array}{l} 1 \times 1.01 \underset{(1-p)}{\overset{p}{\diagdown}} \\ 1 \div 1.01 \underset{(1-p)}{\overset{p}{\diagdown}} \end{array}$$

1 with probability $2 \times p \times (1-p) = 0.376241$

$$\begin{array}{l} 1 \div 1.01 \div 1.01 = 0.980296 \\ \text{with probability } (1-p) \times (1-p) = 0.063124 \end{array}$$

The expected value of this option at maturity is therefore:

$$(0.560636 \times 0.0161) + (0.376241 \times 0) + (0.063124 \times 0) = 0.009026$$

The present value of the option is therefore $\dfrac{0.009026}{\left(1 + 0.06 \times \frac{1}{12}\right)^2} = 0.008937$

0.89% is therefore the price of this 2-month option.

3 months

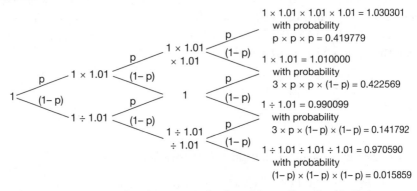

$1 \times 1.01 \times 1.01 \times 1.01 = 1.030301$
with probability
$p \times p \times p = 0.419779$

$1 \times 1.01 = 1.010000$
with probability
$3 \times p \times p \times (1-p) = 0.422569$

$1 \div 1.01 = 0.990099$
with probability
$3 \times p \times (1-p) \times (1-p) = 0.141792$

$1 \div 1.01 \div 1.01 \div 1.01 = 0.970590$
with probability
$(1-p) \times (1-p) \times (1-p) = 0.015859$

From the tree, we can see that the expected value of the option at maturity is:

$(0.419779 \times [1.030301 - 1.004]) + (0.422569 \times [1.01 - 1.004])$

$+ (0.141792 \times 0) + (0.015859 \times 0) = 0.013576$

The option price is therefore the present value of this expected outcome:

$\dfrac{0.013576}{\left(1 + 0.06 \times \frac{1}{12}\right)^3} = 1.34\%$

Risk-free portfolio

It may seem unreasonable, when calculating the probabilities of up and down movements, to equate the expected outcome of investing in the asset with the outcome of investing at a risk-free interest rate. It is possible to justify this however by constructing an investment package which does have a known outcome, as follows.

In the example above for a one-month option, we could sell a call option on one unit of the asset for a premium of 0.004470. Suppose that at the same time we buy 0.301492 units of the asset at the current price of 1. The net cost of this investment package would be:

$0.301492 - 0.004470 = 0.297022$

If the price is 1.01 at the end of the month, the option would be exercised against us, so that we would make a loss on the option of $1.01 - 1.004 = 0.006$. The price of the asset we purchased would also have risen to 1.01 however, so that the total value of our investment at the end of the month would have become:

$0.301492 \times 1.01 - 0.006 = 0.298507$

If the price is 0.990099 at the end of the month however the option would not be exercised against us. The value of the asset we purchased would have fallen to 0.990099, so that the total value of our investment would have become:

$$0.301492 \times 0.990099 = 0.298507$$

In this way we have constructed a package – consisting of a short position in one call option and a long position in 0.301492 units of the asset – which has a known outcome equal to 0.298507 whether the price rises or falls. This outcome represents an annual return on our investment, as expected for a risk-free investment, of:

$$\left(\frac{0.298507}{0.297022} - 1\right) \times \frac{12}{1} = 6\%$$

We now need to consider how to construct such a package in the first place. We need to calculate how much of the asset should be purchased initially in order to make it risk-free. If the amount of asset purchased is A, the two possible outcomes are:

$$A \times 1.01 - 0.006 \text{ (if the price rises)}$$
$$\text{or} \quad A \times 0.990099 \text{ (if the price falls)}$$

If there is to be no risk, these two outcomes must be equal, so that:

$$A \times 1.01 - 0.006 = A \times 0.990099$$

Therefore: $A = \dfrac{0.006}{1.01 - 0.990099} = 0.301492$

and the final outcome is therefore:

$$0.301492 \times 0.990099 = 0.298507$$

If the price of the call option on one unit of the asset is C, we now know that our initial investment in this package must be (0.301492 – C). If the rate of return is 6 percent, we know therefore that:

$$(0.301492 - C) \times \left(1 + 0.06 \times \frac{1}{12}\right) = 0.298507$$

This gives the cost of the option, as before, as:

$$0.301492 - \frac{0.298507}{\left(1 + 0.06 \times \frac{1}{12}\right)} = 0.004470$$

Comparison with Black–Scholes

It can be shown that for a given period to the option expiry, if we build a binomial tree which has more and more branches, each of which is shorter and shorter, the result eventually becomes the same as the result of the Black–Scholes formula – as long as the possible up and down price movements are chosen appropriately.

In the example above, what is the volatility of the asset price? We have two possible values for LN (relative price movements):

$$LN(1.01) = 0.00995 \text{ with probability } 0.748756$$

and $LN(0.990099) = -0.00995$ with probability 0.251244

The mean of these values is:

$$0.00995 \times 0.748756 - 0.00995 \times 0.251244 = 0.00495$$

The variance is therefore:

$$(0.00995 - 0.00495)^2 \times 0.748756 + (-0.00995 - 0.00495)^2 \times 0.251244 = 0.000074$$

The standard deviation is therefore:

$$\sqrt{0.000074} = 0.008631$$

As the data are monthly, the volatility is:

$$0.008631 \times \sqrt{12} = 2.98\%$$

If we now value the 3-month option using the Black–Scholes formula, we have:

$$\text{Call premium} = 1 \times N(d_1) - \frac{1.004 \times N(d_2)}{(1 + 0.06 \times \frac{1}{12})^3}$$

where:

$$d_1 = \frac{LN\left(\frac{(1 + 0.06 \times \frac{1}{12})^3}{1.004}\right) + \frac{(0.0298)^2 \times \frac{3}{12}}{2}}{0.0298 \times \sqrt{\frac{3}{12}}}$$

$$d_2 = \frac{LN\left(\frac{(1 + 0.06 \times \frac{1}{12})^3}{1.004}\right) - \frac{(0.0298)^2 \times \frac{3}{12}}{2}}{0.0298 \times \sqrt{\frac{3}{12}}}$$

This gives:

$$\text{Call premium} = N(0.7437) - 0.9891 \times N(0.7288)$$
$$= 0.7715 - 0.9891 \times 0.7669 = 0.0130 = 1.30\%$$

This option price of 1.30% calculated using the Black–Scholes formula is close to the binomial model's result of 1.34%.

In the example above, we assume that we know in advance the possible up and down price movements. In practice, when using a binomial tree to estimate an option price, we need to choose these possible price movements in such a way as to arrive at a result similar to the Black–Scholes model.

In order for the answers from the two models to converge as the number of branches increases, the possible binomial up and down movements in the price must be chosen to suit the parameters assumed by the Black–Scholes model. One possible way of doing this is to choose them as follows:

$$u = e^{\sigma\sqrt{\frac{t}{n}}}$$

$$d = \frac{1}{u}$$

$$p = \frac{(1 + i \times t)^{\frac{1}{n}} - d}{u - d}$$

where: t = time to expiry expressed in years
$\quad\quad\quad n$ = number of periods in the binomial tree
$\quad\quad\quad \sigma$ = volatility
$\quad\quad\quad u$ = multiplicative up movement
$\quad\quad\quad d$ = multiplicative down movement
$\quad\quad\quad i$ = interest rate per annum to expiry

Put/call relationship, synthetic forwards and risk reversal

Suppose that I pay a premium of C to buy a European call option with a strike price of K for an asset which pays no dividends. Suppose that at the same time I receive a premium P to sell a put option on the same asset, also with a strike of K. Third, suppose that I also sell the asset for forward delivery at the current forward price F. If the asset price is above K at expiry, I will exercise my call option at K. If it is below K at maturity, my counterparty will exercise the put option which I have sold to him. Either way, I buy the asset at a price K. However I also sell the asset at price F, because of the forward deal. I therefore have a profit (F – K). On the basis that "free profits" are not available, this must offset my net payment (C – P). However (F – K) is received/paid at maturity while (C – P) is paid/received up-front. Therefore:

Call premium – put premium = (forward price – strike price) discounted to a present value

Calculation summary

Expressed in terms of the spot price rather than the forward price, this is:

Call premium – put premium = spot price – (strike price discounted to a present value)

Calculation summary

If the strike price is set equal to the forward price, (C – P) must be zero. Therefore, with an option struck at the forward price (at-the-money), the put and call premiums are equal. This is the "put/call parity". This relationship explains the formulas given for the put premium in the section on Black–Scholes.

This relationship is also important because it is related to the creation of synthetic positions. From the above analysis, it can be seen that for any strike price K, it is true that:

sell forward *plus* buy call *plus* sell put = 0

This is the same as saying:

buy forward = buy call *plus* sell put

or

sell forward = sell call *plus* buy put

These two relationships show that a synthetic forward deal can be created from two option deals.

Key Point	Synthetic forwards
	Buying a call and selling a put at the same strike creates a synthetic forward purchase – and vice versa.

The relationship can also be expressed as follows:

buy call = buy put *plus* buy forward
sell call = sell put *plus* sell forward
buy put = buy call *plus* sell forward
sell put = sell call *plus* buy forward

Thus, for example, a trader can either buy a call at a particular strike or, if priced more efficiently, he can buy a put at the same strike and buy forward simultaneously. Viewed from a different standpoint, this is known as "risk reversal". If, for example, a trader already has a position where he is long of a put, he can reverse this position to become effectively long of a call instead, by buying forward.

Key Point	Risk reversal
	A long or short position in a call can be reversed to the same position in a put by selling or buying forward – and vice versa.

OTC OPTIONS vs. EXCHANGE-TRADED OPTIONS

The difference between OTC options and those traded on an exchange is parallel to the difference between OTC instruments such as forwards and exchange-traded futures. In the case of an exchange-traded option, the underlying "commodity" may be the corresponding futures contract. Thus on LIFFE, if an interest-rate option is exercised, the option buyer receives a LIFFE interest rate futures contract. On the Philadelphia Currency Options Exchange, on the other hand, most currency options are deliverable into a cash currency exchange. Exchange-traded options may be either European or American. On LIFFE, for example, most options are American, although there is also a European option on the FTSE 100 index. On the IMM, options are American; on the Philadelphia Exchange, there is a range of both American and European currency options.

One significant difference which can arise between OTC and exchange-traded options concerns the premium payment. On the IMM and other exchanges the option buyer pays a premium up-front as with an OTC option, but pays no variation margin. On LIFFE however the premium is effectively paid via the variation margin. The variation margin paid or received each day represents the change in value of the option. If, for example, an option expires worthless at maturity, the variation margin payments made over the life of the option total the change in value from the original premium to zero. There is therefore no premium payable at the beginning.

On LIFFE the exercise of a call (or put) option on a futures position simply causes a long (or short) futures position to be assigned to the option purchaser and a corresponding short (or long) position to be assigned to the option writer. Positions are assigned at the option exercise price and then marked-to-market in the usual way.

Once an option has been exercised, its price is effectively zero. Therefore, the difference between its market price at the time of exercise and zero is paid as settlement margin. Thus the full option premium will then have been paid partly as variation margin during the life of the option and partly as settlement margin.

Strike prices for OTC options can be set at any level agreed between the two parties – generally at the buyer's request. Exchanges however set a series of strikes, spaced at regular intervals, which are extended as the underlying price moves up and down.

The tick values on exchange-traded options are not always straightforward. US T-bonds and T-bond futures, for example, are priced in multiples of $\frac{1}{32}$. Options on T-bonds however are priced in multiples of $\frac{1}{64}$.

THE GREEK LETTERS

In principle, an option writer could sell options without hedging his position. If the premiums received accurately reflect the expected payouts at expiry, there is theoretically no profit or loss on average. This is analogous to an insurance company not reinsuring its business. In practice however the risk that any one option may move sharply in-the-money makes this too dangerous. In order to manage a portfolio of options, therefore, the option dealer must know how the value of the options he has sold and bought will vary with changes in the various factors affecting their price, so that he can hedge the options.

Delta

An option's delta (Δ) measures how the option's value (which is the same as its current premium) varies with changes in the underlying price:

$$\text{delta } (\Delta) = \frac{\text{change in option's value}}{\text{change in underlying's value}}$$

Mathematically, the delta is the partial derivative of the option premium with respect to the underlying, $\frac{\partial C}{\partial S}$ or $\frac{\partial P}{\partial S}$ (where C is the call premium, P is the put premium and S is the price of the underlying). Based on the Black–Scholes formula given earlier, and with the same notation, the delta can be shown to be $N(d_1)$ for a call and $-N(-d_1)$ for a put. If an option has a delta of 0.7 (or 70%), for example, a $100 increase in the value of the underlying will cause a $70 increase in the value of the option.

For a call option which is deep out-of-the-money, the premium will increase very little as the underlying improves – essentially the option will remain worth almost zero. For an option deep in-the-money, an improvement in the underlying will be reflected completely in the call premium. The delta is therefore close to zero for deep out-of-the-money call options, 0.5 at-the-money, and close to 1 for deep in-the-money call options. For put options, delta is close to zero deep out-of-the-money, –0.5 at-the-money, and close to –1 deep in-the-money.

Consider, for example, a call option on an asset with a strike price of 99. When the current price is 99, the option will have a certain premium value C. If the current price rises to 99.5, the option will have a higher value because it could be exercised for a 0.5 profit if the current price remains at 99.5. However there is still a probability of approximately 50 percent that the price will fall and the option will expire worthless. The premium increase is therefore only approximately 50 percent of the underlying increase.

When an option trader wishes to hedge an option he has written, he has several choices:

- Buy an exactly matching option.
- Buy or sell the underlying. In this case, the trader will buy or sell enough of the underlying so that if the price changes he will make a profit or loss which exactly offsets the loss or profit on the option position. In the example above, he would buy the underlying asset to the

extent of 50 percent of the option amount. In this way, if the price rises from 99 to, say, 100, he will make a profit of 1 on half the amount of the option. This would offset a loss on the option position of 0.5 on the whole amount. In general, the amount of the hedge is equal to:

delta × the notional amount of the option.

This is known as "delta hedging" and demonstrates the importance of knowing the delta.

■ Buy or sell another instrument with the same (but opposite) value for (delta × notional amount), so that again any change in the underlying price gives rise to a change in the hedge value which exactly offsets the change in the option value. In the example above, such a hedge might be the purchase of an option with a different strike price – say, a larger amount of an option on the same asset which is slightly out-of-the-money (and hence has a smaller delta).

If a trader is short of a call (as in this example) or long of a put, he has a negative delta and needs to buy the underlying in order to hedge. If he is long of a call or short of a put, he has a positive delta and needs to sell the underlying in order to hedge.

> **Key Point**
>
> Delta hedging an option can be achieved by buying or selling the correct amount of the underlying so that any change in the option's P & L is offset by a change in the underlying position's P & L.

Gamma

One problem with delta hedging an option or portfolio of options is that the delta itself changes as the underlying price changes, so that although a portfolio may be hedged, or "delta neutral" at one moment, it may not be so the next moment. An option's gamma (Γ) measures how much the delta changes with changes in the underlying price:

$$\text{gamma } (\Gamma) = \frac{\text{change in delta}}{\text{change in price}}$$

Mathematically, this is the second partial derivative of the premium with respect to the underlying price, $\frac{\partial^2 C}{\partial S^2}$ or $\frac{\partial^2 P}{\partial S^2}$. Based on the Black–Scholes formula, Γ can be shown to be $\dfrac{1}{S\sigma\sqrt{2\pi t}\ e^{\frac{d_1^2}{2}}}$ for a call or a put.

As already discussed, the delta does not change rapidly when an option is deep out-of-the-money (the delta remains close to zero) or when an option is deep in-the-money (the delta remains close to 1 or −1), so that gamma is very small. When an option is close to the money however, the delta changes rapidly, and the gamma of a call is at its greatest slightly out-of-the-money. Gamma is positive for long option positions, both calls and puts, and negative for short calls and short puts.

Ideally, a trader who wishes to be fully hedged would like to be gamma-neutral – that is, to have a portfolio of options where the delta does not change at all.

Suppose, for example, that an option portfolio is currently delta-neutral, but has a portfolio gamma (= gamma × portfolio size) of –60. A particular option which could be used to hedge this has a delta of 0.5 and a gamma of 0.6. The gamma of the portfolio could be reduced to zero by adding a long position of $\frac{60}{0.6}$ = 100 units of the option. However the delta of the portfolio would now be $100 \times 0.5 = 50$. It is therefore necessary to superimpose on this, for example, a further hedge of a short position of 50 in the underlying – to reduce the delta back to zero. This will not affect the portfolio's gamma, because the underlying has a delta of 1 but a gamma of zero. The portfolio would still need to be hedged dynamically – because the gamma and the delta will change as the underlying moves – but it would be less vulnerable.

Vega

An option's vega (or epsilon (ε), eta (η), lambda (λ) or kappa (κ)) measures how much an option's value changes with changes in the volatility of the underlying:

$$\text{vega} = \frac{\text{change in option's value}}{\text{change in volatility}}$$

Mathematically, this is the partial derivative of the option premium with respect to volatility, $\frac{\partial C}{\partial \sigma}$ or $\frac{\partial P}{\partial \sigma}$. Based on the Black–Scholes formula, this is $\dfrac{S\sqrt{\frac{t}{2\pi}}}{e^{\frac{d_1^2}{2}}}$ for a call or a put.

Vega is at its highest when an option is at-the-money and falls as the market and strike prices diverge. Options closer to expiration have a lower vega than those with more time to run. Positions with positive vega will generally have positive gamma. To be long vega (to have a positive vega) is achieved by purchasing either put or call options.

Theta

An option's theta (Θ) measures how much an option's value changes with changes in the time to maturity:

$$\text{theta } (\Theta) = -\frac{\text{change in option's value}}{\text{change in time}}$$

Mathematically, this is $-\dfrac{\partial C}{\partial t}$ or $-\dfrac{\partial P}{\partial t}$. Based on the Black–Scholes formula, this is $-\dfrac{S\sigma}{2\sqrt{2\pi t}}e^{-\frac{d_1^2}{2}} - Kre^{-rt}N(d_2)$ for a call or $-\dfrac{S\sigma}{2\sqrt{2\pi t}}e^{-\frac{d_1^2}{2}} + Kre^{-rt}N(-d_2)$ for a put, where K is the strike price.

Theta is negative for a long option position and positive for a short option position. The more the market and strike prices diverge, the less effect time has on an option's price and hence the smaller the theta. Positive theta is generally associated with negative gamma and vice versa.

Rho

An option's rho (ρ) measures how much an option's value changes with changes in interest rates:

$$\text{rho } (\rho) = \frac{\text{change in option's value}}{\text{change in interest rate}}$$

Mathematically, this is $\dfrac{\partial C}{\partial r}$ or $\dfrac{\partial P}{\partial r}$. Based on the Black–Scholes formula, this is $Kte^{-rt} N(d_2)$ for a call or $- Kte^{-rt}N(-d_2)$ for a put.

Rho tends to increase with maturity.

Based on the Black–Scholes formula

Calculation summary

Delta (Δ) = $N(d_1)$ for a call
or $-N(-d_1)$ for a put

Gamma (Γ) = $\dfrac{1}{S\sigma \sqrt{2\pi t}\, e^{\frac{d_1^2}{2}}}$

Vega = $\dfrac{S\sqrt{\frac{t}{2\pi}}}{e^{\frac{d_1^2}{2}}}$

Theta (Θ) = $- \dfrac{S\sigma}{2\sqrt{2\pi t}}\, e^{-\frac{d_1^2}{2}} - Kre^{-rt}N(d_2)$ for a call

or $- \dfrac{S\sigma}{2\sqrt{2\pi t}}\, e^{-\frac{d_1^2}{2}} + Kre^{-rt}N(-d_2)$ for a put

Rho (ρ) = $Kte^{-rt} N(d_2)$ for a call
or $- Kte^{-rt}N(-d_2)$ for a put

where: S = spot price
K = strike price

HEDGING WITH OPTIONS

Comparison with forwards

A company with a short yen position which it wishes to hedge against euros has three basic choices. It can do nothing and remain unhedged, it can buy the yen forward, or it can buy a yen call option. In general, the option will never provide the best outcome because of the premium cost: if the yen rises, the company would be better buying forward; if the yen falls, the company would be better remaining unhedged. On the other hand, the option provides the safest overall result because it protects against a yen rise while preserving opportunity gain if the yen falls. Essentially, if the company firmly believes the yen will rise, it should buy forward; if the company firmly believes the yen will fall, it should do nothing; if the company believes the yen will fall but cannot afford to be wrong, it should buy a yen call option. The outcomes of the three possibilities are as follows. Figure 10.1 shows the effective net outcome (in terms of the EUR/JPY exchange rate achieved net of the option premium cost) for a hedger with an underlying position. It is important to note that, unlike the subsequent figures in this chapter, it is *not* a profit/loss profile on a "naked" position with no underlying exposure.

Figure 10.1 **Hedging a short yen exposure against euros**

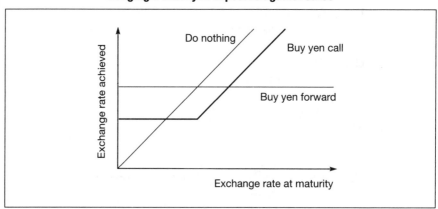

Interest rate guarantees

A parallel situation arises in interest rate hedging. A company with a short-term borrowing rollover in the future also has three basic choices. It can remain unhedged, buy an FRA or buy or sell an option on an FRA (an "interest rate guarantee" or IRG). A currency option is an option to buy an agreed amount of one currency against another currency at an agreed exchange rate on an agreed date. An IRG is the interest rate equivalent of this.

An IRG is effectively an option to buy or sell an agreed amount of an FRA in one particular currency at an agreed rate for an agreed maturity and on an agreed delivery date. An interest rate guarantee can therefore fix the maximum cost on a future borrowing (or the minimum return on a future deposit). The IRG does not entail an actual borrowing or deposit. Like a futures contract, it is a "contract for differences": the difference between the strike rate and the actual rate at settlement is paid or received.

An IRG can be either a "borrower's option" or a "lender's option". This terminology may be safer than thinking in terms of "call" or "put" because a call on an FRA is equivalent to a put on an interest rate futures contract.

Caps and floors

A cap or ceiling is a series of IRGs (borrower's options) generally at the same strike, purchased together to secure a series of borrowing rollovers. Suppose, for example, that a borrower has a 5-year loan which he rolls over each 3 months at the 3-month LIBOR then current. He can buy a 5-year cap which will put a maximum cost on each of the rollovers. Whenever the rollover rate exceeds the cap strike rate, he receives the difference. Whenever the cap strike rate exceeds the rollover rate, nothing is paid or received.

A floor is similarly a series of IRGs (lender's options) purchased to secure a series of deposits, by putting a minimum return on each rollover.

SOME "PACKAGED" OPTIONS

Various OTC option-based products are offered by banks to their customers, some of which can be constructed from straightforward options. The common products available are as follows.

Range forward (or collar, cylinder or tunnel)

A straightforward option provides a fixed worst-case level at which the customer can deal, but allows him to deal at the market rate if this turns out better. A range forward allows the customer to deal at a better market rate only up to a certain level. Beyond that level, the customer must deal at another fixed best-case level. In return for this reduced opportunity, the customer pays a lower premium for the option. Indeed the premium can be zero (a zero-cost option) or even negative.

Such an arrangement can be constructed by buying one option (for example, a USD put option) and selling another (in this case a USD call option). The premium earned from the second option offsets the premium paid on the first option, either partly or (in the case of a zero-cost option) completely. The obligation to deal at the strike rate of the second option, if the counterparty wishes, determines the best-case level. Setting the two strike rates determines the net premium. Alternatively, setting the size of the net premium and one of the strike rates determines the other strike rate.

There is generally a technical difference between a range forward and a collar. With a range forward, the customer is usually obliged to deal with the bank. If neither of the range limits is reached (i.e. neither option is exercised) at expiry, the customer must deal at the spot rate with the bank. With a collar, the customer is not obliged to deal with any particular bank if neither option is exercised. The term "range forward" usually applies to a deal with a single future date, but in general a collar can be applied to any underlying instrument. It is often used, for example, to describe the simultaneous purchase of a cap and sale of a floor. A collar is sometimes called a "cylinder" or a "tunnel".

Break forward (or forward with optional exit)

A break forward is a forward deal at a fixed rate (the worst-case level) with another "break" level at which the customer may reverse the forward deal if he chooses. For example, a break forward to sell USD against CHF at 1.52 with a break at 1.55 obliges the customer to sell USD at 1.52 but allows him to buy USD back at 1.55 if he chooses. If the USD strengthens to 1.61, for example, the customer may buy the USD back again at 1.55 and sell them in the market at 1.61 – an all-in effective rate of 1.58 (= 1.52 – 1.55 + 1.61).

A break forward has exactly the same profit/loss profile as a straightforward option, because it is in fact a straightforward option with deferred payment of the premium. The fixed rate and break rates are set as follows. Suppose that the forward rate for selling USD against CHF is currently 1.56 and the customer asks for a fixed rate of 1.52 as above. The bank calculates what strike rate would be necessary on a USD put option so that the strike rate less the future value of the premium is 1.52. This strike rate then becomes the break rate.

Calculating the necessary strike rate can be done conveniently using the put/call parity. As before, if C is the call premium and P is the put premium:

$$C - P = (\text{forward} - \text{strike}) \text{ discounted to a present value}$$

or

$$\text{Strike} - P^* = \text{forward} - C^*$$

where P^* and C^* are the *future* values of P and C

If the fixed rate set in the transaction is 1.52, this must represent the true strike rate adjusted for the deferred put premium. In other words:

$$\text{Strike} - P^* = 1.52$$

From the put/call relationship, it follows that:

Forward − C* = 1.52

Since the forward rate is 1.56, it follows that:

C* = 1.56 − 1.52 = 0.04

The call premium is therefore the present value of 0.04. This then determines the true strike rate behind the deal, which is used as the break level.

Participation forward

A participation forward provides a worst-case level in the same way as an option. If the customer wishes not to deal at this level because the market level is better, he shares the benefit with the bank. For example, a participation forward to sell USD against CHF at 1.50 with a participation rate of 70 percent provides a worst-case level of 1.50. If the market rate is 1.60, the customer receives 70 percent of the 0.10 benefit – i.e. 0.07 – and sells USD at 1.57. There is no premium to pay for a participation forward, but there is a potential 30 percent loss of advantage compared with a straight-forward option.

A participation forward can be constructed by buying an option (in this case a USD put option) and selling a smaller amount of an opposite option (in this case a USD call option) at the same strike rate.

Setting the strike rates of the two options determines the two premiums. In order for the total net premium to be zero, this then sets the amount of the second option which must be sold, and hence the participation rate. Alternatively, setting the participation rate will determine the strike rate for the options which will result in a net zero premium.

SOME TRADING STRATEGIES

Calls and puts

The most basic trading strategies are the purchase or sale of a call or a put. The purchase of either gives rise to limited potential loss (the premium paid) and almost unlimited potential profit. The sale of either gives the reverse. Assuming that the price of the underlying can fall only as far as zero, the potential profit from holding a put (or the loss from writing a put) is not actually unlimited. The profit/loss profile can be illustrated as shown in Figures 10.2–10.5.

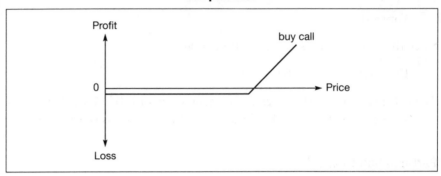

Figure 10.2

Call purchase

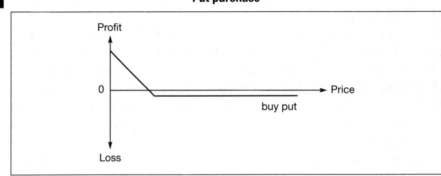

Figure 10.3

Put purchase

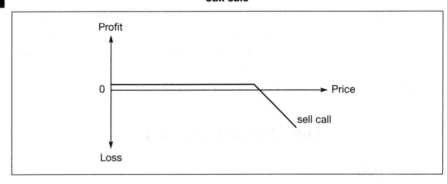

Figure 10.4

Call sale

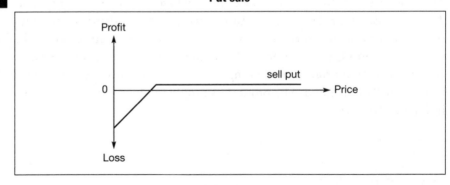

Figure 10.5

Put sale

Covered calls and puts

To sell a call or put as above without any underlying exposure is to write a "naked" option. A "covered" call or put arises when the writer has an offsetting position in the underlying – a long position in the underlying to offset the selling of a call, or a short position in the underlying to offset the selling of a put.

Sale of a covered call can, for example, be used by a fund manager to increase income by receiving option premium. It would be used for a security he is willing to sell only if the underlying goes up sufficiently for the option to be exercised. Generally, covered call writers would undertake the strategy only if they thought implied volatility was too high. The lower the volatility, the less the covered call writer gains in return for giving up potential profit in the underlying. It provides protection against potential loss only to the extent that the option premium offsets a market downturn.

A covered put can be used by a fund manager who is holding cash because he has shorted securities, to increase income by receiving option premium. Covered put writing can also be used as a way of target buying: if an investor has a target price at which he wants to buy, he can set the strike price of the option at that level and receive option premium meanwhile to increase the yield of the asset. Investors may also sell covered puts if markets have fallen rapidly but seem to have bottomed, because of the high volatility typically received on the option in such market conditions. (See Figures 10.6 and 10.7.)

Covered call sale

Figure 10.6

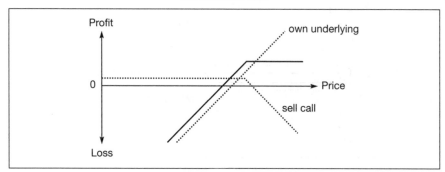

Covered put sale

Figure 10.7

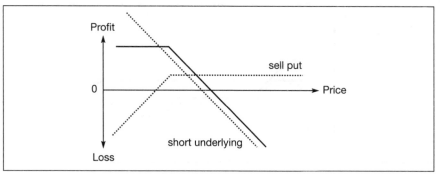

Spread

Spreads involve the simultaneous purchase and sale of two different calls, or of two different puts. A long call spread is the purchase of a call at one strike price, offset by the simultaneous sale of a call at another strike price less in-the-money (or more out-of-the-money) than the first. This limits the potential gain if the underlying goes up, but the premium received from selling the second call partly finances the purchase of the first call. A call spread may also be advantageous if the purchaser thinks there is only limited upside in the underlying. A put spread is similarly the simultaneous purchase of a put at one strike price, offset by the simultaneous sale of a put less in-the-money (or more out-of-the-money) than the first – used if the purchaser thinks there is limited downside for the underlying. To short a spread is the reverse. (See Figures 10.8–10.11.)

A bull spread is either the purchase of a call spread or the sale of a put spread. A bear spread is either the sale of a call spread or the purchase of a put spread.

A calendar spread is the purchase of a call (or put) and the simultaneous sale of a call (or put) with the same strike price but a different maturity. For example, if one-month volatility is high and one-year volatility low, a

Figure 10.8

Call spread purchase

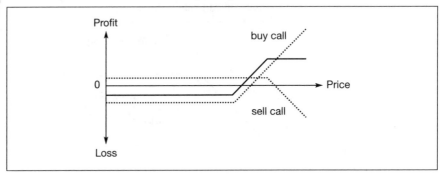

Figure 10.9

Put spread purchase

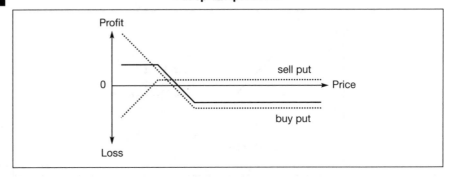

Call spread sale

Figure 10.10

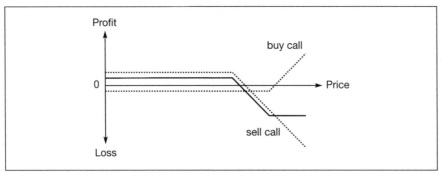

Put spread sale

Figure 10.11

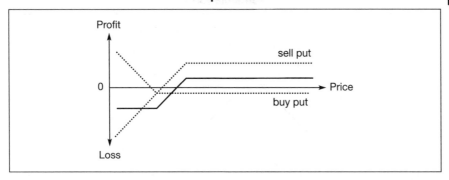

trader might buy one-year options and sell one-month options, thereby selling short-term volatility and buying long-term volatility. If short-term volatility falls relative to long-term volatility, the strategy can be reversed at a profit.

Spreads constructed from options with the same maturity but different strikes are sometimes known as "vertical" spreads, while calendar spreads are "horizontal" spreads. A spread constructed from both different strikes and different maturities is a "diagonal" spread.

Straddle

To go long of a straddle is to buy both a put and a call at the same strike price. In return for paying two premiums, the buyer benefits if the underlying moves far enough in either direction. It is a trade which expects increased volatility. The seller of a straddle assumes unlimited risk in both directions but receives a double premium and benefits if volatility is low. (See Figures 10.12 and 10.13.)

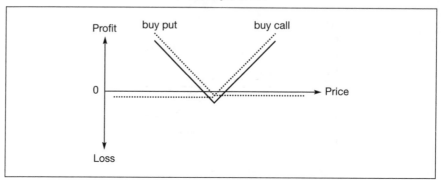

Figure 10.12

Straddle purchase

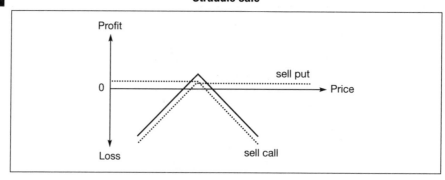

Figure 10.13

Straddle sale

Strangle

A strangle is similar to a straddle but the premiums are reduced by setting the two strike prices apart – generally each strike will be out-of-the-money. Profits are generated on a long strangle position only if the underlying moves significantly. (See Figures 10.14 and 10.15.)

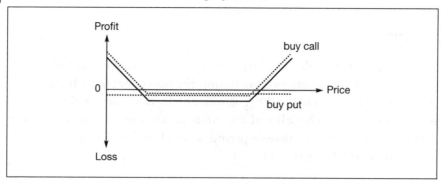

Figure 10.14

Strangle purchase

Strangle sale

Figure 10.15

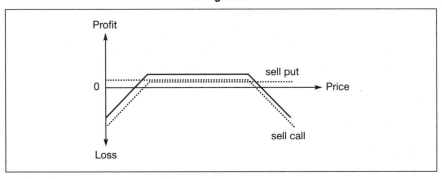

With combination strategies such as straddles and strangles, a "top" combination is one such as a straddle sale or a strangle sale which has a top limit to its profitability and a "bottom" combination is the reverse, such as a straddle purchase or a strangle purchase.

SOME LESS STRAIGHTFORWARD OPTIONS

We conclude, by way of illustration, with a selection of a few of the less straightforward option types available.

Average rate option (or Asian option)

This is a cash-settled option, paying the buyer the difference (if positive) between the strike and the average of the underlying over an agreed period. The volatility of the underlying's average is less than the volatility of the underlying itself, so that the option cost is reduced.

Average strike option

Also cheaper than a straightforward option, this sets the strike to be the average of the underlying over a period, which is then compared with the actual underlying rate at expiry.

Barrier option

A barrier option is one which is either activated (a "knock-in" option) or cancelled (a "knock-out" option) if the underlying reaches a certain trigger level during the option's life. For example, an "up-and-in" option becomes active if the underlying rate moves up to a certain agreed level; if that level is not reached, the option never becomes active, regardless of the strike rate. "Up-and-out", "down-and-in" and "down-and-out" options are defined analogously. The circumstances in which the writer will be required to pay out on a barrier option are more restricted, so the option is cheaper.

Binary option (or digital option)

A binary option has an "all or nothing" profit/loss profile. If the option expires in-the-money, the buyer receives a fixed payout regardless of how far the underlying has moved beyond the strike rate. A "one touch" binary option pays out if the strike is reached at any time during the option's life.

Compound option

An option on an option.

Contingent option

This is an option where the buyer pays no premium unless the option expires in-the-money. If it does expire in-the-money however, the buyer must then pay the premium. The cost is higher than for a straightforward option.

Quanto option (or guaranteed exchange rate option)

A quanto option is one where the underlying is denominated in one currency but payable in another at a fixed exchange rate.

Swaption

A swaption is an option on a swap. Exercising the option delivers the agreed swap from the time of exercise onwards.

EXERCISES

90. What is the estimated annualised volatility of the GBP/USD exchange rate, based on the following daily data, assuming the usual lognormal probability distribution for relative price changes and 252 days in a year?

Day 1	1.6320
Day 2	1.6410
Day 3	1.6350
Day 4	1.6390
Day 5	1.6280
Day 6	1.6300
Day 7	1.6250
Day 8	1.6200
Day 9	1.6280
Day 10	1.6200

91. A 6-month (182 days) NOK call option against USD at a strike of 6.9500 costs 1.5% of the USD amount. What should a NOK put cost at the same strike rate?

USD/NOK spot:	7.0000
USD/NOK 6-month outright:	7.0690
USD 6-month LIBOR:	5%
NOK 6-month LIBOR:	7%

92. Construct a three-step binomial tree to calculate a price for a 3-month put option on an asset at a strike of 101. The current price is 100. At each step, the price either rises or falls by a factor of 2% (that is, either multiplied by 1.02 or divided by 1.02). The risk-free interest rate is 12% per annum.

Part 5

Gold and Other Commodities

"… it is generally not possible to give a clear formula for a theoretical forward price for a commodity in the same way as for a financial instrument."

■ ■ ■

11

Gold and Other Commodities

GOLD

The term "precious metals" covers gold, silver, palladium, platinum and the other "platinum group" metals (rhodium, ruthenium, iridium and osmium). "Bullion" means gold and silver traded in bulk form (for example, gold bars, gold ingots or gold plate, rather than gold coins).

Metal	ISO Code
Gold	XAU
Silver	XAG
Platinum	XPT
Palladium	XPD

Pricing

Prices for the four metals above are mostly quoted and traded in USD, although prices are available against other currencies such as EUR. Traditionally – and still mostly – the price is quoted as USD per ounce. In this context, an "ounce" means a "troy" ounce (rather than an ounce used for weighing vegetables, which is an "avoirdupois" ounce). As with all prices, a dealer quotes a two-way price – the "bid" is the price in USD that he is willing to pay to buy one ounce of metal, and his "offer" is the price in USD that he is willing to receive if he sells one ounce of metal. The abbreviation for "ounce" is "oz". 1 troy ounce is 31.10348 grammes.

A "fine ounce" means an ounce of 100% pure gold. When a trader buys gold at a certain price – say $590 per ounce – he is agreeing to pay $590 for each fine ounce he receives. In practice however, a real bar of gold has impurities – it is not 100% pure gold. The buyer pays only for the pure gold content. The fine weight of a bar is the weight of pure gold contained in the bar – i.e. the "gross weight" (the actual weight of the bar) multiplied by the "fineness" of the bar, which is the proportion of pure gold contained within the bar. The fineness is typically expressed in parts per thousand, so that "995" means 99.5% pure gold content. The maximum purity accepted for normal trading is 999.9 (i.e. 99.99% pure, known as "four nines") and traded gold is typically either 995 or four nines.

For trading purposes, the exact purity and size of a particular bar of gold is not generally significant, in that a purchaser pays only for the fine weight he has purchased. Although the price is quoted in USD per ounce, all OTC trades must take place in terms of so many gold bars, because physical delivery must take place in whole multiples of gold bars. A standard amount for a spot price quotation in the market might be ten 400-ounce bars, or 4,000 ounces of gold.

In practice, there are certain traditionally accepted sizes for a bar – based on different weighting systems traditionally used in different regions – as follows. Each one might be slightly lighter or heavier, within reasonable accepted tolerances.

Key Point

- 400 ounce bar (400 troy ounces = 12.44 kilogrammes)
- 1 kilogramme bar (32.15 troy ounces = 1 kilogramme)
- 10 tael bar (12 troy ounces = 373 grammes) – used in Hong Kong, 990 or 999.9 fine
- 10 tola bar (3.75 troy ounces = 116.6 grammes) – used in India and the Arabian Gulf, 999 fine
- baht (0.47 troy ounces = 14.6 grammes) – used in Thailand, 990 fine

---

Example 11.1

I buy 400 ounces of gold at $601.20 per ounce. I receive a bar weighing 392.475 ounces, with a fineness of 995.1.

On delivery of the gold, I pay:

$601.20 \times 392.475 \times 0.9951 = \$234,799.79$

601.2 ENTER 392.475 × .9951 ×

The principal centre for trading gold is the London market, dominated by the London Bullion Market, which is operated by the London Bullion Market Association (LBMA).

The LBMA sets down standards for gold bars that can be accepted for "good delivery". A good delivery bar for London should be of at least 99.5% purity and have between 350 and 430 ounces fine gold content, with the bar's actual weight expressed in multiples of 0.025 ounces. The gold must have been produced at one of a specified list of refineries, and be kept at one of a list of specified vaults.

Delivery in London (known as "loco London") is the international benchmark for quoting prices. Other trades – either for delivery in a location other than London (for example "loco Zurich" or "loco Tokyo") or in a form other than a good delivery bar – can be priced by taking into account the extra costs involved in shipping to London or in converting the form into a good delivery bar.

As with foreign exchange, in precious metals there is a spot market (for value two days after trade date) and a forward market.

Allocated and unallocated delivery

"Delivery" of gold can mean either physical delivery or "book-entry". With physical delivery, the purchaser of the gold has an "allocated account", meaning that a specific gold bar is delivered to a specific location and allocated to his account. With book entry, the purchaser of the gold has an "unallocated account". This confirms his ownership of a certain number of ounces of gold, but does not associate this holding with any specific physical gold bars. Most settlement is to unallocated accounts, which avoids the transaction costs and security risks of moving the actual metal.

In the case of an unallocated account, the owner of the gold is an unsecured creditor of the bank where the account is held. In this case, it is possible that there is no actual gold backing the account, if the bank where the account is chooses to take a short position in gold. If there is actual gold, it might be held physically by that bank, or might be represented by gold which that bank holds in turn with another bank.

The gold fix

The gold fix is a process of arriving at a market reference price for gold in the market, which takes place twice each day in London at 10:30 a.m. and 3:00 p.m. The five members of the fix commence the fix with a trying price. This trying price is passed to the members' dealing rooms, which are in contact with market participants, who declare how much gold they wish to buy or sell at that price. If the net result of all this is more demand than supply, the price is adjusted upwards and if demand is less than supply, the price is adjusted downwards. The process is repeated until balance is achieved, at which point the price is fixed.

The gold fix provides a reference price analogous to LIBOR as a fixing for interest rates. Some market users use the fix as a price at which they wish to transact – for example, by leaving an order with a dealer to buy or sell at whatever the fix turns out to be.

GOLD BORROWING, FORWARDS, SWAPS AND GOFO

Borrowing gold

As discussed in Chapter 6 on Repos, someone wishing to go short of a bond can do so by selling the bond and then borrowing it in order to be able to deliver to the counterparty. He will then benefit if the bond price falls because he can buy the bond back cheaper in order to return it to the lender.

Gold borrowing is analogous. A gold mining company, for example, might wish to sell its future production and at the same time finance that production. It can do this by selling gold spot for cash. In order to deliver the gold now, it can borrow the gold. It then repays the gold in the future, out of its own future production. The interest rate for borrowing the gold is called the gold "lease rate" (or "gold LIBOR"). It is expressed in gold and payable in gold, with a year basis of 360 days.

Example 11.2

I borrow 100 ounces of gold for 180 days at a gold lease rate of 1.25%. At the end of 180 days I pay back the 100 ounces plus interest of 0.625 ounces of gold:

$$100 \text{ ounces} \times 1.25\% \times 180/360 = 0.625 \text{ ounces}$$

100 ENTER .0125 × 180 × 360 ÷

In practice, the interest is often paid in USD, rather than in gold, by converting the gold interest amount into USD using the London fix price. Central banks, which are big holders of gold, are the major lenders of gold. As with any other interest rate, the level of the gold lease rate is determined by supply and demand in the gold borrowing market.

Forward transactions in gold

We have seen in Chapter 8 on Foreign Exchange how a theoretical forward foreign exchange rate is derived from the spot exchange rate and the interest rates for the two currencies involved. In exactly the same way, a theoretical forward gold price is derived from the spot gold price and the two interest rates — in other words, the interest rate for gold (i.e. the gold lease rate) and the interest rate for cash (i.e. US dollars). We discuss this further below — see "Forward commodity pricing".

Calculation summary

$$\text{Forward price} = \text{spot price} \times \frac{\left(1 + \text{USD interest rate} \times \dfrac{\text{days}}{360}\right)}{\left(1 + \text{gold lease rate} \times \dfrac{\text{days}}{360}\right)}$$

The current spot gold price is $510.35 per ounce. The USD 3-month (91-day) interest rate is 5.21% and the gold lease rate for the same period is 1.31%. What is the theoretical 3-month forward gold price?

Example 11.3

$$\text{Forward price} = 510.35 \times \frac{\left(1 + 0.0521 \times \dfrac{91}{360}\right)}{\left(1 + 0.0131 \times \dfrac{91}{360}\right)} = 515.36$$

.0521 ENTER 91 × 360 ÷ 1 +
.0131 ENTER 91 × 360 ÷ 1 + ÷
510.35 ×

Contango and backwardation

Again analogously to foreign exchange, if the lease rate is lower than the USD interest rate, then the forward gold price is higher than the spot price. In this case, the difference between the spot price and the forward price is known as "contango".

If the lease rate is higher than the USD interest rate, then the forward gold price is lower than the spot price. In this case, the difference between the spot price and the forward price is known as "backwardation".

Key Point	"Contango" is when the forward price is higher than spot. "Backwardation" is when the forward price is lower than spot.

In practice the gold lease rate is almost always lower than the USD interest rate and backwardation is extremely rare. Because only a small proportion of gold is "consumed" in a final sense, most of the gold ever mined still exists, so that available stocks are far greater than demand. Although new demand can of course be greater than new supply, and existing holders can be reluctant to sell their stocks, these holders can still lend to satisfy demand. The large volume available for lending, relative to demand, keeps the lease rate low. This is coupled with a natural reluctance on the part of gold producers to sell forward below the current spot price.

Gold swaps

A forward swap in foreign exchange is a spot sale of one currency against another, combined with a simultaneous agreement to buy the same currency back again for a forward date. As we saw in Chapter 8 on Foreign Exchange, this is equivalent to lending one currency and borrowing the other. In the same way, a gold swap is a spot sale or purchase of gold combined with a simultaneous agreement to reverse the transaction for a forward date – which can again be seen as lending gold and borrowing USD (or vice versa).

Again as explained in Chapter 8, an FX swap price can therefore be seen as representing the interest rate differential between the two currencies involved – so that given the swap price and one of the interest rates, we can calculate the other interest rate. However, in FX, we saw that the swap is only *approximately* the interest differential – a good approximation for much of the time, but nevertheless an approximation:

$$\text{Forward swap} \approx \text{spot} \times \text{interest rate differential} \times \frac{\text{days}}{\text{year}}$$

The precise formulation was:

$$\text{Forward swap} = \text{spot} \times \frac{\left(\text{variable currency interest rate} \times \frac{\text{days}}{\text{year}} - \text{base currency interest rate} \times \frac{\text{days}}{\text{year}}\right)}{\left(1 + \text{base currency interest rate} \times \frac{\text{days}}{\text{year}}\right)}$$

Exactly the same logic, mathematics and approximation apply to gold forward pricing:

> **Calculation summary**
>
> Theoretical gold forward swap =
>
> $$\text{gold spot price} \times \frac{\left(\text{USD interest rate} \times \frac{days}{360} - \text{gold lease rate} \times \frac{days}{360}\right)}{\left(1 + \text{gold lease rate} \times \frac{days}{360}\right)}$$
>
> **Approximation**
>
> $$\text{Forward swap} \approx \text{gold spot price} \times (\text{USD interest rate} - \text{gold lease rate}) \times \frac{days}{360}$$

GOFO

The "gold forward offered rate" ("GOFO") can be defined as the net interest rate at which one would lend gold and borrow USD. As this is equivalent to a gold swap, this is approximately (but *not* precisely) equivalent to saying that GOFO is the difference between the USD interest rate and the lease rate.

> **Key Point**
>
> **GOFO = the net interest rate at which one would lend gold and borrow USD**

From this, and the formulas above for forward prices, we have:

> **Calculation summary**
>
> $$\text{Theoretical gold forward price} = \text{spot price} \times \left(1 + \text{GOFO} \times \frac{days}{360}\right)$$
>
> $$\text{Theoretical gold forward swap} = \text{spot price} \times \left(\text{GOFO} \times \frac{days}{360}\right)$$
>
> $$\text{GOFO} = \frac{\text{USD interest rate} - \text{gold lease rate}}{\left(1 + \text{gold lease rate} \times \frac{days}{360}\right)}$$

This definition of GOFO can be turned round to give:

> **Calculation summary**
>
> $$\text{Gold lease rate} = \frac{\text{USD interest rate} - \text{GOFO}}{\left(1 + \text{GOFO} \times \frac{days}{360}\right)}$$

An alternative approach is not to define GOFO as the net interest rate at which one would lend gold and borrow USD, but instead to define GOFO as *exactly* the difference between the USD interest rate and the gold lease rate:

> GOFO = USD interest rate − gold lease rate

In practice, the gold market sometimes starts from this relationship but then derives the gold lease rate from GOFO, instead of deriving GOFO from the lease rate as suggested above. For example, in the same way that there is a daily fixing for many interest rates (such as USD LIBOR at 11:00 a.m. London time), there is a daily fixing of GOFO (arranged at 11:00 a.m. London time by the LBMA). This GOFO fixing is used as the reference in some financial agreements as well as for the settlement rate (analogous to LIBOR) for gold interest rate swaps and FRAs. From this, the LBMA *derives* a reference rate for the gold lease rate, rather than the lease rate itself being the "raw material".

> **Key Point** Fixing for gold lease rate = GOFO fixing – USD LIBOR fixing

Based on this alternative definition of GOFO, we could rewrite the earlier forward price formulas as:

Calculation summary

$$\text{Theoretical gold forward swap} = \text{gold spot price} \times \frac{\text{GOFO} \times \frac{\text{days}}{360}}{\left(1 + \text{gold lease rate} \times \frac{\text{days}}{360}\right)}$$

Approximations:

$$\text{Gold forward swap} \approx \text{gold spot price} \times \text{GOFO} \times \frac{\text{days}}{360}$$

$$\text{Gold forward price} \approx \text{gold spot price} \times \left(1 + \text{GOFO} \times \frac{\text{days}}{360}\right)$$

From this, we could derive what would then be the correct net interest rate at which one would lend gold and borrow USD, as follows. Again, this is approximately the same as GOFO, but not exactly:

Calculation summary

$$\text{Net interest rate to lend gold and borrow USD} =$$

$$\frac{\text{swap}}{\text{spot}} \times \frac{360}{\text{days}} = \frac{\text{GOFO}}{\left(1 + \text{gold lease rate} \times \frac{\text{days}}{360}\right)}$$

The reason for suggesting this alternative definition is that in practice, the gold market sometimes appears to accept the two definitions as equivalent. This is the same as accepting the approximations we have given above as precisely correct – i.e. the market appears to define GOFO as being the rate at which one would lend gold and borrow USD, but also appears sometimes to work on the basis that GOFO is *exactly* the difference between the USD interest rate and the lease rate, which is mathematically not quite consistent. If the gold lease rate is extremely low, and GOFO is hence very close to the USD interest rate, this is unlikely to lead to significant anomalies. However if the lease rate is relatively high, this might lead to arbitrage opportunities.

The 3-month (92-day) GOFO fixing today is 4.494%. The 3-month USD LIBOR **Example 11.4** fixing is 5.92783%.

The LBMA published reference rate for the gold lease rate is 1.43383%:

$$5.92783\% - 4.494\% = 1.43383\%$$

The lease rate based on GOFO and USD LIBOR should theoretically be 1.41755%:

$$\left(\frac{\left(1 + 0.0592783 \times \frac{92}{360}\right)}{\left(1 + 0.04494 \times \frac{92}{360}\right)} - 1 \right) \times \frac{360}{92} = 1.41755\%$$

```
.0592783 ENTER 92 × 360 ÷ 1 +
.04494 ENTER 92 × 360 ÷ 1 + ÷
1 - 360 × 92 ÷
```

Location swaps

Because of the physical nature of gold, the location of delivery is an element in its trading. The term "swap" in gold trading can therefore also refer to a change of delivery location – i.e. a trade, for example, to sell gold for delivery in London and simultaneously buy gold for delivery in Zurich.

Futures, FRAs, interest rate swaps and options

As well as OTC trading in gold, there are exchange-traded futures on gold. We describe gold futures later in this chapter by comparison with futures in other commodities.

FRAs and fixed/floating interest rate swaps on the gold lease rate, as well as options on gold and options on the lease rate, also all exist and are exactly parallel to these instruments in cash interest rates and currencies; the reader is referred to the earlier chapters on these subjects, as the instruments work in exactly the same way, considering gold to be the same as any currency. Where a reference fixing price or rate is needed for settlement, the London gold fix is typically used for the gold price and the LBMA derived lease rate for the gold lease rate.

I wish to protect against a fall in the lease rate on a gold deposit of 100,000 ounces **Example 11.5** which I anticipate making for a period of 2 months (61 days), starting in 1 month's time (30 days) from spot. I therefore sell a 1 v 3 FRA at 1.07%.

Two days before the start of the forward period (i.e. the spot fixing date for the start of the forward period), the LBMA derived lease rate fixing for 2 months is 1.13%. The difference between the FRA rate and the settlement fixing rate is 0.06%. The settlement amount is therefore 10.14724 ounces of gold:

$$100,000 \times \frac{0.0006 \times \frac{61}{360}}{\left(1 + 0.0113 \times \frac{61}{360}\right)} = 10.14724$$

I sold the FRA to protect against a fall in rates. In fact the rate rose rather than fell, so I pay this settlement amount to my FRA counterparty.

0.0006 ENTER 61 × 360 ÷
0.0113 ENTER 61 × 360 ÷ 1 + ÷
100,000 ×

OTHER COMMODITIES

We have discussed gold so far in this chapter, because it is close to the other instruments discussed in this book. In other words, although it is a commodity, it is very much a "financial" commodity, in that it is used for investment and traded in a way similar to other financial assets such as bonds or currencies. The same can be said, for example, of silver. Most commodities however are traded largely because of their use in real life – i.e. because they are "consumed". There is an extremely wide range of such commodities which can be traded in a way analogous to financial instruments, that is with instruments for trading spot, forward, futures, options, swaps, etc. The particular characteristics of trading each commodity however also vary extremely widely, because of the specific nature of each commodity itself. Whereas the characteristics of trading currencies such as Swiss francs or Australian dollars are essentially the same, the characteristics of trading in two agricultural commodities such as sugar and wheat, for example, are not the same. The discussion here should therefore be taken only as a general one, and care must be taken in considering the details of any specific community.

In some cases, the characteristics of a particular commodity are too specific and limiting to enable it to be widely traded as a core product. In the energy market for example, a very small number of reference grade oils are traded – for example Brent crude oil delivered at a particular location at a particular date or period. In order to price and trade other products, "spreads" are quoted for oils of a different grade, at different delivery locations and at different delivery times, and even for different products (such as coal). "Spread" is used in this sense in the same way as in an IRS (interest rate swap) spread – it is the difference between the reference price (in this case Brent) and whatever other specification is being traded. For example in oil, a commercial contract for future delivery of a particular crude oil might be agreed at a fixed spread above or below whatever the price is at that delivery time for Brent. In a similar way, other commodities can be traded as spreads relative to certain reference prices.

It is not appropriate in a book such as this to detail all the differences in trading all commodities. We therefore mainly cover only two areas here. First, we discuss the general concept of "convenience yield" and forward pricing theory. Second, we look at three very different futures contracts – gold, live cattle and temperature (not a commodity in the same sense, but traded analogously) – to demonstrate the diversity and complexity of such contracts.

FORWARD PRICING AND CONVENIENCE YIELD

Forward commodity pricing

In Chapter 8 on Foreign Exchange, we explained the theoretical forward outright exchange rate as coming from the following "round-trip" of four simultaneous transactions:

1. Borrow dollars for 3 months starting from spot value date.
2. Sell dollars and buy euros for value spot.
3. Deposit the purchased euros for 3 months starting from spot value date.
4. Sell forward now the euro principal and interest which mature in 3 months' time, into dollars.

In general, the market will adjust the forward price for (4) so that these simultaneous transactions generate neither a profit nor a loss. When the four rates involved are not in line (USD interest rate, EUR/USD spot rate, EUR interest rate and EUR/USD forward rate), there is in fact an opportunity for arbitrage – making a profit by round-tripping. That is, either the transactions as shown above will produce a profit or exactly the reverse transactions (borrow EUR, sell EUR spot, deposit USD and sell USD forward) will produce a profit. The supply and demand effect of this arbitrage activity is such as to move the rates back into line. If in fact this results in a forward rate which is out of line with the market's "average" view, supply and demand pressure will tend to move the spot rate or the interest rates until this is no longer the case.

This no-arbitrage approach led to the theoretical forward outright rate formula (which we have already seen above when discussing gold) as follows:

$$\text{Forward outright} = \text{spot} \times \frac{\left(1 + \text{variable currency interest rate} \times \frac{\text{days}}{\text{year}}\right)}{\left(1 + \text{base currency interest rate} \times \frac{\text{days}}{\text{year}}\right)}$$

When considering forward prices for commodities, this no-arbitrage approach does not generally work. This is essentially because a commodity typically does not have a liquid lending / borrowing market in the same way as cash. This means that a round-trip similar to the one detailed above is possible, but the reverse round-trip is less practicable. For example, it is possible to do the following:

1. Borrow cash for 3 months starting from spot value date.
2. Buy the commodity against cash for value spot.
3. Store the purchased commodity for 3 months starting from spot value date.
4. Sell the commodity forward for cash.

If the forward price is so high that a round-trip profit can be made by doing this, market supply and demand will tend to bring the forward price down (or the spot price up) to remove the arbitrage. This suggests that there is at least an upper limit to the forward price. The forward price received should not be greater than the cash amount to be repaid at the end, including cash interest and storage costs (which include, for example, insurance costs) meanwhile:

$$\text{Forward price} \leq \text{spot} \times \left(1 + \text{cash interest rate} \times \tfrac{\text{days}}{\text{year}}\right) + \text{storage costs}$$

Clearly this argument is possible only for commodities which can be stored. For a commodity such as electricity, which by its nature is not storable, this arbitrage disappears because it is not possible to "carry" the commodity. In some cases, such as with agricultural commodities, storage is possible, but limited because of the non-durable nature of the commodity. Metals are generally easier (and relatively cheap) to store.

In reverse however, the round-trip would require the following:

1. Borrow the commodity for 3 months starting from spot value date.
2. Sell the commodity against cash for value spot.
3. Lend the cash for 3 months starting from spot value date.
4. Buy the commodity forward for cash.

As there is typically no effective way of borrowing the commodity, this arbitrage cannot be completed. Therefore this approach provides no lower limit for the forward price. However an alternative way of seeing this round-trip is to assume that someone already has the commodity in stock. In this case, he could effectively "borrow" from himself – i.e. simply cease to hold his stock of commodity (thereby saving himself the costs associated with storage) and sell it instead. In this case, the round-trip does work and implies the following lower limit to the forward price:

$$\text{Forward price} \geq \text{spot} \times \left(1 + \text{cash interest rate} \times \tfrac{\text{days}}{\text{year}}\right) + \text{storage costs}$$

In this case, the no-arbitrage approach would work both ways, so we would have a forward price formula:

$$\text{Forward price} = \text{spot} \times \left(1 + \text{cash interest rate} \times \tfrac{\text{days}}{\text{year}}\right) + \text{storage costs}$$

In practice however, this approach does not work either, because stocks of commodities are typically not held for investment purposes but for "real" consumption purposes. A holder of a stock of copper, for example, is typically holding it because he needs it for processing, either immediately or in the near future. He might wish to be able to benefit from temporary shortages if they occur, and in any case he needs to keep his processes running efficiently. In practice therefore, he is unwilling to sell it, even if he could buy it back forward at a price which is lower than:

$$\text{Spot} \times \left(1 + \text{cash interest rate} \times \tfrac{\text{days}}{\text{year}}\right) + \text{storage costs}$$

As a result, it is generally not possible to give a clear formula for a theoretical forward price for a commodity in the same way as for a financial instrument. Usually therefore, we are left with only the following inequality for a forward commodity price (and even this does not apply for commodities that cannot be stored):

For storable commodities: **Key Point**

$$\text{Forward price} \leq \text{spot} \times \left(1 + \text{cash interest rate} \times \tfrac{\text{days}}{\text{year}}\right) + \text{storage costs}$$

As we have discussed earlier, gold in particular, and similarly silver to a large extent, do have "store value" rather than consumption value – they are both held to a significant extent for investment rather than consumption. Market players should be willing to sell gold and silver stocks spot and buy them back again forward, if there is an arbitrage profit to be made by doing so. Also, there is a liquid market for borrowing gold and silver. Therefore the second arbitrage above does work for gold and silver, so that in these particular cases we can derive a theoretical formula for the forward price, as indeed we did earlier in this chapter.

Convenience yield

In the general case, the reluctance of the holder of a commodity to sell his stock can be expressed as the perceived benefit, or "convenience" to him of holding the stock. The extent of this convenience can be expressed in the same way as an interest rate per year and is then known as the "convenience yield". Although this convenience yield is "real" in the sense that it is an important real factor in the behaviour of participants in the industries to which the commodity relates, it is not a number which those participants are clearly aware of in the same sense that they are aware of a cash interest rate. It cannot be generated somehow as a piece of "raw data" to put into a formula. Rather, it can be measured by observation, as the number implied by definition, by working backwards from the actual forward rate currently available in the market for a particular commodity. The convenience yield can be defined either to exclude factors such as storage costs, or to be the total benefit perceived of holding the commodity, net of all storage and associated costs. If we adopt the latter approach, we have:

Key Point

If "convenience yield" is the total benefit perceived of holding the commodity, net of all storage and associated costs, then by definition:

$$\text{Forward price} = \text{spot price} \times \frac{\left(1 + \text{cash interest rate} \times \frac{\text{days}}{\text{year}}\right)}{\left(1 + \text{convenience yield} \times \frac{\text{days}}{\text{year}}\right)}$$

This is not a formula which can be used to calculate the theoretical forward price. Rather, it is a way of defining what is meant by convenience yield. The forward price can be found only by observing it in the market. Clearly we can turn this formula round to derive the convenience yield from the spot and forward prices:

Calculation summary

$$\text{Convenience yield} =$$

$$\left(\frac{\text{spot price}}{\text{forward price}} \times \left(1 + \text{cash interest rate} \times \frac{\text{days}}{\text{year}}\right) - 1\right) \times \frac{\text{year}}{\text{days}}$$

Example 11.6 The spot price for a particular commodity is quoted as $1,256 and the price for delivery 61 days forward is $1,239. The 2-month USD interest rate is currently 4.93%. What is the implied convenience yield?

$$\text{Convenience yield} = \left(\frac{1,256}{1,239} \times \left(1 + 0.0493 \times \frac{61}{360}\right) - 1\right) \times \frac{360}{61} = 13.10\%$$

```
0.0493 ENTER 61 × 360 ÷ 1 +
1,256 × 1,239 ÷
1 −
360 × 61 ÷
```

There is no reason to suppose that the convenience yield is constant for all maturities, and in practice it is not. The theoretical convenience yield derived in this way from observed market prices is useful for analysing the state of the market in that particular commodity, but it is not something which can be traded directly. If a trader believes that the convenience yield is too high or too low, and wishes to take a position based on that, he would need to trade the commodity itself.

Example 11.7

A trader believes that the convenience yield derived as above is currently too high and is likely to fall – i.e. the forward price is currently too low relative to the spot price and is likely to rise relative to it. He therefore sells spot and buys forward simultaneously. If he is correct, and the convenience yield falls, he can later reverse his position – buy back spot and sell back forward – and make a profit.

If the dealer believes it might take some time for the position to become profitable, he could instead initially sell for value a short time forward (rather than spot) and simultaneously buy forward for a longer period.

The trade above is exactly analogous to taking a speculative position on interest rates by trading an FX swap (or a forward-forward swap), rather than by trading cash interest rates directly through deposits, FRAs or STIR futures.

Contango and backwardation (again!)

The convenience yield might be negative (for example if storage costs are greater than the perceived benefits of holding) or positive. If it is negative – or positive but less than the cash interest rate – the forward is greater than the spot price. As with gold, this is known as "contango". If the convenience yield is greater than the cash interest rate, the forward price is lower than the spot price – "backwardation".

Backwardation is linked to the tightness of supply of a commodity – if supply is short, holders are more reluctant to sell their stocks now. Typically therefore, backwardation is seen in the case of commodities where the market is aware that sudden supply shortages do occur and the user cannot afford to be without the commodity – for example because of the need to keep an industrial process running at all times because of high overhead costs.

COMMODITY FUTURES AND EFP (EXCHANGE FOR PHYSICAL)

Elsewhere in the book, we have discussed futures on short-term interest rates and bonds. Futures exist similarly on a huge range of agricultural and mineral commodities, as well as energy, weather and other underlyings. The general principles of futures trading apply throughout, in terms of standardisation of the contract specification, and the mechanisms of trading, clearing and margin. The details however depend entirely on the specific commodity traded. By way of comparison with the interest rate and currency futures detailed in Chapter 4, we show below the specifications of three more futures contracts – gold, live cattle and temperature. These give an idea of the complexity and wide range of futures contracts available. See Examples 11.8–11.12.

Different commodities of course give rise to different terminology. One term used generally in futures is "prompt month", which is the front month – i.e. the nearest expiring futures contract. In some futures such as gold, this nearest contract is also known – confusingly for those involved in the physical markets – as "spot". In some markets, the "prompt date" means the delivery date for the futures contract. Unlike interest rate futures, where contracts in different currencies all follow the IMM dates, there is no standard system of dates across different commodities; each commodity market has its own standards. In commodity options, the "prompt date" is the date on which the buyer of the option will buy or sell the underlying commodity if the option is exercised.

Example 11.8

Gold futures

Exchange	COMEX, a division of NYMEX in New York.
Commodity	The basis of the contract is 100 troy ounces of gold.
Delivery	The contract can be delivered (although almost all positions are closed out before delivery). The gold delivered must weigh 100 troy ounces ± 5%, with fineness of at least 995. It must consist of either one bar or three 1-kilogramme bars, each bearing a serial number and identifying stamp of a refiner approved and listed by COMEX; delivery must be made from a depository licensed by COMEX.
Delivery date	Delivery can be on any business day in the delivery month. The delivery months available are the current month and the next two months, plus February, April, August and October (for the next 23 months) plus June and December (for the next 5 years).
Trading	It is possible to trade the contract until close of business 2 days before the last business day of the delivery month.
Price	Quoted as USD per troy ounce.
Price movement	Prices are quoted to two decimal places and can move by as little as $0.10 (the tick size) – equivalent to a profit or loss of $10.00 on one contract:

Amount of contract × price movement
= 100 ounces × $0.10 = $10.00

Example 11.9

Live cattle futures

Exchange	Chicago Mercantile Exchange in Chicago.
Commodity	40,000 pounds weight (lb) of cattle, consisting of 55% "choice", 45% "select", yield grade 3 live steers or steer carcasses, as defined by the United States Department of Agriculture (USDA).
Delivery	The contract can be delivered. The details of delivery are complex. Live steers, for example, should average between 1,100 pounds and 1,350 pounds with no individual steer weighing more than 100 pounds above or below the average weight for the unit and no individual animal weighing less than 1,050 pounds or more

than 1,400 pounds, but adjustments can be made for differences in size and quality of what is actually delivered.

Delivery date   Delivery can be on any business day in the delivery month or any of the first 7 business days of the following month, at the seller's choice. The delivery months available are the next 7 of February, April, June, August, October and December.

Trading   It is possible to trade the contract until close of business on the last business day of the delivery month.

Price   Quoted as USD per lb.

Price movement   Prices are quoted to five decimal places and can move by as little as $0.00025 per lb (the tick size) – equivalent to a profit or loss of $10.00 on one contract:

$$\text{Amount of contract} \times \text{price movement}$$
$$= 40{,}000 \text{ lb} \times \$0.00025 = \$10.00$$

European monthly heating degree day futures for Amsterdam   Example 11.10

Exchange   Chicago Mercantile Exchange in Chicago.

Commodity   £20 times the "heating degree day index". This index is calculated as follows:

(1) Each calendar day during the particular month being traded, the "average temperature" is the average of the maximum and minimum temperatures (measured in degrees Celsius) at Amsterdam-Schiphol (Netherlands).

(2) The "heating degree day" (HDD) is 18 minus the daily average from (1) – or zero, if this result would be negative.

(3) The "heating degree day index" for that month is the total of all the HDDs for each calendar day throughout the month.

Delivery   The contract is cash-settled and cannot be delivered. The cash settlement is calculated as £20 times the heating degree day index and settled on the final trading date.

Delivery date   The months available for trading are October, November, December, January, February, March and April, with 7 months always available.

Trading   It is possible to trade the contract until 9:00 a.m. (Chicago) on the first business day which is at least two calendar days after the end of the month.

Price   Quoted in points, with 1 point equal to 1 HDD.

Price movement   The tick size is 1 point, equivalent to a profit or loss of £20.00.

If the winter is particularly warm, this reduces demand for electricity and hence revenue for an electricity-generating company. If such a company wishes to hedge against a warm winter, it could buy puts on the heating degree day index.   Example 11.11

Suppose, for example, that the company buys February puts. Suppose also that during February, there are many days when the temperature is unusually high. This will cause the heating degree day index to be unusually low. The company therefore makes a profit on its puts. This helps to offset the revenue shortfall.

Example 11.12 If the winter is particularly cold, outdoor construction work becomes difficult and the revenues of a construction company therefore fall. If such a company wishes to hedge against this, it could buy calls on the heating degree day index.

Suppose, for example, that the company buys February calls. Suppose also that during February, there are many days when the temperature is unusually low. This will cause the heating degree day index to be unusually high. The company therefore makes a profit on its calls. This helps to offset the revenue shortfall.

EFP – exchange for physical

An "exchange for physical" ("EFP") involves two separate but linked transactions, one a cash transaction in a physical commodity and the other a futures transaction. The EFP takes place privately between two parties, not on a futures exchange, but is designed either to convert a physical off-market transaction between those two counterparties into a futures position, or vice versa. The mechanics involve one party buying the underlying in a physical OTC transaction and simultaneously selling the futures contract, while the other party does the reverse.

The two parties negotiate privately both the price of the cash commodity to be exchanged and the price at which the futures position is exchanged. Once this has been done, the details are given to the clearing house of the futures exchange, which effects the futures contracts as agreed. The futures contracts are registered with the clearing house as the central counterparty in the usual way. From that point, as far as the futures side of the EFP is concerned, the futures margin and delivery obligations of the parties arising from an EFP are exactly the same as with any other futures contracts. In practice, there would usually also be a broker in the chain of transactions, as the two main counterparties are unlikely to be members of the clearing house and would need to effect the whole arrangement through a broker member.

The net result is that the physical position and the counterparty credit exposure are transferred from the OTC market to the futures market – or vice versa.

The underlying of the physical transaction and the underlying of the futures contract must be substantially the same. The exact rules vary between exchanges. For example, the price agreed between the two parties for the futures contracts might be required to be within the day's futures price trading range.

A (a meat processing business) has a long position in live cattle futures on the CME, taken in order to hedge the cost of future supplies. B (a farming business) has a similar short position, taken to hedge future income. The cattle which B has to deliver do not conform to the futures contract specification (they are a different breed and quality).

A arranges with B privately (off the exchange) a purchase of B's cattle. At the same time, A and B also agree a price at which A will sell his long futures position to B. The futures clearing house is informed of the whole arrangement. The clearing house then registers the futures transactions at the agreed price, which has the effect of closing each of A's and B's existing futures positions.

The net result is that A and B have effectively arranged an off-exchange delivery of their futures positions. The difference between the price at which they agree the physical transaction and the price at which they agree the futures exchange is effectively the "spread" or "basis" between the price of the cattle which will actually be delivered and the price of the cattle which underlie the futures contract.

> **Example 11.13**

In reverse, an EFP can be used to replace a physical position by a futures position – see Example 11.14.

An investor wishes to trade PLN/USD currency futures on the CME at a time when the futures market is likely to be rather illiquid. He therefore trades in the OTC market and agrees to transfer the deal to the futures market using an EFP.

The investor buys PLN from the counterparty against USD and agrees simultaneously to transfer the trade to the futures exchange using an EFP. Effectively there are three transactions involved:

1. The investor buys PLN from the counterparty against USD.
2. The investor sells PLN to the counterparty against USD.
3. The investor take a long PLN/USD futures position and the counterparty takes a short PLN/USD futures position, at an agreed rate.

Transactions (2) and (3) make up the EFP and are notified to the futures clearing house. The clearing house then establishes the long PLN/USD futures position for the investor at the agreed price, and an opposite short position for the counterparty.

The net result is that the investor has established a futures position, but he was able to do so at a time when the futures market was not liquid enough to do this in the normal way.

> **Example 11.14**

There is a variety of situations where an EFP can be used:

Converting a futures position to a physical OTC position

■ (As in Example 11.13) because the commodity to be delivered does not conform to the futures specification.

■ Because the physical exchange is to be at a different date from the futures delivery date.

- Because the physical exchange is to be at a different delivery location from the futures specification. In gold for example, an EFP might be because someone has a long position in gold futures, but wants the gold delivered loco London (which is not one of the delivery specifications in the CME gold futures contract).

Converting a physical OTC trade to a futures position

- (As in Example 11.14) to execute a trade at a time when the futures market is closed or illiquid, and then convert the trade to a futures position. The same procedure works for closing an existing futures position when the futures market is closed or illiquid; in this case, the futures contracts created by the EFP close the original futures positions rather than open new ones.

- (As in Example 11.14) to remove the credit risk associated with trading OTC – there is effectively no credit risk in futures because of the margin system and the clearing house as central counterparty.

- To release credit line availability.

- To reduce the balance sheet.

- To realise a cash profit sooner. Suppose someone has a forward physical cash position which is in profit compared with current market rates. The benefit will not be realised until delivery date. By converting the physical position to futures, the position will be marked to market and the profit realised immediately through margin, in the usual way.

FRAs, SWAPS AND OPTIONS

A range of derivatives exists for other commodities as well as gold, which again is analogous to those for the financial instruments we have considered elsewhere in the book, and the concepts and maths are broadly parallel. The details vary of course, in line with the different characteristics of each commodity.

We have already mentioned FRAs and fixed/floating interest rate swaps based on the gold lease rate, exactly analogous to those for interest rates on cash that we have seen earlier in the book. Similarly, there are fixed/floating oil price swaps. For example, a large user of oil might wish to hedge the cost of oil over a long period. It could enter a swap whereby over a long period it agrees to receive the floating price of oil (the spot price for Brent, for example, could be used as a reference fixing rate) and pay a fixed price.

Options

One approach to pricing options on commodities is to consider them analogously to options on currencies – the base currency is the "commodity" and the variable currency is the "cash". The convenience yield of the commodity is analogous to the interest rate of the base currency. When we gave a formula for a currency option price in Chapter 10, we did not in fact use the base currency interest rate – instead, this was implicit in the forward outright price of the base currency. Similarly in the following formulas, the convenience yield does not need to be explicitly derived.

The formulas below depend of course on whether the Black–Scholes / Garman–Kohlhagen model is appropriate for options on the commodity being considered. This might well not be the case. For example, the fundamental assumption that the probability distribution of relative price changes is lognormal may well not be correct. Also, because the convenience yield might vary widely with changing "real-life" conditions, an assumption that the convenience yield is constant might be a significant flaw.

Black–Scholes / Garman–Kohlhagen formula for commodities

Calculation summary

Call premium = (forward price × N(d_1) – strike price × N(d_2)) × e^{-rt}

Put premium = (–forward price × N($-d_1$) + strike price × N($-d_2$)) × e^{-rt}

= call premium + (strike price – forward price) × e^{-rt}

where:

$$d_1 = \frac{LN\left(\frac{forward}{strike}\right) + \frac{\sigma^2 t}{2}}{\sigma\sqrt{t}}$$

$$d_2 = \frac{LN\left(\frac{forward}{strike}\right) - \frac{\sigma^2 t}{2}}{\sigma\sqrt{t}}$$

r = the continuously compounded cash interest rate (as before, the expressions e^{rt} and e^{-rt} in the formulas above can be replaced by $(1 + i \times t)$ and $\frac{1}{(1 + i \times t)}$ respectively, where i is the simple interest rate for the period rather than the continuously compounded rate)

t = the time to expiry of the option expressed as a proportion of a year (365 days)

σ = the annualised volatility

N(d) = the standardised normal cumulative probability distribution

---

Example 11.15	What is the cost of a 3-month (91-day) call on one unit of commodity X, at a strike of $560 per unit of the commodity, using the Black–Scholes formula? The spot price of commodity X is 575, the 3-month forward price is 570, volatility is 9.0%, and the 3-month cash interest rate is 5.0%.

First, convert the cash interest rate to its continuously compounded equivalent:

$$r = \frac{365}{91} \times LN \left(1 + 0.05 \times \frac{91}{360}\right) = 0.0504$$

$$d_1 = \frac{LN\left(\frac{570}{560}\right) + \frac{0.09^2 \times \frac{91}{365}}{2}}{0.09 \sqrt{\frac{91}{365}}} = 0.4163$$

$$d_2 = \frac{LN\left(\frac{570}{560}\right) - \frac{0.09^2 \times \frac{91}{365}}{2}}{0.09 \sqrt{\frac{91}{365}}} = 0.3714$$

Call premium
$$= (570 \times N(0.4163) - 560 \times N(0.3714)) \times e^{-0.0504 \times \frac{91}{365}}$$
$$= (570 \times 0.6614 - 560 \times 0.6448) \times 0.9875$$
$$= 15.71$$

The premium is therefore $15.71.

For further analysis of options, option strategies and the "Greeks", we suggest that the reader refers to Chapter 10.

EXERCISES

93. I sell 400 ounces of gold at $487.60 per ounce. I receive a bar weighing 402.925 ounces, with a fineness of 999.9. How much do I pay for the gold?

94. I borrow 40,000 ounces of gold for 31 days at a gold lease rate of 0.87%. At the end of the loan, I pay back the interest in USD, converted at the gold fix price of 513.70. What is the interest amount in USD?

95. The current spot gold price is $601.95 per ounce. The USD 2-month (61-day) interest rate is 5.48% and the gold lease rate for the same period is 1.02%. What is the theoretical 3-month forward gold price?

96. The 6-month (182-day) GOFO fixing today is 5.203%. The 6-month USD LIBOR fixing is 5.88721%. What is the theoretical gold lease rate consistent with these numbers?

97. I wish to protect against a rise in the gold lease rate because I intend to borrow 40,000 ounces of gold for 6 months (181 days), starting in 1 month's time (31 days) from spot. I am quoted a gold FRA at 0.95%/1.05%. At settlement of the FRA, the LBMA derived lease rate fixing for 6 months is 1.02%. What is the settlement amount (in ounces of gold) and do I pay it or receive it?

98. The spot price for a particular commodity is quoted as $493.2 and the price for delivery 91 days forward is $495.1. The 3-month USD interest rate is currently 4.87%. What is the implied convenience yield?

99. A trader believes that the convenience yields implied by current forward prices for a particular commodity are too low and are therefore likely to rise. He transacts a swap to profit from this. Does he sell the commodity forward for a near date and simultaneously buy it back for a date further forward, or does he1 do the reverse of that?

100. What is the cost of a 6-month (182-day) put on one unit of commodity X, at a strike of $7.95 per unit of the commodity, using the Black–Scholes formula? The spot price of commodity X is 7.96, the 3-month forward price is 7.98, volatility is 15.0%, and the 3-month cash interest rate is 4.95%.

Part 6

Hints and Answers
to Exercises

Hints and Answers
to Exercises

Hints on exercises

Answers to exercises

Hints on exercises

1. Future value = present value $\times \left(1 + \text{yield} \times \dfrac{\text{days}}{\text{year}}\right)$

2. Present value = $\dfrac{\text{future value}}{\left(1 + \text{yield} \times \frac{\text{days}}{\text{year}}\right)}$

3. Yield = $\left(\dfrac{\text{future value}}{\text{present value}} - 1\right) \times \dfrac{\text{year}}{\text{days}}$

4. Future value = present value $\times (1 + \text{yield})^N$

5. Is a present value generally greater or smaller than a future value?

6. Future value = present value $\times (1 + \text{yield})^N$
   Interest = future value $-$ principal

7. Present value = $\dfrac{\text{future value}}{(1 + \text{yield})^N}$

8. Future value = present value $\times (1 + \text{yield})^N$

9. Yield = $\left(\dfrac{\text{future value}}{\text{present value}}\right)^{\frac{1}{N}} - 1$

10. Future value =

    present value $\times \left(1 + \dfrac{\text{first yield}}{\text{frequency}}\right)^{\text{number of periods}} \times \left(1 + \dfrac{\text{second yield}}{\text{frequency}}\right)^{\text{number of periods}}$

11. Future value = present value $\times \left(1 + \dfrac{\text{yield}}{\text{frequency}}\right)^{\text{number of periods}}$

    With reinvestment at a different rate, consider each cashflow separately, reinvested to maturity.

12. Either use the TVM keys on the HP, or calculate the present value of each cashflow and add them together:

    Present value = $\dfrac{\text{future value}}{(1 + \text{yield})^N}$

13. Consider the problem in terms of monthly periods rather than years. On this basis, how many periods are there and what is the interest rate for each period? Then use the TVM keys on the HP.

14. Effective rate $= \left(1 + \dfrac{\text{semi-annual rate}}{2}\right)^2 - 1$

15. Rate $= \left[(1 + \text{annual rate})^{\frac{1}{\text{frequency}}} - 1\right] \times \text{frequency}$

16. Future value $= \text{present value} \times e^{r \times \frac{\text{days}}{\text{year}}}$

Effective rate $= e^r - 1$

Continuously compounded rate $= \text{LN}(1 + i)$

17. Effective rate $= \left(1 + i \times \dfrac{\text{days}}{\text{year}}\right)^{\frac{365}{\text{days}}}$

Daily equivalent rate $= \left[\left(1 + i \times \dfrac{\text{days}}{\text{year}}\right)^{\frac{1}{\text{days}}} - 1\right] \times \text{year}$

Discount factor $= \dfrac{1}{\left(1 + i \times \frac{\text{days}}{\text{year}}\right)}$

18. First known rate $+$

difference between known rates $\times \dfrac{\text{days from first date to interpolated date}}{\text{days between known dates}}$

19. What is the period between cashflows? What is the interest rate for this period? Are there any zero cashflows?

The NPV can be calculated either by using the HP cashflow function, or from first principles:

Present value $= \dfrac{\text{future value}}{(1 + \text{yield})^N}$

20. Use the IRR function on the HP and then consider for what period the result is expressed.

21. Mean $=$ sum of all the values divided by the number of values

Estimated variance $= \dfrac{\text{sum of all the (difference from the mean)}^2}{(\text{the number of values} - 1)}$

Estimated standard deviation $= \sqrt{\text{estimated variance}}$

22. Mean plus one standard deviation

23. Proceeds $= \text{face value} \times \left(1 + \text{coupon rate} \times \dfrac{\text{days}}{\text{year}}\right)$

24. Price = present value = $\dfrac{\text{future value}}{\left(1 + \text{yield} \times \frac{\text{days}}{\text{year}}\right)}$

Simple yield = $\left(\dfrac{\text{future cashflow}}{\text{present cashflow}} - 1\right) \times \dfrac{\text{year}}{\text{days held}}$

Effective yield = $\left(\dfrac{\text{future cashflow}}{\text{present cashflow}}\right)^{\frac{365}{\text{days}}} - 1$

25. Overall return = $\left[\dfrac{\left(1 + \text{yield on purchase} \times \frac{\text{days on purchase}}{\text{year}}\right)}{\left(1 + \text{yield on sale} \times \frac{\text{days on sale}}{\text{year}}\right)} - 1\right] \times \dfrac{\text{year}}{\text{days held}}$

Therefore: yield on sale =

$\left[\dfrac{\left(1 + \text{yield on purchase} \times \frac{\text{days on purchase}}{\text{year}}\right)}{\left(1 + \text{overall return} \times \frac{\text{days held}}{\text{year}}\right)} - 1\right] \times \dfrac{\text{year}}{\text{days on sale}}$

26. Rate on ACT/365 basis = rate on ACT/360 basis $\times \dfrac{365}{360}$

Effective yield (ACT/365 basis) = $\left(1 + \text{interest rate} \times \dfrac{\text{days}}{\text{year}}\right)^{\frac{365}{\text{days}}} - 1$

Effective yield on ACT/360 basis = effective yield $\times \dfrac{360}{365}$

27. What is the day/year count?

price = present value = $\dfrac{\text{future value}}{\left(1 + \text{yield} \times \frac{\text{days}}{\text{year}}\right)}$

28. Discount rate = $\dfrac{\text{rate of true yield}}{\left(1 + \text{yield} \times \frac{\text{days}}{\text{year}}\right)}$

Discount amount = principal × discount rate $\times \dfrac{\text{days}}{\text{year}}$

29. Rate of true yield = $\dfrac{\text{discount rate}}{\left(1 - \text{discount rate} \times \frac{\text{days}}{\text{year}}\right)}$

Amount paid = principal $\times \left(1 - \text{discount rate} \times \dfrac{\text{days}}{\text{year}}\right)$

30. Discount amount = face value − amount paid

Discount rate = $\dfrac{\text{discount amount}}{\text{face value}} \times \dfrac{\text{year}}{\text{days}}$

31. What is the day/year count?

a. Amount paid = principal $\times \left(1 - \text{discount rate} \times \dfrac{\text{days}}{\text{year}}\right)$

b. Rate of true yield $= \dfrac{\text{discount rate}}{\left(1 - \text{discount rate} \times \frac{\text{days}}{\text{year}}\right)}$

Then convert to 365-day basis

32. Yield $= \left(\dfrac{\text{future cashflow}}{\text{present cashflow}} - 1\right) \times \dfrac{\text{year}}{\text{days held}}$

33. Yield $= \left(\dfrac{\text{future cashflow}}{\text{present cashflow}} - 1\right) \times \dfrac{\text{year}}{\text{days held}}$

34. What is the day/year count in each case?
Is the quote a yield or a discount rate in each case?

35. Convert all rates to the same basis in order to compare them – for example, true yield, on a 365-day basis.

36. Taking account of non-working days as appropriate, what was the last coupon date, and what are the remaining coupon dates?

How many days are there between these dates and what are the exact coupon payments?

Discount each cashflow back to the previous date, using exact day counts, add the actual cashflows for that date, and so on back to the settlement date.

37. Forward-forward rate $= \left[\dfrac{\left(1 + \text{longer rate} \times \frac{\text{days}}{\text{year}}\right)}{\left(1 + \text{shorter rate} \times \frac{\text{days}}{\text{year}}\right)} - 1\right] \times \left(\dfrac{\text{year}}{\text{days difference}}\right)$

If the above is based on middle rates rather than offered rates, you should add around 0.06% to benchmark against LIBOR.

38. a. For the FRA, are you a borrower (protecting against the risk of higher rates) or an investor (protecting against the risk of lower rates)?

b. The price-taker always gets the worse price.

c. Consider the cashflows – exactly what amount will you be rolling over?

d. FRA settlement amount $= \text{principal} \times \dfrac{(\text{FRA rate} - \text{LIBOR}) \times \frac{\text{days}}{\text{year}}}{\left(1 + \text{LIBOR} \times \frac{\text{days}}{\text{year}}\right)}$

e. Consider all the exact cashflows and timings and on which side of the market you will be dealing.

39. Remember that the profit / loss relates to a 3-month period rather than a whole year.

40. Create a strip.

41. Calculate the implied 3 v 9 and 6 v 12 rates.
    Interpolate for 3 v 7 and 6 v 10.
    Interpolate further for 4 v 8.
    The hedge follows the same construction.

42. First, calculate the various cash forward-forward rates (3 v 6, 6 v 9, 3 v 9). Then, compare the various combinations possible:
    - forward-forward, FRA or futures for 3 v 6
    - forward-forward, FRA or futures for 6 v 9
    - forward-forward or FRA for 3 v 9

43. Use the TVM function of the HP.

44. What are all the cashflows from the bond?
    Clean price = NPV using the yield
    Clean price = dirty price because there is no accrued coupon

$$\text{Current yield} = \frac{\text{coupon rate}}{\dfrac{\text{clean price}}{100}}$$

$$\text{Simple yield to maturity} = \frac{\text{coupon rate} + \left(\dfrac{\text{redemption amount} - \text{clean price}}{\text{years to maturity}}\right)}{\dfrac{\text{clean price}}{100}}$$

$$\text{Duration} = \frac{\sum(\text{present value of cashflow} \times \text{time to cashflow})}{\text{dirty price}}$$

45. This question is complicated by the fact that the calculation bases for accrued coupon and price are different.

    - Calculate the clean price and the accrued interest assuming that both are calculated on an ACT/ACT basis.
    - Add together to give the correct dirty price.
    - Recalculate the accrued interest on the correct 30/360 basis.
    - Subtract this from the dirty price to give the correct clean price.

    Or, using the bond price formula rather than the functions built into the HP calculator:

$$\text{Dirty price} = \frac{100}{\left(1+\frac{i}{n}\right)^w}\left[\frac{R}{n} \times \frac{\left(1-\dfrac{1}{\left(1+\frac{i}{n}\right)^N}\right)}{\left(1-\dfrac{1}{\left(1+\frac{i}{n}\right)}\right)} + \frac{1}{\left(1+\frac{i}{n}\right)^{N-1}}\right]$$

    Clean price = dirty price − accrued coupon

46. If you use the HP calculator's built-in bond functions, it is again necessary to make an adjustment for the fact that the price/yield calculation is on a 30/360 basis but the accrued coupon is on an ACT/365 basis, as follows:

   ■ Calculate the correct accrued interest.
   ■ Add to the clean price to give the correct dirty price.
   ■ Calculate the accrued coupon as if it were on a 30/360 basis.
   ■ Subtract from the dirty price to give an adjusted clean price.

47. What is the fraction of a period to the next quasi-coupon date?

$$\text{Price} = \frac{100}{\left(1 + \dfrac{\text{yield}}{2}\right)^{(\text{number of periods to maturity})}}$$

48. True yield on bond year basis $= \dfrac{\text{discount rate}}{\left(1 - \text{discount rate} \times \frac{\text{days}}{360}\right)} \times \dfrac{365}{360}$

49. Yield $= \dfrac{-\frac{\text{days}}{365} + \left(\left(\frac{\text{days}}{365}\right)^2 \times 2 \times \left(\frac{\text{days}}{365} - \frac{1}{2}\right) \times \left(\dfrac{1}{\left(1 - D \times \frac{\text{days}}{360}\right)} - 1\right)\right)^{\frac{1}{2}}}{\left(\frac{\text{days}}{365} - \frac{1}{2}\right)}$

50. This needs the same equation as the previous question. However you need to manipulate the equation into the form "D = ..." rather than "i = ...".

51. The HP calculator bond function cannot be used for a bond with stepped coupons. The easiest method is to work from first principles, as follows:

   ■ Discount the final cashflow to a value one year earlier.
   ■ Add the coupon cashflow paid then and discount back a further year.
   ■ Repeat the process back to the first remaining coupon.
   ■ Discount back to settlement date (what is the $\frac{\text{day}}{\text{year}}$ basis?) to give the current dirty price.
   ■ Subtract the accrued interest to give the clean price.

52. Because bond price/yield formulas generally assume a redemption amount of 100, one approach is to scale down every cashflow by the same factor to correspond to a redemption amount of 100.

$$\text{Simple return} = \left(\frac{\text{sale proceeds}}{\text{amount invested}} - 1\right) \times \frac{\text{year}}{\text{days}}$$

$$\text{Effective return} = \left(\frac{\text{sale proceeds}}{\text{amount invested}}\right)^{\frac{365}{\text{days}}} - 1$$

53. For each one:

   ■ Are coupons paid annually or semi-annually?
   ■ What was the last coupon date?
   ■ What is the day/year basis?

54. Compare the cost of funding with the current yield. The difference between the futures price and the bond price should compensate for this.

55. Either build up the price from the arbitrage mechanism:

   ■ Buy the bond.
   ■ Borrow to finance the bond purchase.
   ■ At delivery of the futures contract, repay the financing plus interest.
   ■ Deliver the bond in return for payment plus accrued.

   Or

   Theoretical futures price =

   $$\frac{\left([\text{bond price} + \text{accrued coupon now}] \times \left[1 + i \times \dfrac{\text{days}}{\text{year}}\right]\right) - (\text{accrued coupon at delivery of futures})}{\text{conversion factor}}$$

56. Implied repo rate = $\left[\dfrac{(\text{futures price} \times \text{conversion factor}) + (\text{accrued coupon at delivery of futures})}{(\text{bond price} + \text{accrued coupon now})} - 1\right] \times \dfrac{\text{year}}{\text{days}}$

57. Assume the cash-and-carry arbitrage is:

   ■ Buy the cash CTD bond now.
   ■ Fund this purchase by repoing the bond.
   ■ Sell the bond futures contract.
   ■ Deliver the bond at maturity of the futures contract.

   Accrued coupon for CTD bond = ?

   Cost of buying CTD bond per €100 nominal = ?

   Total borrowing (principal + interest) to be repaid at the end = ?

   Anticipated receipt from selling futures contract and delivering bond per €100 nominal = ?

   Profit per €100 nominal = ?

   Size of euro bond futures contract = ?

   Face value of bond purchased in the arbitrage = ?

   Therefore profit per futures contract = ?

58. For each bond, calculate the yield, the modified duration, the accrued interest, the dirty price, then the total value.

$$\text{Modified duration of portfolio} \approx \frac{\sum(\text{modified duration} \times \text{value})}{\text{portfolio value}}$$

Change in value $\approx -$ value $\times$ change in yield $\times$ modified duration

59. For each bond, calculate the yield, the modified duration, the accrued interest and the dirty price.

Hedge ratio =

$$\frac{\text{notional amount of futures contract required to hedge a position in bond A}}{\text{face value of bond A}} =$$

$$\frac{\text{dirty price of bond A}}{\text{dirty price of CTD bond}} \times \frac{\text{modified duration of bond A}}{\text{modified duration of CTD bond}}$$

$$\times \frac{\text{conversion factor for CTD bond}}{\left(1 + i \times \frac{\text{days}}{\text{year}}\right)}$$

where i = short-term funding rate

60. What is the value of the T-bill?
Adjust for the haircut.

61. a. How frequent are the bond coupons?
What is the accrual method for this bond?
Calculate the accrued coupon on the bond on 13 March 2009.

Calculate the dirty price.
Adjust the dirty price for the haircut.
Calculate the nominal amount of bond required.

b. At the end of the repo, the original cash amount is repaid with interest (money market basis).

62. Calculate the value of the cash originally lent plus interest accrued to 28 March.
The collateral value required (A) is this cash value adjusted for the haircut.

Calculate the accrued coupon on the bond on 28 March.
Calculate the dirty price of the bond on 28 March.
Calculate the value (B) of the bond on 28 March.

The margin call is the difference between A and B.

63. **a.** Calculate the accrued coupon on the bond.
    Calculate the dirty price of the bond.
    Calculate the value of the bond.
    Adjust for the haircut to give the cash amount at the start.
    Convert to USD.

    b. The cash amount at the end is the start cash amount plus interest (on a money market basis).

64. How frequent are BTP coupons?
    What is the accrual method for this bond?
    Calculate the accrued coupon on the bond on 4 April.
    Calculate the dirty price.

    Calculate the value of the cash originally lent plus interest accrued so far.
    Convert to EUR.
    Adjust for the haircut to calculate the value of collateral required.

    Calculate the face value of collateral required.

65. How often do gilts pay coupons?
    What is the amount of the coupon paid?
    Add interest from coupon payment date to the end of the buy / sell-back (calculated at what interest rate?).

66. Calculate the accrued coupon on the bond.
    Calculate the dirty price of the bond.
    Calculate the value of the bond.
    Adjust for the haircut to give the cash amount at the start.

    The cash amount at the end in a repo would be the start cash amount plus interest (on a money market basis).

    How much is the coupon payment during the buy / sell-back?
    Add interest to this.
    Subtract from the cash amount that would be at the end of a repo.

    Calculate the forward dirty price.
    Calculate accrued coupon on the bond at the forward date.
    Subtract to give the forward clean price.

67. **a.** Calculate accrued coupon on the security borrowed.
    Calculate the dirty price of the security borrowed.
    Calculate the value of the security borrowed.
    Adjust for the margin, to give the value of collateral required.

Calculate accrued coupon on the collateral.
Calculate the dirty price of the collateral.
Calculate the face value of collateral required.

b. The lending fee is calculated on the value of the security lent, at the lending fee rate, for the time of the loan, on a money market basis.

68. The difference between the GC rate and the fee.

69. a. Calculate accrued coupon on the security lent.
Calculate the dirty price of the security lent.
Calculate the value of the security lent.
Adjust for the margin, to give the value of collateral required.

Calculate the "price" of the collateral (money market CD calculation).
Calculate the face value of collateral required.

b. The lending fee is calculated on the value of the security lent, at the lending fee rate, for the time of the loan, on a money market basis.

70. Calculate the accrued coupon on the bond.
Calculate the dirty price of the bond.
Calculate the value of the bond to give the cash consideration of the deal.
Calculate the profit based on this amount.

71. Bootstrap to create the zero-coupon yields and discount factors.

$$1 \text{ year v 2 year forward-forward} = \frac{1\text{-year discount factor}}{2\text{-year discount factor}} - 1 \text{ etc.}$$

72. a. Create the zero-coupon yields from strips of the 1-year rate and forward-forwards.

Calculate the discount factors.

The par yield is the coupon of a bond such that the NPV of the bond's cashflows (using the discount factors) is par.

b. Calculate the NPV of the cashflows using the discount factors.
Use the TVM function of the HP to calculate the yield.

73. Bootstrap to create the 18-month and 24-month discount factors.

$$\text{Forward-forward rate} = \left[\frac{18\text{-month discount factor}}{24\text{-month discount factor}} - 1 \right] \times \frac{\text{year}}{\text{days}}$$

74. What are the day/year bases?

$$\text{Forward swap} = \text{spot} \times \frac{\left(\text{variable currency rate} \times \frac{\text{days}}{\text{year}} - \text{base currency rate} \times \frac{\text{days}}{\text{year}}\right)}{\left(1 + \text{base currency rate} \times \frac{\text{days}}{\text{year}}\right)}$$

75. a. Indirect rates: divide opposite sides. Customer gets the worse price.

    b. One direct rate and one indirect: multiply same sides.

    c. Add or subtract the forward points?

    d. Add or subtract the forward points?

    e. Is sterling worth more forward than spot or vice versa?

    f. Similar to (d) and (e).

    g. Forward points = outright − spot.

76. a. The value date is after spot (add or subtract forward points?).

    b. The value date is before spot (add or subtract forward points?).

    c. The customer gets the worse price.

    d. Similar to (c).

    e. Take the difference between opposite sides.

    f. Should the price be bigger or smaller than the one-month swap? Take care with +/− signs.

77. a. Calculate NOK and JPY outrights against the USD.
       Calculate cross-rate spots and outrights.
       Cross-rate swap = outright − spot.
       Forward-forward price is difference between opposite sides.

    b. For a swap from before spot to after spot, add the same sides.

78. a. You need to interpolate between the 1-month and the 2-month dates. Then the method is similar to 77(a).

    b. Similar to 77(b) but combine the O/N price as well as the T/N.

    c. Again, combine the O/N and T/N.

79. a. The 6-month USD/JPY forward swap price means ¥2.69/2.63.

    b. Assume that the expected changes happen, and calculate the effect on the forward outright price, using middle prices for the comparison.

80. Either consider the exact cashflows:

- Initial USD investment = ?
- Total proceeds at maturity of CP = ?
- Buy and sell EUR (sell and buy USD) spot against 3 months.

Or use the formula for covered interest arbitrage:

Variable currency rate =

$$\left[\left(1 + \text{base currency rate} \times \frac{\text{days}}{\text{base year}}\right) \times \frac{\text{outright}}{\text{spot}} - 1\right] \times \frac{\text{variable year}}{\text{days}}$$

81. **Action now**
   (i)   Arrange FRA on a notional 3 v 9 borrowing of USD.
   (ii) Convert this notional loan from USD to NOK via a foreign exchange swap.

   Action in 3 months' time
   (iii) Assume a borrowing of NOK.
   (iv) Convert this borrowing to a USD borrowing to match (i), via a foreign exchange swap.

   Settlement at the end of 9 months
   (v)   Receive deferred FRA settlement.

82. Write out all the resulting cashflows, then calculate present values.

83. **a.** Value the USD cashflows in EUR using current outrights. Recalculate the outrights after the spot rate movement, then revalue the USD cashflows.

   b. Calculate the NPV of these net future cashflows using an appropriate EUR interest rate for each period.

   Calculate the NPV of the original USD positions using an appropriate USD interest rate for each period; the appropriate spot hedge should offset this NPV.

84. On what basis is the swap quoted? Convert the absolute swap rate and the bond coupon both to semi-annual money market. The difference represents the approximate sub-LIBOR spread.

85. **a.** Convert the futures prices to implied interest rates. Then for each maturity, create a zero-coupon rate from a strip of 3-month rates. Is this on a bond basis or a money market basis? Calculate the effective annual equivalent.

b. Calculate the par rate in the same way that you would calculate a par bond yield – the coupon and yield are the same for an instrument priced at par. The quarterly coupon cashflows need to be calculated on a quarterly money market basis.

86. a The USD swap cashflows match the remaining bond cashflows (including the principal). What is the NPV in USD of these cashflows? Convert to GBP at spot. The GBP side of the swap must have an NPV equal to this. The GBP swap cashflows can therefore be 11% per annum plus principal, based on this NPV amount.

b. Long-dated forward outright $= \text{spot} \times \dfrac{(1 + \text{variable interest rate})^N}{(1 + \text{base interest rate})^N}$

Convert the USD bond cashflows to GBP at the forward rates.

c. What is the NPV of the alternative GBP cashflow streams, using various rates of discount to calculate the NPV?

87. Convert the USD cash raised from the bond issue to CHF and create CHF swap cashflows (floating rate interest payments plus principal) on this amount. Calculate the NPV of the USD swap cashflows (which match all the bond cashflows) and convert to CHF at spot; the NPV of the CHF swap cashflows needs to equal this amount.

Therefore adjust the CHF interest payments by a regular amount which brings the NPV of all the CHF cashflows to this amount.

88. Write out the cashflows in each currency, remembering to include the final principal payments. Calculate the NPV of the USD cashflows using the USD discount factors.

Some of the SEK cashflows are unknown because they depend on future LIBOR fixings. Eliminate these by adding an appropriate FRN structure beginning on 27 May 2010. Alternatively, calculate forward-forward rates for the future LIBOR fixings. Then calculate the NPV of the net SEK cashflows using the SEK discount factors. Convert this NPV to USD and net against the USD NPV already calculated.

89. Write out all the cashflows arising from issuing USD 100 face value of the bond. Add the cashflows arising from a swap based on a notional amount of USD 100. Consider the net result as a structure of 100 borrowed, 100 repaid at maturity and $(100 \times \text{LIBOR} \times \frac{1}{2} \times \frac{365}{360})$ each six months plus some irregular cashflows.

Calculate the NPV of these irregular cashflows.

Offset them by matching cashflows and replace by a series of regular six-monthly cashflows with the same NPV.

What spread above or below LIBOR is necessary to generate these regular six-monthly cashflows?

90. From the ten price data, calculate nine daily relative price changes ($\frac{\text{day 2 price}}{\text{day 1 price}}$ etc.).

Take the natural logarithm of each relative price change.

Calculate the standard deviation of these nine logarithms, as usual:

- Calculate the mean.
- Calculate the differences from the mean.
- Square the differences.
- Add the squares and divide by eight (one less than the number of data) to give the variance.
- The standard deviation is the square root of the variance.

The annualised volatility is:

$$\text{Standard deviation} \times \sqrt{\text{number of data observations per year}}$$

91. Convert the NOK call option premium to a cost in NOK.
Use the put / call relationship expressed in units of the variable currency:

Premium for call on base currency − premium for put on base currency = present value of (forward − strike).

Convert the result back to percentage of the USD amount.

92. Calculate the probability (p) of an up movement in the price and of a down movement (1 − p):

The expected outcome after 1 month is [p × increased price + (1 − p) × decreased price]. This should equal the result of depositing 100 for 1 month at the risk-free interest rate.

Construct a tree showing all the possible outcomes at the end of three months.

Calculate the probability of arriving at each of these outcomes by combining the probabilities along each route along the tree.

Which of these outcomes would make the option in-the-money at expiry?

What would the profit be for each outcome?

Multiply each profit by the probability of it happening, and add to give the expected value of the option.

The PV of this expected value is the option's premium.

93. Cost = price per ounce × ounces actually delivered × proportion of pure gold in the bar delivered

94. Interest = amount of gold × lease rate × days/year, then converted to USD

95. Forward price = spot price × $\dfrac{\left(1 + \text{USD interest rate} \times \frac{\text{days}}{360}\right)}{\left(1 + \text{gold lease rate} \times \frac{\text{days}}{360}\right)}$

96. Theoretical lease rate = $\left(\dfrac{\left(1 + \text{USD interest rate} \times \frac{\text{days}}{360}\right)}{\left(1 + \text{GOFO} \times \frac{\text{days}}{360}\right)} - 1\right) \times \dfrac{\text{days}}{360}$

97. To determine on which side of the FRA quote you deal – do you buy or sell the FRA?

Settlement amount = amount of FRA × $\dfrac{(\text{FRA rate} - \text{fixing rate}) \times \frac{\text{days}}{\text{year}}}{\left(1 + \text{fixing rate} \times \frac{\text{days}}{\text{year}}\right)}$

To determine whether you pay or receive the settlement amount – have rates moved in the direction you expected?

98. Implied convenience yield =

$\left(\dfrac{\text{spot price}}{\text{forward price}} \times \left(1 + \text{cash interest rate} \times \dfrac{\text{days}}{\text{year}}\right) - 1\right) \times \dfrac{\text{days}}{\text{year}}$

99. If the convenience yields are too low, does that mean the forward prices are too low or too high, relative to the spot price?

100. Put premium = $(- \text{forward outright price} \times N(-d_1) + \text{strike price} \times N(-d_2)) \times e^{-rt}$

where:

$$d_1 = \frac{LN\left(\frac{\text{forward}}{\text{strike}}\right) + \frac{\sigma^2 t}{2}}{\sigma\sqrt{t}} \qquad d_2 = \frac{LN\left(\frac{\text{forward}}{\text{strike}}\right) - \frac{\sigma^2 t}{2}}{\sigma\sqrt{t}}$$

Answers to exercises

1. Future value = £43 × $\left(1 + 0.075 \times \frac{120}{365}\right)$ = **£44.06**

   .075 ENTER 120 × 365 ÷ 1 + 43 ×

2. Present value = $\dfrac{£89}{\left(1 + 0.101 \times \frac{93}{365}\right)}$ = **£86.77**

   .101 ENTER 93 × 365 ÷ 1 + 89 □ $x \gtreqless y$ ÷

3. Yield = $\left(\dfrac{83.64}{83.00} - 1\right) \times \dfrac{365}{28}$ = **10.05%**

   83.64 ENTER 83 ÷ 1 − 365 × 28 ÷

4. £36 × $(1 + 0.09)^{10}$ = **£85.23**

   1.09 ENTER 10 □ ∧ 36 ×

5. Choose **€1,000 now** unless interest rates are negative. With positive rates, €1,000 now must be worth more than a smaller amount in the future.

6. £342 × $(1 + 0.06)^5$ = £457.67

   £457.67 − £342 = **£115.67**

   1.06 ENTER 5 □ ∧ 342 × 342 −

7. € $\dfrac{98}{(1 + 0.11)^5}$ = **€58.16**

   1.11 ENTER 5 □ ∧ 98 □ $x \gtreqless y$ ÷

8. £1,000 × $(1 + 0.054)^4$ = **£1,234.13**

> 1.054 ENTER 4 □ ∧ 1,000 ×
>
>   *OR*
>
> FIN TVM
> 4 N
> 1,000 ⁺/₋ PV
> 0 PMT
> 5.4 I% YR
> FV

9. $\left(\dfrac{1,360.86}{1,000}\right)^{\frac{1}{7}} - 1 = 4.50\%$

> 1,360.86 ENTER 1,000 ÷
> 7 □ ¹/ₓ □ ∧ 1 −
>
>   *OR*
>
> FIN TVM
> 7 N
> 1,000 ⁺/₋ PV
> 0 PMT
> 1360.86 FV
> I%YR

10. $£1,000,000 \times \left(1 + \dfrac{0.06}{4}\right)^{20} \times \left(1 + \dfrac{0.065}{2}\right)^{10} = £1,854,476.99$

> .06 ENTER 4 ÷ 1 + 20 □ ∧
> .065 ENTER 2 ÷ 1 + 10 □ ∧ ×
> 1,000,000 ×

11. $£1,000,000 \times \left(1 + \dfrac{0.085}{4}\right)^{4} = £1,087,747.96$

> .085 ENTER 4 ÷ 1 + 4 □ ∧ 1,000,000 ×

With reinvestment at 8.0%:

First interest payment plus reinvestment:

$$£1,000,000 \times \frac{0.085}{4} \times \left(1 + \frac{0.08}{4}\right)^{3}$$

Second interest payment plus reinvestment:

$$£1,000,000 \times \frac{0.085}{4} \times \left(1 + \frac{0.08}{4}\right)^{2}$$

Third interest payment plus reinvestment:

$$£1,000,000 \times \frac{0.085}{4} \times \left(1 + \frac{0.08}{4}\right)$$

Fourth interest payment plus reinvestment: $£1,000,000 \times \dfrac{0.085}{4}$

Principal amount:	£1,000,000
Total:	£1,087,584.17

```
.08 ENTER 4 ÷ 1 + 3 □ ∧
.08 ENTER 4 ÷ 1 + 2 □ ∧ +
.08 ENTER 4 ÷ 1 + +
1,000,000 × .085 × 4 ÷
.085 ENTER 4 ÷ 1 + 1,000,000 × +
```

12. £32,088.29

```
FIN TVM
10 N
9 I%YR
5,000 PMT
0 FV
PV
```

13. There are 300 payment periods. The interest for each period is $\dfrac{7.25\%}{12}$.

The regular payment must be £650.53.

```
FIN TVM
300 N
7.25 ENTER 12 ÷ I%YR
90,000 PV
0 FV
PMT
```

14. $\left(1 + \dfrac{0.114}{2}\right)^{2} - 1 = 11.72\%$

```
.114 ENTER 2 ÷ 1 + 2 □ ∧ 1 −
```

15. $[(1 + 0.12)^{\frac{1}{4}} - 1] \times 4 = 11.49\%$
$[(1 + 0.12)^{\frac{1}{12}} - 1] \times 12 = 11.39\%$

```
1.12 ENTER 4 □ 1/x □ ∧ 1 − 4 ×
1.12 ENTER 12 □ 1/x □ ∧ 1 − 12 ×
```

16. $£1,000,000 \times e^{0.07} = £1,072,508.18$

Effective rate is 7.2508% per annum

☐ MATH LOGS .07 EXP 1,000,000 ×

LN(1.09) = **8.6178%** is the continuously compounded rate.

☐ MATH LOGS 1.09 LN

---

17. Effective rate $= \left(1 + 0.065 \times \dfrac{138}{365}\right)^{\frac{365}{138}} - 1 = \mathbf{6.6321\%}$

Daily equivalent rate $= \left[\left(1 + 0.065 \times \dfrac{138}{365}\right)^{\frac{1}{138}} - 1\right] \times 365 = \mathbf{6.4220\%}$

Discount factor $= \dfrac{1}{\left(1 + 0.065 \times \frac{138}{365}\right)} = \mathbf{0.9760}$

.065 ENTER 138 × 365 ÷ 1 + 365 ENTER 138 ÷ ☐ ∧ 1 −
.065 ENTER 138 × 365 ÷ 1 + 138 ☐ ¹/ₓ ☐ ∧ 1 − 365 ×
.065 ENTER 138 × 365 ÷ 1 + ☐ ¹/ₓ ☐

---

18. $5.2\% + (5.4\% - 5.2\%) \times \dfrac{(41 - 30)}{(60 - 30)} = \mathbf{5.2733\%}$

---

41 ENTER 30 − 60 ENTER 30 − ÷
5.4 ENTER 5.2 − ×
5.2 +

---

19. Because the cashflows are 6-monthly, the effective annual interest rate must be converted to an equivalent rate for this 6-monthly period, rather than an annual rate:

$(1.10)^{\frac{1}{2}} - 1 = 4.88\%$

The NPV can then be calculated either by using the HP cashflow function (remembering that the 30-month cashflow is zero), or from first principles as:

$-\$105 - \dfrac{\$47}{(1.0488)} - \dfrac{\$47}{(1.0488)^2} - \dfrac{\$47}{(1.0488)^3} - \dfrac{\$93}{(1.0488)^4} + \dfrac{\$450}{(1.0488)^6} = \mathbf{\$27.95}$

FIN CFLO ☐ CLEAR DATA YES
105 ⁺/− INPUT
47 ⁺/− INPUT 3 INPUT
93 ⁺/− INPUT INPUT
0 INPUT INPUT

```
450 INPUT INPUT
CALC
1.1 ENTER □ √x 1 – 100 × I%
NPV
                          OR
1.1 ENTER □ √x STO 1
6 □ ∧ 450 □ x⇄y ÷
93 RCL 1 4 □ ∧ ÷ –
47 RCL 1 3 □ ∧ ÷ –
47 RCL 1 2 □ ∧ ÷ –
47 RCL 1 ÷ –
105 –
```

20. 7.047% is the IRR on the basis of the semi-annual periods. This is then annualised:

$$(1 + 0.07047)^2 - 1 = 14.59\%$$

```
Following on from the previous calculation using the HP cashflow function:
IRR%
100 ÷ 1 + 2 □ ∧ 1 –
```

21.

	Price	(Difference from mean)^2
	95	4,761
	250	7,396
	160	16
	124	1,600
	180	256
	175	121
Sum	984	14,150
Mean = $\dfrac{\text{sum}}{6}$	164	
Estimated variance = $\dfrac{\text{sum}}{5}$		2,830
Estimated standard deviation = $\sqrt{\text{variance}}$		53

```
95 ENTER 250 + 160 + 124 + 180 + 175 + 6 ÷     [Mean]
STO 1
95 RCL 1 – 2 □ ∧
250 RCL 1 – 2 □ ∧ +
160 RCL 1 – 2 □ ∧ +
124 RCL 1 – 2 □ ∧ +
180 RCL 1 – 2 □ ∧ +
175 RCL 1 – 2 □ ∧ +
5 ÷                                            [Variance]
□ √x                                           [Standard deviation]
```

22. Mean plus one standard deviation = 164 pence plus 53 pence = 217 **pence**

23. $£1,000,000 \times \left(1 + 0.11 \times \dfrac{181}{365}\right) = £1,054,547.95$

> .11 ENTER 181 × 365 ÷ 1 + 1,000,000 ×

24. $\dfrac{£1,000,000 \times \left(1 + 0.11 \times \frac{181}{365}\right)}{\left(1 + 0.10 \times \frac{134}{365}\right)} = £1,017,204.02$ **price**

> .11 ENTER 181 × 365 ÷ 1 + 1,000,000 ×
> .1 ENTER 134 × 365 ÷ 1 + ÷

$$\left[\frac{\left(1 + 0.10 \times \frac{134}{365}\right)}{\left(1 + 0.095 \times \frac{71}{365}\right)} - 1\right] \times \frac{365}{63} = 10.37\% \text{ simple return}$$

> .1 ENTER 134 × 365 ÷ 1 +
> .095 ENTER 71 × 365 ÷ 1 + ÷
> 1 − 365 × 63 ÷

$$\left[\frac{\left(1 + 0.10 \times \frac{134}{365}\right)}{\left(1 + 0.095 \times \frac{71}{365}\right)}\right]^{\frac{365}{63}} - 1 = 10.83\% \text{ effective return}$$

> .1 ENTER 134 × 365 ÷ 1 +
> .095 ENTER 71 × 365 ÷ 1 + ÷
> 365 ENTER 63 ÷ □ ∧ 1 −

25. $\left[\dfrac{\left(1 + 0.10 \times \frac{134}{365}\right)}{\left(1 + i \times \frac{71}{365}\right)} - 1\right] \times \frac{365}{63} = 10.00\%$

Therefore $i = \left[\dfrac{\left(1 + 0.10 \times \frac{134}{365}\right)}{\left(1 + 0.10 \times \frac{63}{365}\right)} - 1\right] \times \frac{365}{71} = 9.83\%$

> .1 ENTER 134 × 365 ÷ 1 +
> .1 ENTER 63 × 365 ÷ 1 + ÷
> 1 − 365 × 71 ÷

26. $11.5\% \times \frac{365}{360} = 11.66\%$

$$\left(1 + 0.115 \times \frac{91}{360}\right)^{\frac{365}{91}} - 1 = 12.18\%$$

$$12.18\% \times \frac{360}{365} = 12.01\%$$

> 11.5 ENTER 365 × 360 ÷
> .115 ENTER 91 × 360 ÷ 1 + 365 ENTER 91 ÷ □ ∧ 1 −
> 360 × 365 ÷

27. Day / year count is ACT/365 basis – that is, $\frac{62}{365}$ in this case.

Purchase price $= \dfrac{£2,000,000}{\left(1 + 0.082 \times \frac{62}{365}\right)} = £1,972,525.16$

> .082 ENTER 62 × 365 ÷ 1 + 2,000,000 □ $x \gtrless y$ ÷

28. $\dfrac{9.5\%}{\left(1 + 0.095 \times \frac{60}{365}\right)} = 9.35\%$

$$9.35\% \times £1,000,000 \times \frac{60}{365} = £15,369,86$$

> .095 ENTER 60 × 365 ÷ 1 + .095 □ $x \gtrless y$ ÷
> .0935 ENTER 1,000,000 × 60 × 365 ÷

29. $\dfrac{9.5\%}{\left(1 - 0.095 \times \frac{60}{365}\right)} = 9.65\%$

$$9.5\% \times £1,000,000 \times \frac{60}{365} = £15,616.44$$

Amount paid $= £1,000,000 - £15,616.44 = £984,383.56$

> .095 ENTER 60 × 365 ÷ 1 − $^+/-$ .095 □ $x \gtrless y$ ÷
> .095 ENTER 60 × 365 ÷ 1 − $^+/-$ 1,000,000 ×

30. $\left(\dfrac{1,000,000 - 975,000}{1,000,000}\right) \times \dfrac{365}{60} = 15.21\%$

> 1,000,000 ENTER 975,000 − 1,000,000 ÷ 365 × 60 ÷

31. a. Amount paid = $1,000,000 $\times \left(1 - 0.065 \times \dfrac{91}{360}\right)$ = **$983,569.44**

    b. Yield = $\dfrac{6.5\%}{\left(1 - 0.065 \times \frac{91}{360}\right)} \times \dfrac{365}{360}$ = **6.70%**

    ```
    .065 ENTER 91 × 360 ÷ 1 – +/– 1,000,000 ×
    .065 ENTER 91 × 360 ÷ 1 – +/– 6.5 □ x⪵y ÷ 365 × 360 ÷
    ```

32. $\left[\dfrac{\left(1 - 0.067 \times \frac{112}{360}\right)}{\left(1 - 0.070 \times \frac{176}{360}\right)} - 1\right] \times \dfrac{365}{64}$ = **7.90%**

    ```
    .067 ENTER 112 × 360 ÷ 1 –
    .07 ENTER 176 × 360 ÷ 1 – ÷
    1 – 365 × 64 ÷
    ```

33. $\left[\dfrac{\left(1 - 0.075 \times \frac{172}{360}\right)}{\left(1 - 0.070 \times \frac{176}{360}\right)} - 1\right] \times \dfrac{365}{4}$ = **–15.22%**

    ```
    .075 ENTER 172 × 360 ÷ 1 –
    .07 ENTER 176 × 360 ÷ 1 – ÷
    1 – 365 × 4 ÷
    ```

34. **US**

    US$1,000,000 $\times \left(1 - 0.05 \times \dfrac{91}{360}\right)$ = **US$987,361.11**

    UK

    £1,000,000 $\times \left(1 - 0.05 \times \dfrac{91}{365}\right)$ = **£987,534.25**

    Australia

    $\dfrac{AUD1,000,000}{\left(1 + 0.05 \times \frac{91}{365}\right)}$ = **AUD987,687.73**

    France

    $\dfrac{€1,000,000}{\left(1 + 0.05 \times \frac{91}{360}\right)}$ = **€987,518.86**

    ```
    .05 ENTER 91 × 360 ÷ 1 – +/– 1,000,000 ×
    .05 ENTER 91 × 365 ÷ 1 – +/– 1,000,000 ×
    .05 ENTER 91 × 365 ÷ 1 + 1,000,000 □ x⪵y ÷
    .05 ENTER 91 × 360 ÷ 1 + 1,000,000 □ x⪵y ÷
    ```

35. Convert all rates, for example to true yield on a 365-day basis to compare:

30-day T-bill (£) $8\frac{1}{4}$% discount rate

$$\text{Yield} = \frac{8.25\%}{\left[1 - 0.0825 \times \frac{30}{365}\right]} = \mathbf{8.3063\%}$$

.0825 ENTER 30 × 365 ÷ 1 – +/– 8.25 □ $x \gtreqless y$ ÷

30-day UK CP (£) **8.1875%** yield

30-day ECP (£) **8.125%** yield

30-day US T-bill 8.3125% discount rate

$$\text{Yield} = \frac{8.3125\%}{\left[1 - 0.083125 \times \frac{30}{360}\right]} = 8.3705\% \text{ on 360-day basis}$$

$$= 8.3705\% \times \frac{365}{360} = \mathbf{8.4867\%} \text{ on 365-day basis}$$

.083125 ENTER 30 × 360 ÷ 1 – +/– 8.3125 □ $x \gtreqless y$ ÷ 365 × 360 ÷

30-day interbank deposit (£) **8.25%** yield

30-day US CP 8.5% discount rate on 360-day basis

$$\text{Yield} = \frac{8.5\%}{\left[1 - 0.085 \times \frac{30}{360}\right]} = 8.5606\% \text{ on 360-day basis}$$

$$= 8.5606\% \times \frac{365}{360} = \mathbf{8.6795\%} \text{ on 365-day basis}$$

.085 ENTER 30 × 360 ÷ 1 – +/– 8.5 □ $x \gtreqless y$ ÷ 365 × 360 ÷

30-day US\$ CD 8.625% yield on ACT/360 basis

$$= 8.625\% \times \frac{365}{360} = \mathbf{8.7448\%} \text{ on 365-day basis}$$

30-day French T-bill 8.5% yield on ACT/360 basis

$$= 8.5\% \times \frac{365}{360} = \mathbf{8.6181\%} \text{ on 365-day basis}$$

Therefore in descending order:

US$ CD	8.7448%
US CP	8.6795%
French T-bill	8.6181%
US T-bill	8.4867%
UK T-bill	8.3063%

Interbank deposit (£)	8.25%
UK CP	8.1875%
ECP (£)	8.125%

36. The last coupon date was: (0) 25 March 2011

The remaining coupon dates are: (1) 26 September 2011 (25 September is a Sunday)

(2) 26 March 2012 (25 March is a Sunday)

(3) 25 September 2012

(4) 25 March 2013

with the same notation as before,

$$
\begin{aligned}
F &= 1{,}000{,}000 \\
R &= 0.075 \\
\text{year} &= 360 \\
d_{p1} &= 130 \\
d_{01} &= 185 \\
d_{12} &= 182 \\
d_{23} &= 183 \\
d_{34} &= 181 \\
i &= 0.08
\end{aligned}
$$

$$A_1 = \left(1 + 0.08 \times \frac{130}{360}\right) = 1.028889$$

$$A_2 = 1.028889 \times \left(1 + 0.08 \times \frac{182}{360}\right) = 1.070502$$

$$A_3 = 1.070502 \times \left(1 + 0.08 \times \frac{183}{360}\right) = 1.114035$$

$$A_4 = 1.114035 \times \left(1 + 0.08 \times \frac{181}{360}\right) = 1.1158844$$

$$P = F \times \left[\frac{R}{\text{year}} \times \left(\frac{d_{01}}{A_1} + \frac{d_{12}}{A_2} + \frac{d_{23}}{A_3} + \frac{d_{34}}{A_4}\right) + \frac{1}{A_4}\right]$$

$$= \$1{,}000{,}000$$

$$\times \left[\frac{0.075}{360} \times \left(\frac{185}{1.028889} + \frac{182}{1.070502} + \frac{183}{1.114035} + \frac{181}{1.158844}\right) + \frac{1}{1.158844}\right]$$

$$= \$1{,}002{,}569.65$$

```
.08 ENTER 130 × 360 ÷ 1 + STO1
.08 ENTER 182 × 360 ÷ 1 + × STO2
.08 ENTER 183 × 360 ÷ 1 + × STO3
.08 ENTER 181 × 360 ÷ 1 + × STO4
185 ENTER RCL1 ÷
182 ENTER RCL2 ÷ +
```

```
183 ENTER RCL3 ÷ +
181 ENTER RCL4 ÷ +
.075 × 360 ÷
RCL4 □ 1/x ÷ +
1,000,000 ×
```

37. Using middle-market rates:

$$\left(\frac{1 + 0.1006 \times \frac{273}{360}}{1 + 0.09935 \times \frac{91}{360}} - 1 \right) \times \frac{360}{(273 - 91)} = 9.87\%$$

As we have used middle rates, we need to add approximately 0.06% to give a rate which can be settled against LIBOR:

9.87% + 0.06% = **9.93% middle FRA**

```
.1006 ENTER 273 × 360 ÷ 1 +
.09935 ENTER 91 × 360 ÷ 1 + ÷
1 – 360 × 273 ENTER 91 – ÷
```

An only slightly different result can be calculated by using the offer side of the 3-month and 6-month rates instead of middle rates, and then not adding 0.06%.

38. a. **Sell the FRA** to cover the deposit which will need to be rolled over

b. 3 v 6 FRA at **7.10%**

c. Ideally, cover the maturing amount of the 3-month deposit:

$$€5 \text{ million} \times \left(1 + 0.0675 \times \frac{91}{360}\right) = €5,085,312.50$$

d. $$\frac{€5,085,312.50 \times (7.10\% - 6.90\%) \times \frac{92}{360}}{\left(1 + 0.069 \times \frac{92}{360}\right)}$$

= **€2,554.12 received by you** (the FRA seller)

```
.071 ENTER .069 – 92 × 360 ÷ 5,085,312.50 ×
.069 ENTER 92 × 360 ÷ 1 + ÷
```

e. Roll over the maturing deposit plus FRA settlement amount at LIBID to give:

$$€(5,085,312.50 + 2,554.12) \times \left(1 + 0.0685 \times \frac{92}{360}\right)$$

= €5,176,932.55

Total borrowing repayment = $€5 \text{ million} \times \left(1 + 0.07 \times \frac{183}{360}\right)$

= €5,177,916.67

Net loss = **€984.12**

> 2,554.12 ENTER 5,085,312.5 + .0685 ENTER 92 × 360 ÷ 1 + ×
> .07 ENTER 183 × 360 ÷ 1 + 5,000,000 × −

39. Selling a futures contract implies **expecting interest rates to rise.**

$$\text{Profit}/\text{loss} = \text{size of contract} \times \frac{\text{change in price}}{100} \times \frac{1}{4}$$

$$= \text{USD 1 million} \times \frac{(94.20 - 94.35)}{100} \times \frac{1}{4} = \textbf{USD 375 loss}$$

40. Create a strip from the implied forward interest rates for each 3-month period:

$$\left[\left(1 + 0.0455 \times \frac{92}{360}\right) \times \left(1 + 0.048 \times \frac{91}{360}\right) \times \left(1 + 0.0495 \times \frac{90}{360}\right) - 1\right] \times \frac{360}{273}$$

$$= \textbf{4.82\%}$$

> .0455 ENTER 92 × 360 ÷ 1 +
> .048 ENTER 91 × 360 ÷ 1 + ×
> .0495 ENTER 90 × 360 ÷ 1 + ×
> 1 − 360 × 273 ÷

41. The FRA rates implied by the futures prices are:

3 v 6 (92 days):	4.55%
6 v 9 (91 days):	4.80%
9 v 12 (90 days):	4.95%

The implied 3 v 9 rate is $\left[\left(1 + 0.0455 \times \frac{92}{360}\right) \times \left(1 + 0.048 \times \frac{91}{360}\right) - 1\right] \times \frac{360}{183}$

$$= 4.7021\%$$

> .0455 ENTER 92 × 360 ÷ 1 + .048 ENTER 91 × 360 ÷ 1 + ×
> 1 − 360 × 183 ÷

The implied 6 v 12 rate is $\left[\left(1 + 0.048 \times \frac{91}{360}\right) \times \left(1 + 0.0495 \times \frac{90}{360}\right) - 1\right] \times \frac{360}{181}$

$$= 4.9044\%$$

> .048 ENTER 91 × 360 ÷ 1 + .0495 ENTER 90 × 360 ÷ 1 + ×
> 1 − 360 × 181 ÷

Interpolation gives:

$$3 \text{ v } 7 \text{ rate} = 3 \text{ v } 6 \text{ rate} + (3 \text{ v } 9 \text{ rate} - 3 \text{ v } 6 \text{ rate}) \times \frac{30}{91} = 4.6001\%$$

$$6 \text{ v } 10 \text{ rate} = 6 \text{ v } 9 \text{ rate} + (6 \text{ v } 12 \text{ rate} - 6 \text{ v } 9 \text{ rate}) \times \frac{31}{90} = 4.8360\%$$

Further interpolation gives:

4 v 8 rate = 3 v 7 rate + (6 v 10 rate − 3 v 7 rate) × $\frac{30}{92}$ = 4.68%

For the hedge, use effectively the same construction by interpolation, but in "round amounts" because futures contracts can be traded only in standardised sizes:

FRA 4 v 8 is equivalent to $\frac{2}{3}$ (FRA 3 v 7) + $\frac{1}{3}$ (FRA 6 v 10)

$= \frac{2}{3}\left[\frac{2}{3} \text{ (FRA 3 v 6)} + \frac{1}{3} \text{ (FRA 3 v 9)}\right] + \frac{1}{3}\left[\frac{2}{3} \text{ (FRA 6 v 9)} + \frac{1}{3} \text{ (FRA 6 v 12)}\right]$

$= \frac{4}{9}$ (FRA 3 v 6) + $\frac{2}{9}$ (FRA 3 v 6 + FRA 6 v 9) + $\frac{2}{9}$ (FA 6 v 9) + $\frac{1}{9}$ (FRA 6 v 9 + FRA 9 v 12)

$= \frac{6}{9}$ (FRA 3 v 6) + $\frac{5}{9}$ (FRA 6 v 9) + $\frac{1}{9}$ (FRA 9 v 12)

Therefore for each USD 9 million FRA sold to the customer, you sell 6 June futures, 5 September futures and 1 December futures. When the June futures contracts expire, replace them by 6 September futures. This will create a basis risk, hedged by selling a further 6 September futures and buying 6 December futures, giving a net position then of short 17 September futures and long 5 December futures.

42. Forward-forward borrowing costs created from the cash market are as follows:

$$3 \text{ v } 6: \quad \left[\frac{\left(1 + 0.0475 \times \frac{183}{360}\right)}{\left(1 + 0.045 \times \frac{92}{360}\right)} - 1\right] \times \frac{360}{91} = 4.9549\%$$

$$6 \text{ v } 9: \quad \left[\frac{\left(1 + 0.049 \times \frac{273}{360}\right)}{\left(1 + 0.046 \times \frac{183}{360}\right)} - 1\right] \times \frac{360}{90} = 5.3841\%$$

$$3 \text{ v } 9: \quad \left[\frac{\left(1 + 0.049 \times \frac{273}{360}\right)}{\left(1 + 0.045 \times \frac{92}{360}\right)} - 1\right] \times \frac{360}{181} = 5.0453\%$$

```
.0475 ENTER 183 × 360 ÷ 1 + .045 ENTER 92 × 360 ÷ 1 + ÷
1 − 360 × 91 ÷                                                    (3 v 6)
.049 ENTER 273 × 360 ÷ 1 + .046 ENTER 183 × 360 ÷ 1 + ÷
1 − 360 × 90 ÷                                                    (6 v 9)
.049 ENTER 273 × 360 ÷ 1 + .045 ENTER 92 × 360 ÷ 1 + ÷
1 − 360 × 181 ÷                                                   (3 v 9)
```

3 v 6 period
Forward-forward: 4.9459%
FRA: 4.96%   } forward-forward is cheapest
September futures (100 − 95.03): 4.97%

6 v 9 period
Forward-forward: 5.3841%
FRA: 5.00% } December futures is cheapest
December futures (100 − 95.05): 4.95%

3 v 9 period
Forward-forward: 5.0453% } forward-forward is cheaper
FRA: 5.07%

Combining the 3 v 6 forward-forward and December futures gives a cost of:

$$\left[\left(1 + 0.049459 \times \frac{91}{360}\right) \times \left(1 + 0.0495 \times \frac{90}{360}\right) - 1\right] \times \frac{360}{181} = 4.98\%$$

.049459 ENTER 91 × 360 ÷ 1 + .0495 ENTER 90 × 360 ÷ 1 + × 1 − 360 × 181 ÷

This is cheaper than the 3 v 9 forward-forward. Therefore the cheapest cover is provided by borrowing for 6 months at 4.75% and depositing for 3 months at 4.50% to create a 3 v 6 forward-forward, and selling 10 December futures at 95.05. (This ignores any balance sheet costs of the forward-forward.)

43. Using HP calculator: **7.23%**

FIN TVM 15 N 102.45 +/− PV 7.5 PMT 100 FV I%YR

44. Cashflows remaining are €8 million after 1 year, €8 million after 2 years and €108 million after 3 years. Discount to NPV at 7.0%:

$$\text{Cost} = € \frac{8,000,000}{(1 + 0.07)} + \frac{8,000,000}{(1 + 0.07)^2} + \frac{108,000,000}{(1 + 0.07)^3}$$

$$= €102,624,316.04$$

8,000,000 ENTER 1.07 ÷ 1.07 ENTER 2 ☐ ∧ 8,000,000 ☐ x⩾y ÷ + 1.07 ENTER 3 ☐ ∧ 108,000,000 ☐ x⩾y ÷ +

$$\text{Current yield} = \frac{8}{102.62} = 7.80\%$$

$$\text{Simple yield to maturity} = \frac{8 + \frac{(100 - 102.62)}{3}}{102.62} = 6.94\%$$

> 8 ENTER 102.62 ÷   (current yield)
> 100 ENTER 102.62 − 3 ÷ 8 + 102.62 ÷   (simple yield to maturity)

$$\text{Duration} = \frac{\frac{8}{1.07} \times 1 + \frac{8}{(1.07)^2} \times 2 + \frac{108}{(1.07)^3} \times 3}{102.62} \text{ years} = 2.79 \text{ years}$$

> 8 ENTER 1.07 ÷
> 1.07 ENTER 2 □ ∧ 8 □ $x{\geq}y$ ÷ 2 × +
> 1.07 ENTER 3 □ ∧ 108 □ $x{\geq}y$ ÷ 3 × +
> 102.62 ÷

45. Clean price =

$$\frac{3.4}{\left(1 + \frac{0.074}{2}\right)^{\frac{134}{181}}} + \frac{3.4}{\left(1 + \frac{0.074}{2}\right)^{1 + \frac{134}{181}}} + \frac{3.4}{\left(1 + \frac{0.074}{2}\right)^{2 + \frac{134}{181}}} \ldots\ldots + \frac{103.4}{\left(1 + \frac{0.074}{2}\right)^{14 + \frac{134}{181}}} - \left(6.8 \times \frac{46}{360}\right)$$

The price is **96.64**. The accrued coupon amount is **43,444.44**.

This question is complicated by the fact that the calculation bases for accrued coupon and price are different. To make the calculation using the HP it is therefore necessary to:

■ Calculate the clean price (96.6261) and the accrued interest (0.8829) using HP, assuming that both are calculated on an ACT/ACT basis.
 96.621 + 0.8829 = 97.5090
■ Add together to give the correct dirty price.
■ Recalculate the accrued interest on the correct 30/360 basis.
 $6.8 \times \frac{46}{360} = 0.8689$
■ Subtract this from the dirty price to give the correct clean price.
 97.5090 − 0.8689 = 96.64

> FIN BOND
> TYPE A/A SEMI EXIT
> 6.112009 SETT
> 20.032017 MAT
> 6.8 CPN%
> MORE 7.4 YLD%
> PRICE   (Clean price assuming ACT/ACT accrued)
> ACCRU   (Accrued coupon assuming ACT/ACT)
> +   (Actual dirty price)
> MORE TYPE 360 EXIT
> MORE ACCRU   (Actual accrued coupon)
> −   (Actual clean price)
> ACCRU 100 ÷ 5,000,000 ×   (Amount of accrued coupon)

Or, using the bond price formula rather than the functions built into the HP calculator:

$$\text{Dirty price} = \frac{100}{\left(1 + \frac{0.074}{2}\right)^{\frac{134}{181}}} \left[\frac{0.068}{2} \times \frac{\left(1 - \frac{1}{\left(1 + \frac{0.074}{2}\right)^{15}}\right)}{\left(1 - \frac{1}{\left(1 + \frac{0.074}{2}\right)}\right)} + \frac{1}{\left(1 + \frac{0.074}{2}\right)^{14}}\right]$$

$$= 97.5090$$

$$\text{Accrued coupon amount} = 5{,}000{,}000 \times 0.068 \times \frac{46}{360} = 43{,}444.44$$

```
TIME CALC
20.092009 DATE1
6.112009 DATE2 360D                    (30/360 days accrued coupon)
20.032010 DATE2 DAYS                   (ACT/ACT days in coupon period)
6.112009 DATE1 DAYS                    (ACT/ACT days to next coupon)

.074 ENTER 2 ÷ 1 + 14 ☐ ∧ ☐ ¹/ₓ
.068 ENTER 2 ÷ +
.068 ENTER .074 ÷ +
.074 ENTER 2 ÷ 1 + 14 ☐ ∧ .074 × .068 ☐ x⋛y ÷ −
100 ×
.074 ENTER 2 ÷ 1 +
134 ENTER 181 ÷ ☐ ∧ ÷               (Dirty price)
6.8 ENTER 46 × 360 ÷                  (Accrued coupon)
−                                     (Clean price)
```

46. The yield is 7.7246%. If you use the HP calculator's bond functions, it is again necessary to make an adjustment for the fact that the price/yield calculation is on a 30/360 basis but the accrued coupon is on an ACT/365 basis as follows:

■ Calculate the correct accrued interest: $8.3 \times \frac{129}{365} = 2.933425$

■ Add to the clean price to give the correct dirty price:

$$102.48 + 2.933425 = 105.413425$$

■ Calculate the accrued coupon as if it were on a 30/360 basis:

$$8.3 \times \frac{127}{360} = 2.928056$$

■ Subtract from the dirty price to give an adjusted clean price:

$$105.413425 - 2.928056 = 102.485369$$

```
FIN BOND
TYPE 360 ANN EXIT
19.102009 SETT
12.062015 MAT
8.3 CPN%
EXIT EXIT TIME CALC
12.062009 DATE1
19.102009 DATE2 DAYS        (ACT/365 days accrued coupon)
365 ÷ 8.3 ×                 (Accrued coupon)
102.48 +                    (Dirty price]
EXIT EXIT FIN BOND
MORE ACCRU                  (Accrued coupon on 30/360 basis)
–                           (Clean price assuming 30/360 accrued)
PRICE
YLD%
```

47. The last quasi-coupon date was 26 March 2010

    The next quasi-coupon date is 26 September 2010

    The quasi-coupon period is 184 days

    The fraction of a period (ACT/ACT) from settlement to 26 September 2010 is $\frac{69}{184}$.

    Therefore $65.48 = \dfrac{100}{\left(1 + \frac{i}{2}\right)^{\left(\frac{69}{184}+15\right)}}$

    Therefore $i = \left[\left(\dfrac{100}{65.48}\right)^{\frac{1}{\left(\frac{69}{184}+15\right)}} - 1\right] \times 2 = 5.5845\%$

```
100 ENTER 65.48 ÷
69 ENTER 184 ÷ 15 + □ 1/x □ ∧
1 – 2 ×

                        OR

FIN BOND
TYPE A/A SEMI EXIT
19.072010 SETT
26.032018 MAT
0 CPN%
MORE 65.48 PRICE
YLD%
```

48. $\dfrac{8.0\%}{1 - 0.08 \times \frac{97}{360}} \times \dfrac{365}{360} = 8.29\%$

```
.08 ENTER 97 × 360 ÷ 1 – +/– 8 □ x⇄y ÷ 365 × 360 ÷
```

49. With the same notation as before, the number of days from purchase to maturity is 205:

$$i = \frac{-\frac{205}{365} + \left(\left(\frac{205}{365}\right)^2 + 2\left(\frac{205}{365} - \frac{1}{2}\right) \times \left(\frac{1}{\left(1 - 0.08 \times \frac{205}{360}\right)} - 1\right)\right)^{\frac{1}{2}}}{\left(\frac{205}{365} - \frac{1}{2}\right)} = 8.46\%$$

```
.08 ENTER 205 x 360 ÷ 1 – +/– □ 1/x 1 –
205 ENTER 365 ÷ .5 – × 2 ×
205 ENTER 365 ÷ □ x² + □ √x
205 ENTER 365 ÷ –
205 ENTER 365 ÷ .5 – ÷
```

50. The same equation as in the previous question can be manipulated to give:

$$D = \frac{360}{\text{days}}\left(1 - \frac{2}{i^2 \times \left(\frac{\text{days}}{365} - \frac{1}{2}\right) + 2i \times \frac{\text{days}}{365} + 2}\right)$$

$$= \frac{360}{205}\left(1 - \frac{2}{(0.09)^2 \times \left(\frac{205}{365} - \frac{1}{2}\right) + 2 \times 0.09 \times \frac{205}{365} + 2}\right)$$

$$= 8.49\%$$

```
205 ENTER 365 ÷ .5 – .09 × .09 ×
2 ENTER .09 × 205 × 365 ÷ +
2 +
2 □ x⪥y ÷ 1 – +/–
360 × 205 ÷
```

51. The HP bond calculation function cannot be used for a bond with stepped coupons. The easiest method is to work from first principles, as follows:

■ Discount the final cashflow of 105.75 to a value one year earlier:

$$\frac{105.75}{1.0524} = 100.4846$$

■ Add the coupon cashflow of 5.50 paid then and discount back a further year:

$$\frac{100.4846 + 5.50}{1.0524} = 100.7075$$

- Repeat the process back to 2 March 2010:

$$\frac{100.7075 + 5.25}{1.0524} = 100.6818$$

$$\frac{100.6818 + 5.00}{1.0524} = 100.4198$$

$$\frac{100.4198 + 4.75}{1.0524} = 99.9333$$

$$99.9333 + 4.5 = 104.4333$$

- Discount the value of 104.4333 back to settlement date (112 days on a 30/360 basis) to give the current dirty price:

$$\frac{104.4333}{(1.0524)^{\frac{112}{360}}} = 102.7870$$

- Subtract the accrued interest (248 days on a 30/360 basis) to give the clean price:

$$102.7870 - 4.5 \times \frac{248}{360} = \mathbf{99.69}$$

105.75 ENTER 1.0524 ÷
5.5 + 1.0524 ÷
5.25 + 1.0524 ÷
5 + 1.0524 ÷
4.75 + 1.0524 ÷
4.5 +
1.0524 ENTER 112 ENTER 360 ÷ ☐ ∧ ÷   (Dirty price)
248 ENTER 360 ÷ 4.5 × −   (Clean price)

52. Because bond price / yield formulas generally assume a redemption amount of 100, a straightforward method is to scale down every cash-flow by the same factor to correspond to a redemption amount of 100. Thus for each $(\frac{100}{1.10})$ nominal amount of bond, the price paid is $(\frac{98}{1.10})$, the coupons paid are $(\frac{3.3}{1.10})$ and the redemption payment is 100. This gives a yield of **4.39%**.

Using the HP bond function, however, it is possible to achieve the answer more simply by entering 110 as the "call value".

FIN BOND TYPE 360 ANN EXIT
7.122009 SETT
19.092019 MAT
3.3 ENTER 1.1 ÷ CPN%

```
98 ENTER 1.1 ÷ MORE PRICE
YLD%
                                    OR
FIN BOND TYPE 360 ANN EXIT
7.122009 SETT
19.092019 MAT
3.3 CPN%
110 CALL
MORE 98 PRICE
YLD%
MORE 100 CALL
(Remember afterwards to reset the call value to 100 for future calculations!)
```

All-in initial cost $= 98 + 3.3 \times \dfrac{78}{360} = 98.715$

All-in sale proceeds $= 98.50 + 3.3 \times \dfrac{85}{360} = 99.279$

Simple rate of return (ACT/360) $= \left(\dfrac{99.279}{98.715} - 1\right) \times \dfrac{360}{7} = 29.39\%$

Effective rate of return (ACT/365) $= \left(\dfrac{99.279}{98.715}\right)^{\frac{365}{7}} - 1 = 34.60\%$

```
3.3 ENTER 85 × 360 ÷ 98.5 +
3.3 ENTER 78 × 360 ÷ 98 + ÷ STO 1
1 – 360 × 7 ÷                                    (Simple rate)
RCL1 365 ENTER 7 ÷ □ ∧ 1 –                       (Effective rate)
```

53. **a.** Last coupon 6 June 2009

   ACT/ACT basis: $\dfrac{51}{366} \times 7.5 = \mathbf{1.045082}$

   b. Last coupon 14 February 2009
   Next coupon 14 August 2009 (181-day coupon period)

   ACT/ACT basis: $\dfrac{163}{362} \times 5.625 = \mathbf{2.532804}$

   c. Last coupon 25 October 2008

   30/360 basis: $\dfrac{272}{360} \times 6.25 = \mathbf{4.722222}$

   d. Last coupon 24 October 2008
   Next coupon 24 October 2009 (365-day coupon period)

   ACT/ACT basis: $\dfrac{276}{365} \times 7.25 = \mathbf{5.482192}$

e. Last coupon 19 March 2009

ACT/365 basis: $\dfrac{130}{365} \times 3.00 = 1.068493$

54. The futures price would be **less than 100**. Between now and delivery of the futures contract, the purchaser of the futures contract is earning a lower yield on the money market than the coupon he would earn by buying the bond in the cash market. The price is therefore lower to compensate.

55. Payment for the bond purchased by the futures seller to hedge himself is made on 25 April. Coupon on the purchase of the bond is accrued for 113 days. Therefore:

Accrued coupon now = $7.375 \times \dfrac{113}{366} = 2.276981$

Delivery of the bond to the futures buyer would require payment to the futures seller on 10 September. The futures seller must therefore fund his position from 25 April to 10 September (138 actual days) and coupon on the bond on 10 September will be accrued for 251 days. Therefore:

Accrued coupon then = $7.375 \times \dfrac{251}{366} = 5.057719$

Theoretical futures price =

$$\dfrac{(106.13 + 2.276981) \times \left(1 + 0.0335 \times \frac{138}{360}\right) - 5.057719}{1.1247} = \mathbf{93.13}$$

7.375 ENTER 113 × 366 ÷	(Accrued coupon now)
106.13 +	
.0335 ENTER 138 × 360 ÷ 1 + ×	
7.375 ENTER 251 × 366 ÷	(Accrued coupon in September)
− 1.1247 ÷	

56. Implied repo rate = $\left[\dfrac{(93.10 \times 1.1247) + 5.057719}{(106.13 + 2.276981)} - 1\right] \times \dfrac{360}{138} = \mathbf{3.27\%}$

93.1 ENTER 1.1247 × 5.057719 +
106.13 ENTER 2.276981 + ÷
1 − 360 × 138 ÷

57. Assume to start with that the implied repo rate is higher than the actual current repo rate.

Cost of buying CTD bond per €100 nominal is (clean price + accrued coupon) = €(102.71 + 3.599) = €106.309

Total borrowing (principal + interest) to be repaid at the end

$$= €106.309 \times \left(1 + 0.068 \times \frac{24}{360}\right) = €106.790934$$

Anticipated receipt from selling futures contract and delivering bond per €100 nominal = (futures price × conversion factor) + accrued coupon

$$= €(85.31 \times 1.2030) + 4.182 = €106.809930$$

Profit = €(106.809930 − 106.790934) = 0.018996 per €100 nominal

Size of EUR bond futures contract is €100,000 nominal

Therefore face value of bond purchased against each futures contract is

$$€\frac{100,000}{1.2030} = €83,126$$

Therefore profit per futures contract

$$= €0.018996 \times \frac{83,126}{100} = €15.79$$

58.

	Bond A	Bond B	Bond C
Yield (from HP):	7.92%	7.17%	7.52%
Duration:	4.41	2.31	3.61
Modified duration = $\frac{duration}{(1+yield)}$:	4.09	2.16	3.36
Accrued coupon (from HP):	0.51	4.83	5.00
Clean price:	88.50	111.00	94.70
Dirty price (= clean price + accrued):	89.01	115.83	99.70
Face value:	10 million	5 million	15 million
Total value (= face value × $\frac{dirty\ price}{100}$):	8.9 million	5.79 million	14.955 million

$$\text{Modified duration of portfolio} \approx \frac{\sum(\text{modified duration} \times \text{value})}{\text{portfolio value}}$$

$$= \frac{4.09 \times 8.9 + 2.16 \times 5.79 + 3.36 \times 14.955}{8.9 + 5.79 + 14.955} = 3.34$$

Change in value ≈ − change in yield × modified duration × total value

$$= -0.001 \times 3.34 \times 29.645 \text{ million} = \mathbf{-99,014}$$

59.

	Bond A	Bond B
Yield (from HP):	7.92%	8.92%
Duration:	4.41	7.56
Modified duration $= \frac{\text{duration}}{(1+\text{yield})}$:	4.09	6.94
Accrued coupon (from HP):	0.51	3.51
Clean price:	88.50	107.50
Dirty price (= clean price + accrued):	89.01	111.01

For an increase of say 1 basis point in yield, the change in value of bond A is:

$$-0.0001 \times \text{modified duration of bond A} \times \text{face value of bond A}$$

$$\times \frac{\text{dirty price of bond A}}{100}$$

$$= -0.0001 \times 4.09 \times 10 \text{ million} \times 0.89 = -3{,}640$$

For an increase of 1 basis point in yield, the change in value of bond B is:

$$-0.0001 \times \text{modified duration of bond B} \times \text{face value of bond B}$$

$$\times \frac{\text{dirty price of bond B}}{100}$$

$$= -0.0001 \times 6.94 \times \text{face value} \times 1.1100 = -0.0007703 \times \text{face value}$$

Therefore face value of bond B required for a hedge is $\dfrac{3{,}640}{0.0007703}$

$$= 4{,}725{,}186$$

The ratio for using futures to hedge a position in the CTD bond is:

$$\frac{\text{conversion factor}}{\left(1 + \text{funding cost} \times \frac{\text{days}}{\text{year}}\right)} = \frac{1.2754}{\left(1 + 0.10 \times \frac{32}{360}\right)} = 1.2642$$

Therefore notional value of futures required to hedge 10 million in bond A is:

$$4{,}725{,}186 \times 1.2642 = 5{,}973{,}580$$

As each contract has a notional size of 100,000, you need **60 contracts**.

60. Value of the T-bill:

$$\frac{€40{,}000{,}000}{\left(1 + \left(0.052 \times \dfrac{28}{360}\right)\right)} = €39{,}838{,}873.89$$

Reduce by the haircut:

$$\frac{€39,838,873.89}{1.02} = €39,057,719.50$$

To the nearest €1,000, this is **€39,058,000**

40,000,000 ENTER	
.052 ENTER 28 × 360 ÷ 1 + ÷	(Value of T-bill)
1.02 ÷	(Reduce by haircut)

61. **a.** The bond pays semi-annual coupons. Accrual is ACT/ACT. The current coupon period 17/2/2009 to 17/8/2009 is 181 days. The accrual period 17/2/2009 to 13/3/2009 is 24 days. Therefore:

Accrued coupon on bond on 13 March 2009 = 24/362 × 5.75 = 0.381215

Dirty price = 97.32 + 0.381215 = 97.701215

Dirty price adjusted for 2.5% haircut = 97.701215 / 1.025 = 95.318259

Nominal amount of bond required = $30,000,000 / 0.95318259 = **$31,473,508**

b. The original cash amount is repaid with interest (money market basis):

$$\$30,000,000 \times \left(1 + \left(.0397 \times \frac{31}{360}\right)\right) = \$30,102,558$$

24 ENTER 362 ÷ 5.75 ×	(Accrued coupon)
97.32 +	(Dirty price)
1.025 ÷	(Adjust for haircut)
100 ÷ 30,000,000 □ x≷y ÷	(Face value required)
.0397 ENTER 31 × 360 ÷ 1 + 30,000,000 ×	(Repurchase price)

62. *Collateral value required:*
Cash originally lent plus interest accrued to 28 March at 3.97%

$$= \$30,000,000 \times \left(1 + \left(0.0397 \times \frac{15}{360}\right)\right) = \$30,049,625.00$$

Allowing for the 2.5% haircut, the buyer will require that the collateral is now worth:

$$\$30,049,625.00 \times 1.025 = \$30,800,865.63$$

Existing collateral:
The accrual period 17/2/2009 to 28/3/2009 is 39 days. Therefore:

Accrued coupon on the bond on 28 March

$$= \frac{39}{362} \times 5.75 = 0.619475$$

New dirty price = 99.14 + 0.619475 = 99.759475

Value of existing collateral

$$= \$31,473,508.13 \times \frac{99.759475}{100} = \$31,397,806.52$$

Margin call:
The seller will therefore call for the excess of $31,397,806.52 − $30,800,865.63 = **$596,940.89** to be returned, either in cash or in securities worth this amount. The margin call is transferred from the buyer to the seller.

.0397 ENTER 15 × 360 ÷ 1 + 30,000,000 ×	("Value" of cash)
1.025 ×	(Value of collateral required)
39 ENTER 362 ÷ 5.75 ×	(Accrued coupon)
99.14 +	(Dirty price)
100 ÷ 31,473,508.13 ×	(Value of existing collateral)
$\square$ $x \gtreqless y$ −	(Margin call)

63. a. Accrued coupon on bond = $50 \times \dfrac{104}{360} = 1.444444$

Dirty price of bond = 98.00 + 1.444444 = 99.444444

Adjusted price allowing for haircut = $\dfrac{99.444444}{1.05} = 94.708995$

Cash loan = CHF 20 million $\times \dfrac{99.708994}{100} = $ CHF 18,941,798.94

Converted at 1.4735: **$12,854,970.44** on 5 July

b. On 5 September, repay cash plus interest (on a money market basis):

$$\$12,854,970.34 \times \left(1 + \left(0.048 \times \frac{62}{360}\right)\right) = \$12,961,238.19$$

104 ENTER 360 ÷ 5 ×	(Accrued coupon)
98 +	(Dirty price)
1.05 ÷	(Adjust for haircut)
100 ÷ 20,000,000 ×	(Cash lent)
1.4735 ÷	(Convert to USD)
.048 ENTER 62 × 360 ÷ 1 + ×	(Repurchase price)

64. *New collateral price:*

BTPs pay semi-annual coupons and accrual is ACT/ACT. The current coupon period from 14/1/2008 to 14/7/2008 is 182 days. The accrual period from 14/1/2008 to 4/4/2008 is 81 days. Therefore:

$$\text{Accrued coupon} = \frac{81}{364} \times 4.8 = 1.068132$$

Dirty price of new collateral = 101.24 + 1.068132 = 102.308132

New collateral value required:
Cash originally lent plus interest accrued so far at 5.9%

$$= £40,000,000 \times \left(1 + \left(0.059 \times \frac{14}{365}\right)\right) = £40,090,520.55$$

Allowing for the 3% haircut, the buyer will require that the new collateral is worth:

£40,090,520.55 × 1.03 = £41,293,236.16

Converted at EUR/GBP 0.6540, this is equivalent to €63,139,504.84.

New collateral face value required:
The face value of the new collateral required is therefore:

$$\frac{€63,139,504.84}{\left(\frac{102.308132}{100}\right)} = €61,715,040$$

81 ENTER 364 ÷ 4.8 ×	(Accrued coupon)
101.24 +	(Dirty price)
.059 ENTER 14 × 365 ÷ 1 + 40,000,000 ×	("Value" of cash)
1.03 ×	(Value of collateral required)
.6540 ÷	(Convert to EUR)
☐ $x \gtrless y$ ÷ 100 ×	(Face value of collateral required)

65. Gilts pay semi-annual coupons. The amount of the coupon is therefore half the annual coupon:

£20,000,000 × 0.02875 = £575,000

Interest is calculated on this coupon payment for the 15 days until the end of the transaction, at the original repo rate of 4.63%:

$$£575,000 \times 0.0463 \times \frac{15}{365} = £1,094.08$$

The final cash settlement will therefore be reduced by:

£575,000 + £1,094.08 = **£576,094.08**

20,000,000 ENTER .02875 ×	(Cash coupon paid)
.0463 × 15 × 365 ÷	(Interest on the coupon)
575,000 +	(Total)

66. Accrued coupon (ACT/ACT basis) at start

$$= 8.0 \times \frac{316}{365} = 6.926027$$

Market dirty price at start = 103.42 + 6.926027 = 110.346027

Dirty price adjusted for haircut $= \dfrac{110.346027}{1.025} = 107.654661$

Cash consideration at start

= €200 million × 107.654661/100 = €215,309,321.75

Cash principal plus interest at maturity

$$= €215,309,321.75 \times \left(1 + \left(0.0552 \times \frac{91}{360}\right)\right)$$

= €218,313,604.49

The coupon received by the buyer during the buy / sell-back is €16,000,000 on 6 June 2009

Reinvest this coupon at 5.52% to give total proceeds on 18 July 2009 of:

$$€16,000,000 \times \left(1 + \left(0.0552 \times \frac{42}{360}\right)\right) = €16,103,040.00$$

Therefore forward dirty value of bond is (total final amount – reinvested coupon received)

= €218,313,604.49 – 16,103,040.00 = €202,210,564.49

Therefore forward dirty price

$$= \frac{202,210,564.49}{200,000,000} \times 100 = 101.105282$$

Accrued coupon at maturity $= 8.0 \times \dfrac{42}{365} = 0.920548$

Clean forward price = dirty price – accrued coupon
= **100.184734**

```
8 ENTER 316 × 365 ÷              (Accrued coupon)
103.42 +                        (Dirty price)
1.025 ÷                         (Adjust for haircut)
100 ÷ 200,000,000 ×             (Start cash)
.0552 ENTER 91 × 360 ÷ 1 + ×    (Start cash plus interest)
200,000,000 ENTER .08 ×         (Cash coupon)
.0552 ENTER 42 × 360 ÷ 1 + ×    (Cash coupon plus interest)
−                               (Repurchase price)
200,000,000 ÷ 100 ×             (Forward dirty price)
8 ENTER 42 × 365 ÷              (Accrued coupon)
−                               (Forward clean price)
```

67. a. *The security lent:*

Bonos pay annual coupons and accrual is ACT/ACT. The coupon period 21/3/2009 to 21/3/2010 is 365 days. The accrual period 21/3/2009 to 16/6/2009 is 87 days. Therefore:

$$\text{Accrued coupon} = \frac{87}{365} \times 5.45 = 1.299041$$

Dirty price = 98.73 + 1.299041 = 100.029041

Value of security borrowed

$$€50,000,000 \times \frac{100.029041}{100} = €50,014,520.55$$

Value of collateral required:

Because the initial margin of 1% is required by the *lender*, the value of the collateral must be 1% *greater* than this:

€50,014,520.55 × 1.01 = €50,514,665.75

The collateral:

OLOs pay annual coupons and accrual is ACT/ACT. The coupon period 9/10/2008 to 9/10/2009 is 365 days. The accrual period 9/10/2008 to 16/6/2009 is 250 days. Therefore:

$$\text{Accrued coupon} = \frac{250}{365} \times 5.85 = 4.006849$$

Dirty price = 100.34 + 4.006849 = 104.346849

Therefore nominal amount of collateral required is:

$$\frac{€50,514,665.76}{\left(\frac{104.346849}{100}\right)} = €48,410,341.17$$

(In practice, the face value of the collateral would be rounded up.)

b. €50,014,520.55 × 0.0035 × $\dfrac{7}{360}$ = **€3,403.77**

5.45 ENTER 87 × 365 ÷	(Accrued coupon)
98.73 +	(Dirty price)
100 ÷ 50,000,000 ×	(Value of security borrowed)
1.01 ×	(Value of collateral required)
5.85 ENTER 250 × 365 ÷	(Accrued coupon on collateral)
100.34 +	(Dirty price of collateral)
100 ÷ ÷	(Face value of collateral required)
50,014,520.55 ENTER .0035 × 7 × 360 ÷	(Lending fee)

68. 6.37% − 0.60% = **5.77%**

6.37 ENTER .6 −

69. a. *The security lent:*

Accrued coupon on security lent (30/360 basis) =

$$\frac{312}{360} \times 6.0 = 5.2$$

Dirty price = 105.23 + 5.2 = 110.43

Value of security lent =

$$€50,000,000 \times \frac{110.43}{100} = €55,215,000.00$$

Value of collateral required:
Because the initial margin of 3% is required by the *lender*, the value of the collateral must be 3% *greater* than this:

€55,215,000.00 × 1.03 = €56,871,450.00

The collateral:
Original maturity of CD is 184 days; remaining maturity is 149 days.

Therefore price of each €1 of CD is:

$$\frac{\left(1 + \left(0.04 \times \frac{184}{360}\right)\right)}{\left(1 + \left(0.0585 \times \frac{149}{360}\right)\right)} = 0.99632102$$

Therefore face value of CD required as collateral is:

$$\frac{€56,871,450.00}{0.99632102} = €57,081,451.42$$

(In practice, the face value of the CD would be rounded up as appropriate.)

b. $€55,215,000.00 \times 0.0045 \times \dfrac{91}{360} = €62,807.06$

6 ENTER 312 × 360 ÷	(Accrued coupon)
105.23 +	(Dirty price)
100 ÷ 50,000,000 ×	(Value of security lent)
1.03 ×	(Value of collateral required)
.04 ENTER 184 × 360 ÷ 1 +	(Maturity proceeds of €1 of CD)
.0585 ENTER 149 × 360 ÷ 1 + ÷	(Value of €1 of CD)
÷	(Face value of collateral required)
55,215,000 ENTER .0045 × 91 × 360 ÷	(Lending fee)

70. Accrued coupon $= 9.0 \times \dfrac{45}{365} = 1.109589$

Dirty price of bond $= 111.649589$

Cash consideration $= €50,000,000 \times 111.649589/100$
$= €55,824,794.52$

Profit $= €55,824,794.52 \times (0.041 - 0.0215) \times \dfrac{30}{360}$

$= €90,715.29$

9 ENTER 45 × 365 ÷	(Accrued coupon)
110.54 +	(Dirty price)
100 ÷ 50,000,000 ×	(Cash consideration)
.041 ENTER .0215 – 30 × 360 ÷ ×	(Profit)

71. Bootstrap to create 2-year zero-coupon yield:

Year			Net flows
0	−97.700	$+\frac{9}{1.1}$	−89.518
1	+9.000	−9.000	
2	+109.000		+109.000

2-year zero-coupon yield is $\left(\dfrac{109}{89.518}\right)^{\frac{1}{2}} - 1 = \mathbf{10.35\%}$

2-year discount factor is $\dfrac{89.518}{109} = \mathbf{0.8213}$

Bootstrap to create 3-year zero-coupon yield:

Year				Net flows
0	−90.900	$+\frac{7}{1.1}$	$+(7 \times 0.8213)$	−78.787
1	+7.000	−7.000		
2	+7.000		−7.000	
3	+107.000			+107.000

3-year zero-coupon yield is $\left(\dfrac{107}{78.787}\right)^{\frac{1}{3}} - 1 = \mathbf{10.74\%}$

3-year discount factor is $\dfrac{78.787}{107} = \mathbf{0.7363}$

Bootstrap to create 4-year zero-coupon yield:

Year					Net flows
0	−99.400	$+\frac{11}{1.1}$	$+(11 \times 0.8213)$	$+(11 \times 0.7363)$	−72.266
1	+11.000	−11.000			
2	+11.000		−11.000		
3	+11.000			−11.000	
4	+111.000				+111.000

4-year zero-coupon yield is $\left(\dfrac{111}{72.266}\right)^{\frac{1}{4}} - 1 = \mathbf{11.33\%}$

4-year discount factor is $\dfrac{72.266}{111} = \mathbf{0.6510}$

1-year discount factor is $\dfrac{1}{1.10} = 0.9091$

1 year v 2 year forward-forward $= \dfrac{\text{1-year discount factor}}{\text{2-year discount factor}} - 1$

$$= \dfrac{0.9091}{0.8213} - 1 = \mathbf{10.69\%}$$

2 year v 3 year forward-forward $= \dfrac{0.8213}{0.7363} - 1 = \mathbf{11.54\%}$

3 year v 4 year forward-forward $= \dfrac{0.7363}{0.6510} - 1 = \mathbf{13.10\%}$

72. **a.** Strip to create zero-coupon yields:

$$2\text{-year: } (1.08 \times 1.0824)^{\frac{1}{2}} - 1 = \mathbf{8.12\%}$$
$$3\text{-year: } (1.08 \times 1.0824 \times 1.09)^{\frac{1}{3}} - 1 = \mathbf{8.41\%}$$
$$4\text{-year: } (1.08 \times 1.0824 \times 1.09 \times 1.095)^{\frac{1}{4}} - 1 = \mathbf{8.68\%}$$

Discount factors are:

$$1\text{-year: } \frac{1}{1.08} = 0.9259$$

$$2\text{-year: } \frac{1}{(1.0812)^2} = 0.8554$$

$$3\text{-year: } \frac{1}{(1.0841)^3} = 0.7849$$

$$4\text{-year: } \frac{1}{(1.0868)^4} = 0.7168$$

If i is the 2-year par yield, then:

$$i \times 0.9259 + (1 + i) \times 0.8554 = 1$$

$$\text{Therefore } i = \frac{1 - 0.8554}{0.9259 + 0.8554} = \mathbf{8.12\%}$$

$$\text{Similarly, 3-year par yield} = \frac{1 - 0.7849}{0.9259 + 0.8554 + 0.7849} = \mathbf{8.38\%}$$

$$4\text{-year par yield} = \frac{1 - 0.7168}{0.9259 + 0.8554 + 0.7849 + 0.7168}$$

$$= \mathbf{8.63\%}$$

b. Discounting each cashflow at a zero-coupon yield, the price of the 4-year bond is:

$$(12 \times 0.9259) + (12 \times 0.8554) + (12 \times 0.7849) + (112 \times 0.7168) = 111.076$$

Using the **TVM** function of the calculator, this gives the yield to maturity as 8.61%.

73. Bootstrap using middle rates to create 18-month discount factor:

Time				Net flows
0	−100	$\dfrac{+8.85 \times \frac{183}{360}}{(1 + 0.0875 \times \frac{365}{360})}$	$\dfrac{+8.85 \times \frac{182}{360}}{(1 + 0.0865 \times \frac{182}{360})}$	−91.581
6	$+8.85 \times \frac{182}{360}$		$-8.85 \times \frac{182}{360}$	
12	$+8.85 \times \frac{183}{360}$	$-8.85 \times \frac{183}{360}$		
18	$+100 + 8.85 \times \frac{183}{360}$			+104.499

18-month discount factor is $\dfrac{91.581}{104.499} = 0.8764$

Bootstrap to create 24-month discount factor:

Time					*Net flows*
0	-100	$+8.95 \times \frac{183}{360} \times 0.8764$	$\dfrac{+8.95 \times \frac{183}{360}}{\left(1 + 0.0875 \times \frac{365}{360}\right)}$	$\dfrac{+8.95 \times \frac{182}{360}}{\left(1 + 0.0865 \times \frac{182}{360}\right)}$	-87.499
6	$+8.95 \times \frac{182}{360}$			$-8.95 \times \frac{182}{360}$	
12	$+8.95 \times \frac{183}{360}$		$-8.95 \times \frac{183}{360}$		
18	$+8.95 \times \frac{183}{360}$	$-8.95 \times \frac{183}{360}$			
24	$+100 + 8.95 \times \frac{182}{360}$				$+104.525$

24-month discount factor is $\dfrac{87.499}{104.525} = 0.8371$

18 v 24 FRA $= \left[\dfrac{\frac{1}{0.8371}}{\frac{1}{0.8764}} - 1 \right] \times \dfrac{360}{183} = 9.24\%$

Assuming FRA is benchmarked against LIBOR, add .05% (half the bid–offer spread) to this calculation: **9.29%**

74. Remember that Eurosterling is on a 365-day basis and EuroSwiss Francs are on a 360-day basis.

Middle swap price $= 2.1585 \times \dfrac{\left(0.03 \times \frac{365}{360} - 0.06 \times \frac{365}{365}\right)}{\left(1 + 0.06 \times \frac{365}{365}\right)}$

$= -0.0602$

$= \textbf{602 points}$ Swiss Franc premium

```
.03 ENTER 365 × 360 ÷ .06 –
1.06 ÷ 2.1585 ×
```

75. **a.** 7.1020 ÷ 1.5145 = 4.6893
7.1040 ÷ 1.5140 = 4.6922
Spot CHF/NOK is **4.6893 / 4.6922.**
Customer buys NOK at **4.6893.**

b. 1.6490 × 7.1020 = 11.7112
1.6500 × 7.1040 = 11.7216
Spot GBP/NOK is **11.7112 / 11.7216.**
Customer sells GBP at **11.7112.**

c. 7.1020 / 7.1040
   246 /   259
   _____
   7.1266 / 7.1299 USD/NOK 3 months forward outright

d. 1.6490 / 1.6500
   268 /   265
   _____
   1.6222 / 1.6235 GBP/USD 3 months forward outright

e. $1.6222 \times 7.1266 = 11.5608$
   $1.6235 \times 7.1299 = 11.5754$
   3 months forward outright GBP/NOK is 11.5608 / 11.5754.
   GBP interest rates are higher than NOK rates because sterling is worth fewer NOK forward than spot.

f. 1.5140 / 1.5145
     29 /   32
   _____
   1.5169 / 1.5177 USD/CHF 3 months forward outright

   $7.1266 \div 1.5177 = 4.6957$
   $7.1299 \div 1.5169 = 4.7003$
   3 months forward outright CHF/NOK is 4.6957 / 4.7003.
   NOK interest rates are higher than CHF rates because the CHF is worth more NOK forward than spot.

g. Outright 4.6957 / 4.7003
   Spot   4.6893 / 4.6922
   _____
            64 /   81 CHF/NOK 3 months forward swap

76. a. 7.1020   /   7.1040 Spot
           18 /   20 S/W
   _____
     7.1038   /   **7.1060** USD/NOK 1 week outright

b. 7.1020   /   7.1040 Spot
       2.3 /   2.9 T/N
   _____
   7.10171   / 7.10377 USD/NOK tomorrow outright
   Before spot, use the opposite side of the forward swap price.

c. 7.1020   /   7.1040 Spot
       2.3 /   2.9 T/N
       2.0 /   2.5 O/N
   _____
   7.10146   / **7.10357** USD/NOK today outright
   Customer buys NOK value today at **7.10146**.

d.

1.2490	/	1.2500	Spot
3.5	/	3.3	T/N
10.6	/	10.1	O/N

1.25034 / 1.25141   EUR/USD today outright
Customer buys EUR value today at 1.25141.

e. 96 / 94   1-month swap
    23 / 22   1-week swap

74 / 71   1 week against 1 month forward-forward swap EUR/
       USD
  Customer "buys and sells" EUR at 74.

The forward-forward price is the difference between opposite sides of the prices. The bank buys the base currency on the left on the far date.

f. 96   / 94   1-month swap
    3.5 / 3.3   T/N swap

99.5 / 97.3   Tomorrow against 1-month forward-forward swap.
  Customer "buys and sells" EUR at 99.5.

77. Calculate the USD/JPY and USD/NOK forward outrights as usual:

USD/JPY		*USD/NOK*
126.965 / 127.175	(tomorrow outright)	6.76195 / 6.76398
123.85 / 124.25	(3-month outright)	6.7605 / 6.7655
121.45 / 122.05	(6-month outright)	6.7670 / 6.7740

Calculating the cross-rate spot, outrights and swaps as usual gives:

	NOK/JPY		
(spot)	18.7685 / 18.8036		
(tomorrow outright)	18.7708 / 18.8074	(T/N swap)	3.8 / 2.3
(3-month outright)	18.306 / 18.379	(3-month swap)	462 / 425
(6-month outright)	17.929 / 18.036	(6-month swap)	839 / 768

(Remember to "reverse" the T/N swap price.)

a. 3 months v 6 months forward-forward price is:

(839 − 425) / (768 − 462) − i.e. **414 / 306**

The bank buys the base currency (in this case NOK) on the far date on the left side. You therefore deal on a price of 414.

b. Tomorrow v 3 months forward-forward price is:

(462 + 3.8) / (425 + 2.3) − i.e. **465.8 / 427.3**

Your customer wishes to buy NOK on the far date, which is the right side. You therefore deal on a price of 427.3. This can be broken down into the two swaps as follows. First, between tomorrow and spot, he is "selling and buying" the base currency (NOK); as the bank is selling the base currency on the far date, this is the right side (minus 2.3). Second, between spot and 3 months, he is again "selling and buying" the base currency (NOK); as the bank is selling the base currency on the far date, this is again the right side (minus 425 points). The combination is (minus 2.3 points) plus (minus 425 points) = (minus 427.3 points).

78. a. Today is Friday 19 April.
Spot is Tuesday 23 April.
Spot-a-week is Tuesday 30 April.
1 month is Thursday 23 May.
2 months is Monday 24 June (23 June is a Sunday).

Number of days from 23 May to 24 June is 32.
Number of days from 23 May to 3 June is 11.

Therefore price for 3 June is:

1-month price + ($\frac{11}{32}$ × difference between 2-month price and 1-month price)

USD/NOK		GBP/USD
7.2590	(middle spot)	1.6162
25 / 23	(swap to 30 April)	11 / 9
133 / 119	(swap to 3 June)	69 / 62

Your customer is "buying and selling" NOK (in that order). The bank buys the variable currency on the far date on the right side. In the USD/NOK swap prices, you therefore need the right side of "133 / 119" but the left side of "25 / 23". In the GBP/USD prices however the customer is "selling and buying" (in that order) the base currency GBP. Therefore you again need the right side of "69 / 62" and the left side of "11 / 9".

The GBP/NOK prices you need are therefore as follows:

(outright value 3 June):
$(7.2590 - 0.0119) \times (1.6162 - 0.0062) = 11.6678$

(outright value 30 April):
$(7.2590 - 0.0025) \times (1.6162 - 0.0011) = \underline{11.7200}$
$$- 0.0522$$

The forward-forward price where the customer can buy NOK value 30 April and sell NOK value 3 June is therefore **522 points**

GBP discount – that is 522 points in the customer's favour (because he is selling on the *far* date the currency which is worth more in the future).

b. For short dates you need to combine the swaps, because you are rolling an existing contract from today to tomorrow, from tomorrow to the next day and from then until a week later. The total swap from today to a week after spot is therefore:

O/N	– 0.4 /	+ 0.1
T/N	– 1.5 /	– 1
S/W	– 11 /	– 9
	– 12.9 /	– 9.9

Your customer needs to sell GBP / buy USD on the far date. The bank buys the base currency (GBP) on the far date on the left, at 12.9 **points GBP discount** – that is, 12.9 points against the customer.

OR

Your customer needs to "buy and sell" GBP (in that order) today against tomorrow. The bank buys the base currency (GBP) on the far date on the left side. The prices are all bigger on the left – GBP is at a discount, worth less in the future. As the customer is selling GBP on the far date, 0.4 points will be against him.

Similarly, he needs to "buy and sell" GBP tomorrow against spot – another 1.5 points against him. He also needs to "buy and sell" GBP spot against 1 week – another 11 points against him. The total swap price will therefore be 0.4 + 1.5 + 11 = **12.9 points against him.**

c. Spot: 1.6157 /   67
   T/N: 1.5 /   1
   Outright value tomorrow: 1.6158   / 1.61685 ("reverse" the short-date)

   O/N: –0.4 /   +0.1
   Outright value today: **1.61579 / 1.61689** ("reverse" the short-date)

   Deal at **1.61689**

79. a. USD/JPY

Spot:	127.30 /	127.35
Swap:	2.66 /	2.60
Outright:	124.64 /	124.75

The bank sells the base currency (USD) on the right side, so the outright price quoted is **124.75**.

The USD is worth less in the future and the JPY is worth more, so the **JPY is at a premium.**

b. The current interest rates are consistent with the current swap price. Assume that the expected changes do happen, and calculate the effect on the forward outright price, using middle prices for the comparison.

After the rates have moved, they will be as follows:

Spot rates
$$\left. \begin{array}{l} \text{EUR/USD } 1.1900 \\ \text{EUR/JPY } 151 \end{array} \right\} \text{USD/JPY} = 151 \div 1.1900 = 126.89$$

Interest rates

USD	4.75% / 4.875%	(middle: 4.8125%)
JPY	2.00% / 2.25%	(middle: 2.125%)

$$\text{Middle swap price} = 126.89 \times \frac{(0.02125 - 0.048125) \times \frac{180}{360}}{(1 + 0.048125 \times \frac{180}{360})} = -1.67$$

The outright middle rate would therefore be $126.89 - 1.67 = 125.22$

This is slightly worse than the current outright middle rate of USD/JPY 124.69, so it is not worth waiting according to these expectations; the improvement in the spot rate would be more than offset by the movement in the swap rate – even though the swap is for a slightly shorter period.

The movement in the swap price could be approximated as follows:

Interest rate differential narrows by 1.50%; period is half a year. Therefore swap price moves by approximately:

$$\text{Spot} \times 0.015 \times \tfrac{1}{2} = 0.95$$

The customer is selling the currency which is at a premium (worth more in the future) but the premium is decreasing, so this movement in the swap price of approximately 0.95 must be against him. He must therefore expect a spot movement of at least this much in his favour for it to be worthwhile waiting.

80. Invest USD 15 million for 91 days.

Investor buys and sells EUR (sells and buys USD) spot against 3 months at 1.2730 and 1.2598.

Investor's cashflows spot:
invest USD 15 million
sell USD 15 million and buy EUR 11,783,189.32 at 1.2730
invest EUR 11,783,189.32 in EUR CP

CP yields EURIBOR + 4 bp $= 8.375\% + 0.04\% = 8.415\%$

Total proceeds at maturity of CP

$$= \text{EUR } 11{,}783{,}189.32 \times \left(1 + 0.08415 \times \frac{91}{360}\right)$$

$$= \text{EUR } 12{,}033{,}832.49$$

Investor sells EUR 12,033,832.49 forward at 1.2598 against USD 15,160,222.17.

Investor's cashflows after 3 months:
    receive EUR 12,033,832.49 from CP
    sell EUR 12,033,832.49
    buy USD 15,160,222.17

$$\text{Overall USD return} = \left(\frac{15{,}160{,}222.17}{15{,}000{,}000.00} - 1\right) \times \frac{360}{91} = 4.23\%$$

This is effectively **USD LIBOR minus 2 bp**. Assuming that the investor's alternative would be a deposit at USD LIBID, the covered interest arbitrage is more attractive.

Note that, in practice, the investor could probably not buy EUR commercial paper with a face value of EUR 12,033,832.49 (the total maturity proceeds for CP are the same as its face value); he would instead need to purchase a round amount but this would not affect the rate of return.

Note also that the amounts dealt on each leg of the swap are mismatched. The bank would therefore typically base the prices on the left side of the spot price (rather than the middle) because that is the "correct" side for a forward outright for the mismatch difference.

15,000,000 ENTER 1.2730 ÷	(Amount invested)
.08415 ENTER 91 × 360 ÷ 1 + ×	(Maturity proceeds in EUR)
1.2598 ×	(Maturity proceeds in USD)
15,000,000 ÷ 1 − 360 × 91 ÷	(Rate of return)

Alternatively, using the formula for covered interest arbitrage:

Variable currency rate =

$$\left[\left(1 + \text{base currency rate} \times \frac{\text{days}}{\text{base year}}\right) \times \frac{\text{outright}}{\text{spot}} - 1\right] \times \frac{\text{variable year}}{\text{days}}$$

$$= \left[\frac{1.2598}{1.2730} \times \left(1 + 0.08415 \times \frac{91}{360}\right) - 1\right] \times \frac{360}{91} = \mathbf{4.23\%}$$

.08415 ENTER 91 × 360 ÷ 1 + 1.2598 × 1.2730 ÷ 1 − 360 × 91 ÷

81. Action now

(i) Arrange FRA 3 v 9 on a notional 6-month borrowing

of USD $\left(\dfrac{1{,}000{,}000}{6.0600}\right)$ = USD 165,016.50

Assuming FRA settlement at the end of 9 months (rather than discounted after 3 months as is conventional), the total notional repayment on this borrowing would be:

USD 165,016.50 $\times \left(1 + 0.0575 \times \dfrac{182}{360}\right)$ = USD 169,813.44

(ii) Convert this notional borrowing from USD to NOK:

- sell USD 165,016.50 / buy NOK 1,000,000.00 (at 6.0600) for value 3 months forward

- buy USD 169,813.44 / sell NOK 1,050,839.53 (at 6.1882) for value 9 months forward

Action in 3 months' time

(iii) Assume borrowing of NOK (165,016.50 × 6.2060)

= NOK 1,024,092.40 for 6 months

Total repayment will be:

NOK 1,024,092.40 $\times \left(1 + 0.1062 \times \dfrac{182}{360}\right)$ = NOK 1,079,075.92

(iv) Convert this borrowing to a notional USD borrowing to match (i):

- buy USD 165,016.50 / sell NOK 1,024,092.40 (at 6.2060) for value spot

- sell USD 170,022.00 / buy NOK 1,078,857.60 (at 6.3454) for value 6 months forward

(USD 170,022.00 is the total repayment which would be due on a 6-month loan of USD 165,016.50 taken at the rate of 6.00% now prevailing.)

Settlement at the end of 9 months

Receive FRA settlement of USD 165,016.50 × (0.06 − 0.0575) $\times \dfrac{182}{360}$

= USD 208.56

Total flows

	NOK		USD
After 3 months:	+1,024,092.40	(iii)	
	− 1,024,092.40	(iv)	+ 165,016.50
	+1,000,000.00	(ii)	− 165,016.50
	+1,000,000.00		−
After 9 months:	− 1,079,075.92	(iii)	
	+1,078,857.60	(iv)	− 170,022.00
		(i)	+ 208.56
	− 1,050,839.53	(ii)	+ 169,813.44
	− 1,051,057.85		−

Effective cost is $\dfrac{51,057.85}{1,000,000} \times \dfrac{360}{(273-91)} = 10.10\%$

Note that, in practice, the USD FRA settlement would be received after 3 months on a discounted basis but could then be invested until 9 months. If this investment were at only 5.87% (LIBID), the final result would be changed very slightly.

82. The GBP cashflows net to zero both spot and forward.

USD cashflows

	spot	6 months
(a)	−16,510,000	+16,350,000
(b)	+16,495,000	−16,325,000
Net:	− 15,000	+ 25,000

$$\text{NPV} = -\,\text{USD } 15,000 + \text{USD } \frac{25,000}{(1 + 0.045 \times \frac{182}{360})} = \text{USD } 9,443.90$$

83. a. USD cashflows:

3 months	6 months	12 months
+ 10,164,306	+ 10,000,000	− 10,000,000
		− 10,709,722

Valuation in EUR at current forward exchange rates:

+ 8,451,240	+ 8,292,562	− 17,095,693

New rates after EUR/USD moves from 1.20 to 1.30:

	EUR/USD	EUR%	USD%
Spot:	1.3000		
3 months:	1.3029	6.5	7.4
6 months:	1.3064	6.5	7.5
12 months:	1.3123	7.0	8.0

Valuation in EUR at new forward rates:

3 months	6 months	12 months
+ 7,801,294	+ 7,654,623	− 15,781,241

Change in valuation in EUR:

3 months	6 months	12 months
− 649,946	− 637,939	+ 1,314,452

Total net profit = **EUR 26,567**

b. The profits / losses discounted to spot become:

3 months	6 months	12 months
− 639,440	− 617,643	+ 1,227,345

Total net present value of profits / losses: − **EUR 29,738**

It is possible to hedge this exposure by a spot transaction of the net present value of the forward USD positions:

	3 months	6 months	12 months
Actual USD cashflows:	+ 10,164,306	+ 10,000,000	− 20,709,722
Discounted to PV:	+ 9,977,668	+ 9,634,685	− 19,155,961
Total NPV:	+ 456,392		

This NPV is the amount of USD which should be sold to achieve a hedge. Suppose that this had been done spot at 1.20. A move to a spot rate of 1.30 would then have produced a profit on the hedge of:

$$\text{EUR} \left(\frac{456,392}{1.20} - \frac{456,392}{1.30} \right) = \textbf{EUR 29,256}$$

Allowing for rounding differences, this would offset the loss shown above. (Try calculating the theoretical forward exchange rates consistent with the interest rates to seven decimal places, and then repeating the exercise. This removes the rounding difference.)

84. As you will be receiving fixed payments under the swap, the spread over treasuries will be 80 basis points (rather than 90). The receipt will therefore be 9.80% on a semi-annual bond basis.

Your cashflows are therefore:

pay: 8.90% annual money market ≈ 8.71% semi-annual money market
receive: 9.80% semi-annual bond = 9.67% semi-annual money market
pay: LIBOR semi-annual money market
net pay: **LIBOR − 96 basis points**

This answer does not discount the cashflows precisely.

85. a. Convert the futures price to implied forward-forward interest rates and then create strips to calculate the effective (annual equivalent) zero-coupon swap rates for each quarterly period up to 18 months:

18-month rate =

$$
\left[
\begin{array}{l}
\left(1 + 0.0625 \times \dfrac{91}{360}\right) \times \left(1 + 0.0659 \times \dfrac{91}{360}\right) \\[2ex]
\times \left(1 + 0.0716 \times \dfrac{91}{360}\right) \times \left(1 + 0.0737 \times \dfrac{92}{360}\right) \\[2ex]
\times \left(1 + 0.0762 \times \dfrac{91}{360}\right) \times \left(1 + 0.0790 \times \dfrac{91}{360}\right)
\end{array}
\right]^{\frac{365}{547}} - 1 = 7.4470\%
$$

15-month rate =

$$
\left[
\begin{array}{l}
\left(1 + 0.0625 \times \dfrac{91}{360}\right) \times \left(1 + 0.0659 \times \dfrac{91}{360}\right) \\[2ex]
\times \left(1 + 0.0716 \times \dfrac{91}{360}\right) \times \left(1 + 0.0737 \times \dfrac{92}{360}\right) \\[2ex]
\times \left(1 + 0.0762 \times \dfrac{91}{360}\right)
\end{array}
\right]^{\frac{365}{456}} - 1 = 7.2868\%
$$

12-month rate =

$$
\left[
\begin{array}{l}
\left(1 + 0.0625 \times \dfrac{91}{360}\right) \times \left(1 + 0.0659 \times \dfrac{91}{360}\right) \\[2ex]
\times \left(1 + 0.0716 \times \dfrac{91}{360}\right) \times \left(1 + 0.0737 \times \dfrac{92}{360}\right)
\end{array}
\right] - 1 = 7.1214\%
$$

9-month rate =

$$
\left[
\begin{array}{l}
\left(1 + 0.0625 \times \dfrac{91}{360}\right) \times \left(1 + 0.0659 \times \dfrac{91}{360}\right) \\[2ex]
\times \left(1 + 0.0716 \times \dfrac{91}{360}\right)
\end{array}
\right]^{\frac{365}{273}} - 1 = 6.9325\%
$$

6-month rate =

$$
\left[\left(1 + 0.0625 \times \dfrac{91}{360}\right) \times \left(1 + 0.0659 \times \dfrac{91}{360}\right)\right]^{\frac{365}{182}} - 1 = 6.6699\%
$$

3-month rate =

$$
\left[\left(1 + 0.0625 \times \dfrac{91}{360}\right)\right]^{\frac{365}{91}} - 1 = 6.4891\%
$$

b. The 18-month par swap rate on a quarterly money market basis is then i, where the NPV of a par investment with quarterly money market coupon i is itself par:

$$1 = \frac{i \times \frac{91}{360}}{(1.064891)^{\frac{91}{365}}} + \frac{i \times \frac{91}{360}}{(1.066699)^{\frac{182}{365}}} + \frac{i \times \frac{91}{360}}{(1.069325)^{\frac{273}{365}}} + \frac{i \times \frac{92}{360}}{(1.071214)^{\frac{365}{365}}}$$

$$+ \frac{i \times \frac{91}{360}}{(1.072868)^{\frac{456}{365}}} + \frac{1 + i \times \frac{91}{360}}{(1.074470)^{\frac{547}{365}}}$$

This gives 1 = 0.248846i + 0.244769i + 0.240418i + 0.238566i + 0.231514i + 0.226981i + 0.897948

Therefore i = 7.13%

86. a. Discount the USD cashflows at 9% to an NPV (= USD 102.531 million). Convert to sterling at the current spot exchange rate (= GBP 66.149 million). Apply 11% to this amount to create a stream of equivalent sterling flows (= GBP 7.276 million per year plus GBP 66.149 million at maturity). All flows below are in millions:

	(i) Remaining bond cashflows	(ii) Equivalent of (i) discounted at 9%	(iii) Swap receipts	(iv) Swap payments
	USD	USD	USD	GBP
Year 1:	−10	−9.174	+10	−7.276
Year 2:	−10	−8.417	+10	−7.276
Year 3:	−10	−7.722	+10	−7.276
	−100	−77.218	+100	−66.149
NPV:		−102.531		

Your total cashflows are (i), (iii) and (iv); your net cashflows are (iv).

b. To calculate the long-dated forward prices, remember that USD money market rates are on a 360-day basis. The forward rates (assuming there are actually 365 days in each year) are as follows:

1 year: $1.55 \times \dfrac{(1 + 0.09 \times \frac{365}{360})}{(1 + 0.14 \times \frac{365}{365})} = 1.4837$

2 years: $1.55 \times \dfrac{(1 + 0.085 \times \frac{365}{360})^2}{(1 + 0.12 \times \frac{365}{365})^2} = 1.4578$

3 years: $1.55 \times \dfrac{(1 + 0.08 \times \frac{365}{360})^3}{(1 + 0.10 \times \frac{365}{365})^3} = 1.4715$

At these rates, the cashflows can be converted as follows:

	(i) Remaining bond cashflows USD	(iv) Cashflows converted at forward rates GBP
Year 1:	−10	−6.740
Year 2:	−10	−6.860
Year 3:	−110	−74.754

c. You might perhaps prefer the second cashflow profile because it defers the net cash outflows slightly. Apart from that, you would prefer the cashflow profile with the lower NPV. Unless the rate of discount is at least 23.4%, this is the first method.

87. The USD 10 million raised from the bond issue can be converted to CHF 15 million at the spot exchange rate. We therefore need to base the floating side of the swap on CHF 15 million:

Year	Bond cashflows	Swap cashflows	
1	− $ 650,000	+ $ 650,000	− (LIBOR − i) on CHF 15 m
2	− $ 650,000	+ $ 650,000	− (LIBOR − i) on CHF 15 m
3	− $ 650,000	+ $ 650,000	− (LIBOR − i) on CHF 15 m
4	− $ 650,000	+ $ 650,000	− (LIBOR − i) on CHF 15 m
5	− $ 10,650,000	+ $ 10,650,000	− (LIBOR − i) on CHF 15 m − CHF 15 m

The NPV of the USD flows in the swap (using 6.8%) is 9,876,333. This is equivalent to CHF 14,814,499 at the spot exchange rate. If i = 0, the CHF flows in the swap would have an NPV of CHF 15,000,000. In order for the two sides of the swap to match therefore, the NPV of ($i \times 15$ million $\times \frac{1}{2} \times \frac{365}{360}$) each six months for 5 years must be $(15,000,000 − 14,814,499) = 185,501$.

Convert 4.5% per annum to an equivalent rate of 2.225% for a 6-monthly period ($\sqrt{1.045} = 1.02225$). Then, using the TVM function of an HP calculator:

N = 10, I%YR = 2.225, PV = 185,501, FV = 0 gives PMT = 20,895

You therefore need $15,000,000 \times i \times \frac{1}{2} \times \frac{365}{360} = 20,895$. This gives i = 0.27%. You can therefore achieve (**LIBOR − 27 basis points**) in CHF.

88. The remaining cashflows are as follows:

Date	Swap	
	USD	SEK
24 May 2010:	+10 m × 8%	−75 m × 5.3% × $\frac{181}{360}$
24 Nov 2010:		−75 m × L$_1$ × $\frac{184}{360}$
24 May 2011:	+10 m × 8%	−75 m × L$_2$ × $\frac{181}{360}$
	+10 m	−75 m

where   L$_1$ is LIBOR from 24 May 2010 to 24 November 2010
        L$_2$ is LIBOR from 24 November 2010 to 24 May 2011

Without upsetting the NPV valuation, add the cashflows for a SEK 75 million "FRN" which starts on 24 May 2010, matures on 24 May 2011 and pays LIBOR semi-annually. The resulting cashflows will then be:

Date	Swap		"FRN"	Net SEK
	USD	SEK	SEK	cashflows
24 May 2010:	+10 m × 8%	−75 m × 5.3% × $\frac{181}{360}$	−75 m	−75 m × (1 +5.3% × $\frac{181}{360}$)
24 Nov 2010:		−75 m × L$_1$ × $\frac{184}{360}$	+75 m × L$_1$ × $\frac{184}{360}$	
24 May 2011:	+10 m × 8%	−75 m × L$_2$ × $\frac{181}{360}$	+75 m × L$_2$ × $\frac{181}{360}$	
	+10 m	−75 m	+75 m	

These cashflows can be valued using the discount factors to give:

USD (800,000 × 0.9850 + 10,800,000 × 0.9300)
  − SEK (76,998,542 × 0.9880)

  = USD 10,832,000 − SEK 76,074,559

Converted at 7.65 spot, this gives an NPV of USD 887,613.

89. Receive 99.00 at the start and transact a par swap based on 100. The bond and swap cashflows are then as follows:

Date	Bond	Swap	
Now:	+99		
6 months:			−100 × LIBOR × $\frac{1}{2}$ × $\frac{365}{360}$
1 year:	−7	+100 × 7.5%	−100 × LIBOR × $\frac{1}{2}$ × $\frac{365}{360}$
1$\frac{1}{2}$ years:			−100 × LIBOR × $\frac{1}{2}$ × $\frac{365}{360}$
2 years:	−7	+100 × 7.5%	−100 × LIBOR × $\frac{1}{2}$ × $\frac{365}{360}$
2$\frac{1}{2}$ years:			−100 × LIBOR × $\frac{1}{2}$ × $\frac{365}{360}$
3 years:	−100 −7	+100 × 7.5%	−100 × LIBOR × $\frac{1}{2}$ × $\frac{365}{360}$

You can provide a par / par liability swap based on 100, by eliminating, you need to eliminate the uneven fixed cashflows of -1 ($= 99 - 100$) now and $+0.5$ ($= -7 + 7.5$) each year. Discounting at 7.5%, these cashflows have an NPV of:

$$-1 + \frac{0.5}{1.075} + \frac{0.5}{(1.075)^2} + \frac{0.5}{(1.075)^3} = 0.3003$$

You can eliminate these cashflows if you replace them by a series of semi-annual cashflows with the same NPV. The rate of discount you are using is 7.5% (annual). You therefore need an interest rate i (money market basis) such that:

$$\frac{100 \times i \times \frac{1}{2} \times \frac{365}{360}}{(1.075)^{0.5}} + \frac{100 \times i \times \frac{1}{2} \times \frac{365}{360}}{(1.075)} + \frac{100 \times i \times \frac{1}{2} \times \frac{365}{360}}{(1.075)^{1.5}}$$
$$+ \frac{100 \times i \times \frac{1}{2} \times \frac{365}{360}}{(1.075)^{2}} + \frac{100 \times i \times \frac{1}{2} \times \frac{365}{360}}{(1.075)^{2.5}} + \frac{100 \times i \times \frac{1}{2} \times \frac{365}{360}}{(1.075)^{3}} = 0.3003$$

The solution to this is: $i = 0.11\%$

You can therefore replace the 30/360 annual swap inflows of (100 × 7.5%) by a combination of 30/360 annual swap inflows of (100 × 7%) and ACT/360 semi-annual inflows of (100 × 0.11%). This 0.11% can be deducted from the ACT/360 semi-annual swap outflows of (100 × LIBOR) which you already have.

The net effect is therefore a par / par liability swap based on an amount of 100, at **(LIBOR − 11 basis points)**.

90.

Day	Price	Relative price change	LN (price change)	(Difference from mean)²
1	1.6320			
2	1.6410	1.005515	0.005500	0.000040
3	1.6350	0.996344	-0.003663	0.000008
4	1.6390	1.002446	0.002443	0.000011
5	1.6280	0.993289	-0.006734	0.000035
6	1.6300	1.001229	0.001228	0.000004
7	1.6250	0.996933	-0.003072	0.000005
8	1.6200	0.996923	-0.003082	0.000005
9	1.6280	1.004938	0.004926	0.000033
10	1.6200	0.995086	-0.004926	0.000017

sum:			-0.007380	0.000158
mean $= \frac{\text{sum}}{9}$			-0.000820	
variance $= \frac{\text{sum}}{8}$				0.000020
standard deviation $= \sqrt{\text{variance}}$				0.004444

volatility = annualised standard deviation = $\sqrt{252} \times 0.004444 = 7.1\%$

91. USD put premium expressed in NOK = percentage of USD amount × spot rate

$$= 1.5\% \times 7.0000 = 0.10500$$

USD call premium = USD put premium + PV of (forward − strike)

$$= 0.10500 + \frac{7.0690 - 6.9500}{(1 + 0.07 \times \frac{182}{360})} = 0.21993$$

Converted to percentage of USD amount at spot rate:

$$\frac{0.21993}{7.0000} = 3.14\%$$

92. **To calculate probabilities of up and down movement**
Say there is a probability p of a 2% increase in price and a probability (1 − p) of a 2% decrease.

Expected outcome after 1 month is:

$$p \times 100 \times 1.02 + (1 - p) \times \frac{100}{1.02}$$

$$= 3.960784p + 98.039216$$

This should equal the outcome of 100 invested at 12% for 1 month:

$$= 100 \times \left(1 + \frac{0.12}{12}\right) = 101$$

Therefore $3.960784p + 98.039216 = 101$

Therefore $p = \dfrac{101 - 98.039216}{3.960784} = 0.7475$

Therefore: probability of increase to 102 is 74.75%
probability of decrease to $\frac{100}{1.02}$ is 25.25%

Possible outcomes after three months

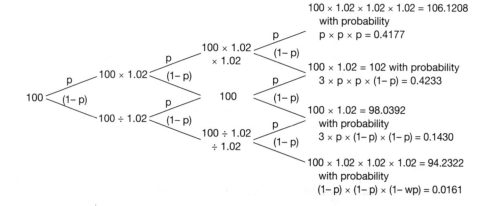

$100 \times 1.02 \times 1.02 \times 1.02 = 106.1208$
with probability
$p \times p \times p = 0.4177$

$100 \times 1.02 = 102$ with probability
$3 \times p \times p \times (1- p) = 0.4233$

$100 \times 1.02 = 98.0392$
with probability
$3 \times p \times (1- p) \times (1- p) = 0.1430$

$100 \times 1.02 \times 1.02 \times 1.02 = 94.2322$
with probability
$(1- p) \times (1- p) \times (1- wp) = 0.0161$

The expected value of the put option at the end of 3 months is therefore:

$$(101 - 98.0392) \times 0.1430 + (101 - 94.2322) \times 0.0161 = 0.5324$$

The premium for the option is therefore the present value of this expected value:

$$\frac{0.5324}{(1 + 0.12 \times \frac{3}{12})} = 0.517$$

93. $\$487.60 \times 402.925 \times 0.9999 = \$196,446.58$

> 487.6 ENTER 402.925 × .9999 ×

94. $40,000 \times 0.87\% \times 31/360 \times \$513.7 = \$15,393.88$

> 40,000 ENTER .0087 × 31 × 360 ÷ 513.17 ×

95. $601.95 \times \dfrac{\left(1 + 0.0548 \times \frac{61}{360}\right)}{\left(1 + 0.0102 \times \frac{61}{360}\right)} = 606.49$

> .0548 ENTER 61 × 360 ÷ 1 +
> .0102 ENTER 61 × 360 ÷ 1 + ÷
> 601.95 ×

96. $\left(\dfrac{\left(1 + 0.0588721 \times \frac{182}{360}\right)}{\left(1 + 0.05203 \times \frac{182}{360}\right)} - 1\right) \times \dfrac{360}{182} = 0.667\%$

> .0588721 ENTER 182 × 360 ÷ 1 +
> .05203 ENTER 182 × 360 ÷ 1 + ÷
> 1 − 360 × 182 ÷

97. I buy the FRA at 1.05% to protect against a rise in rates.

$$40,000 \text{ ounces} \times \frac{(0.0105 + 0.0102) \times \frac{181}{360}}{\left(1 + 0.0102 \times \frac{181}{360}\right)} = 6.003 \text{ ounces}$$

```
.0105 ENTER .0102 – 181 × 360 ÷
.0102 ENTER 181 × 360 ÷ 1 + ÷
40,000 ×
```

I buy the FRA but rates fall, so I pay the settlement amount.

98. $\left(\dfrac{493.2}{495.1} \times \left(1 + 0.0487 \times \dfrac{91}{360}\right) - 1\right) \times \dfrac{360}{91} = 3.33\%$

```
.0487 ENTER 91 × 360 ÷ 1 +
493.2 × 495.1 ÷
1 –
360 × 91 ÷
```

99. If the convenience yields are too low, that means the forward prices are too high, relative to the spot price. Therefore **he buys for a near date and sells back for a date further forward.**

100. Convert the cash interest rate to its continuously compounded equivalent:

$$r = \frac{365}{182} \times LN\left(1 + 0.0495 \times \frac{182}{360}\right) = 0.0489$$

$$d_1 = \frac{LN\left(\frac{7.98}{7.95}\right) + \frac{0.15^2 \times \frac{182}{365}}{2}}{0.15\sqrt{\frac{182}{365}}} = 0.0885$$

$$d_2 = \frac{LN\left(\frac{7.98}{7.95}\right) - \frac{0.15^2 \times \frac{182}{365}}{2}}{0.15\sqrt{\frac{182}{365}}} = -0.0174$$

Put premium = (–forward outright price × N(–d$_1$) + strike price × N(–d$_2$)) × e^{-rt}

$= (-7.98 \times N(-0.0885) + 7.95 \times N(0.0174)) \times e^{-0.0489 \times \frac{182}{365}}$

$= (-7.98 \times 0.4647 + 7.95 \times 0.5070) \times 0.9759$

$= 0.31$

The premium is therefore **$0.31**.

Appendices

Appendix 1
Using an HP calculator

INTRODUCTION

We have not tried to give full instructions here for using Hewlett-Packard calculators, but have set out only those operations necessary for the examples and exercises in this book.

The HP calculators generally used fall into two categories:

The HP12C calculator

It is essential first to understand the logic of this calculator, which is called "reverse Polish notation" (RPN). On a traditional calculator, the steps are entered in the same order as on a piece of paper. Thus, for example, the calculation $4 \times 5 + 6 = 26$ would be performed by entering 4, ×, 5, +, 6 and = in that order. The result appears as 26.

With an HP12C using RPN however, it is necessary instead to enter 4, ENTER, 5, ×, 6 and +, in that order. The first number is generally followed by ENTER; thereafter, each number is followed (rather than preceded as is traditional) by its operator. In this example, we are multiplying by 5. The × therefore follows the 5 instead of the other way round.

The HP17BII and HP19BII

With these calculators, the user can choose whether to use RPN or the more traditional algebraic logic, using the calculators' MODES function. The labels shown on the calculators' keys for the various operation functions are also different in a few cases from the HP12C.

In this Appendix, we show the essential steps for the HP12C and for the HP19BII in each mode. This would be very cumbersome for all the examples in the book however, and we have therefore shown steps elsewhere in the text for the HP19BII in RPN mode only. This will not give a problem to a user of the HP12C and HP17BII in RPN, as the steps are the same even though a few keys are labelled differently. The steps in algebraic mode are in any case more familiar.

Basic operations

In the steps shown below, "f" and "g" refer to the yellow and blue shift keys marked "f" and "g" on the HP12C and "□" refers to the yellow shift key on the HP19BII. Also, the key "∧" may alternatively be marked "y^x".

Switching between algebraic and RPN modes

To switch the HP19BII to algebraic mode: □ MODES MORE ALG
To switch the HP19BII to RPN mode: □ MODES MORE RPN

Deleting an incorrect entry

To delete the current entry without affecting the calculation so far:

HP12C	HP19BII (RPN mode)	HP19BII (algebraic)
CL*x*	□ CLEAR	□ CLEAR

To delete the entire calculation so far:

HP12C	HP19BII (RPN mode)	HP19BII (algebraic)
f CLEAR REG	□ CLEAR DATA	□ CLEAR DATA

To correct the current entry before pressing another key:

HP12C	HP19BII (RPN mode)	HP19BII (algebraic)
not available	←	←
	Works as a backspace key	

Number of decimal places

The number of decimal places displayed can be adjusted, without affecting the accuracy of the calculation. For example, to display four decimal places:

HP12C	HP19BII (RPN mode)	HP19BII (algebraic)
f 4	DISP FIX 4 INPUT	DISP FIX 4 INPUT

Addition

Example: 5 + 4 = 9

HP12C	HP19BII (RPN mode)	HP19BII (algebraic)
5 ENTER 4 +	5 ENTER 4 +	5 + 4 =

Example: $-5 + 4 = -1$

HP12C	HP19BII (RPN mode)	HP19BII (algebraic)
5 ENTER CHS 4 +	5 ENTER +/- 4 +	$-5 + 4 =$
(Because the first entry in RPN must be a number rather than an operator, it is necessary to enter the 5 and then change its sign from positive to negative)		

Subtraction

Example: $7 - 3 = 4$

HP12C	HP19BII (RPN mode)	HP19BII (algebraic)
7 ENTER 3 −	7 ENTER 3 −	$7 - 3 =$

Multiplication, division

Example: $8 \div 2 \times 5 = 20$

HP12C	HP19BII (RPN mode)	HP19BII (algebraic)
8 ENTER 2 ÷ 5 ×	8 ENTER 2 ÷ 5 ×	$8 \div 2 \times 5 =$

Example: $3 \times 4 + 7 = 19$

HP12C	HP19BII (RPN mode)	HP19BII (algebraic)
3 ENTER 4 × 7 +	3 ENTER 4 × 7 +	$3 \times 4 + 7 =$

Example: $3 + 4 \times 7 = 31$

HP12C	HP19BII (RPN mode)	HP19BII (algebraic)
4 ENTER 7 × 3 +	4 ENTER 7 × 3 +	$3 + (4 \times 7) =$

Note that in the expression "$3 + 4 \times 7$", you must do the multiplication *before* the addition. It is a convention of the way mathematical formulas are written that any exponents (5^4, x^2, $4.2^{\frac{1}{4}}$, etc.) must be done first, followed by multiplication and division (0.08×92, $x \div y$, $\frac{17}{38}$ etc.) and addition and subtraction last. This rule is applied first to anything inside brackets (...) and then to everything else.

Exponents

Example: $3^5 = 243$

HP12C	HP19BII (RPN mode)	HP19BII (algebraic)
3 ENTER 5 y^x	3 ENTER 5 ☐ ∧	3 ☐ ∧ 5 =

Chaining

"Chaining" is performing a series of calculations in succession without the need to keep stopping and starting or using memory stores.

Example: $\left[\dfrac{(1 + 0.4 \times \frac{78}{360})}{(1 + 0.5 \times \frac{28}{360})} - 1 \right] \times \dfrac{360}{50} = 0.3311$

HP12C	HP19BII (RPN mode)	HP19BII (algebraic)
.4 ENTER 78 × 360 ÷ 1 + .5 ENTER 28 × 360 ÷ 1 + ÷ 1 − 360 × 50 ÷ *(Note that the ÷ in the fifth line divides the result of the fourth line into the result of the second line without the need to re-enter any interim results)*	.4 ENTER 78 × 360 ÷ 1 + .5 ENTER 28 × 360 ÷ 1 + ÷ 1 − 360 × 50 ÷	((1 + (.4 × 78 ÷ 360)) ÷ (1 + (.5 × 28 ÷ 360)) −1) × 360 ÷ 50 =

Reversing the order of the current operation

This can be useful in the middle of chaining.

Example: $\dfrac{85}{1 + 8 \times 2} = 5$

HP12C	HP19BII (RPN mode)	HP19BII (algebraic)
8 ENTER 2 × 1 + 85 $x\gtrless y$ ÷ *("$x\gtrless y$" switches the order, so that 85 is divided by the result of "1 + 8 × 2", instead of the other way round)*	8 ENTER 2 × 1 + 85 ☐ $x\gtrless y$ ÷ *("☐ $x\gtrless y$" switches the order, so that 85 is divided by the result of "1 + 8 × 2", instead of the other way round)*	*not available*

Square roots

Example: $\sqrt{(9 + 7)}$ [the same as $(9 + 7)^{\frac{1}{2}}$] = 4

HP12C	HP19BII (RPN mode)	HP19BII (algebraic)
9 ENTER 7 + g $\sqrt{x}$	9 ENTER 7 + □ $\sqrt{x}$	9 + 7 = □ $\sqrt{x}$

Reciprocals

Example: $\dfrac{1}{16} = 0.625$

HP12C	HP19BII (RPN mode)	HP19BII (algebraic)
16 $1/x$	16 □ $1/x$	16 □ $1/x$

Example: $\dfrac{1}{4 \times 5} = 0.05$

HP12C	HP19BII (RPN mode)	HP19BII (algebraic)
4 ENTER 5 × $1/x$	4 ENTER 5 × □ $1/x$	4 × 5 = □ $1/x$

Example: $(21 + 43)^{\frac{1}{6}} = 2$

HP12C	HP19BII (RPN mode)	HP19BII (algebraic)
21 ENTER 43 + 6 $1/x$ y^x	21 ENTER 43 + 6 □ $1/x$ □ ∧	21 + 43 = □ ∧ 6 □ $1/x$ =

Function menus

Various functions on the HP19BII are available through special menus and sub-menus accessed by pressing the calculator's top row of keys. Pressing "EXIT" moves from the current level menu to the previous level. Pressing "□ MAIN" moves from the current level to the highest level menu.

Date calculations

The calculator can be switched to accept dates in either European format (e.g. 18 August 2009 entered as 18.082009) or American format (e.g. 18 August 2009 entered as 08.182009). This switching is done as follows:

HP12C	HP19BII (RPN mode)	HP19BII (algebraic)
g D.MY *(for European format)* or g M.DY *(for American format)*	*Select* TIME *menu* *Select* SET *menu* *Select* M/D *(This switches from the* *existing format to the* *other one)* ☐ MAIN	*Select* TIME *menu* *Select* SET *menu* *Select* M/D *(This switches from the* *existing format to the* *other one)* ☐ MAIN

All our examples are shown using the European format.

Example: What is the number of true calendar days between 18 August 2009 and 12 December 2009?
Answer: 116

HP12C	HP19BII (RPN mode)	HP19BII (algebraic)
18.082009 ENTER 12.122009 g ΔDYS	*Select* TIME *menu* *Select* CALC *menu* 18.082009 DATE1 12.122009 DATE2 DAYS ☐ MAIN	*Select* TIME *menu* *Select* CALC *menu* 18.082009 DATE1 12.122009 DATE2 DAYS ☐ MAIN

Example: What is the number of days between 18 August 2009 and 12 December 2009 on a 30(A)/360 basis? (For an explanation of this, see the section "Day / year conventions" in Chapter 5.)
Answer: 114

HP12C	HP19BII (RPN mode)	HP19BII (algebraic)
Repeat the steps *above, followed by* *x≷y or R ▮*	*Repeat the steps* *above, but type* 360D *instead of* DAYS	*Repeat the steps* *above, but type* 360D *instead of* DAYS

(Note that the HP calculators can perform date calculations based on the 30/360 (ISDA) (or 30(A)/360) convention but not on the very similar 30/360 (ICMA) (or 30(E)/360) convention.)

Example: What date is 180 calendar days after 18 August 2009?
Answer: 14 February 2010

HP12C	HP19BII (RPN mode)	HP19BII (algebraic)
18.082009 ENTER 180 g DATE	*Select* TIME *menu* *Select* CALC *menu* 18.082009 DATE1 180 DAYS DATE2 ☐ MAIN	*Select* TIME *menu* *Select* CALC *menu* 18.082009 DATE1 180 DAYS DATE2 ☐ MAIN

Other operations

Hewlett-Packard calculators – particularly the HP17II and HP19II – have a number of more sophisticated inbuilt functions on which the calculators' manuals are the best source of information. Several of these functions are however described elsewhere in this book in the appropriate chapters as they become relevant. These are:

■ **Time value of money:** covered in Chapter 1.

■ **Irregular cashflows:** covered in Chapter 1.

■ **Bond calculations:** covered in Chapter 5.

■ **Maths functions:** examples of use are given in Chapter 1.

■ **Solving equations:** an example is given in Chapter 5.

Appendix 2
A summary of market day / year conventions for money markets and government bond markets

Instrument	Day / year basis	Yield or discount
Australia		
Money market	ACT/365	Y
Bond (semi-annual coupons)	ACT/ACT	
Austria		
Money market	ACT/360	Y
Bond (annual coupons)	ACT/ACT	
Belgium		
Money market	ACT/360	Y
OLO (annual coupons)	ACT/ACT	
Canada		
Money market	ACT/365	Y
Bond (semi-annual coupons)	ACT/365 (accrued coupon)	
	ACT/ACT (dirty price calculation)	
Denmark		
Money market	ACT/360	Y
Bond (annual coupons)	ACT/ACT	
Eire		
Money market	ACT/360	Y
Bond (annual and semi-annual coupons)	ACT/ACT[1]	
Finland		
Money market	ACT/360	Y
Bond (annual coupons)	ACT/ACT	

France
Money market	ACT/360	Y
OAT, BTAN (annual coupons)	ACT/ACT	

Germany
Money market	ACT/360	Y
Bund, OBL (annual coupons)	ACT/ACT	

Italy
Money market	ACT/360	Y
BTP (semi-annual coupons)	ACT/ACT	

Japan
Money market	ACT/365	Y
JGB (semi-annual coupons)	ACT/365	

Netherlands
Money market	ACT/360	Y
Bond (annual coupons)	ACT/ACT	

Norway
T-bills	ACT/365	Y
Other money market	ACT/360	Y
Bond (annual coupons)	ACT/365 (accrued coupon)	
	30/360 (dirty price calculation)	

Spain
Money market	ACT/360	Y
Bono (annual coupons)	ACT/ACT	

Sweden
Money market	ACT/360	Y
Bond	30(E)/360	

Switzerland
Money market	ACT/360	Y
Bond (annual coupons)	30/360	

UK
Depo / CD / £CP	ACT/365	Y
BA / T-bill	ACT/365	D
Gilt (almost all semi-annual coupons; a few quarterly coupons)	ACT/ACT	

USA

Depo / CD	ACT/360	Y
BA / $CP / T-bill	ACT/360	D
T-bond / note		
(semi-annual coupons)	ACT/ACT	
Federal agency & corporate		
bonds	30/360	

Euro (*the single "domestic" currency for the European Monetary Union countries*)

Money market	ACT/360	Y
Bond	ACT/ACT	

Euromarket (*non-domestic markets generally, regardless of the currency*)

Money market	ACT/360 (exceptions using ACT/365 include GBP, SGD, HKD, MYR, TWD, THB, ZAR)	Y

Eurobond (almost all annual coupons)

USD bonds	30/360 (ICMA)
other currencies	ACT/ACT[2]

Notes

1. Some older bonds still use ACT/365 or 30/360.
2. Bonds issued before 1999 use 30(E)/360. Yields are quoted on an annual basis, even for Eurobonds with semi-annual coupons.

Appendix 3
A summary of calculation procedures

Notation

The following general notation is used throughout these formulas, unless something different is specifically mentioned:

D	=	discount rate
FV	=	future value, or future cashflow
i	=	interest rate or yield per annum
n	=	number of times per year an interest payment is made
N	=	number of years or number of coupon periods
P	=	price (dirty price for a bond)
PV	=	present value, or cashflow now
r	=	continuously compounded interest rate
R	=	coupon rate paid on a security
year	=	number of days in the conventional year
z_k	=	zero-coupon yield for k years

Financial arithmetic basics (Chapter 1)

Effective and nominal rates

If the interest rate with n payments per year is i, the effective rate (equivalent annual rate) i* is:

$$i^* = \left[\left(1 + \frac{i}{n}\right)^n - 1\right]$$

Similarly:

$$i = \left[(1 + i^*)^{\frac{1}{n}}\right] \times n$$

$$\text{Effective rate} = \left(1 + i \times \frac{\text{days}}{\text{year}}\right)^{\frac{365}{\text{days}}} - 1$$

$$\text{Effective rate on a 360-day basis} = \text{effective rate} \times \frac{360}{365}$$

Continuously compounded interest rate

$$r = \frac{365}{\text{days}} \times \text{LN}\left(1 + i \times \frac{\text{days}}{\text{year}}\right)$$

$$\text{Discount factor} = e^{r \times \frac{\text{days}}{365}}$$

where i is the nominal rate for that number of days

In particular, when i is the effective rate:

$$r = \text{LN}(1 + i)$$

and:

$$i = \frac{\text{year}}{\text{days}} \times \left(e^{r \times \frac{\text{days}}{365}} - 1\right)$$

Short-term investments

$$FV = PV \times \left(1 + i \times \frac{\text{days}}{\text{year}}\right)$$

$$PV = \frac{FV}{(1 + i \times \frac{\text{days}}{\text{year}})}$$

$$i = \left(\frac{FV}{PV} - 1\right) \times \frac{\text{year}}{\text{days}}$$

$$\text{Effective yield} = \left(\frac{FV}{PV}\right)^{\frac{365}{\text{days}}} - 1$$

$$\text{Discount factor} = \frac{1}{1 + i \times \frac{\text{days}}{\text{year}}}$$

Long-term investments over N years

$$FV = PV \times (1 + i)^N$$

$$PV = \frac{FV}{(1 + i)^N}$$

$$i = \left(\frac{FV}{PV}\right)^{\frac{1}{N}} - 1$$

$$\text{Discount factor} = \left(\frac{1}{1 + i}\right)^N$$

NPV and internal rate of return

$$NPV = \text{sum of all the present values}$$

The internal rate of return is the interest rate which discounts all the future cashflows to a given NPV. This is equivalent to the interest rate which discounts all the cashflows *including* any cashflow *now* to zero.

Annuities

Annuity paying a constant amount at the end of each year

$$\text{initial cost} = \frac{\text{annual amount}}{\text{yield}} \times \left(1 - \left(\frac{1}{(1 + \text{yield})^{\text{number of years}}} \right) \right)$$

$$\text{annual amount} = \frac{\text{initial cost} \times \text{yield}}{\left(1 - \left(\frac{1}{(1 + \text{yield})^{\text{number of years}}} \right) \right)}$$

Annuity paying a constant amount at the beginning of each year

$$\text{initial cost} = \frac{\text{annual amount}}{\text{yield}} \times \left(1 + \text{yield} - \left(\frac{1}{(1 + \text{yield})^{(\text{number of years} -1)}} \right) \right)$$

$$\text{annual amount} = \frac{\text{initial cost} \times \text{yield}}{\left(1 + \text{yield} - \left(\frac{1}{(1 + \text{yield})^{(\text{number of years} -1)}} \right) \right)}$$

Perpetual annuity paying a constant amount at the end of each year

$$\text{initial cost} = \frac{\text{annual amount}}{\text{yield}}$$

$$\text{annual amount} = \text{initial cost} \times \text{yield}$$

Interpolation and extrapolation

$$i = i_1 + (i_2 - i_1) \times \frac{(d - d_1)}{(d_2 - d_1)}$$

where: i is the rate required for d days
   i_1 is the known rate for d_1 days
   i_2 is the known rate for d_2 days

Basic statistics

Mean (μ) = sum of all the values divided by the number of values

Variance (σ^2) = mean of (difference from mean)^2

When estimating the variance from only a sample of the data rather than all the data, divide by one less than the number of values used.

Standard deviation (σ) = $\sqrt{\text{variance}}$

Historic volatility

Historic volatility = standard deviation of LN(relative price movement) × $\sqrt{\text{frequency of data per year}}$

Take a series of n price data.

Divide each price by the previous day's price to give the relative price change – so that you now have only (n–1) data.

Take the natural logarithms (LN) of these (n–1) relative price changes. These are now the data from which to calculate the annualised standard deviation (= volatility). This is calculated as above:

- Calculate the mean
- Calculate the differences from the mean
- Square the differences
- Add these squares and divide by (n–2)
- Calculate the square root

To annualise volatility, multiply by the square root of the frequency of data per year.

The money market (Chapter 2)

$$\text{Interest rate on 360-day basis} = \text{interest rate on 365-day basis} \times \frac{360}{365}$$

$$\text{Interest rate on 365-day basis} = \text{interest rate on 360-day basis} \times \frac{365}{360}$$

Certificate of deposit

$$\text{Maturity proceeds} = \text{face value} \times$$

$$\left(1 + \text{coupon rate} \times \frac{\text{days from issue to maturity}}{\text{year}}\right)$$

$$\text{Secondary market proceeds} = \frac{\text{maturity proceeds}}{\left(1 + \text{market yield} \times \frac{\text{days left to maturity}}{\text{year}}\right)}$$

$$\text{Return on holding a CD} =$$

$$\left[\frac{\left(1 + \text{purchase yield} \times \frac{\text{days from purchase to maturity}}{\text{year}}\right)}{\left(1 + \text{sale yield} \times \frac{\text{days from sale to maturity}}{\text{year}}\right)} - 1\right] \times \frac{\text{year}}{\text{days held}}$$

Discount instrument

$$\text{Maturity proceeds} = \text{face value}$$

$$\text{Secondary market proceeds} = \frac{\text{face value}}{\left(1 + \text{market yield} \times \frac{\text{days left to maturity}}{\text{year}}\right)}$$

Instruments quoted on a discount rate

$$\text{Rate of true yield} = \frac{\text{discount rate}}{(1 - \text{discount rate} \times \frac{\text{days}}{\text{year}})}$$

$$\text{Discount rate} = \frac{\text{rate of true yield}}{(1 + \text{yield} \times \frac{\text{days}}{\text{year}})}$$

$$\text{Amount of discount} = \text{face value} \times \text{discount rate} \times \frac{\text{days}}{\text{year}}$$

$$\text{Amount paid} = \text{face value} \times (1 - \text{discount rate} \times \frac{\text{days}}{\text{year}})$$

Instruments quoted on a discount rate:

US:	T-bill	UK:	T-bill
	BA		BA
	CP		

Medium-term CD

$$P = F \times \left[\frac{1}{A_N} + \left(\frac{R}{\text{year}} \times \sum_{k=1}^{N} \left[\frac{d_{k-1;k}}{A_k} \right] \right) \right]$$

where: $A_k = (1 + i \times \frac{d_{p1}}{\text{year}}) \times (1 + i \times \frac{d_{12}}{\text{year}}) \times (1 + i \times \frac{d_{23}}{\text{year}})$

$$... \times (1 + i \times \frac{d_{k-1;k}}{\text{year}})$$

N = number of coupons not yet paid

$d_{k-1;k}$ = number of days between $(k-1)^{th}$ coupon and k^{th} coupon

d_{p1} = number of days between purchase and first coupon

Forward-forwards and forward rate agreements (Chapter 3)

For periods up to one year:

$$\text{Forward-forward rate} = \left[\frac{\left(1 + i_L \times \frac{d_L}{\text{year}}\right)}{\left(1 + i_S \times \frac{d_S}{\text{year}}\right)} - 1 \right] \times \left(\frac{\text{year}}{d_L - d_S} \right)$$

where: i_L = interest rate for longer period

i_S = interest rate for shorter period

d_L = number of days in longer period

d_S = number of days in shorter period

$$\text{FRA settlement amount} = \text{principal} \times \frac{(f - L) \times \frac{\text{days}}{\text{year}}}{(1 + L \times \frac{\text{days}}{\text{year}})}$$

where: f   = FRA rate
        L   = LIBOR at the beginning of the FRA period
        days = number of days in the FRA period

For periods longer than a year but less than 2 years:

$$\text{FRA settlement} = \text{principal} \times \frac{(f - L) \times \frac{d_1}{\text{year}}}{(1 + L \times \frac{d_1}{\text{year}})} + \frac{(f - L) \times \frac{d_2}{\text{year}}}{(1 + L \times \frac{d_1}{\text{year}}) \times (1 + L \times \frac{d_2}{\text{year}})}$$

where: d_1 = number of days in the first year of the FRA period
        d_2 = number of days from d_1 until the end of the FRA period

Constructing a strip

The interest rate for a longer period up to 1 year =

$$\left[\left(1 + i_1 \times \frac{d_1}{\text{year}}\right) \times \left(1 + i_2 \times \frac{d_2}{\text{year}}\right) \times \left(1 + i_3 \times \frac{d_3}{\text{year}}\right) \times \dots - 1\right] \times \frac{\text{year}}{\text{total days}}$$

where: i_1, i_2, i_3, ... are the cash interest rate and forward-forward rates for a series of consecutive periods lasting d_1, d_2, d_3, ... days.

Interest rate futures (Chapter 4)

Price = 100 − (implied forward-forward interest rate × 100)

Profit / loss on long position in a 3-month contract =

$$\text{notional contract size} \times \frac{(\text{sale price} - \text{purchase price})}{100} \times \frac{1}{4}$$

Basis   = implied cash price − actual futures price
Theoretical basis = implied cash price − theoretical futures price
Value basis   = theoretical futures price − actual futures price

Bond market calculations (Chapter 5)

General dirty price formula

$$P = \text{NPV of all future cashflows} = \sum_k \frac{C_k}{\left(1 + \frac{i}{n}\right)^{\frac{d_k \times n}{\text{year}}}}$$

where: C_k = the kth cashflow arising
   d_k = number of days until C_k
   i = yield on the basis of n interest payments per year

Conventional dirty price formula

$$P = \frac{100}{(1 + \frac{i}{n})^W} \left[\frac{R}{n} \times \frac{\left(1 - \frac{1}{(1 + \frac{i}{n})^N}\right)}{\left(1 - \frac{1}{(1 + \frac{i}{n})}\right)} + \frac{1}{(1 + \frac{i}{n})^{N-1}} \right]$$

where: R = the annual coupon rate paid n times per year
   W = the fraction of a coupon period between purchase and
       the next coupon to be received
   N = the number of coupon payments not yet made
   i = yield per annum based on n payments per year

$$\text{Accrued coupon} = 100 \times \text{coupon rate} \times \frac{\text{days since last coupon}}{\text{year}}$$

For ex-dividend prices, accrued coupon is negative:

$$\text{Accrued coupon} = - 100 \times \text{coupon rate} \times \frac{\text{days to next coupon}}{\text{year}}$$

Clean price = dirty price − accrued coupon

Price falls as yield rises and vice versa.

Generally, if a bond's price is greater than par, its yield is less than the coupon rate.

Other yields

$$\text{Current yield} = \frac{\text{coupon}}{\text{clean price}}$$

$$\text{Simple yield to maturity} = \frac{\text{coupon} + \left(\frac{\text{redemption amount} - \text{clean price}}{\text{years to maturity}}\right)}{\text{clean price}}$$

Alternative yield in final coupon period (simple)

$$i = \left[\frac{\text{total final cashflow including coupon}}{\text{dirty price}} - 1\right] \times \frac{\text{year}}{\text{days to maturity}}$$

where days and year are measured on the relevant bond basis.

Bond equivalent yield for US T-bill

If 182 days or less to maturity:

$$i = \frac{D}{1 - D \times \frac{days}{360}} \times \frac{365}{360}$$

If more than 182 days to maturity:

$$i = \frac{-\frac{days}{365} + \left(\left(\frac{days}{365}\right)^2 + 2 \times \left(\left(\frac{days}{365} - \frac{1}{2}\right) \times \left(\frac{1}{\left(1 - D \times \frac{days}{360}\right)} - 1\right)\right)\right)^{\frac{1}{2}}}{\left(\frac{days}{365} - \frac{1}{2}\right)}$$

If 29 February falls in the 12-month period starting on the purchase date, replace 365 by 366.

Money market yield

$$P = \frac{100}{(1 + \frac{i}{n} \times W)} \left[\frac{R}{n} \times \frac{\left(1 - \frac{1}{(1 + \frac{i}{n} \times \frac{365}{360})^N}\right)}{\left(1 - \frac{1}{(1 + \frac{i}{n} \times \frac{365}{360})}\right)} + \frac{1}{(1 + \frac{i}{n} \times \frac{365}{360})^{N-1}} \right]$$

where i and W are the yield and fraction of a coupon period on a money market basis rather than a bond basis.

Moosmüller yield

$$P = \frac{100}{(1 + \frac{i}{n} \times W)} \left[\frac{R}{n} \times \frac{\left(1 - \frac{1}{(1 + \frac{i}{n})^N}\right)}{\left(1 - \frac{1}{(1 + \frac{i}{n})}\right)} + \frac{1}{(1 + \frac{i}{n})^{N-1}} \right]$$

where i and W are the yield and fraction of a coupon period on a bond basis.

Duration and convexity

$$(\text{Macaulay}) \text{ duration} = \frac{\sum (\text{present value of cashflow} \times \text{time to cashflow})}{\sum (\text{present value of cashflow})}$$

$$\text{Modified duration} = -\frac{dP}{di} \Big/ \text{dirty price} = \frac{\text{duration}}{(1 + i/n)}$$

DV01 = modified duration × dirty price × 0.0001

Approximation

Change in price $\approx$ – dirty price $\times$ change in yield $\times$ modified duration

Convexity =

$$-\frac{d^2P}{di^2}\bigg/ \text{dirty price} = \Sigma_k\left[\frac{C_k}{(1 + i/_n)^{n\frac{d_k}{\text{year}}+2}} \times \frac{d_k}{\text{year}}\left(\frac{d_k}{\text{year}} + \frac{1}{n}\right)\right]\bigg/ \text{dirty price}$$

where d_k is the number of days to cashflow C_k

Better approximation

Change in price $\approx$ – dirty price $\times$ modified duration $\times$ change in yield + $\frac{1}{2}$ dirty price $\times$ convexity $\times$ (change in yield)^2

Approximations for a portfolio

$$\text{Duration} = \frac{\Sigma(\text{duration of investment} \times \text{value of each investment})}{\text{value of portfolio}}$$

$$\text{Modified duration} = \frac{\Sigma(\text{mod. dur. of each investment} \times \text{value of each investment})}{\text{value of portfolio}}$$

$$\text{Convexity} = \frac{\Sigma(\text{convexity of each investment} \times \text{value of each investment})}{\text{value of portfolio}}$$

Bond futures

Conversion factor = clean price at delivery for one unit of the deliverable bond, at which that bond's yield equals the futures contract notional coupon rate

Theoretical bond futures price =

$$\frac{\left([\text{bond price} + \text{accrued coupon now}] \times \left[1 + i \times \frac{\text{days}}{\text{year}}\right]\right) - (\text{accrued coupon at delivery}) - (\text{intervening coupon reinvested})}{\text{conversion factor}}$$

where i = short-term funding rate

Implied repo rate =

$$\left[\frac{(\text{futures price} \times \text{conversion factor}) + (\text{accrued coupon at delivery of futures}) + (\text{interim coupon reinvested})}{(\text{bond price} + \text{accrued coupon now})} - 1\right] \times \frac{\text{year}}{\text{days}}$$

Basis = bond price – futures price $\times$ conversion factor

Net cost of carry = coupon income – financing cost

Net basis = basis – net cost of carry

Forward bond price =

$$\Big([\text{bond price} + \text{accrued coupon now}] \times \Big[1 + i \times \tfrac{\text{days}}{\text{year}}\Big]\Big) -$$
$$(\text{accrued coupon at delivery}) - (\text{intervening coupon reinvested})$$

where i = short-term funding rate

Generally, a forward bond price is at a premium (discount) to the cash price if the short-term funding cost is greater than (less than) $\dfrac{\text{coupon rate}}{\text{cash price} / 100}$.

Hedge ratio

$$\frac{\text{notional amount of futures contract required to hedge a position in bond A}}{\text{face value of bond A}} =$$

$$\frac{\text{dirty price of bond A}}{\text{dirty price of CTD bond}} \times \frac{\text{modified duration of bond A}}{\text{modified duration of CTD bond}} \times$$

$$\frac{\text{conversion factor for CTD bond}}{(1 + i \times \tfrac{\text{days to futures delivery}}{\text{year}})}$$

where i = short-term funding rate

Cash-and-carry arbitrage

Assume the arbitrage is achieved by buying the cash bond and selling the futures:

Cash cost at start = nominal bond amount
$$\times (\text{cash bond price} + \text{accrued coupon at start})/100$$

$$\text{Total payments} = (\text{cash cost at start}) \times \Big(1 + \text{repo rate} \times \frac{\text{days to futures delivery}}{\text{year}}\Big)$$

$$\text{Total receipts} = \text{nominal bond amount} \times (\text{futures price} \times \text{conversion factor} + \text{accrued coupon at delivery of futures}) \big/ 100$$

Profit = total receipts – total payments

For each futures, the bond amount above is $\dfrac{\text{notional contract size}}{\text{conversion factor}}$

Zero-coupon rates and yield curves (Chapter 7)

$$\text{Par yield for N years} = \frac{1 - df_N}{\displaystyle\sum_{k=1}^{N} df_k}$$

where df_k = zero-coupon discount factor for k years

Forward-forward zero-coupon yield from k years to m years =

$$\left[\frac{(1 + z_m)^m}{(1 + z_k)^k}\right]^{\frac{1}{(m-k)}} - 1$$

In particular:

Forward-forward yield from k years to (k + 1) years =

$$\frac{(1 + z_{k+1})^{k+1}}{(1 + z_k)^k} - 1$$

Creating a strip

$$z_k = [(1 + i_1) \times (1 + i_2) \times (1 + i_3) \times \dots \times (1 + i_k)]^{\frac{1}{k}} - 1$$

where i_1, i_2, i_3 ... i_k are the 1-year cash interest rate and the 1-year v 2-year, 2-year v 3-year, ... , (k − 1)-year v k-year forward-forward rates.

Conversion between yield curves

To create a zero-coupon yield from coupon-bearing yields: **bootstrap.**

To calculate the yield to maturity on a non-par coupon-bearing bond from zero-coupon yields: **calculate the NPV of the bond using the zero-coupon yields, then calculate the yield to maturity of the bond from this dirty price.**

To create a par yield from zero-coupon yields: **use the formula above.**

To create a forward-forward yield from zero-coupon yields: **use the formula above.**

To create a zero-coupon yield from forward-forward yields: **create a strip of the first cash leg with a series of forward-forwards.**

Foreign exchange (Chapter 8)

To calculate cross-rates

From two rates with the same base currency or the same variable currency: divide opposite sides of the exchange rates.

From two rates where the base currency in one is the same as the variable currency in the other: multiply the same sides of the exchange rates.

In general:

Given two exchange rates A/B and A/C, the cross-rates are:

B/C = A/C ÷ A/B
C/B = A/B ÷ A/C

Given two exchange rates B/A and A/C, the cross-rates are:

B/C = B/A × A/C
C/B = 1 ÷ (B/A × A/C)

When dividing, use opposite sides. When multiplying, use the same sides.

Forwards

$$\text{Forward outright} = \text{spot} \times \frac{\left(1 + \text{variable currency interest} \times \frac{\text{days}}{\text{year}}\right)}{\left(1 + \text{base currency interest rate} \times \frac{\text{days}}{\text{year}}\right)}$$

$$\text{Forward swap} = \text{spot} \times$$

$$\frac{\left(\text{variable currency interest rate} \times \frac{\text{days}}{\text{year}} - \text{base currency interest rate} \times \frac{\text{days}}{\text{year}}\right)}{\left(1 + \text{base currency interest rate} \times \frac{\text{days}}{\text{year}}\right)}$$

Forward outright = spot + forward swap

Approximations

$$\text{Forward swap} \approx \text{spot} \times \text{interest rate differential} \times \frac{\text{days}}{\text{year}}$$

$$\text{Interest rate differential} \approx \frac{\text{forward swap}}{\text{spot}} \times \frac{\text{year}}{\text{days}}$$

Premiums and discounts

1. The currency with higher interest rates (= the currency at a "discount") is worth less in the future.
   The currency with lower interest rates (= the currency at a "premium") is worth more in the future.

2. The bank quoting the price buys the base currency / sells the variable currency on the far date on the left.
   The bank quoting the price sells the base currency / buys the variable currency on the far date on the right.

3. For outrights later than spot, if the swap price is larger on the right than the left, add it to the spot price. If the swap price is larger on the left than the right, subtract it from the spot price.

4. For outrights later than spot, the right-hand swap price is added to (or subtracted from) the right-hand spot price; the left-hand swap price is added to (or subtracted from) the left-hand spot price.

5. For outright deals earlier than spot, calculate as if the swap price is reversed and follow (3) and (4).

6. Of the two prices available, the customer gets the worse one. Thus if the swap price is 3 / 2 and the customer knows that the points are "in his

favour" (the outright will be better than the spot), the price will be 2. If he knows that the points are "against him" (the outright will be worse than the spot), the price will be 3.

7. The effect of combining the swap points with the spot price will always be to widen the spread, never to narrow it.

A forward dealer expecting the interest rate differential to move in favour of the base currency (for example, base currency interest rates rise or variable currency interest rates fall) will "buy and sell" the base currency. This is equivalent to borrowing the base currency and depositing in the variable currency. And vice versa.

Covered interest arbitrage

Variable currency rate created =

$$\left[\left(1 + \text{base currency rate} \times \frac{\text{days}}{\text{base year}}\right) \times \frac{\text{outright}}{\text{spot}} - 1\right] \times \frac{\text{variable year}}{\text{days}}$$

Base currency rate created =

$$\left[\left(1 + \text{variable currency rate} \times \frac{\text{days}}{\text{variable year}}\right) \times \frac{\text{spot}}{\text{outright}} - 1\right] \times \frac{\text{base year}}{\text{days}}$$

Forward-forward price after spot

Left side = (left side of far-date swap) – (right side of near-date swap)
Right side = (right side of far-date swap) – (left side of near-date swap)

Time option

A time option price is the best for the bank / worst for the customer over the time option period.

Long-dated forwards

$$\text{Forward outright} = \text{spot} \times \frac{(1 + \text{variable interest rate})^N}{(1 + \text{base interest rate})^N}$$

Covered interest arbitrage (forward)

Variable currency FRA rate =

$$\left[\left(1 + \text{base currency FRA} \times \frac{\text{days}}{\text{year}}\right) \times \frac{\text{outright to far date}}{\text{outright to near date}} - 1\right] \times \frac{\text{variable year}}{\text{days}}$$

Base currency FRA rate =

$$\left[\left(1 + \text{variable currency FRA} \times \frac{\text{days}}{\text{variable year}}\right) \times \frac{\text{outright to near date}}{\text{outright to far date}} - 1\right] \times \frac{\text{base year}}{\text{days}}$$

Forward-forward swap =

$$\text{outright to near date} \times \frac{\left(\text{variable currency FRA} \times \frac{\text{days}}{\text{year}} - \text{base currency FRA} \times \frac{\text{days}}{\text{year}}\right)}{\left(1 + \text{base currency FRA} \times \frac{\text{days}}{\text{year}}\right)}$$

Interest rate swaps and currency swaps (Chapter 9)

Pricing interest rate swaps from futures or FRAs

- For each successive futures maturity, create a strip to generate a discount factor.

- Use the series of discount factors to calculate the yield of a par swap.

Valuing swaps

To value a swap, calculate the NPV of the cashflows, preferably using zero-coupon swap yields or the equivalent discount factors.

To value floating rate cashflows, superimpose offsetting floating rate cash-flows known to have an NPV of zero – effectively an FRN.

To value cashflows in a different currency, convert the resulting NPV at the spot exchange rate.

A swap at current rates has an NPV of zero.

If a current swap involves an off-market fixed rate, this is compensated by a one-off payment or by an adjustment to the other side of the swap, so as to maintain the NPV at zero.

The current swap rate for a swap based on an irregular or forward-start notional principal is again the rate which gives the swap an NPV of zero.

Options (Chapter 10)

Price quotation

Currency option price expressed as points of the variable currency =
(price expressed as percentage of the base currency amount) × spot exchange rate.

Currency option price expressed as percentage of base currency amount =
(price expressed as points of the variable currency) ÷ spot exchange rate.

Black–Scholes

Option-pricing formula for a non-dividend-paying asset

Call premium = spot price × $N(d_1)$ – strike price × $N(d_2)$ × e^{-rt}

$$\text{Put premium} = -\text{spot price} \times N(-d_1) + \text{strike price} \times N(-d_2) \times e^{-rt}$$
$$= \text{call premium} + \text{strike price} \times e^{-rt} - \text{spot price}$$

where: $\quad d_1 = \dfrac{LN\left(\dfrac{\text{spot} \times e^{rt}}{\text{strike}}\right) + \dfrac{\sigma^2 t}{2}}{\sigma\sqrt{t}}$

$\quad d_2 = \dfrac{LN\left(\dfrac{\text{spot} \times e^{rt}}{\text{strike}}\right) - \dfrac{\sigma^2 t}{2}}{\sigma\sqrt{t}}$

t $\quad$ = $\quad$ the time to expiry of the option as a proportion of a year

σ $\quad$ = $\quad$ the annualised volatility

r $\quad$ = $\quad$ the continuously compounded interest rate

N(d) = $\quad$ the standardised normal cumulative probability distribution

The normal distribution function can be approximated by:

$$N(d) = 1 - \dfrac{\dfrac{0.4361836}{1+0.33267d} - \dfrac{0.1201676}{(1+0.33267d)^2} + \dfrac{0.937298}{(1+0.33267d)^3}}{\sqrt{2\pi}\, e^{\frac{d^2}{2}}} \quad \text{when } d \geq 0 \text{ and}$$

$$N(d) = 1 - N(-d) \qquad\qquad\qquad \text{when } d < 0$$

Currency option pricing formula (Garman-Kohlhagen)

Call premium = (forward price $\times$ N(d$_1$) – strike price $\times$ N(d$_2$)) $\times$ e^{-rt}

Put premium = (– forward price $\times$ N(–d$_1$) + strike price $\times$ N(–d$_2$)) $\times$ e^{-rt}
$\qquad\qquad\quad$ = call premium + (strike price – forward price) $\times$ e^{-rt}

where: the option is a call on a unit of the base currency (that is, a put on the variable currency) and the premium is expressed in units of the variable currency

$\quad d_1 = \dfrac{LN\left(\dfrac{\text{forward}}{\text{strike}}\right) + \dfrac{\sigma^2 t}{2}}{\sigma\sqrt{t}}$

$\quad d_2 = \dfrac{LN\left(\dfrac{\text{forward}}{\text{strike}}\right) - \dfrac{\sigma^2 t}{2}}{\sigma\sqrt{t}}$

r = the continuously compounded interest rate for the variable currency

Put–call relationship

Call premium = put premium + spot – strike $\times$ e^{-rt}
$\qquad\qquad\quad$ = put premium + (forward – strike) $\times$ e^{-rt}

$$\text{Put premium} = \text{call premium} - \text{spot} + \text{strike} \times e^{-rt}$$
$$= \text{call premium} - (\text{forward} - \text{strike}) \times e^{-rt}$$

where: r = continuously compounded interest rate

t = time to expiry as a proportion of a year

In particular, when the strike is the same as the simple forward, the call and put premiums are equal (put–call parity).

The expressions e^{rt} and e^{-rt} in the various formulas above can be replaced by $(1 + i \times t)$ and $\frac{1}{(1 + i \times t)}$ respectively, where i is the simple interest rate for the period.

Synthetic forwards

Buy forward = buy call *plus* sell put

Sell forward = sell call *plus* buy put

Risk reversal

Buy call	= buy put *plus* buy forward
Sell call	= sell put *plus* sell forward
Buy put	= buy call *plus* sell forward
Sell put	= sell call *plus* buy forward

Option price sensitivities

$$\text{delta } (\Delta) = \frac{\text{change in option's value}}{\text{change in underlying's value}}$$

$$\text{gamma } (\Gamma) = \frac{\text{change in delta}}{\text{change in underlying's value}}$$

$$\text{vega} = \frac{\text{change in option's value}}{\text{change in volatility}}$$

$$\text{theta } (\Theta) = -\frac{\text{change in option's value}}{\text{change in time}}$$

$$\text{rho } (\rho) = \frac{\text{change in option's value}}{\text{change in interest rate}}$$

Based on the Black–Scholes formula

$$\Delta = N(d_1) \text{ for a call}$$
$$\text{or } -N(-d_1) \text{ for a put}$$

$$\Gamma = \frac{1}{S\sigma\sqrt{2\pi t}\, e^{\frac{d_1^2}{2}}} \text{ for a call or a put}$$

$$\text{vega} = \frac{S\sqrt{\frac{t}{2\pi}}}{e^{\frac{d_1^2}{2}}} \text{ for a call or a put}$$

$$\text{theta } (\Theta) = -\frac{S\sigma}{2\sqrt{2\pi t}} \, e^{-\frac{d_1^2}{2}} - Kre^{-rt}N(d_2) \text{ for a call}$$

$$\text{or} - \frac{S\sigma}{2\sqrt{2\pi t}} \, e^{-\frac{d_1^2}{2}} + Kre^{-rt}N(-d_2) \text{ for a put}$$

rho $(\rho) = Kte^{-rt}N(d_2)$ for a call
or $-Kte^{-rt}N(-d_2)$ for a put

where: S = spot price for the asset
K = strike price

Gold and other commodities (Chapter 11)

Forward prices

$$\text{Gold forward price} = \text{spot price} \times \frac{\left(1 + \text{USD interest rate} \times \frac{\text{days}}{360}\right)}{\left(1 + \text{lease rate} \times \frac{\text{days}}{360}\right)}$$

Gold forward swap =

$$\text{spot price} \times \frac{\left(\text{USD interest rate} \times \frac{\text{days}}{360} - \text{lease rate} \times \frac{\text{days}}{360}\right)}{\left(1 + \text{lease rate} \times \frac{\text{days}}{360}\right)}$$

Approximation

Gold forward swap $\approx$
gold spot price $\times$ (USD interest rate – gold lease rate) $\times \frac{\text{days}}{360}$

If GOFO is defined as the net interest rate to lend gold and borrow USD, *then*:

$$\text{GOFO} = \left(\frac{\left(1 + \text{USD interest rate} \times \frac{\text{days}}{360}\right)}{\left(1 + \text{lease rate} \times \frac{\text{days}}{360}\right)} - 1\right) \times \frac{360}{\text{days}}$$

$$\text{Lease rate} = \left(\frac{\left(1 + \text{USD interest rate} \times \frac{\text{days}}{360}\right)}{\left(1 + \text{GOFO} \times \frac{\text{days}}{360}\right)} - 1\right) \times \frac{360}{\text{days}}$$

Gold forward price = spot price $\times \left(1 + \text{GOFO} \times \frac{\text{days}}{360}\right)$

Gold forward swap = spot price $\times \left(\text{GOFO} \times \frac{\text{days}}{360}\right)$

Alternatively, *if* GOFO is defined as GOFO = USD interest rate – gold lease rate, *then*:

$$\text{Gold forward swap} = \text{spot price} \times \frac{\left(\text{GOFO} \times \frac{\text{days}}{360}\right)}{\left(1 + \text{lease rate} \times \frac{\text{days}}{360}\right)}$$

Approximation

$$\text{Gold forward swap} \approx \text{spot price} \times \text{GOFO} \times \frac{\text{days}}{360}$$

Approximation

$$\text{Gold forward price} \approx \text{spot price} \times \left(1 + \text{GOFO} \times \frac{\text{days}}{360}\right)$$

The net interest rate to lend gold and borrow USD =

$$\frac{\text{swap}}{\text{spot}} \times \frac{360}{\text{days}} = \frac{\text{GOFO}}{\left(1 + \text{lease rate} \times \frac{\text{days}}{360}\right)}$$

Forwards and convenience yield

Convenience yield =

$$\left(\frac{\text{spot price}}{\text{forward price}} \times \left(1 + \text{cash interest rate} \times \frac{\text{days}}{\text{year}}\right) - 1\right) \times \frac{\text{year}}{\text{days}}$$

For storable commodities

$$\text{Forward price} \leq \text{spot} \times \left(1 + \text{cash interest rate} \times \frac{\text{days}}{\text{year}}\right) + \text{storage costs}$$

Appendix 4
Glossary

30/360 (Or 360/360). A day/year count convention assuming 30 days in each calendar month and a "year" of 360 days; sometimes adjusted for certain periods ending on 31st day of the month or the last day of February.

360/360 Same as 30/360.

Accreting An accreting principal is one which increases during the life of the deal. *See* **amortising, bullet.**

Accrued interest The proportion of interest or **coupon** earned on an investment from the previous coupon payment date until the **value date.**

Accumulated value Same as **future value.**

ACT/360 A day/year count convention taking the number of calendar days in a period and a "year" of 360 days.

ACT/365 (Or ACT/365 fixed). A day/year count convention taking the number of calendar days in a period and a "year" of 365 days. Under the ISDA definitions used for **interest rate swap** documentation, ACT/365 means the same as **ACT/ACT.**

ACT/365 fixed See ACT/365.

ACT/ACT A day/year count convention taking the number of calendar days in a period and a "year" equal to the number of days in the current coupon period multiplied by the coupon frequency. For an **interest rate swap,** that part of the interest period falling in a leap year is divided by 366 and the remainder is divided by 365.

Allocated account Ownership of specific gold bars held in a specific location and allocated to the holder's account. See **unallocated account.**

American An American **option** is one which may be **exercised** at any time during its life. *See* **European.**

Amortising An amortising principal is one which decreases during the life of the deal, or is repaid in stages during a loan.

Amortising an amount over a period of time also means accruing for it pro rata over the period. *See* **accreting, bullet.**

Annuity An investment providing a series of (generally equal) future cashflows.

Appreciation An increase in the market value of a currency in terms of other currencies. *See* **depreciation, revaluation**.

Arbitrage Arbitrage is the simultaneous operation in two different but related markets in order to take advantage of a discrepancy between them which will lock in a profit. The arbitrage operation itself usually tends to cause the different markets to converge. *See* **covered interest arbitrage**.

Asian An Asian **option** depends on the average value of the **underlying** over the option's life.

Ask *See* **offer**.

Asset-backed security A security which is collateralised by specific assets – such as mortgages – rather than by the intangible creditworthiness of the issuer.

Asset swap An **interest rate swap** or **currency swap** used in conjunction with an underlying asset such as a bond investment. *See* **liability swap**.

At-the-money (Or ATM.) An **option** is at-the-money if the current value of the **underlying** is the same as the **strike** price. *See* **in-the-money, out-of-the-money**.

ATM *See* **at-the-money**.

Backwardation A situation where the forward price of a commodity is lower than the spot price. See **contango**.

Baht A weight measurement for gold (0.47 troy ounces = 14.6 grammes), used in Thailand.

Banker's acceptance *See* **bill of exchange**.

Barrier option A barrier **option** is one which ceases to exist, or starts to exist, if the **underlying** reaches a certain barrier level. *See* **knock out/in**.

Base currency Exchange rates are quoted in terms of the number of units of one currency (the **variable** or **counter** or **quoted currency**) which corresponds to one unit of the other currency (the base currency).

Basis The underlying **cash market** price minus the **futures** price. In the case of a bond futures contract, the futures price must be multiplied by the **conversion factor** for the cash bond in question.

Basis points In interest rate quotations, 0.01 percent.

Basis risk The risk that the prices of two instruments will not move exactly in line – for example, the price of a particular bond and the price of a **futures** contract being used to hedge a position in that bond.

Basis swap An **interest rate swap** where both legs are based on **floating** rate payments.

Basis trade Buying the basis means selling a **futures** contract and buying the commodity or instrument **underlying** the futures contract. Selling the basis is the opposite.

Bear spread A **spread** position taken with the expectation of a fall in value in the **underlying**.

Bearer security A security where the issuer pays **coupons** and principal to the **holders** of the security from time to time, without the need for the holders to register their ownership; this provides anonymity to investors.

Bid In general, the price at which the dealer quoting a price is prepared to buy or borrow. The bid price of a foreign exchange quotation is the rate at which the dealer will buy the **base currency** and sell the **variable** currency. The bid rate in a deposit quotation is the interest rate at which the dealer will borrow the currency involved. The bid rate in a **repo** is the interest rate at which the dealer will borrow the **collateral** and lend the cash. *See* **offer**.

Big figure In a foreign exchange quotation, the exchange rate omitting the last two decimal places. For example, when EUR/USD is 1.1910/20, the big figure is 1.19. *See* **points**.

Bill of exchange A short-term, zero-coupon debt issued by a company to finance commercial trading. If it is guaranteed by a bank, it becomes a **banker's acceptance**.

Binomial tree A mathematical model to value **options**, based on the assumption that the value of the **underlying** can move either up or down a given extent over a given short time. This process is repeated many times to give a large number of possible paths (the "tree") which the value could follow during the option's life.

Black–Scholes A widely used **option** pricing formula devised by Fischer Black and Myron Scholes.

Bond basis An interest rate is quoted on a bond basis if it is on an **ACT/365**, **ACT/ACT** or **30/360** basis. In the short term (for **accrued interest**, for example), these three are different. Over a whole (non-leap) year, however, they all equate to 1. In general, the expression "bond basis" does not distinguish between them and is calculated as ACT/365. *See* **money market basis**.

Bond-equivalent yield The **yield** which would be quoted on a US treasury bond which is trading at par and which has the same economic return and maturity as a given **treasury bill**.

Bootstrapping Building up successive **zero-coupon** yields from a combination of coupon-bearing **yields**.

Bräss/Fangmeyer A method for calculating the **yield** of a bond similar to the **Moosmüller** method but, in the case of bonds which pay coupons more frequently than annually, using a mixture of annual and less than annual compounding.

Break forward A product equivalent to a straightforward **option**, but structured as a **forward** deal at an **off-market** rate which can be reversed at a penalty rate.

Broken date (Or odd date.) A maturity date other than the standard ones (such as 1 week, 1, 2, 3, 6 and 12 months) normally quoted.

Bull spread A **spread** position taken with the expectation of a rise in value in the **underlying**.

Bullet A loan / deposit has a bullet maturity if the principal is all repaid at maturity. *See* **amortising**.

Bullion Gold and silver traded in bulk form.

Buy / sell-back Opposite of **sell / buy-back**.

Cable The exchange rate for sterling against the US dollar.

Calendar spread The simultaneous purchase / sale of a **futures** contract for one date and the sale / purchase of a similar futures contract for a different date. *See* **spread**.

Call option An option to purchase the commodity or instrument **underlying** the option. *See* **put**.

Cap Equivalent to a series of borrower's **IRGs**, designed to protect a borrower against rising interest rates on each of a series of dates.

Capital market Long-term market (generally longer than one year) for financial instruments. *See* **money market**.

Cash *See* **cash market**.

Cash-and-carry A round trip (**arbitrage**) where a dealer buys bonds, **repos** them out for cash to fund their purchase, sells bond **futures** and delivers the bonds to the futures buyer at maturity of the futures contract.

Cash market The market for trading an **underlying** financial instrument, where the whole value of the instrument will potentially be settled on the normal delivery date – as opposed to **contracts for differences**, **futures**, **options**, etc. (where the cash amount to be settled is not intended to be the full value of the underlying) or **forwards** (where delivery is for a later date than normal). *See* **derivative**.

CD *See* **certificate of deposit**.

Ceiling Same as **cap**.

Certificate of deposit (Or CD.) A security, generally coupon-bearing, issued by a bank to borrow money.

Cheapest to deliver (Or CTD.) In a bond futures contract, the one underlying bond among all those that are **deliverable**, which is the most price-efficient for the seller to deliver.

Classic repo (Or **repo** or US-style repo.) Repo is short for "sale and repurchase agreement" – a simultaneous **spot** sale and **forward** purchase of a **security**, equivalent to borrowing money against a loan of **collateral**. A **reverse repo** is the opposite. The terminology is usually applied from the perspective of the repo dealer. For example, when a central bank does repos, it is lending cash (the repo dealer is borrowing cash from the central bank).

Clean deposit Same as **time deposit**.

Clean price The price of a bond excluding accrued coupon. The price quoted in the market for a bond is generally a clean price rather than a **dirty price**.

Collar The simultaneous sale of a **put** (or **call**) option and purchase of a call (or put) at different **strikes** – typically both **out-of-the-money**.

Collateral (Or **security**.) Something of value, often of good creditworthiness such as a government bond, given temporarily to a counterparty to enhance a party's creditworthiness. In a **repo**, the collateral is actually sold temporarily by one party to the other rather than merely lodged with it.

Commercial paper A short-term security issued by a company or bank, generally with a zero **coupon**.

Compound interest When some interest on an investment is paid before maturity and the investor can reinvest it to earn interest on interest, the interest is said to be compounded. Compounding generally assumes that the **reinvestment rate** is the same as the original rate. *See* **simple interest**.

Contango A situation where the forward price of a commodity is higher than the spot price. See **backwardation**.

Continuous compounding A mathematical, rather than practical, concept of **compound interest** where the period of compounding is infinitesimally small.

Contract date The date on which a transaction is negotiated. *See* **value date**.

Contract for differences A deal such as an **FRA** and some **futures contracts**, where the instrument or commodity effectively bought or sold cannot be delivered; instead, a cash gain or loss is taken by comparing the price dealt with the market price, or an index, at maturity.

Convenience yield The perceived benefit of holding a commodity expressed as an interest rate per year.

Conversion factor (Or price factor.) In a bond **futures contract**, a factor to make each **deliverable bond** comparable with the contract's **notional** bond specification. Defined as the price of one unit of the deliverable bond required to make its yield equal the notional **coupon**. The price paid for a bond on delivery is the futures settlement price times the conversion factor.

Convertible currency A currency that may be freely exchanged for other currencies.

Convexity A measure of the curvature of a bond's price / **yield** curve (mathematically, $\dfrac{d^2P}{di^2}\bigg/$ dirty price).

Cost of carry The net running cost of holding a position (which may be negative) – for example, the cost of borrowing cash to buy a bond less the **coupon** earned on the bond while holding it.

Counter currency *See* **variable currency.**

Coupon The interest payment(s) made by the issuer of a security to the **holders,** based on the coupon rate and **face value.**

Coupon swap An **interest rate swap** in which one leg is fixed-rate and the other floating-rate. See **basis swap.**

Cover To cover an **exposure** is to deal in such a way as to remove the risk – either reversing the position, or **hedging** it by dealing in an instrument with a similar but opposite risk profile.

Covered call / put The sale of a covered **call** option is when the option **writer** also owns the **underlying.** If the underlying rises in value so that the option is **exercised,** the writer is protected by his position in the underlying. Covered **puts** are defined analogously. *See* **naked.**

Covered interest arbitrage Creating a loan / deposit in one currency by combining a loan / deposit in another with a forward foreign exchange **swap.**

CP *See* **commercial paper.**

Cross *See* **cross-rate.**

Cross-rate Historically, an exchange rate between two currencies, neither of which is the US dollar. Nowadays, any exchange rate calculated from two or more other exchange rates. In the American market, spot cross is the exchange rate for US dollars against Canadian dollars in its **direct** form.

CTD *See* **cheapest to deliver.**

Cum-dividend When (as is usual) the next **coupon** or other payment due on a **security** is paid to the buyer of a security. *See* **ex-dividend.**

Currency swap An agreement to exchange a series of cashflows determined in one currency, possibly with reference to a particular fixed or **floating** interest payment schedule, for a series of cashflows based in a different currency. *See* **interest rate swap.**

Current yield Bond **coupon** as a proportion of clean price per 100; does not take principal gain / loss or **time value of money** into account. *See* **yield to maturity, simple yield to maturity.**

Cylinder Same as **collar.**

DAC – RAP Delivery against collateral – receipt against payment. Same as **DVP.**

Deliverable bond One of the bonds which is eligible to be delivered by the seller of a bond **futures contract** at the contract's maturity, according to the specifications of that particular contract.

Delta (Δ) The change in an **option**'s value relative to a change in the **underlying**'s value.

Depreciation A decrease in the market value of a currency in terms of other currencies. *See* **appreciation, devaluation**.

Derivative Strictly, any financial instrument whose value is derived from another, such as a **forward** foreign exchange rate, a **futures contract**, an **option**, an **interest rate swap**, etc. Forward deals to be settled in full are not always called derivatives, however.

Devaluation An official one-off decrease in the value of a currency in terms of other currencies. *See* **revaluation, depreciation**.

Direct An exchange rate quotation against the US dollar in which the dollar is the **variable currency** and the other currency is the **base currency**.

Dirty price The price of a security including **accrued coupon**. *See* **clean price**.

Discount The amount by which a currency is cheaper, in terms of another currency, for future delivery than for spot, is the forward discount (in general, a reflection of interest rate differentials between two currencies). If an exchange rate is "at a discount" (without specifying to which of the two currencies this refers), this generally means that the **variable currency** is at a discount. *See* **premium**.

To discount a future cashflow means to calculate its **present value**.

Discount rate The method of market quotation for certain securities (US and UK treasury bills, for example), expressing the return on the security as a proportion of the face value of the security received at maturity – as opposed to a **yield** which expresses the return as a proportion of the original investment.

Duration (Or Macaulay duration.) A measure of the weighted average life of a bond or other series of cashflows, using the present values of the cashflows as the weights. *See* **modified duration**.

DVP Delivery versus payment, in which the settlement mechanics of a sale or loan of securities against cash is such that the securities and cash are exchanged against each other simultaneously through the same clearing mechanism and neither can be transferred unless the other is.

Effective rate An effective interest rate is the rate which, earned as simple interest over one year, gives the same return as interest paid more frequently than once per year and then compounded. *See* **nominal rate**.

EFP See **exchange for physical**.

End-end A money market deal commencing on the last working day of a month and lasting for a whole number of months, maturing on the last working day of the corresponding month.

Epsilon (ε) Same as **vega**.

Equivalent life The weighted average life of the principal of a bond where there are partial **redemptions**, using the **present values** of the partial redemptions as the weights.

Eta (η) Same as **vega**.

Euro The name for the "domestic" currency of the European Monetary Union. Not to be confused with **Eurocurrency**.

Eurocurrency A Eurocurrency is a currency owned by a non-resident of the country in which the currency is legal tender. Not to be confused with **euro**.

Euromarket The international market in which **Eurocurrencies** are traded.

European A European **option** is one that may be **exercised** only at **expiry**. *See* **American**.

Exchange controls Regulations restricting the free convertibility of a currency into other currencies.

Exchange for physical An exchange of opposite futures positions plus an offsetting physical transaction, both agreed simultaneously with the same counterparty off-market.

Exchange-traded **Futures** contracts are traded on a futures exchange, as opposed to **forward** deals which are **OTC**. Some **option** contracts are similarly exchange traded rather than OTC.

Ex-dividend When the next **coupon** or other payment due on a **security** is paid to the seller of a security after he has sold it, rather than to the buyer, generally because the transaction is settled after the **record date**. See **cum-dividend**.

Exercise To exercise an **option** (by the **holder**) is to require the other party (the **writer**) to fulfil the underlying transaction. Exercise price is the same as **strike** price.

Expiry An option's expiry is the time after which it can no longer be **exercised**.

Exposure Risk.

Extrapolation The process of estimating a price or rate for a particular value date, from other known prices, when the value date required lies outside the period covered by the known prices. *See* **interpolation**.

Face value (Or nominal value.) The principal amount of a security, generally repaid ("redeemed") all at maturity, but sometimes repaid in stages, on which the **coupon** amounts are calculated.

Fence Same as **collar**.

Fine ounce An ounce of pure gold.

Fine weight The weight of pure gold contained in a bar of gold.

Fineness The proportion of pure gold contained in a particular bar of gold, expressed in parts per thousand.

Floating rate In interest rates, an instrument paying a floating rate is one where the rate of interest is refixed in line with market conditions at regular intervals such as every three or six months.

In the currency market, an exchange rate determined by market forces with no government intervention.

Floating rate CD (Or FRCD.) **CD** on which the rate of interest payable is refixed in line with market conditions at regular intervals (usually six months).

Floating rate note (Or FRN.) **Capital market** instrument on which the rate of interest payable is refixed in line with market conditions at regular intervals (usually six months).

Floor Equivalent to a series of lender's **IRG**s, designed to protect an investor against falling interest rates on each of a series of dates.

Forward In general, a deal for value later than the normal value date for that particular commodity or instrument. In the foreign exchange market, a forward price is the price quoted for the purchase or sale of one currency against another where the value date is at least one month after the **spot** date. *See* **short date**.

Forward-forward An FX **swap**, loan or other interest-rate agreement starting on one **forward** date and ending on another.

Forward rate agreement (Or FRA.) **A contract for differences** based on a forward-forward interest rate.

FRA *See* **forward rate agreement**.

FRCD *See* **floating rate CD**.

FRN *See* **floating rate note**.

Funds The USD/CAD exchange rate for value on the next business day (standard practice for USD/CAD in preference to **spot**).

Future value The amount of money achieved in the future, including interest, by investing a given amount of money now. *See* **time value of money, present value**.

Futures contract A deal to buy or sell some financial instrument or commodity for value on a future date. Unlike a **forward** deal, futures contracts are traded only on an exchange (rather than **OTC**), have standardised contract sizes and value dates, and are often only **contracts for differences** rather than deliverable.

Gamma (Γ) The change in an **option**'s **delta** relative to a change in the **underlying**'s value.

GOFO *See* **gold forward offered rate**.

Gold forward offered rate The rate at which dealers lend gold and borrow dollars.

Gross redemption yield The same as **yield to maturity**; "gross" because it does not take tax effects into account.

GRY *See* **gross redemption yield**.

Hedge ratio The ratio of the size of the position it is necessary to take in a particular instrument as a hedge against another, to the size of the position being hedged.

Hedging Protecting against risks. *See* **cover, arbitrage, speculation**.

Historic rate rollover A **forward swap** in FX where the settlement exchange rate for the near date is based on a historic **off-market** rate rather than the current market rate. This is prohibited by many central banks.

Historic volatility The actual **volatility** recorded in market prices over a particular period.

Holder The holder of an **option** is the party that has purchased it.

Immunisation The construction of a portfolio of securities so as not to be adversely affected by yield changes, provided it is held until a specific time.

Implied repo rate The break-even interest rate at which it is possible to sell a bond **futures contract**, buy a **deliverable bond**, and **repo** the bond out. *See* **cash-and-carry**.

Implied volatility The **volatility** used by a dealer to calculate an **option** price; conversely, the volatility implied by the price actually quoted.

Index swap Sometimes the same as a **basis swap**. Otherwise a swap like an **interest rate swap** where payments on one or both of the legs are based on the value of an index – such as an equity index, for example.

Indirect An exchange rate quotation against the US dollar in which the dollar is the **base currency** and the other currency is the **variable currency**.

Initial margin *See* **margin**.

Interest rate guarantee (Or IRG.) An **option** on an **FRA**.

Interest rate swap (Or IRS.) An agreement to exchange a series of cashflows determined in one currency, based on fixed or **floating** interest payments on an agreed **notional** principal, for a series of cashflows based in the same currency but on a different interest rate. May be combined with a **currency swap**.

Internal rate of return (Or IRR.) The **yield** necessary to discount a series of cashflows to an **NPV** of zero.

Interpolation The process of estimating a price or rate for value on a particular date by comparing the prices actually quoted for value dates either side. *See* **extrapolation.**

Intervention Purchases or sales of currencies in the market by central banks in an attempt to reduce exchange rate fluctuations or to maintain the value of a currency within a particular band, or at a particular level. Similarly, central bank operations in the money markets to maintain interest rates at a certain level.

In-the-money A **call** (**put**) **option** is in-the-money if the **underlying** is currently more (less) valuable than the **strike** price. *See* **at-the-money, out-of-the-money.**

IRG *See* **interest rate guarantee.**

IRR *See* **internal rate of return.**

IRS *See* **interest rate swap.**

Iteration The repetitive mathematical process of estimating the answer to a problem, by trying how well this estimate fits the data, adjusting the estimate appropriately and trying again, until the fit is acceptably close. Used, for example, in calculating a bond's **yield** from its price.

Kappa (κ) Same as **vega.**

Knock out / in A knock out (in) **option** ceases to exist (starts to exist) if the **underlying** reaches a certain trigger level. *See* **barrier option.**

Lambda (λ) Same as **vega.**

LBMA London Bullion Market Association, the trade association for the physical gold and silver markets.

Lease rate (Or "gold **LIBOR**"). The interest rate borne by gold.

Liability swap An **interest rate swap** or **currency swap** used in conjunction with an underlying liability such as a borrowing. *See* **asset swap.**

LIBID *See* **LIBOR.**

LIBOR London inter-bank offered rate, the rate at which banks are willing to lend to other banks of top creditworthiness. The term is used both generally to mean the interest rate at any time, and specifically to mean the rate at 11:00 a.m. published as a reference for the purpose of providing a benchmark to fix an interest payment such as on an **FRN**. LIBID is similarly London inter-bank bid rate. LIMEAN is the average between LIBID and LIBOR.

LIMEAN *See* **LIBOR.**

Limit up / down **Futures** prices are generally not allowed to change by more than a specified total amount in a specified time, in order to control risk in very volatile conditions. The maximum movements permitted are referred to as limit up and limit down.

Location swaps An exchange of gold (or other commodity) to be delivered in one location for delivery in another location.

Loco The physical delivery point for gold – e.g. "loco London" means delivery in London.

Lognormal A variable's **probability distribution** is lognormal if the logarithm of the variable has a **normal** distribution.

Long A long position is a surplus of purchases over sales of a given currency or asset, or a situation which naturally gives rise to an organisation benefiting from a strengthening of that currency or asset. To a money market dealer, a long position is a surplus of borrowings taken in over money lent out (which gives rise to a benefit if that interest rate rises). *See* **short**.

Macaulay duration *See* **duration**.

Margin Initial margin is **collateral**, placed by one party with a counterparty at the time of a deal, against the possibility that the market price will move against the first party, thereby leaving the counterparty with a credit risk.

Variation margin is a payment or extra collateral transferred subsequently from one party to the other because the market price has moved. Variation margin payment is either in effect a settlement of profit/loss (for example, in the case of a **futures** contract) or the reduction of credit exposure (for example, in the case of a **repo**). In gilt repos, variation margin refers to the fluctuation band or threshold within which the existing collateral's value may vary before further cash or collateral needs to be transferred.

In a loan, margin is the extra interest above a benchmark (e.g. a margin of 0.5 percent over **LIBOR**) required by a lender to compensate for the credit risk of that particular borrower.

Margin call A call by one party in a transaction for **variation margin** to be transferred by the other.

Margin transfer The payment of a **margin call**.

Mark-to-market Generally, the process of revaluing a position at current market rates.

Mean Average.

Modified duration A measure of the proportional change in the price of a bond or other series of cashflows, relative to a change in yield.
(Mathematically $-\dfrac{dP}{di}\Big/\text{dirty price.}$) See **duration**.

Modified following The convention that if a value date in the future falls on a non-business day, the value date will be moved to the next following business day, unless this moves the value date to the next month, in which case the value date is moved back to the last previous business day.

Money market Short-term market (generally up to one year) for financial instruments. *See* **capital market**.

Money market basis An interest rate quoted on an **ACT/360** basis is said to be on a money market basis. *See* **bond basis**.

Moosmüller A method for calculating the yield of a bond.

Naked A naked **option** position is one not protected by an offsetting position in the **underlying**. *See* **covered call/put**.

Negotiable A security which can be bought and sold in a **secondary market** is negotiable.

Net present value (Or NPV.) The net present value of a series of cashflows is the sum of the present values of each cashflow (some or all of which may be negative).

Nominal amount Same as **face value** of a security.

Nominal rate A rate of interest as quoted, rather than the **effective rate** to which it is equivalent.

Normal A normal **probability distribution** is a particular distribution assumed to prevail in a wide variety of circumstances, including the financial markets. Mathematically, it corresponds to the probability density function $\dfrac{1}{\sqrt{2\pi}}\,e^{-\frac{1}{2}\phi^2}$.

Notional In a bond **futures** contract, the bond bought or sold is a standardised non-existent notional bond, as opposed to the actual bonds which are **deliverable** at maturity. **Contracts for differences** also require a notional principal amount on which settlement can be calculated.

NPV *See* **net present value**.

O/N *See* **overnight**.

Odd date *See* **broken date**.

Offer (Or ask.) In general, the price at which the dealer quoting a price is prepared to sell or lend. The offer price of a foreign exchange quotation is the rate at which the dealer will sell the **base currency** and buy the **variable currency**. The offer rate in a deposit quotation is the interest rate at which the dealer will lend the currency involved. The offer rate in a **repo** is the interest rate at which the dealer will lend the **collateral** and borrow the cash.

Off-market A rate which is not the current market rate.

Open interest The quantity of **futures** contracts (of a particular specification) which have not yet been closed out by reversing. Either all **long** positions or all **short** positions are counted but not both.

Option An option is the right, without any obligation, to undertake a particular deal at predetermined rates. *See* **call**, **put**.

Option forward *See* **time option**.

OTC *See* **over the counter**.

Out-of-the-money A **call** (**put**) **option** is out-of-the-money if the **underlying** is currently less (more) valuable than the **strike** price. *See* **at-the-money**, **in-the-money**.

Outright An outright (or **forward** outright) is the sale or purchase of one foreign currency against another for value on any date other than spot. *See* **spot**, **swap**, **forward**, **short date**.

Over the counter (Or OTC.) An OTC transaction is one dealt privately between any two parties, with all details agreed between them, as opposed to one dealt on an exchange – for example, a **forward** deal as opposed to a **futures contract**.

Overborrowed A position in which a dealer's liabilities (borrowings taken in) are of longer maturity than the assets (loans out).

Overlent A position in which a dealer's assets (loans out) are of longer maturity than the liabilities (borrowings taken in).

Overnight (Or O/N or today/tomorrow.) A deal from today until the next working day ("tomorrow").

Par In foreign exchange, when the **outright** and **spot** exchange rates are equal, the **forward swap** is zero or par.

When the price of a **security** is equal to the face value, usually expressed as 100, it is said to be trading at par.

A par swap rate is the current market rate for a fixed **interest rate swap** against **LIBOR**.

Par yield curve A curve plotting maturity against **yield** for bonds priced at par.

Parity The official rate of exchange for one currency in terms of another which a government is obliged to maintain by means of intervention.

Participation forward A product equivalent to a straightforward **option** plus a **forward** deal, but structured as a forward deal at an **off-market** rate plus the opportunity to benefit partially if the market rate improves.

Path-dependent A path-dependent **option** is one which depends on what happens to the **underlying** throughout the option's life (such as an **American** or **barrier** option) rather than only at **expiry** (a **European** option).

Pips *See* **points**.

Plain vanilla *See* **vanilla**.

Points The last two decimal places in an exchange rate. For example, when EUR/USD is 1.1910/1.1920, the points are 10/20. *See* **big figure**.

Precious metals Gold, silver, palladium, platinum, and the other platinum group metals (rhodium, ruthenium, iridium and osmium).

Premium The amount by which a currency is more expensive, in terms of another currency, for future delivery than for spot, is the forward premium (in general, a reflection of interest rate differentials between two currencies). If an exchange rate is "at a premium" (without specifying to which of the two currencies this refers), this generally means that the **variable currency** is at a premium. *See* **discount**.

An **option** premium is the amount paid up-front by the purchaser of the option to the **writer**.

Present value The amount of money which needs to be invested now to achieve a given amount in the future when interest is added. *See* **time value of money, future value**.

Price factor *See* **conversion factor**.

Primary market The primary market for a security refers to its original issue. *See* **secondary market**.

Probability distribution The mathematical description of how probable it is that the value of something is less than or equal to a particular level.

Prompt date The delivery date for a commodity futures contract or the date on which the buyer of an option will buy or sell the underlying commodity if the option is exercised.

Prompt month The front month - i.e. the nearest expiring futures contract - in commodities.

Put A put option is an option to sell the commodity or instrument **underlying** the option. *See* **call**.

Quanto swap A **swap** where the payments on one or both legs are based on a measurement (such as the interest rate) in one currency but payable in another currency.

Quasi-coupon date The regular date for which a **coupon** payment would be scheduled if there were one. Used for price/yield calculations for **zero-coupon** instruments.

Range forward A **zero-cost collar** where the customer is obliged to deal with the same bank at spot if neither limit of the collar is breached at **expiry**.

Record date A coupon or other payment due on a **security** is paid by the issuer to whoever is registered on the record date as being the owner. *See* **ex-dividend, cum-dividend**.

Redeem A security is said to be redeemed when the principal is repaid.

Reinvestment rate The rate at which interest paid during the life of an investment is reinvested to earn interest-on-interest, which in practice will generally not be the same as the original yield quoted on the investment.

Repo (Or RP.) Usually refers in particular to **classic repo**. Also used as a term to include classic repos and **buy/sell-backs**.

Repurchase agreement *See* repo.

Revaluation An official one-off increase in the value of a currency in terms of other currencies. *See* **devaluation**.

Reverse *See* **reverse repo**.

Reverse repo (Or reverse.) The opposite of a **repo**.

Rho (ρ) The change in an **option**'s value relative to a change in interest rates.

Risk reversal Purchase (or sale) of a call option at a higher strike, combined with the sale (or purchase) of a put option at a lower strike.

Rollover *See* **tom/next**. Also refers to renewal of a loan.

RP *See* repo.

Running yield Same as **current yield**.

Secondary market The market for buying and selling a security after it has been issued. *See* **primary market**.

Securities lending (Or stock lending.) When a specific security is lent against some form of collateral.

Security A financial asset sold initially for cash by a borrowing organisation (the "issuer"). The security is often **negotiable** and usually has a maturity date when it is **redeemed**.

Same as **collateral**.

Sell / buy-back Simultaneous **spot** sale and **forward** purchase of a **security**, with the **forward** price calculated to achieve an effect equivalent to a **classic repo**.

Short A short position is a surplus of sales over purchases of a given currency or asset, or a situation which naturally gives rise to an organisation benefiting from a weakening of that currency or asset. To a money market dealer, a short position is a surplus of money lent out over borrowings taken in (which gives rise to a benefit if that interest rate falls). *See* **long**.

Short date A deal for value on a date other than **spot** but less than one month after spot.

Simple interest When interest on an investment is paid all at maturity or not reinvested to earn interest on interest, the interest is said to be simple. *See* **compound interest**.

Simple yield to maturity Bond **coupon** plus principal gain / loss **amortised** over the time to maturity, as a proportion of the clean price per 100. Does not take **time value of money** into account. *See* **yield to maturity, current yield.**

S/N *See* spot/next.

Speculation A deal undertaken because the dealer expects prices to move in his favour, as opposed to **hedging** or **arbitrage.**

Spot A deal to be settled on the customary value date for that particular market. In the foreign exchange market, this is for value in two working days' time. In some futures such as gold, the nearest expiring futures contract.

A spot curve is a yield curve using **zero-coupon** yields.

Spot-a-week (Or S/W.) A transaction from **spot** to a week later.

Spot/next (Or S/N.) A transaction from **spot** until the next working day.

Spread The difference between the **bid** and **offer** prices in a quotation.

Also a strategy involving the purchase of an instrument and the simultaneous sale of a similar related instrument, such as the purchase of a **call option** at one **strike** and the sale of a call option at a different strike.

Also the difference between the prices of two different but associated things, such as the difference between the price of oil and the price of coal, or the yield on a bond and an IRS rate.

Square A position in which sales exactly match purchases, or in which assets exactly match liabilities. *See* **long, short.**

Standard deviation (σ) A measure of how much the values of something fluctuate around its **mean** value. Defined as the square root of the **variance.**

Stock lending *See* **securities lending.**

Straddle A position combining the purchase of both a **call** and a **put** at the same **strike** for the same date. *See* **strangle.**

Strangle A position combining the purchase of both a **call** and a **put** at different **strikes** for the same date. *See* **straddle.**

Street The "street" is a nickname for the market. The street convention for quoting the price or yield for a particular instrument is the generally accepted market convention.

Strike (Or **exercise** price.) The strike price or strike rate of an **option** is the price or rate at which the **holder** can insist on the underlying transaction being fulfilled.

Strip A strip of **futures** is a series of short-term futures contracts with consecutive delivery dates, which together create the effect of a longer term instrument (for example, four consecutive 3-month futures contracts as a hedge against a one-year swap). A strip of **FRAs** is similar.

To strip a bond is to separate its principal amount and its **coupons** and trade each individual cashflow as a separate instrument ("*s*eparately *t*raded and *r*egistered for *i*nterest and *p*rincipal").

S/W *See* **spot-a-week.**

Swap A foreign exchange swap is the purchase of one currency against another for delivery on one date, with a simultaneous sale to reverse the transaction on another value date.

See also **interest rate swap, currency swap.**

Swaption An **option** on an **interest rate swap** or **currency swap.**

Synthetic A package of transactions which is economically equivalent to a different transaction (for example, the purchase of a **call option** and simultaneous sale of a **put** option at the same **strike** is a synthetic **forward** purchase).

Tael A weight measurement for gold (1.2 troy ounces = 37.3 grammes), used in Hong Kong.

Tail The **exposure** to interest rates over a **forward-forward** period arising from a mismatched position (such as a two-month borrowing against a three-month loan).

A **forward** foreign exchange dealer's exposure to **spot** movements.

Term The time between the beginning and end of a deal or investment.

Theta (Θ) The change in an **option**'s value relative to a change in the time left to **expiry.**

Tick The minimum change allowed in a **futures** price.

Time deposit A non-**negotiable** deposit for a specific **term.**

Time option (Or option forward.) A **forward** currency deal in which the **value date** is set to be within a period rather than on a particular day. The customer sets the exact date two working days before settlement.

Time value of money The concept that a future cashflow can be valued as the amount of money which it is necessary to invest now in order to achieve that cashflow in the future. *See* **present value, future value.**

T/N *See* **tom/next.**

Today/tomorrow *See* **overnight.**

Tola A weight measurement for gold (0.375 troy ounces = 11.66 grammes), used in India and the Arabian Gulf.

Tom/next (Or T/N or rollover.) A transaction from the next working day ("tomorrow") until the day after ("next" day – i.e. **spot** in the foreign exchange market).

Treasury bill A short-term security issued by a government, generally with a zero **coupon.**

Troy ounce Standard unit of weight in precious metals, equal to 31.10348 grammes.

True yield The yield which is equivalent to the quoted **discount rate** (for a US or UK treasury bill, for example).

Tunnel Same as **collar**.

Unallocated account Ownership of a certain weight of gold, without its holding being associated with any specific physical gold bars. The holder is an unsecured creditor of the bank where the account is held. See **allocated account**.

Underlying The underlying of a **futures** or **option** contract is the commodity or financial instrument on which the contract depends. Thus the underlying for a bond option is the bond; the underlying for a short-term interest rate futures contract is typically a three-month deposit.

Value date (Or settlement date or maturity date.) The date on which a deal is to be consummated. In some bond markets, the value date for **coupon** accruals can sometimes differ from the settlement date.

Vanilla A vanilla transaction is a straightforward one.

Variable currency (Or counter currency.) Exchange rates are quoted in terms of the number of units of one currency (the variable or counter currency) which corresponds to one unit of the other currency (the **base currency**).

Variance (σ^2) A measure of how much the values of something fluctuate around its **mean** value. Defined as the average of (value − mean)^2. *See* **standard deviation**.

Variation margin *See* **margin**.

Vega (Or epsilon (ε), eta (η), kappa (κ) or lambda (λ).) The change in an option's value relative to a change in the **underlying**'s **volatility**.

Volatility The **standard deviation** of the continuously compounded return on the **underlying**. Volatility is generally annualised. *See* **historic volatility, implied volatility**.

Also the price sensitivity of a bond as measured by **modified duration**.

Warrant An **option**, generally referring to a **call** option – often a call option on a security where the warrant is purchased as part of an investment in another or the same security.

Writer Same as "seller" of an **option**.

Yield The interest rate which can be earned on an investment, currently quoted by the market or implied by the current market price for the investment – as opposed to the **coupon** paid by an issuer on a security, which is based on the coupon rate and the face value.

For a bond, generally the same as **yield to maturity** unless otherwise specified.

Yield to equivalent life The same as **yield to maturity** for a bond with partial redemptions.

Yield to maturity (Or YTM.) The **internal rate of return** of a bond – the yield necessary to discount all the bond's cashflows to an **NPV** equal to its current price. *See* **simple yield to maturity, current yield.**

YTM *See* **yield to maturity.**

Zero-cost collar A **collar** where the premiums paid and received are equal, giving a net zero cost.

Zero-coupon A zero-coupon security is one that does not pay a **coupon.** Its price is correspondingly less to compensate for this.

A zero-coupon **yield** is the yield which a zero-coupon investment for that term would have if it were consistent with the **par yield curve.**

Appendix 5
ISO (SWIFT) currency codes

Country	Currency	Code
Abu Dhabi	UAE dirham	AED
Afghanistan	afghani	AFN
Ajman	UAE dirham	AED
Albania	lek	ALL
Algeria	dinar	DZD
Andorra	euro	EUR
Angola	kwanza	AOA
Anguilla	E Caribbean dollar	XCD
Antigua	E Caribbean dollar	XCD
Argentina	peso	ARS
Armenia	dram	AMD
Aruba	guilder	AWG
Australia	Australian dollar	AUD
Austria	euro	EUR
Azerbaijan	manat	AZN
Azores	euro	EUR
Bahamas	Bahama dollar	BSD
Bahrain	dinar	BHD
Bangladesh	taka	BDT
Barbados	Barbados dollar	BBD
Belarus	rouble	BYR
Belgium	euro	EUR
Belize	Belize dollar	BZD
Benin	CFA franc	XOF
Bermuda	Bermuda dollar	BMD
Bhutan	ngultrum	BTN
Bolivia	boliviano	BOB
Bosnia and Herzegovina	convertible mark	BAM
Botswana	pula	BWP
Brazil	real	BRL
Brunei	Brunei dollar	BND

Country	Currency	Code
Bulgaria	lev	BGN
Burkina Faso	CFA franc	XOF
Burundi	Burundi franc	BIF
Cambodia	riel	KHR
Cameroon	CFA franc	XAF
Canada	Canadian dollar	CAD
Canary Islands	euro	EUR
Cape Verde	escudo	CVE
Cayman Islands	CI dollar	KYD
Central African Republic	CFA franc	XAF
Chad	CFA franc	XAF
Chile	peso	CLP
China	renminbi yuan	CNY
Colombia	peso	COP
Congo	CFA franc	XAF
Congo Dem. Rep.	Congolese franc	CDF
Comoros	franc	KMF
Costa Rica	colon	CRC
Croatia	kuna	HRK
Cuba	peso	CUP
Cyprus	Cyprus pound	CYP
Czech Republic	koruna	CZK
Denmark	krone	DKK
Djibouti	Djibouti franc	DJF
Dominica	E Caribbean dollar	XCD
Dominican Republic	peso	DOP
Dubai	UAE dirham	AED
Ecuador	sucre	ECS
Egypt	Egyptian pound	EGP
El Salvador	US dollar	USD
Equatorial Guinea	CFA franc	XAF
Eritrea	nafka	ERN
Estonia	kroon	EEK
Ethiopia	birr	ETB
European Monetary Union	euro	EUR
Falkland Islands	pound	FKP
Faroe Islands	Danish krone	DKK
Fiji Islands	Fiji dollar	FJD

Country	Currency	Code
Finland	euro	EUR
France	euro	EUR
French Pacific Islands	CFP franc	XPF
Fujairah	UAE dirham	AED
Gabon	CFA franc	XAF
Gambia	dalasi	GMD
Georgia	lari	GEL
Germany	euro	EUR
Ghana	cedi	GHC
Gibraltar	Gibraltar pound	GIP
Great Britain	pound	GBP
Greece	euro	EUR
Greenland	Danish krone	DKK
Grenada	E Caribbean dollar	XCD
Guadeloupe	euro	EUR
Guatemala	quetzal	GTQ
Guinea Republic	Guinean franc	GNF
Guinea-Bissau	CFA franc	XOF
Guyana	Guyana dollar	GYD
Haiti	gourde	HTG
Honduras	lempira	HNL
Hong Kong	Hong Kong dollar	HKD
Hungary	forint	HUF
Iceland	krona	ISK
India	rupee	INR
Indonesia	rupiah	IDR
Iran	rial	IRR
Iraq	dinar	IQD
Irish Republic	euro	EUR
Israel	shekel	ILS
Italy	euro	EUR
Ivory Coast	CFA franc	XOF
Jamaica	Jamaican dollar	JMD
Japan	yen	JPY
Jordan	dinar	JOD

Country	Currency	Code
Kazakhstan	tenge	KZT
Kenya	shilling	KES
Kiribati	Australian dollar	AUD
Korea (North)	won	KPW
Korea (South)	won	KRW
Kuwait	dinar	KWD
Kyrgizstan	som	KGS
Laos	kip	LAK
Latvia	lat	LVL
Lebanon	Lebanese pound	LBP
Lesotho	loti	LSL
Liberia	Liberian dollar	LRD
Libya	dinar	LYD
Liechtenstein	Swiss franc	CHF
Lithuania	litas	LTL
Luxembourg	euro	EUR
Macao	pataca	MOP
Macedonia	denar	MKD
Madeira	euro	EUR
Malagasy Republic	ariary	MGA
Malawi	kwacha	MWK
Malaysia	ringgitt	MYR
Maldives	rufiyaa	MVR
Mali	CFA franc	XOF
Malta	lira	MTL
Martinique	euro	EUR
Mauritania	ouguiya	MRO
Mauritius	rupee	MUR
Mexico	peso nuevo	MXN
Moldova	leu	MDL
Monaco	euro	EUR
Mongolia	tugrik	MNT
Montserrat	E Caribbean dollar	XCD
Morocco	dirham	MAD
Mozambique	metical	MZN
Myanmar	kyat	MMK
Namibia	dollar	NAD
Nauru Isles	Australian dollar	AUD

Country	Currency	Code
Nepal	rupee	NPR
Netherlands	euro	EUR
Netherlands Antilles	guilder	ANG
New Caledonia	CFP franc	XPF
New Zealand	NZ dollar	NZD
Nicaragua	cordoba	NIO
Niger	CFA franc	XOF
Nigeria	naira	NGN
Norway	krone	NOK
Oman	riyal	OMR
Pakistan	rupee	PKR
Panama	balboa	PAB
Papua New Guinea	kina	PGK
Paraguay	guarani	PYG
Peru	sol nuevo	PEN
Philippines	peso	PHP
Poland	zloty	PLN
Portugal	euro	EUR
Qatar	riyal	QAR
Ras Al Khaimah	UAE dirham	AED
Reunion Island	euro	EUR
Romania	leu	RON
Russia	rouble	RUB
Rwanda	franc	RWF
São Tomé	dobra	STD
Saudi Arabia	riyal	SAR
Senegal	CFA franc	XOF
Serbia	dinar	RSD
Seychelles	rupee	SCR
Sharjah	UAE dirham	AED
Sierra Leone	leone	SLL
Singapore	Singapore dollar	SGD
Slovakia	koruna	SKK
Slovenia	euro	EUR
Solomon Islands	dollar	SBD
Somalia	shilling	SOS

Country	Currency	Code
South Africa	rand	ZAR
Spain	euro	EUR
Sri Lanka	rupee	LKR
St Christopher	E Caribbean dollar	XCD
St Helena	pound	SHP
St Kitts & Nevis	E Caribbean dollar	XCD
St Lucia	E Caribbean dollar	XCD
St Pierre et Miquelon	euro	EUR
St Vincent	E Caribbean dollar	XCD
Sudan	dinar	SDD
Surinam	Surinam dollar	SRD
Swaziland	lilangeni	SZL
Sweden	krona	SEK
Switzerland	Swiss franc	CHF
Syria	Syrian pound	SYP
Taiwan	dollar	TWD
Tajikistan	somoni	TJS
Tanzania	shilling	TZS
Thailand	baht	THB
Togo	CFA franc	XOF
Tonga	pa' anga	TOP
Trinidad & Tobago	TT dollar	TTD
Tunisia	dinar	TND
Turkey	lira	TRY
Turkmenistan	manat	TMM
Uganda	shilling	UGX
Ukraine	hryvnia	UAH
Um Al Quwain	UAE dirham	AED
United Arab Emirates	dirham	AED
Uruguay	peso	UYU
USA	US dollar	USD
Uzbekistan	som	UZS
Vanuatu	vatu	VUV
Venezuela	bolivar	VEB
Vietnam	dong	VND
Virgin Islands (USA)	US dollar	USD

Country	*Currency*	*Code*
Wallis & Futuna Islands	CFP franc	XPF
Western Samoa	tala	WST
Yemen	rial	YER
Zambia	kwacha	ZMK
Zimbabwe	Zimbabwe dollar	ZWD

Select Bibliography

General

Adams, A. Bloomfield, D. Booth, P. and England, P. (1993) *Investment Mathematics and Statistics*, Graham & Trotman, London.

Blake, D. (1990) *Financial Market Analysis*, McGraw Hill, Maidenhead.

Risk Magazine, monthly periodical, Risk Publications Ltd.

Money market

Stigum, M. (1981) *Money Market Calculations: Yields, Break-evens and Arbitrage*, Dow Jones Irwin, Illinois.

Quarterly Review, quarterly periodical, LIFFE, London.

Bond market calculations

Fabozzi, F. (1988) *Fixed Income Mathematics*, Probus, Illinois.

Repos

Steiner, R. (1997) *Mastering Repo Markets*, FT Pitman, London.

Corrigan, D. Georgiou, C. and Gollow, J. (1995) *Natwest Markets Handbook of International Repo*, IFR Publishing, London.

Swaps

Marshall, J. and Kapner, K. (1993) *Understanding Swaps*, John Wiley, Chichester.

Price, J. and Henderson, S. (1988) *Currency and Interest Rate Swaps*, Butterworths, London.

Options

Wilmot, P. Howison, S. and Dewynne, J. (1995) *The Mathematics of Financial Derivatives*, Cambridge University Press, Cambridge.

Hull, J. (1989) *Options, Futures and Other Derivative Securities*, Prentice-Hall, New Jersey.

Cox, J. and Rubinstein, M. (1985) *Options Markets*, Prentice-Hall, New Jersey.

Commodities

Hélyette, G. (2005) *Commodities and Commodity Derivatives*, John Wiley, Chichester.

Index